THE OFFICIAL 1986 BLACKBOOK PRICE GUIDE OF UNITED STATES COINS

TWENTY-FOURTH EDITION

BY MARC HUDGEONS, N.L.G.

Y0-CMF-054

Published by: The House of Collectibles, Inc.
Orlando Central Park
1904 Premier Row
Orlando, FL 32809
Phone: (305) 857-9095

Printed in the United States of America
Library of Congress Card Number 79-643730
ISBN: 0-87637-284-1

TABLE OF CONTENTS

OFFICIAL BOARD OF CONTRIBUTORS TO THE 24TH EDITION

Mr. Aubrey E. Bebee
Mr. Q. David Bowers
Mr. Roger Bryan
Mr. James H. Cohen
Mr. Robert Cornely
Col. Grover C. Criswell
Mr. Dennis Forgue

Mr. Lawrence Goldberg
Mr. Robert L. Hughes
Mr. Curtis Iversen
Mr. Kurt R. Krueger
Mr. Julian Leidman
Mr. Clifford Mishler
Mr. Glenn Smedley
Mr. Rick Sundman

The publisher also wishes to express special thanks to the American Numismatic Association for their continuing support and assistance. Certain photographs are courtesy of the Bowers and Merena Galleries, Inc., Wolfboro, NH 03894.

PUBLISHER'S NOTE

This book is presented as a guide to the values of U. S. coins, as an aid for the beginner, advanced collector and dealer. We are not dealers. We do not buy or sell coins. Prices listed are intended as a guide only and are not warranted for accuracy.

MARKET REVIEW

The coin market was hectic and somewhat erratic in the past year. It was aided by the overall economic growth, but at the same time hurt by sluggish bullion prices. Analysts had a decidedly bad time of it, all during the year, trying to make sense out of what was happening. Buying trends came and went almost weekly. Never in the history of the coin market were there as many short-lived buying trends. Yet there were some strongly positive chords struck: the heavy competition (adding up to $3,640,110.65) at the Jerry Buss sale, and the unmistakable resurgence of investors as a potential market force. Investors were more prominent in the coin market this past year than in any year since 1981. A number of the nation's largest coin firms are now doing business with investors than with collectors, just as happened in the years from 1979 to 1981. Other news of the year included the much-publicized "quality crisis," or market shortage of many coins in grades higher than MS-60, and the controversy surrounding the American Numismatic Association's certification service (known as A.N.A.C.S.). Nor did the U.S. Mint escape the spotlight, as there were a number of Congressional hearings involving our coins, one of them concerning a possible readoption of 95% copper for the cent.

Apparently the increased investment activity and the "quality crisis" are related. Today's investors are going very heavily into BU rolls, much more so than the investors of 1979-81. When spending (say) $2000, they would rather buy a roll of forty $50 coins than a single $2000 rarity. Silver denominations from the 1920s up to 1964 have been their favorite target up to this point, but there are also investors for BU rolls of Lincoln Cents and Buffalo/Indian Nickels. Most of them are not terribly concerned about dates or mint marks. They *are* concerned about condition and are looking for rolls in the MS-63, MS-65 and even higher grades. This is an extremely interesting development, as it's reminiscent of the approach to coin investment in the 1970s when the average investor was not a hobbyist and did not care about the numismatic aspects of coins. The philosophy behind that sort of investing is that medium priced coins, within the financial reach of most hobbyists, have a firmer foundation than rarities. The vast demand for MS-63, MS-65 and higher grade rolls seems directly responsible for the shortage of such coins on the market. There is no even flow between buying and selling. At the present time, buyers are far outnumbering sellers, and the coins they buy are going into bank deposit boxes for five years or longer.

The Dr. Jerry Buss collection of United States coins was auctioned in Los Angeles on January 28, 29 and 30, 1985. While this was by no means another Garrett collection, as it was weak in certain areas such as Colonials, it did include a number of the fabled rarities among U.S. coins. There is some difference of opinion in the hobby, on the validity of auction results as a barometer of the market. Still, strong prices for high priced rarities are normally taken to indicate a bullish market. The bulls carried the day in Los Angeles, as many prices far exceeded their estimates. Tops for the sale was $350,000 paid for a 1913 Liberty Nickel, against an estimate of "$250,000-up." This was the first specimen sold at public auction since the 1970s so of course it was difficult to estimate a price. But a coin which *has* been sold rather frequently, the 1804 Dollar, did almost as well in beating its pre-sale estimate. It fetched $280,000, while estimated at

"$200,000-up." This was not the record price for an 1804 Dollar but it was the record, so far as is known, for the 1913 Liberty Nickel. The total realized for this sale exceeded the total pre-sale estimate. What proportion of the buyers were investors? A good question but one that cannot be answered, as the majority of successful bidders were dealers acting as agents for undisclosed clients.

The zinc cent, introduced on a trial basis in 1982 and later adopted for full production, may be on the verge of extinction. It was assailed from various quarters throughout the year and has an uncertain future as this edition is going to press. A widely publicized news report told of a family's pet dog which died from zinc poisoning as the result of swallowing one of the zinc cents. Speculation was immediately raised as to possible dangers to small children. At the same time it was pointed out that the original reason for switching to zinc — the rising price of raw copper — no longer exists. Copper prices have been coming down. The Mint is not anxious to readopt the 95% copper cent and probably would do so only by an Act of Congress. Such an Act is well within the realm of possibility. While the Mint would not lose money by switching back to 95% copper, it could not save nearly as much as it does by using zinc. The profit on cents was $36,000,000 in the last fiscal year, using zinc. With copper it would be a fraction of that sum. Amazing as it sounds, the Mint can manufacture about 17 zinc cents for every 1¢ of production cost. Using copper it would not even be able to manufacture two cents for 1¢. The Mint is also telling Congress that a "conversion cost" would be involved if it went back to copper. One Congressman arguing for a return to 95% copper cents cites the fact that copper mines are suffering by losing such a large share of the Mint's business. While this is perhaps true, the Mint remains the largest U.S. purchaser of copper, as copper is used to some degree in all our coins. Of course there is the very real possibility that if the Mint returned to 95% copper cents, copper prices would be driven up again and the exact same situation faced in 1982 would return.

SPECIAL REPORT: UNDERVALUED SILVER COINS?

Are modern silver coins undervalued in relation to their availability?

The possibility that some (or even a majority) of silver coins are undervalued has become a topic of considerable attention. Within the past two decades, enormous quantities of U.S. 90% silver coins have been melted down. Two peak periods of melting occurred, in the late 1960s and again in 1979 and 1980. But even between these two periods, and in fact from 1980 to the present, coin melting has been substantial. More silver coins are melted when silver's bullion value is high, but some are melted regardless of "spot price."

Melting has hit hardest at 90% silver coins of the twentieth century, which in collector terminology are referred to as modern coins. These were the coins readily available to melters during the two periods of massive silver coin melting. In all cases, the melters obtained their coins in the least expensive manner. They took silver coins from ordinary circulation when obtainable, and bought others at the lowest possible premium over face value. Both methods led to acquiring, for melting, coins that consisted primarily of late dates. Some nineteenth century coins were melted, but the percentage of such coins melted was much lower. Thus, the current situation finds hundreds of twentieth century silver coins to be potentially underpriced in relation to their actual availability.

While no exact figures are available on the total quantity of 90% silver coins melted, various estimates have been made based on the extent of melting and the numbers of silver coins available to melters. It is known that the U.S. Government melted more than two billion silver coins in the late 1960s, consisting entirely of dimes and quarters. In estimating total quantities melted, by the Government and private parties combined, the following should be taken into account:

1. Private parties were melting half dollars and silver dollars in addition to the two lower denominations being melted by the Government.

2. Private smelters not only took their coins from circulation (the source for all coins melted by the Government), but bought coins for melting, which the Government of course did not do.

3. The Government did not melt any 90% silver coins during the silver melt of 1979-80, while private melting was extremely heavy at that time.

Thus it would seem reasonable that the two billion figure, representing 90% silver coins melted by the Government, would need to be multiplied at least fifteen to twenty times, to arrive at the grand total melted down by all parties. This would give a tentative figure of 30 to 40 billion.

Many silver coins have increased in value, some substantially, since the last period of heavy melting in 1979-80. Does this mean that the market has fully reacted to the decreased availability? On the surface it may appear so, but when one looks at 90% silver coins as a whole it is clear that the market values do not reflect actual current scarcity.

On examination it becomes clear that values have adjusted only on certain coins or coins in certain condition grades. Adjustment has occurred chiefly on coins that were already somewhat better than "common dates," before any extensive melting was done. There has been some noticeable adjustment in the MS category for most 90% silver coins. However, values as they stand today do not appear to reflect the current availabilities on circulated specimens (which suffered most in melting). Nor are the MS prices, in many instances, a real reflection of actual availability. They have increased over the years but much of the increase would have taken place simply due to more collectors entering the hobby, more investment buying, etc. It seems evident, then, that buyers of 90% silver coins (both collectors and investors, and perhaps even dealers to some degree) have not recognized their decreased availability. We are of the opinion that many coins deserve to be selling for higher sums, if true market availabilities are taken into account.

In its quarter century of continuous publication, *The Official Blackbook to Coins* has always presented coin prices as they are, not as they might be or should be. The actual price of a coin is the price that matters; anything else is in the realm of speculation. This edition of *The Official Blackbook to Coins* once again shows prices as they stand in the marketplace. However, since 90% silver coin availabilities have received such widespread attention, the following analysis has been prepared to shed light on the subject. It is not intended as a prediction of future coin values. However, as the coin traditionally adjusts along lines of availability, it is reasonable to presume that these undervalued 90% silver coins will rise in price. Actual adjustment of values would depend on a greater public awareness of their decreased availability and true scarcity.

A further purpose in publishing the following information is to some of the false assumptions currently circulating on this subject. Numerous theories have been advanced by writers and market analysts, all in apparent good faith but with varying degrees of merit. While we do not present these pages as the "definitive analysis' of the subject, we do feel that our position permits us to take a fully objective, independent, and informative view of the situation, inasmuch as the publishers are not involved in the buying or selling of coins.

While silver can be recycled from all articles containing silver, coins are greatly preferred by refineries and those who supply silver to refineries. With coins there is no question about the fineness or weight. Most other silver items have to be weighed or tested, or both, and the labor costs involved reduce the profitability of handling such items.

Except for early issues which are not melted because of their collector value, nearly all U.S. silver coins contain .900 or 90% silver. This means a ratio of nine parts .999 fine silver to one part copper alloy. In refining, the copper alloy is removed and the coins yield .999 fine silver. The chief exception to the .900 standard is the 40% Kennedy Half Dollar struck from 1965 to 1970. After 1970, the Kennedy Half Dollar did not contain silver.

Silver coins are bought by refineries in $1,000 bags. This does not refer to the value of the silver, which can change from day to day, but to the face value of the coins. A bag of $1,000 face value contains coins of one denomination only. A $1,000 dime bag contains 10,000 coins (10¢ × 10,000 = $1,000); a $1,000 quarter bag contains 4,000 coins; a $1,000 half dollar bag contains 2,000 coins. While a $1,000 bag of Silver Dollars contains 1,000 coins, it will have slightly more silver that the other bags because the old Silver Dollars (Morgan and Peace) were heavy in relation to their face value. Thus, the refineries will pay slightly more for a $1,000 bag of Silver Dollars than for a $1,000 bag of coins of a lower denomination. As far as the other denominations are concerned, a $1,000 bag of one will contain the identical amount of silver as a $1,000 bag of another. Thus, the prices are always the same. The price of a $1,000 bag is based on the current "spot" price of silver bullion. It is always higher than face value, and can be considerably higher when the price of silver is rising.

The bags are made up by various suppliers who sell to the refineries. Mostly the suppliers are professional coin dealers, who buy "bullion coins" in varying quantities from the public when available. Many small purchases from the public may be required before the $1,000 face value is attained. On the other hand it is not unusual, especially during times of high silver bullion prices, for sellers to bring full bags to the coin dealers.

Of course, these $1,000 bags are not always automatically melted. This depends on circumstances and the preferences of the coin dealer or other supplier. The dealer can choose to advertise his $1,000 bags and sell them to a silver bullion investor, perhaps doing slightly better this way then selling to a refinery. But the majority of bags are melted sooner or later, particularly when the price of silver is high.

The specific coin-by-coin content of "melting bags' has been a subject of considerable discussion, and for apt reasons.

A widely held belief is that these $1,000 refinery bags consist wholly of coins that could not be sold for more than "bullion value." In other words, common date coins in the lower grades of circulated condition. Most dealers involved in supplying $1,000 face value bags to melters are well aware of the fact that some better grade coins are included. The methods by which these bags are normally assembled do not entail any really tight safeguards, and during periods of stampede buying there are likely to be no safeguards whatsoever. Also, there have been intentional inclusion of better grade coins in $1,000 refinery bags.

These are the two chief reasons for coins other than those of "bullion value" reaching refinery bags:

1. Virtually no sorting occurs when the price of silver is rising by $3 or $4 per day.

2. Intentional inclusion of better coins. While this does not happen frequently, it will invariably happen when the price of silver bullion is very high (as in January, 1980). The dealers will take better grade coins from their stock and include them in the $1,000 refinery bags, for the sole purpose of delivering more bags. Coins worth $25 to collectors but only $20 as bullion may go into the bags — by the thousands.

Why would the dealer throw away $5?

Simply because he is making a very healthy profit at $20 — healthy and immediate. If he keeps the coin in stock, he might sell it to a collector for $25, he might not. The price of silver could go down, and the coin may end up being worth much less than $20 by the time someone buys it. If he paid only a few dollars for the coin, he will not hesitate to melt it for $20.

In fact, many coins that could be sold to collectors for double their bullion values are melted, when the price of silver is skyrocketing.

These better coins include BU rolls of common dates, as well as scarce coins in various grades of circulated condition. Scarce date BU coins are not melted, but this could occur if silver reached an extraordinarily high price.

Thus the premise that melting decreases availability of the commonest coins, but has no effect on scarcer coins or coins in BU condition, is erroneous. It has its greatest (by far) effect on circulated common date coins, but there is some measure of effect on others as well

Early Meltings

The U.S. Mint issued its first silver coins in 1793, though some were dated 1792. Dies were prepared in 1792 in the hope that sufficient quantities of silver could be obtained, but the supply at first was minimal and no coins were released that year. The 1792 dies were used in the early part of 1793, until they began to show signs of wear, at which point they were replaced with dies reading 1793. Thus the silver coins released by the Mint in 1793 included those dated 1792 and 1793 (and there are no separate mint-age figures).

There were no known silver mints in the country at that time, though a number were discovered in the 1800s. The method used by the Mint in obtaining silver was a public advertising campaign. Private citizens brought scrap silver to the Mint, received a receipt for its value, and could then redeem the receipt for like value in finished coins. There was no direct distribution, at that time, of silver coins to banks. They went exclusively from the Mint to private citizens, and the hope was that they would be spent and thus released into circulation.

It was decided, in a rather daring move, to set silver prices lower in the U.S. than in Europe. This prevented the government from buying silver overseas and importing it, but also established a favorable exchange rate for our silver against foreign currencies and encouraged foreign nations to do business with the U.S.

It also resulted in some foreign business of the wrong kind.

U.S. speculators promptly began gathering up kegs and boxes of silver coins and selling them to the sea captains and merchants who called at the major eastern ports. They were easily resold for a profit when the ship returned to its native port. In a short time, the demand was so great that the supply of coins rapidly decreased.

While all U.S. silver coins were involved in this operation, the dollar suffered the worst assault. As the largest silver piece, dollars were sorted and counted out much faster than the smaller coins, and they did not escape as easily through the cracks in boxes or barrels. In 1795 the Mint struck about 160,000 silver dollars, and at least 100,000 of them are thought to have gone overseas into foreign smelting furnaces by 1803. In 1798 the total output was 327,536, of which about half had been smelted by 1803. The Mint tried to step up its production to counteract this activity but it was a lost cause. As the proportion of Silver Dollars coming from the Mint increased, so did the proportion vanishing across the Atlantic. This sale and exportation of dollars was illegal but little could be done to halt it.

President Jefferson, fully realizing that the Mint was doing little more than playing into the hands of profiteers, ordered production of Silver Dollars terminated in 1803. They did not resume until 1836, although a few dollars dated 1804 were struck for inclusion in special presentation sets. While the dollar was out of production, the reason usually given for its discontinuance was a shortage of raw silver. There was in fact no real shortage, as supplies of silver coming into the Mint had been steadily increasing since 1792.

While dollars were flowing abroad to be melted, many of those remaining home suffered the same fate. The U.S. Silver Dollar was mercilessly melted on American soil from the time of its inception until the mid 1800s, except for the years when dollars were not struck and therefore unavailable. Domestic melters simply wanted the silver for use in manufacturing. By utilizing coins to obtain silver they paid only a slight advance, sometimes none at all, over the actual bullion value. Silversmiths were the chief consumers of Silver Dollars in the period from about 1795 to 1850. Many of them had their own furnaces and did their own coin melting. They simply used the silver/copper alloy as it came from the molten coins and made it into teapots, serving dishes, knives, spoons, candelabrum, coal hods and other standard wares of their trade. At first the fineness varied slightly but by 1836 it had become established at a strict .900, as it remained for our silver coins until their withdrawal in 1964. When used in manufacturing, this grade of silver came to be known as "coin silver." Today "coin silver" is merely an expression to denote .900 fineness, but in the early days of American silversmithing it actually meant silver derived from melted coins.

The First Great Melt

The "great melt" began in 1853, and resulted in what may be termed the first sweeping silver coin melt in the U.S., far exceeding what had occurred earlier in connection with Silver Dollars. It was short-lived but must have claimed millions of coins, ranging all the way from the tiny silver 5¢ piece to the 50¢ piece. Unlike the earlier melting of Silver Dollars, its motive was clearly for profit. The year 1853 yielded far-reaching changes in our silver coinage. All silver coins with the exception of the dollar were reduced in silver content. The fineness remained the same, .900, but the weight of each coin was brought down slightly. The difference in actual pure silver (.999) content was very minimal in a single coin, especially in a coin of low denomination which had only a little silver to begin with. But in a hundred coins, or a thousand, or ten thousand, it added up. The weight reduction occurred in midyear, after a number of coins dated 1853 had been struck with the old specifications. To call attention to the new coins, the Mint placed arrows at the date and rays behind the eagle on the reverse side. Profiteers simply sifted through change and picked out all silver coins dating prior to 1853, and those dating 1853 without the rays and arrows.

Melters poured every old-weight silver coin into their furnaces. The silver yielded was made into bars and sold for the going rate. Each bar sold for more than the face value of the coins melted to make it. This enterprise led directly to a shortage of silver coinage in general circulation. The government attempted to counteract this by increasing the production of silver coins. In 1854 it struck over seven million half dollars, the largest quantity manufactured in a single year up to that date. Nevertheless the coin shortage prevailed for a number of years and became more extreme during the Civil War, which encouraged hoarding of both silver and gold coins.

While coin melting continued to some extent following the conclusion of the Civil War, no large scale private or commercial melting occurred during the remainder of the nineteenth century. The only U.S. silver coin to be substantially melted in the years from 1865 to 1900 was the Trade Dollar, and this took place over a long period of time. Both the government and commercial smelters melted Trade Dollars. Trade Dollars, which contained more silver than ordinary Silver Dollars but had the same face value, were struck from 1873 to 1885. In 1887 their legal tender statue was revoked, which in effect was an invitation from the government to melt them. As they could no longer be spent as money, they became useful only as collector's items (which few people considered them, at that time) or for melting. Their high silver content in relation to standard dollars made them ideal for melting. It is not known how many were melted but quite likely all available specimens in the U.S., with the exception of those belonging to coin collectors and coin dealers, were melted. The only reason why Trade Dollars exist today in rather large numbers is the fact that millions of them were not in the U.S while this melting was taking place. They were traveling through the Orient, where most had been distributed originally. By the time they eventually returned to the U.S — decades later in some instances — they had acquired some value as collectibles and were not melted.

While it is a fact known beyond doubt that the government extensively melted Trade Dollars, official figures are few. It was announced that a melting of Trade Dollars on July 19, 1878, consumed over 44,000 specimens. As the Carson City striking of the 1878 Trade Dollar is very scarce, it is presumed that most, or all, melted specimens were from that facility.

The Pittman Act

The melting of Trade Dollars by the government, however does not begin to equal the volume of Morgan Dollars melted. The U.S. government has the distinction of engineering the largest official coin melt in recorded history. Unlike most coin melting done by the government it was publicly announced and the figures published.

Production of the Morgan Dollar began in 1878 and continued until 1904. Just a century earlier, Jefferson had called a halt to Silver Dollars — and once again the same action was taken. The reason given was precisely the same: a shortage of raw bullion supplies. Actually the dollar was taken out of production for somewhat more complex reasons, which were probably a slight source of embarrassment to the government. For years the Mint had not been releasing its entire output of Morgans. A portion of the yearly production was released while a portion was stockpiled. As this had been going on for more than twenty years, the stockpile was reaching enormous proportions. The purpose of stockpiling was to insure that the Treasury Department would always have enough Silver Dollars available to redeem Silver Certificates. No great rush to redeem Silver Certificates ever developed, however, and the government eventually realized that its supply of Silver Dollars was a bit over abundant. It could have released some of these coins over the years, bit by bit, but it did not wish to place coins with old dates into circulation. The decision to halt Silver Dollar production in 1904 was based on the assumption that Treasury stockpiles were more than adequate to meet any demand that might arise over a long time. This proved correct, as the redemption of Silver Certificates continued for the next dozen years without the need for additional supplies of Silver Dollars. Just as in the past there was no stampede for redemption. Even the outbreak of World War I saw only a modest increase in the number of Silver Certificates turned in for redemption. And of course many of the Silver Dollars paid out by the Treasury Department found their way back to the government via banking transactions.

In 1918, with World War I at an end, agitation began for resumption of the Silver Dollar. The government still had its enormous stockpiles but every coin was dated 1904 and earlier. After lengthy Congressional debate it was resolved to melt a quantity of the stockpiled dollars. This resulted in the Pittman Act, one of the major coin-related rulings handed down by Congress. The total of Morgan Dollars melted under terms of the Pittman Act was a staggering 270,232,700. This was more than ten times the largest annual output of Morgans from any single Mint, as the record was 19,963,886 struck at Philadelphia in 1886. The government did not, however, deplete its supply of Morgans. Redemption of Silver Certificates continued, and it was necessary to have dollars for that purpose. Just how many dollars were kept on hand was not announced, but the quantity melted must have greatly exceeded the supply retained.

Resumption of striking the Silver Dollar did not occur until 1921. In that year the Morgan design was revived and all three Mints (Philadelphia, Denver and San Francisco) turned out the coin in prodigious numbers. In just a single year, more than 85,000,000 Morgans were struck — but this still meant a deficit of nearly 200 million compared to those in existence prior to the Pittman Act. It is little wonder that the 1921 Morgan is the most common date of the series. its commonness is hardly noticeable in market value, however, as the circulated specimens are still "bullion coins" and command just as much as other common dates in the Morgan group.

Late in 1921 the Silver Dollar design was switched to the Peace type, and this new version remained in production until 1935. The silver used in striking Peace Dollars all during that period was derived from the melted Morgans. The total number of Peace Dollars struck, coupled with the number of 1921 Morgans struck, did not equal the number of Morgans melted by the Pittman Act. When striking of Silver Dollars concluded in 1935 the government still had a surplus of "Pittman silver" on hand.

The action by the government in melting more than 270 million Morgan dollars had an immediate impact on coin collecting. Morgans were already popular with numismatists, but interest had been largely directed on the established scarcities such as the 1894 and 1895 Philadelphia strikings. With so many Morgans destroyed, their desirability was considerably enhanced. Collectors and dealers rushed en masse to banks to change paper currency for Morgans. It no longer was a question of sifting out the good dates and spending the rest; now they were all good dates, though the majority brought only a small premium over face. The excitement was intensified by the shroud of mystery surrounding the specific dates and mintmarks melted by the government. For all anyone knew at that time, some instant rarities may have been created by the melt.

The Second Great Melt

The next significant melting of silver U.S. coinage did not occur until the 1960s. It was unquestionably the largest in terms of the total number of coins destroyed, and unique in that both the government and private individuals participated. It was also the most indiscriminate melt in the nation's history up to that time, as it involved silver coins of all denominations and ages. (The smaller silver denominations, 3¢ and 5¢, were saved from this melt only because of their premium collector value.) Nor was it confined exclusively to U.S. coins, as those of Canada, Mexico and numerous foreign countries were likewise melted.

The silver melt of the 1960s was also of significance for its effect on coin collecting. Wholesale destruction of coins by the hundreds of thousands, in some cases by the millions, meant that "common dates" were no longer as common. Any scarce dates that went into the melting furnaces, and some surely did, increased the scarcity factor for those coins. Though the numismatic hobby was well aware of what was occurring, no immediate assessment was made. It was known only that a gross volume of silver U.S. coinage was being melted daily.

The series of events leading to this "second great silver melt," and the first in modern history, began with the withdrawal of silver from the dime and quarter in 1965, and the reduction of the 50¢ piece to .400 silver rather rather than .900. All three coins were switched to a "clad" composition in 1965, with silver removed entirely from the 10¢ and 25¢. A coating of nickel gave them an appearance of silver.

The market value ("spot" price) of silver bullion had been inching upward in the early sixties, mainly because of increased use in industry and the jewelry trade. Projections by the Treasury Department indicated that silver coinage would soon be worth more than its face value. This would make it impossible to continue striking silver coins, as a manufacturing loss would result. Various possible solutions existed: reduce the silver content, raise the face values, or drop the silver entirely.

The switch to basemetal for the 10¢ and 25¢, and reduction of silver in the 50¢, focused international attention on silver. Many persons who had not previously paid the slightest attention to the silver market, or to coins, began accumulating silver in anticipation of price increases. Also, beginning in 1965 but becoming more widespread thereafter, numerous persons got into the practice of putting aside silver coins received in pocket change. They were not coin collectors and most of them were unaware of scarce dates or mintmarks. These people believed that silver coins would eventually be worth a premium over and above face value; and since the coins could always be spent there was no risk involved. The number of people doing this must have been considerable, as silver coins rapidly decreased in general circulation. As early as 1966, just a year after cladding began, the ratio of silver coins traveling in circulation had dropped to only slightly more than 50%. It was down to around 20% the following year, and to less than 1% by 1970.

The government saved vast sums of money with the new clad coins, which cost far less to manufacture than the old ones. It was not wholly out of the woods in its battle against the silver bullion market, however. Silver Certificates were still redeemable for their face value in Silver Dollars. There was no limit to the number of Silver Dollars that could be obtained this way. In the mid 1960s the official "fixed" price of silver was $1.29 per troy ounce, but in actual transactions it was frequently selling higher. On July 14, 1967, the government removed its controls from silver prices, realizing that a fixed price for silver bullion was no longer feasible. This brought an immediate upsurge in the price, and a rush to cash in Silver Certificates. At some banks, throngs of more than one thousand persons queued up to redeem their paper money. They received an instant profit. Soon the government announced that redemption of Silver Certificates would be halted.

Two months before the lifting of fixed prices for silver, the Treasury Department sought to control profiteering by placing a ban on the melting of U.S. silver coins. While the ban was chiefly aimed at the Silver Dollar, since that was the coin exchanged for Silver Certificates, it was written to include silver coins of all denominations. Exporting U.S coins was likewise prohibited, to prevent a recurrence of the "Jefferson dilemma" some century and a half earlier. Since the U.S. had no control on coin melting in foreign countries, the only way to prevent our coins from being melted abroad was to insure that they remained in the confines of U.S. law. However, coin melting occurred in secret locations unknown to federal investigators, not in the established refineries where inspections were made. Fully realizing that the law could not be effectively enforced, it was abandoned in May of 1969. Other factors were also involved in lifting the ban, chiefly that the availability of 90% U.S. silver coins to legitimate refineries would increase the domestic supply of silver bullion and hold its price within bounds. The government did not wish great quantities of silver bullion to be imported from abroad, as that would not only raise the price of silver but weaken the U.S. dollar on foreign currency exchanges.

Meanwhile the Treasury Department was doing a fair amount of melting. In July, 1967, it instituted a new policy with regard to used coins received from Federal Reserve Banks. The twelve Federal Reserve Banks located in various parts of the country regularly ship bags of used coins to the Treasury Department, in exchange for new ones. Traditionally the incoming coins were not sorted or inspected. Under the new policy all bags containing dimes and quarters are opened and a coin-by-coin check was made to segregate those dated 1964 and earlier from those dated 1965 and later. The half dollar bags were not included as the coins they contained, regardless of date, had some silver content (either .900 or .400). Coins containing silver were not redistributed, but sent to the Mint's furnaces for melting. In this fashion the Treasury Department obtained more than enough silver bullion to supply the needs of the 50¢ piece, without purchasing any silver. As silver coins were still found in rather substantial quantities in ordinary circulation in 1967, the incoming bags contained a fair proportion of them. This policy continued until the close of the 1970 fiscal year (June, 1970), at which time it was no longer worthwhile to inspect incoming bags because few silver coins remained in circulation. Precise records were kept on the number of coins melted, though no effort was made to record the dates, mintmarks, varieties or other numismatic data. During the length of this operation a total of 563,882,690 quarters were melted and 1,552,903,056 dimes, for a combined total of more than two billion coins. The government's statistics provide vivid testimony of the declining numbers of 90% silver coins in circulation throughout that period. While more than 192 million dimes were melted in April, 1969, the total for April of the following year was down to 39 million. Such figures cannot be regarded as an exact reflection of the percentages of silver coins in circulation, as they indicate the time of melting only, not the period during which the coins were collected. Presumably there was a long time gap between receiving the coins and melting them, during which the arduous sorting process took place. Thus the true totals of 90% silver coins available in circulation were undoubtedly much lower than one would gather from the quantities melted. When the government was melting 39 million silver dimes in April, 1970, this very likely exceeded the entire total of silver dimes remaining in circulation.

The activities of the Treasury Department in melting 90% silver dimes and quarters, even though more than two billion pieces were involved, paled before the actions of private and commercial coin melters during this era. These melters started before July, 1967, and kept on going long after the government stopped; and the number of numismatically significant coins they destroyed was probably far greater than those melted by the government. Just taking into account the fact that private melters destroyed Morgan and Peace Dollars, while the government did not, should turn the majority of numismatic wrath against them.

The single action having the greatest impetus on coin melting was the end of price controls in July, 1967. This was the clarion call to melt, melt, melt. The fact that such melting was illegal discouraged only a minority of potential coin melters. Smelting furnaces were set up in basements and other secluded places. Foreign coins were melted as a cover for illicit operations. Smelters kept junk silver on the premises which could be displayed in the event of a raid. Since smelting silver was perfectly legal in itself, they had only to show that they were melting articles other than U.S. coins. Once the coins were melted, refined and made into .999 bars, the origin of the silver was impossible to determine.

The prospect of impending doom constantly hung over the smelters, which made them work with lightning speed. With so much coinage being melted the supply of .999 fine silver bullion was increasing. Also, with the government no longer buying silver for its coins, the nation's largest customer was out of the market. Silver prices could, indeed, reverse themselves overnight.

Because the illicit smelters had to work quickly, they could not depend upon coins pulled from circulation. They had to get their supplies of 90% silver coins from people who had access to large amounts, preferably presorted with the clad specimens removed. There were several ways of accomplishing this and the illicit smelters relied upon all of them. One source was the private citizen who had been filling up his jars and boxes with 90% silver coins. This was considered the best source, as many people were not aware of current bullion values and would turn over their coins for a slight profit. Illicit smelters often bought $1,000 in face value for $1,100 when the silver bullion content was worth over $2,000. Private owners were reached through classified newspaper ads and the smelter never revealed who he was, beyond "Jim" or "Harry." Of course he paid in cash. There was no real danger in placing the ads, since many non-smelters were doing the same thing, in an effort to buy silver coins for investment. Another source, which was excellent in terms of available quantities but not as good on price, was the professional coin dealer. Coin dealers had silver coins by the bag, but they wanted full bullion value for them. While smelters did not care to pay that much, they still bought heavily from coin dealers, feeling that in a rising market they would still end up far ahead. There were other sources, too. Operators of vending machines, such as the owners of coin laundromats, would sell their weekly proceeds to smelters for a very small advance over face, say 10%. The problem with vending machine coins was that they usually came unsorted, and the proportion of clad coins was high.

Regardless of how the coins were obtained, they were almost always melted very quickly without any visual inspection. Such inspection, if it occurred at all, was aimed at ascertaining whether the bag or lot was wholly 90% silver or mixed silver and clad. If it seemed to be 90% silver, after spot checking some of the coins at random, the average smelter did not concern himself about the possible presence of scarce dates or obsolete types.

While the pace of silver coin melting was fast and furious during the two years of its illegality, it increased to an even greater level following removal of the no-melt law in May, 1969. There were probably more silver coins melted in 1969 than in the two prior years combined, though this cannot be proved. The increased supplies of silver entering the marketplace caused fluctuations in the price, and silver was no longer the hot item of the moment. Also, many owners of silver bullion coins became unwilling to sell.

So the second great silver melt, having begun more than a century after the first, gradually stopped. By the close of 1970 it was all but a thing of the past, though some melting was still going on.

In those approximately three and a half years of unprecedented melting, the toll taken of silver coinage numbered well into the multi billions of pieces. It was possibly as high as twenty billion, which would place the government's share at only about 10%. Of any particular coin (that is, date and mintmark), the total destroyed just in that period may have been 50%

of the quantity struck. It was certainly a minimum of 20% for the more recent 90% silver coins struck in the years from 1960 to 1964 at all three Mint facilities. For the older coins, especially those dating before 1950, the percentages may have been quite a bit lower. Interestingly enough, this very rapid diminishing of available quantities had little effect on the coin market. The coins did not become more expensive to collectors because of melting. When prices rose, it was usually because of a corresponding rise in bullion value and had nothing to do with availability. They were still treated as "common dates," because of their mintage figures.

Looking at the situation as it existed in 1970 and the years immediately thereafter, it is easy to understand why collectors (and coin dealers for that matter) failed to become more enthusiastic about silver coins. Of course they may have underestimated the quantities of coins destroyed. But even assuming they knew the extent of melting, it was difficult for them to relate this to enhanced desirability. Most of the coins being melted were circulated, so the numbers of surviving "uncs" decreased by lower percentages. The coin dealers appeared to have these coins in just as abundant a supply as before, so the matter received little attention. If a certain date did seem to be getting scarce on the market, many collectors blamed the speculators and hoarders rather than the smelters. It was thought to be a temporary condition which would right itself as soon as a few hundred rolls entered the market.

THE THIRD GREAT MELT

If this second big melt had been the last one, followed only by low-volume refinery melting and the normal attrition of coins over the years, it is entirely possible that the effect on values would have been slight. Coupled with the "third melt" of 1979-80, a situation was created wherein available quantities of even the most common 90% silver coins were drastically diminished. This third melt, though of shorter duration, had a more far-reaching impact on numismatics. This was largely because practically none of the billions of silver coins melted in 1979-80 came from ordinary circulation. The overall nature of the coins melted in 1979-80 was different than those consumed in the 1967-70 melt. A much higher percentage of "uncs" was involved, as dealers were very willingly tossing their common date "uncs" in bullion bags. There were more coins of scarce dates, more older coins, more coins that would not have been melted if 90% silver coins could have been obtained from circulation. The 1979-80 "third melt" claimed Barber coins in denominations of 10¢, 25¢ and 50¢, whereas it is probable that very few Barber coins were melted in 1967-70. The 1979-80 melt claimed Seated Liberty Dollars and even some Trade Dollars, coins that under normal circumstances would never be melted because of their premium value. It is not hard to see why. The price of silver reached $50 during the third melt, while it never even touched $5 during the second melt. At $50 per troy ounce, there are many individuals who will not stop to consider premium collector value, or age, or anything else. Some dealers were throwing half, or more, of their silver coin stocks into the bullion bags. Whole BU rolls were going into bullion bags by the dozen, coins that had a very clear premium collector value. While these may not have included too many Morgan or Peace Dollars, it is well known that BU rolls of virtually every other coin, including high premium Franklin Halves, were being sacrificed.

The third silver melt was even more frenzied than the second. Silver prices were not only much higher but climbing considerably faster. Also, everything was done openly, as the third melt occurred at a time when no laws prevented the melting or other use of U.S. silver coins.

Silver bullion had been rising in price more or less steadily throughout 1979, as the result of various pressures (chiefly U.S. economic inflation, dissatisfaction with paper investments, and the faltering position of the U.S. dollar on foreign currency exchanges). Unknown at that time to the general public was another major reason for the sharp upturn in silver prices during 1979: the fact that the Hunt family of Texas, one of the wealthiest American families, was buying several hundred million dollars, worth of silver. The price of silver was $8 per troy ounce in July. It cracked $10 in August, surpassed $15 in September, and was just below $20 at the end of November. By the end of December it was a shade under $25, and ready to take a stunning leap. In January it doubled the December price, hitting $50 briefly. While a decline did set in toward the close of January, the price was still a fantastic $45 by the month's end. That was 5½ times higher than it had been just five months earlier.

The coin market reacted very strongly to silver's surge. But the reaction was far from evenly balanced and did not accurately reflect the circumstances that were unfolding. For one thing, investments in "hard assets," including coins, had become widespread on all financial levels. Most of the investment capital was going into rare coins rather than bullion coins. Of those who did buy bullion coins, the majority sold when the price of bullion reached $40 or $50 and their coins were melted. All silver coins, even some really rare coins in low grade condition were getting melted. The most noticeable result was that coin prices no longer gave a true reflection of scarcity. Though the "third great silver melt" is now five to six years behind us, values of silver coins still fail to show its effects. In general, coin hobbyists and perhaps even dealers are not aware of the current availabilities of many silver coins. If the precise availabilities were known — which unfortunately is impossible — it is almost certain that demand would increase for many dates and mintmarks, and thereby result in increased values. Though we cannot know the exact figures, logical deduction based on mintages, coins available for melting, and the extent of silver coin melting allows us to obtain some insight into current scarcities.

The Publisher's Analysis

In analyzing all available information relating to silver coin melting and the coins involved, our basic conclusions are as follows:

1. Considerably more 90% silver coins have been destroyed by melting than generally realized.

2. Scarce date coins did not escape melting, but the common dates were melted in far greater proportion.

3. Scarce date coins that were melted were almost exclusively circulated.

4. Of common dates coins melted, a fairly substantial number were uncirculated.

5. Early (pre-1900) coins were melted, but not in very large quantities, and almost exclusively circulated.

In applying these findings to the current numismatic market, the following conclusions are reached:

1. On the whole, silver coins of many series are undervalued in relation to the quantities now in existence.

2. Undervaluation is most extreme on common date coins in all condition grades and scarce dates in lower condition grades. Little undervaluation exists on scarce dates in MS-60 condition, as these coins were not heavily melted and their loss has, in most instances, been reflected in upward marked values.

A few words of explanation regarding these findings are in order.

Though we will never know coin-by-coin statistics, approximate estimates are possible, and from these estimates a fair picture of current availabilities can be drawn.

The editors have analyzed each coin involved in melting according to a set of factors, some rigid and some variable.

Briefly, these included:

1. Mintage figures.

2. Normal attrition not related to melting.

3. Wear suffered in circulation, as the result of age and softness of design. While this may not appear an important factor in our study, it bears directly on the survival ratio of circulated specimens. During the second large-scale melt (1967-70) many of the coins were coming from daily circulation, and were in less than MS condition. Additionally there were high grade specimens intentionally consigned to melting by coin dealers, not so much in the second melt (1967-70) but by the millions in the third (1979-80), when the high price of silver bullion made it irresistible to melt such coins.

4. Values of coins during the 1967-70 melt and 1979-80 melt. This is an important consideration in determining the specific coins deemed fit for melting by coin dealers. All bullion coins that could not be sold to collectors for more than "bullion value" were considered fit for melting. This automatically included all common dates in the lower condition grades. Coins in that group suffered the greatest proportion of melting, but we know they were not, by any means, the only coins intentionally melted by dealers. Many dealers melted coins which could be sold to collectors for fractionally more than bullion value; and quite a few ended up melting coins with a fair premium value during the 1979-80 melt. At the height of the 1979-80 melt, any coin — circulated or uncirculated — which could not be sold for at least *double* its bullion value was likely to be melted. This is difficult for many collectors to understand, but it was simply a matter of economics. The dealers could clear huge, fast profits by melting silver coins, and they were anxious to do this *so long as their investment in each melted coin was less than the then-current bullion value.* Since this attitude was short-lived, however, the total number of premium-value coins melted fell well short of the quantities melted of "bullion coins."

Thus in our calculations we have made the presumption that very few coins selling for double their bullion value (or higher) were ever intentionally melted. Some specimens were, of course, unknowingly melted.

5. Market availability of common date BU rolls during the 1979-80 meltdown. Only a relatively small number of BU rolls were involved in the 1967-70 melting, but they were sacrificed in vast quantities in 1979-80. These included rolls of Mercury and Roosevelt Dimes, Washington

Quarters, Franklin Halves, 1964 Kennedy Halves, and possibly Morgan and Peace Dollars (as unbelievable as that sounds). The two most heavily hit BU rolls were Roosevelt Dimes of 1964 and 1964-D, because of their abundance. Reviewing the market availability of BU rolls in late 1979 and early 1980 provides some clues to the coins most heavily melted in uncirculated condition. The reader should also realize that it was not just a matter of dealers disposing of rolls from their own stocks. BU rolls were coming on the market at an unprecedented pace in 1979-80. Speculators who bought them early in 1979, or before, were selling every roll they owned and literally tens of thousands of BU rolls were reaching the market every day. Of these, perhaps 20% escaped melting.

6. Grade dropping. In estimating quantities destroyed, the condition of a coin when melted is the primary consideration. If 200,000 F-12 specimens of a certain coin were melted, 200,000 fewer F-12 specimens remain in existence. *But the overall loss of F-12 specimens will be somewhat higher than the total melted.* Let us say that 100,000 VF-20 specimens are melted, many of which came from circulation. If they had been allowed to remain in circulation, many would have "grade dropped" to F-12 and contributed to the existing supply of F-12 specimens. Thus we can estimate that perhaps 10,000 of the 100,000 VF-20 specimens that were melted were actually losses to the F-12 category.

7. Dateless coins. Certainly a proportion of the circulated 90% silver coins that have been melted were in very low grade condition, lacking their dates and mintmarks. Some confusion may prevail over the correct method of dealing with dateless coins in making an analysis such as ours. Some readers may feel the dateless coins should be wholly disregarded and not entered into the calculations at all. It is our feeling, however, that the melting of dateless coins should not be entirely overlooked. It is possible to estimate, based on rate of wear and softness of design, the quantities of dateless 90% silver coins that were in circulation in 1967-70, and from these estimates we can gain a rough knowledge of the years and mintmarks involved. Any destroyed coin means one less specimen of that type and date. The fact that many dateless specimens existed, before melting, was proof that the total number of existing dated specimens was far less than the mintage figures would indicate. Thus the melting of dated specimens, which we know was extremely heavy, reduced their survival total from a quantity that was already lower than many persons realized.

However, to what extent were "good dates" saved from melting?

It is a quite natural assumption that the good dates were saved from melting. Any coin collector would certainly make a careful examination of a large batch of Mercury Dimes, or other 90% silver coins, to find the scarce dates. But there are several good reasons for us to believe that scarce dates, perhaps large numbers of them, were melted.

For one thing, the persons involved in melting operations included many amateurs, many cloak-and-dagger individuals who worked outside the law, and numerous others who had no knowledge of numismatics. Where did the melters get their silver coins? From a vast variety of sources. At the time of the first large scale silver melt-down in the late 1960s, many silver coins were still to be found in ordinary circulation and even in bank rolls. They were being pulled from circulation by persons who knew that the 1964 date was magic, but who did not necessarily know about scarce dates. These individuals, or many of them, were looking only for 90% silver content. When they saw a date of 1964 or earlier they put the coin aside; they could have thrown a 1916D Dime into their silver accumulation.

Admittedly there could not have been too many rare silver coins in circulation in the 1960s. But what about persons who already owned miscellaneous old coins? Not collectors, but individuals who had coins in the attic, remnants of an ancestor's collection, or just a tin of old coins? The lure of selling coins for more than face value brought many such caches of odds-and-ends on the market. Most people selling 90% silver coins for melting were not collectors, as the collectors were not about to part with their coins for a mere advance over face value. They did not know about scarce dates, and quite a few of them (it can logically be concluded) did not try to find out. They just wanted to make a sale.

We will make the presumption that coins sold by the general public for melting, at least during the first melt, contained a fair percentage of scarce dates. By percentage we mean the number of specimens vs. the mintage figures for those dates.

There was yet another checkpoint, or several of them, at which the better coins could have been segregated. Dealers buying from the public may have carefully examined all incoming coins and sifted out the good ones. Some of the intermediaries (the dealers who bought from the public and then resold to smelters) were professional coin dealers. They certainly knew a good coin when they saw it. But what about the economics of the situation? During the second big melt (1979-80) hardly anybody was checking dates or mintmarks. Things were simply happening too fast. For the coin dealer to do this would have been near-suicide under the circumstances. Silver was increasing in spot (bullion) value by $4 or $5 per day, but no one knew if it would continue increasing. Everyone buying silver coins wanted to resell them immediately, to avoid being caught with a substantial supply when the price declined. Picking through thousands upon thousands of coins for "good dates" was hardly a sensible proposition. Even if a dealer found $1,000 worth of scarce dates in a day by careful picking, a drop of $10 in silver's spot price could mean a loss of $50,000 or $100,000 in one afternoon. Most dealers would not have searched their incoming silver coins without the absolute guarantee of finding an 1804 dollar.

Aside from the professional coin dealers, other dealers were buying 90% silver coins from the public and reselling them to refineries. They wanted to get on the silver bandwagon, which meant obtaining quantities of 90% silver coins and selling them as fast as possible to refineries. Speed counted first and foremost because of the unpredictability of the silver market. Most of the quasi-dealers worked alone. If any sorting and sifting was to be done, they attended to it personally. We can safely assume that the vast bulk of coins they bought from the public were bagged for refineries without any spot checking.

One is tempted to believe that if any really extensive date-searching was done, it occurred at the place of melting.

However, the melters were just as rushed as the dealers who supplied them with coins. The silver ingots and bars they produced had to be sold on the open market, and any drop in silver bullion "spot" price would have hurt them just as much as the suppliers. It was certainly in their interest to waste no time in refining their silver and sending the finished bars on their way. Considering the profits they were making on the silver, and the potential for even greater profits if the market went higher, anything gained from "scarce date" would have seemed minimal by comparison.

A prime example of the disregard for scarce dates and early types ("type" is the numismatic term for a coin design, such as Walking Liberty) was shown in the actions of many professional coin dealers during the second melt of 1979-80. In addition to buying 90% silver coins from the public and reselling them to melters, dealers naturally wanted to contribute some of their own coin stock to the supply. This was more profitable for them, as they could sell silver coins at a spot price of $30 or $40 per troy for which they had paid possibly a tiny fraction of that value when originally acquired, whereas incoming coins from the public had to be bought at the prevailing current price. So they milked their stocks, bypassing only the coins which could easily be sold to collectors for large premiums over "spot." All low grade"type coins' went for melting and many medium grades as well. Numerous specimens of the Barber Half in circulated grades were consigned to melting; so were a good many Seated Liberty Silver Dollars in AG and G. It was a paying proposition. Before silver bullion started its meteoric price climb in the fall of 1979, many dealers were overstocked with these coins. They were glad to sell an Ag or G Seated Liberty Silver Dollar (with its three quarters of an ounce of .999 fine silver) for $15. When silver bullion was $7 per ounce, the coin contained only $5 worth of silver, so a $15 sale to a collector on a low-grade specimen was quite satisfactory. With silver at $40 per troy ounce, the Seated Liberty Dollar suddenly had a bullion value over $30. Yes, the dealers could have retained these coins and marker them up to $40 or $50 with the intention of selling them to collectors. That would have been more than the refineries paid, since the refineries never (obviously) gave a premium for numismatic factors. But — once again — it just wasn't worthwhile. The dealers had a $5 or $6 investment in these coins and a $30 sale was irresistible . . . not just for the profit, but the fact that all their stock of such coins could be sold simultaneously. By waiting for collectors to buy, sales would be made piecemeal and very likely the value of silver bullion would drop before all were sold. During the big melts, everybody was trying desperately to beat the inevitable price decline. Everybody was trying to make the most of the situation while it existed, knowing or at least suspecting that it could not last forever.

Naturally the dealer had enormous amounts of coins to contribute for melting. Barber coins in all three denominations were melted in the multi millions, and it is undeniable that nearly all came from the stocks of dealers. The general public would not be in a position to supply coins of that age. All of these specimens, with the exception of those with dates missing or really serious damage, were better than bullion coins. Yet they were, unquestionably, melted. They were treated as bullion coins because the silver bullion market gave them considerably more bullion value than collector value. Of course the dealers did not send any 1892 San Francisco Barber halves for melting, regardless of condition. It was very simple for them to select the specimens for melting, as a quick glance at the prices showed which coins were justifiable to melt. If the spot price was $40 and the dealer had a $40 investment in a certain coin, he was not going to include it in a 90% silver bag. But if silver had reached $100 per troy ounce, as some felt it would, even these coins would have gone. One need only look through the ad pages of coin periodicals for December, 1979 and

January, 1980 to see what was being melted. Some dealers were buying Franklin Mint medals for melting, and in act the quantity of Franklin Mint items reaching the smelters' furnaces was huge.

It is a myth that few "scarce dates" or "good coins" were melted in the first or second big silver melt-downs. They were indeed melted but the proportion was much less than that of common dates. Also, the proportion of scarce dates melted in uncirculated condition was considerably less than common date"uncs." The professional coin dealers would not have consigned scarce date "uncs" for melting. They could have been included in bags assembled from miscellaneous sources, but the scarce dates in these bags were mainly circulated.

GENERAL CONCLUSIONS

It is the publisher's opinion that:

1. Current market values of many 90% silver coins do not reflect actual availability.

2. Melting consumed a large percentage of scarce dates, but many of these coins have adjusted to their decreased availability (i.e., climbed in price) while the common dates generally have not.

3. Melting may have accidentally consumed some very rare coins, but most likely these would be specimens unknown to the coin trade (owned by non-collectors who were unaware of their rarity of value), and their loss did not materially change the number of specimens available to collectors.

4. Market values are likely to increase on coins that suffered the greatest destruction by melting.

Probable Future Effects on the Coin Market. At the present time, mintage figures continue to be a prime factor in the prices that collectors are willing to pay for 90% silver coins. Coin prices — not just those of silver coins but all coins — have been traditionally aligned to mintage figures, in the belief that mintage figures are the most reliable barometer of scarcity. Some investors have already perceived that many 90% silver coins are, as the result of melting, much scarcer than their mintage figures indicate, and are buying selected coins accordingly. It is likely that the coming months will witness a growth in this trend, and if this happens it is inevitable that market values will climb. Many of the coins involved, such as late date Washington Quarters, have never been the target of heavily concentrated buying. Thus the dealers have had little, if any, problems resupplying their stocks at modest prices. Should heavy demand develop, the true scarcity of such coins will become apparent. Dealers will be obliged to bid against each other for the available supplies, Thus raising the wholesale prices, and these increases will then be translated into higher retail prices. It may require just such a situation before collectors are willing to admit that a majority of 90% silver coins are scarce in relation to their mintage figures. It is difficult at the present time for most collectors to recognize the reduced availability of 90% silver coins, as they are still readily obtainable from coin dealers. This camouflages the true picture: the fact that the total numbers of silver coins passing through the market are considerably less than twenty years ago. The fact that prices have not risen dramatically is not an indication that the coins are still available in the same quantities as before. Prices have simply not reached — yet — to the reduced availabilities. Hundreds of 90% silver coins are currently underpriced.

If prices do increase substantially, will this bring hidden caches of silver coins on the market, coins that are now nestled away as bullion investments? This possibility cannot fail to occur to investors and may cause them to hesitate to pay higher prices. Certainly a sharp rise in prices would lead to some silver coins coming on the market which would not otherwise have been sold. This happened in the sixties and again in the period from 1970 to early 1980. One must understand, however, that circumstances are very different today. In the sixties, 90% silver coins could still be skimmed from daily circulation and vending machines. In 1979-80 there were the accumulations held by private parties, who had been saving silver coins for a decade or more waiting until silver bullion reached an irresistible price. Almost everyone who had quantities of silver coins sold them in 1979-80, and most of those sold were melted. It is unlikely that any further jars or trunks of silver coins will be coming out of attics. Virtually all 90% silver coins now in existence are divided between three groups of owners: (1) investors, (2) coin collectors, (3) coin dealers. If prices begin to readjust, to reflect actual scarcity, it can be expected that some investors now holding silver coins will sell. These will be the investors who bought at very favorable low prices and are content to accept a modest profit. The actual quantity of silver coins returned to the market in this fashion would undoubtedly amount to nothing more than a trickle. Not all investors would be tempted to sell, even by a fairly substantial price increase. Some would automatically hold their coins in the prospect of still higher prices. Some would refuse to sell because they purchased when prices were high. So the coin dealers, faced with increased demand for 90% silver coins, could not depend on investors as their source of supply. Quite the reverse: investors would probably be doing far more buying than selling.

Price readjustments on silver coins would have a number of side effects. One of these would surely be the breaking up of numerous BU rolls now on the market. Many of today's dealers do a heavier business in rolls than single coins, and are accustomed to regard common date 90% silver coins as "roll coins." They put aside single specimens for the purpose of making up rolls. A price readjustment will see the opposite happening: rolls will be broken to meet collector demands for single specimens. Dealers will no longer discount BU rolls but will gladly take the time and trouble to place each specimen in a holder. The higher prices will make this worthwhile. As rolls disappear from the market, many investors will inevitably begin buying single specimens, even of coins valued at only $5 or $10. This will intensify the price increases, as they will be buying without the "roll discount." They will be paying full prices the same as collectors who buy individual coins.

Another side effect will be increased traffic in circulated common dates. This is where some of the really gross undervaluing exists, in series such as Walking Liberty Halves and Standing Liberty Quarters. While these coins have the potential to gain considerably in value, uncirculated specimens will probably have to lead the way. Few collectors or investors would be willing to pay a 50% increase for an F or VF specimen if the MS price has risen by only 10% or 20%. Our feeling is that the "uncs" will be at the forefront of price adjustment in its early stages, but that circulated grades will eventually register the same increases or possibly even higher ones. With circulated grades there could be a real difficulty for the dealers in resupplying their stocks. Few of the common dates now exist in circulated rolls graded under AU-50 and many cannot even be found in AU-50 rolls.

Over the years they have been made up into BU rolls with hardly anyone bothering to roll circulated specimens. Thus the potential for obtaining single specimens by breaking rolls will not be offered to most dealers.

NOTE TO READERS

"Silver Coins: The Aftermath of Melting" presents an analysis of the latest information as available to the editors of the Blackbook. As this situation is likely to have far reaching effects on the coin market, we want to continue our investigations and gather as much additional information as possible.

We would like to hear from you, whether you are a coin collector, coin dealer or silver coin investor. Do you agree that many 90% silver coins are undervalued? Have you found certain dated more difficult to obtain than their present values would suggest? Do 90% silver coins appear misvalued in just one condition grade, or several? Most important, do you have any specific information (not previously published) relating to the melting of silver coins? For example, do you know of large scale meltings of specific solid-date BU rolls? Can you contribute anything in the way of background information to what is presented in this article?

During the course of this entire year, until the 1987 Blackbook is published, the editors will conduct a huge information-gathering survey on 90% silver coins, to bring our readers fully up-to-date with the most reliable data. The results will be summarized in the next edition. Anyone who can contribute information will help to place this matter in focus and will be doing a service for the entire numismatic hobby.

We cannot promise personal replies but all letters will be carefully read. Please address to:

Blackbook Editor,
The House Of Collectibles
1904 Premier Row
Orlando, FL 32809

Information contained in letters may be published but names and addresses will not be used.

THE AMERICAN NUMISMATIC ASSOCIATION

Most of today's coin collectors probably know that there is an American Numismatic Association, the largest organization of "coin" collectors in the world. However, many may not realize that the Association is nearly 100 years old, with a current operating budget of more than a million dollars.

DR. GEORGE F. HEATH
FOUNDER OF A.N.A.

Q. DAVID BOWERS
CURRENT A.N.A. PRESIDENT

An educational, nonprofit organization, the American Numismatic Association invites and welcomes to membership all worthy persons eleven years of age and older who have a sincere interest in numismatics, whether they collect coins, paper money, tokens or medals; whether advanced collectors or those noncollectors only generally interested in the subject. Members, located in every state of the Union and in many other countries, total some 40,000.

A factor that deterred the Association's development during its first three-quarters of a century was the geographic dispersal of its functional offices: the executive secretary was in Phoenix, Arizona; the treasurer in Washington, D.C.; the editor in Chicago, Illinois; and the librarian in Lincoln, Nebraska. None of the staff was full-time or received pay and most operated out of their homes or private offices. Obviously, this situation limited and hampered communication and made for inefficient operation in general.

Since 1967 ANA operations have been centered in Colorado Springs, Colorado, and in 1982 the building was expanded to almost twice its original size. A board of governors, which establishes policy is determining all bylaws and regulations, is elected from the membership on a regular basis and serves without pay. Implementing established policy is a full-time salaried professional staff in Colorado Springs that includes an executive vice president, editor, librarian, authenticators, and assistants and clerical staff.

The principal objectives of the Association are the advancement of numismatic knowledge and better relations among numismatists. Collectors will find the annual membership dues low compared to the tremendous value to be found in the prestige and services that membership offers.

The ANA does not buy or sell coins. Its revenue comes from membership dues and is supplemented by gifts, bequests and contributions. It receives no operating funds from any governmental body. Any net income from various activities is used on behalf of its members and for the advancement of the hobby.

When the ANA was organized in October 1891, Dr. George F. Heath, the motivating force, was honored with membership No. 1. Member No. 1,000 was admitted in March 1908; No. 10,000 in March 1944; No. 50,000 in August

1963; and No. 100,000 in August 1979. Of course, the passing of time has taken its toll, and today's membership is slightly less than a third of the total number enrolled during the Association's 92 years.

The Numismatist, the Association's monthly magazine, is actually older than the ANA itself, having been started by Dr. Heath in 1888 (September-October) and published privately through 1910. It did, however, cooperate with and champion the cause of the Association — before and after its organization. In 1910 the vice president of ANA, W. W. C. Wilson of Montreal, purchased the magazine from publisher Farran Zerbe and gifted it to the Association, which has continued its publication without interruption.

More recent and rapidly growing is the American Numismatic Association Certification Service (ANACS), available to the public, but with lower fees for members. The ANACS staff examines and conducts nondestructive tests on numismatic items and furnishes the person submitting an item with a statement of expert opinion of the item's genuineness. A permanent record is kept by ANACS of all coins it examines.

Using the system of grading established and published by the ANA, the ANACS staff will express an opinion upon the condition of a United States coin and record it on the coin's certificate. Only authenticated coins will be graded. The fee for grading is, in most cases, appreciably less than for certification.

Collectors between the ages of 11 and 17 are encouraged in the hobby by lower membership dues, special articles in *The Numismatist,* special exhibit classes and programs at conventions, and other educational programs.

Classes of membership are as follows: **Regular** — adults 18 years of age and older (eligible for all benefits, including receipt of *The Numismatist); **Club** — nonprofit numismatic organizations, (entitled to all benefits); **Junior** — 11 through 17 years of age (entitled to all benefits but cannot hold office; **Associate** — limited to the spouse or child of a Regular or Life Member (cannot hold office or receive *The Numismatist);* and **Life Member** — corresponding to Regular members but a one-time fee is paid for lifetime membership. Memberships are not transferrable from one person to another, and membership numbers are never reassigned.

The amounts of dues and a few other details of membership follow:

DUES

Regular *(adult) — U.S. only*	$ 21.00*
Regular *(adult) — all other countries*	13.00*
Club — *any country*	25.00*
Junior *(11 through 17 years old)*	11.00
Associate *(child or spouse of Regular or Life Member living at member's address)*	4.00
Life *(adult individual)*	350.00
(Installment ($60 with application**, plus $25 per month for 12 months)	
Life *(club)*	1000.00

*Add $5 application fee, first year only
**Includes $10 bookkeeping fee, deducted from final payment if made within 90 days of application. Life Membership is not effective until full $350 fee is paid.

Nonmember annual subscription — *U.S. only* . . . . $ 28.00
Subscription — *all other countries* 33.00

The Numismatist continues to be the official publication and voice of the Association. Published monthly, it contains well illustrated articles about various phases of collecting, identifying and caring for coins, tokens, medals and paper money. Included are news items regarding Association activities, new issues of coins, medals and paper money, and developments within the hobby.

The advertising pages of the magazine are open only to ANA members, who must agree to abide by a strict "Code of Ethics". Members, except Associates, receive the magazine as one of the advantages of membership.

Aside from the magazine, one of the earliest services offered to ANA members was use of a circulating numismatic library, which has grown to be the world's largest facility of its kind. The library houses more than 12,000 books and more than 20,000 periodicals and other items, all of which are loaned by mail to members and are available to non-members for use in the Colorado Springs headquarters.

Related to the library is a visual education service that maintains and loans numismatic slide sets to member clubs for their meeting programs. These sets cover many different phases of numismatics and are available without cost except for shipping charges.

An important date in the history of ANA is May 9, 1912, when it was granted a Federal Charter by the U.S. Congress. Signed by President Taft, the Act gave the Charter a fifty-year life. A Congressional amendment dated April 10, 1962, allowed for an increase in the number of ANA board members and perpetuated the Charter indefinitely. One of very few such charters ever granted, it has given the Association prestige and has been a stabilizing influence on its management.

The ANA produces books of articles reprinted from *The Numismatist*, as well as pamphlets about coin collecting and "ANACS Counterfeit Detection Reports". In addition, numismatic books are offered at reduced prices through the Reference Book of the Month Club. Members of the book club are not required to purchase books, although membership will be automatically renewed only if one or more titles are purchased during a calendar year.

Persons having specific questions, wanting to see a copy of *The Numismatist* or obtain an application for membership are invited to write to: ANA Executive Vice President, P. O. Box 2366, Colorado Springs, CO 80901-2366, Phone (303) 632-COIN.

COLONIAL COINS, PATTERNS AND TOKENS

The history of our coinage begins not with the first federal issues but the coin used earlier by colonists. This period in American coin use, from exploration of Florida and the first Virginia settlements up to 1792, spans 200 years and is considered one of the most fascinating specialties for collectors. It is rich in types, designs and methods of production. While a great deal of colonial coinage is rare, some falls into the moderate price range. Here are historical objects of undisputed significance, purchasable in some for less than the cost of key-date modern coins. The celebrated "Rosa Americana," circulated before George Washington was born, can be held in good condition for less than $100. Even some of the 17th century "elephant tokens" sell for under $100, though this series also includes rarities of high price. The belief that colonial coinage is only for the wealthy just isn't so.

The story of this nation's beginnings is probably better told by its early money than by any other antiquities. Pilgrim settlers are often pictured as hunters and trappers living off the land. This is partly true but even in the 1600's there were cities with shops and a real need existed for coinage. When nothing better was available the old barter system was resorted to, as used in ancient times, with goods traded for other goods of similar value. In Massachusetts iron nails were accepted as legal tender, as well as Indian wampum (shells strung together on cords, each having a set value). As early as the 1640's, 20 years after the Mayflower, serious thought was given by the Bay Colony to striking its own money. In 1652 the Massachusetts General Court authorized experimental efforts in this direction, the first attempts were no more than rough metal discs stamped with small symbols. Compared to Europe's elaborate coinage they were meager but proved that this country had the ability to produce a medium of exchange. These were followed by improved domestic efforts as well as importation of coins from abroad, struck expressly for colonial use. These include the "Lord Baltimore" coins of Maryland and the Colonial Plantation Token. By the 17th century's close a variety of coins and pseudo-coins circulated. Some were private or merchant tokens, of British or Dutch manufacture. These were largely speculative issues brought to this country in large quantites by persons hoping to acquire vast land parcels. There was little confidence in the integrity of such coinage but it was nevertheless accepted, on the basis of weight.

Coins of both England and Spain, brought over by immigrants and traders, circulated pretty freely. Other foreign coins were also met with. Rather than being changed at face value they were, in the early years, valued at metal content, every merchant having a scale to weigh coins brought to him. Spain's dollar or "piece of eight" became the most familiar coin in the colonies, replaced thereafter by the coins of Great Britain. By the time of the Revolution, probably as many as 90% of the coins in American circulation were of British mintage.

Because colonial coins and tokens were not issued by a central government and were produced under challenging conditions, standardization cannot be expected. Sizes, denominations and quality of workmanship all vary sometimes to an extreme degree. Included are crude pieces hardly recognizable as coins, and works of considerable artistic merit. Some were not milled but hammered, struck by hammering the dies into metal blanks just as the Romans and Greeks made their coins 2,000 years ago. They also vary in scarcity. The collector should not be duped into paying inflated prices for coins merely on grounds of their being pre- Revolutionary. This in itself is no assurance of rarity. Each issue has its own established value, as shown in the listings section of this book. Allowance must be made for the condition of hammered pieces (whose shape will be somewhat irregular) and for specimens of great rarity, as these are almost impossible to find in the kind of condition one would expect of later coins. On the whole, condition standards are less rigid for colonial than federal issues. On the other hand, the buyer should not accept badly damaged examples in the belief that nothing better can be found.

THE UNITED STATES MINT

For 16 years following the Declaration of Independence this country still relied upon British and other foreign coinage. This was not only unsatisfactory but objectionable to many citizens, as Britain's coins bore the likeness of the not-too-popular George III. In 1791 Congress approved the establishment of a federal Mint. Presses for milling were purchased, designers and die-cutters hired. But the question remained whether to fashion U.S. coinage after Britain's or devise an entirely new series with different denominations. After much debate the latter plan was adopted, with the dollar (named for Thalers of the Dutch, who were not out enemies) as the chief currency unit and our coinage based upon divisions or multiples of it. The metal standard was fixed at 15 parts silver to one part of gold. When finalized on April 2, 1792, the Mint Act provided for coins in values of $10, $5, $2.50, $1, 50¢, 25¢, 10¢, 5¢, 1¢ and ½¢. The 1¢ and ½¢ were of copper, other denominations up to $1 silver, those over $1 gold. The $5 piece was regarded as the equivalent to Britain's pound sterling, the 25¢ to the British shilling, while the ½¢ was the counterpart to Britain's farthing or "fourthling" (¼th part of a British penny). It may seem odd that necessity was felt for a coin valued under one cent but at this remote period even the penny had considerable buying power and fractional pricing of goods was common — apples at 1¢ each or 5½¢ per half dozen for example. If such a coin was not available the situation would have invited an onslaught of merchant tokens.

Philadelphia was selected as home for the first Mint building, whose cornerstone was laid July 31, 1792. George Washington, then serving as President, contributed silverware from which the first federal coins were struck — a few half dimes or half dismes as they were called (5¢ pieces). Proceeding cautiously, the Mint's first purchase of metal was six pounds of copper. This was used for cents and half cents, delivered to the Treasurer of the United States in 1793. The following year a deposit of $80,715.73½ worth.of French silver coins was made to the Mint by the State of Maryland, to be melted down and used for coinage. They yielded a quantity of 1794-dated dollars and half dollars. Gold was not obtained until 1795 when a Boston merchant turned over $2,276.72 in ingots, which were quickly transformed (apparently along with gold from other sources) into 744 Half Eagles ($5 pieces). Later that year 400 Eagles ($10) were produced. By the close of the year 1800 the Mint had milled $2,534,000 worth of coins and succeeded in distributing them pretty widely throughout the then-inhabited regions of the country, as far west as Michigan and Missouri.

HOW UNITED STATES COINS ARE MINTED

THE COIN ALLOY CONTENT

In the coinage process, the first step is to prepare the alloy to be used. Except for nickels and one cent pieces, the alloys formerly (1964 and earlier) used in the coining of United States coins, were as follows:

a. **Silver coins**—90% silver and 10% copper
b. **Five-cent pieces**—75% copper and 25% nickel
c. **One-cent pieces**—95% copper and 5% zinc
(The cents of 1943 consisted of steel coated with zinc; and the nickels of 1942 to 1945 consisted of 35% silver, 56% copper, and 9% manganese.) In 1982 the cent was changed to a zinc interior with copper coating.

WHAT ARE THE NEW CLAD COINS MADE OF?

a. **(1971 TO DATE)** cupro-nickel dollars and half dollars. **(1965 TO DATE)** quarters and dimes. The outer surfaces are 75% copper and 25% nickel and the inner core is 100% copper.
b. **(1965-1970)** half-dollars. The outer surface is 80% silver and 20% copper. The inner core is 21% silver and 79% copper. The overall silver content of the coin is 40%.

When clad coinage was introduced in 1965, the designs then in use were retained: the Roosevelt dime, Washington quarter and Kennedy half. (The U. S. was not at that time minting dollar coins.) The only alteration since then was for the special 1976 Bicentennial designs.

Because of the ever-increasing demand for coinage, the mint introduced new time-saving steps in its coin minting. Raw metal is cast into giant ingots 18 feet long, 16 inches wide and 6 inches thick, weighing 6,600 pounds. Previously, they had weighed 400 pounds and were 16 times smaller in measurement. The ingot is rolled red hot and scaled to remove imperfections. It's then ready for the coins to be stamped; no longer are blanks made and annealed (heated). The excess metal that's left behind is used to make new ingots, in a continuing, never-ending process. The new coins are electronically scanned, counted and automatically bagged. These facilities are in use at the new, ultra-modern Mint in Philadelphia. It has a production capacity of eight billion coins per year and is open to the public, featuring interesting displays and guided tours.

HOW PROOF COINS ARE MINTED

1. Perfect planchets are picked out.
2. They are washed with a solution of cream of tartar.
3. Washed again and alcohol dipped.
4. The dies for making proof coins receive a special polishing for mirror-like finish.
5. The planchets are then milled.
6. The coins are minted by special hydraulic presses at a much slower rate than regular coins. The fine lines are much more visible on a proof coin.

MINTING: FROM METAL TO COINS

1.
Casting

2.
Rolled   Rolled again (18-22 times)

3.
Blanks punched out of strip

4.
Annealed (softened) in gas flame

5.
Tumbled (Polished)   Washed   Centrifugally dried

6.
Raised edge formed

7.
Coins weighed

8.
Obverse die
Reverse die
Reeded (milled) and stamped

9.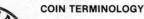
Final coins counted and bagged

COIN TERMINOLOGY

BORDERS
BEADED ·······
ORNAMENTED ━━━
SERRATED ▬▬ OR ▬▬ AND ∿∿∿

EDGES
MILLED • LETTERED • ORNAMENTED • VINE & BARS
• PLAIN • DIAGONALLY REEDED • ENGRAILED

THE MINTS AND THEIR MINT MARKS

By separate Acts of Congress, the government has established mints in different parts of the country.

1. **"P"**   **PHILADELPHIA,** *Pennsylvania* — 1973 to date — No Mint Mark. Until 1973, coins minted at Philadelphia did not carry mint marks, except for the silver-content nickels of 1942 to 1945.
2. **"C"**   **CHARLOTTE,** *North Carolina* — gold coins only 1838 to 1861.
3. **"CC"**   **CARSON CITY,** *Nevada* — 1870 to 1893.
4. **"D"**   **DAHLONEGA,** *Georgia* — on gold coins only 1838 to 1861.
5. **"D"**   **DENVER,** *Colorado* — 1906 to Date.
6. **"O"**   **NEW ORLEANS,** *Louisiana* — 1838 to 1861 and 1879 to 1909.
7. **"S"**   **SAN FRANCISCO,** *California* — 1854 to 1955. 1968 to Date.

The mint mark is a small letter, denoting which mint made the coin. Mint marks appear on either the obverse or reverse.

WHERE TO BUY AND SELL COINS

There are many potential sources for buying and selling coins: coin shops, auction sales, approval selections, coin shows and conventions, mail order and other collectors. If a coin shop is located in your area, this is the best place to begin buying. By examining the many coins offered in a shop you will become familiar with grading standards. Later you may wish to try buying at auction. When buying from dealers be sure to do business only with reputable parties. Be wary of rare coins offered at bargain prices as they could be counterfeits or improperly graded. Some bargain coins are specimens that have been amateurishly cleaned and are not considered desirable by collectors. The best "bargains" are popular coins in good condition, offered at fair prices.

Selling Coins to a Dealer. All coin dealers buy from the public. They must replenish their stock and the public is a much more economical source of supply than buying from other dealers. Damaged, very worn, or common coins are worthless to a dealer. So, too, usually, are sets in which the "key" coins are missing. If you have a large collection or several valuable coins to sell it might be wise to check the pages of coin publications for addresses of dealers handling major properties, rather than selling to a local shop.

Visit a coin show or convention. There you will find many dealers at one time, and you will experience the thrill of an active trading market in coins. You will find schedules of conventions and meetings of regional coin clubs listed in such publications as:

Coin World ($1.25)
Post Office Box 150
Sidney, Ohio 45365

Coins Magazine ($1.25)
Iola, Wisconsin 54945

The Numismatist ($2.50)
Published by the A.N.A.
P. O. 2366, Colo. Springs,
Colorado 80901

Numismatic News ($.85)
Iola, Wisconsin 54945

The Coin Wholesaler ($6.00 yr.)
P. O. Box 1028
Chattanooga, TN 37401

To find your local dealer, check the phone book under
"Coin Dealers".

CLEANING COINS

Under no circumstances should any effort be made to clean coins. Their value is likely to be reduced by such attempt.

ABOUT THE PRICES IN THIS BOOK

Prices shown in this book represent the current *retail* selling prices at the time of going to press. In the first column of each listing, a current *average buying price* is also indicated. This is the price at which coin dealers are buying from the public. Readers should understand that the actual prices charged, or paid, by any given dealer (there are more than 12,000 coin dealers in the U.S.) can vary somewhat. Hence the *Blackbook* is presented merely as a guide to the average buying and selling prices.

Prices are shown for each coin in various condition grades. It is of utmost importance that a coin be accurately graded, before a value can be placed on it. So-called "slider coins," such as MS-62, are not included in this book, because of space limitations and the difficulties of gathering reliable information on their values. Nor are split-grade coins included (such as AU-55/MS-60), but with some simple mathematics their values can be estimated, based on the prices shown.

When a price is omitted, there is not enough reliable pricing information available. This is usually because the coin, in that particular condition grade, is seldom publicly sold. However, this should not lead to the assumption that all such coins are more valuable than those for which prices are indicated. This is not necessarily the case.

For some scarce coins which are not regularly sold, an example will be given of a specific auction sale result, along with the year in which the sale occurred. These are given purely in the interest of supplying some tangible pricing information, but *may not* (especially in the case of older prices) accurately reflect the price that would be obtained for the same coin if sold today.

When a coin is said to be "unique," this indicates that only one single specimen is recorded to exist. It does not preclude the possibility that other specimens might exist, which have escaped the notice of numismatists.

Price are given for the major or traditionally acknowledged die varieties, for coins on which die varieties occurred. Many additional die varieties will be noticed in dealers' and auctioneers' literature. The collector status of many of these "minor" die varieties — that is, whether they deserve to be recognized as separate varieties — is a point on which no general agreement has been, or is likely to be, reached. It is important however to note, whether discussing major or minor die varieties, that the market values of such coins are not automatically higher than those of the normal die type. Nor can it always be assumed that the variety is scarcer than the normal die type.

In the case of common date silver and gold coins of the late nineteenth and twentieth centuries, it must be borne in mind that the values (for buying or selling) are influenced by the current value of the metal they contain. Most coin shops display the current "spot" prices for silver and gold bullion.

HOW TO USE THIS BOOK

Listings are provided in this book for all coins of the U.S. Mint plus colonial coins and several other groups of coins (please consult index).

Each listing carries the following information:

Denomination of coin.

Date (this is the date appearing on the coin, which is not necessarily the year in which it was actually manufactured).

Mintage (quantity manufactured by the Mint). In some cases this information is not available. In others, the totals announced by the Mint may not be entirely accurate. This is particularly true of coins dating before 1830.

Average Buying Price (A.P.B.). This is the price at which dealers are buying the coin in the condition grade noted. Buying prices can vary somewhat from one dealer to another.

Current Retail Value, in various grades of condition. The price columns following the A.B.P. or Average Buying Price show retail prices being charged by dealers. Prices for each coin are given in various grades of condition. Check the column head, then refer to the Grading Guide if you have any doubt about the condition of your coin. Be sure you have correctly identified your coin and its condition. If the date is missing from your coin, it qualifies only as a "type filler" (that is, a "type" coin in low grade condition), and its value will be lower than the price shown for a coin of that series.

OFFICIAL ANA GRADING SYSTEM

The descriptions of coin grades given in this book are intended for use in determining the relative condition of coins in various states of preservation. The terms and standards are based on the commonly accepted practices of experienced dealers and collectors. Use of these standards is recommended by the American Numismatic Association to avoid misunderstandings during transactions, cataloging and advertising.

The method of grading described in this book should be referred to as the Official ANA Grading System. When grading by these standards, care must be taken to adhere to the standard wording, abbreviations and numbers used in this text.

When a coin first begins to show signs of handling, abrasion, or light wear, only the highest parts of the design are affected. Evidence that such a coin is not Uncirculated can be seen by carefully examining the high spots for signs of a slight change in color, surface texture, or sharpness of fine details.

In early stages of wear the highest points of design become slightly rounded or flattened, and the very fine details begin to merge together in small spots.

After a coin has been in circulation for a short time, the entire design and surface will show light wear. Many of the high parts will lose their sharpness, and most of the original mint luster will begin to wear except in recessed areas.

Further circulation will reduce the sharpness and relief of the entire design. High points then begin to merge with the next lower parts of the design.

After the protective rim is worn away the entire surface becomes flat, and most of the details blend together or become partially merged with the surface.

It should be understood that because of the nature of the minting process, some coins will be found which do not conform exactly with the standard definitions of wear as given in this text. Specific points of wear may vary slightly. Information given in the notes at the end of some sections does not cover all exceptions, but is a guide to the most frequently encountered varieties.

Also, the amount of mint luster (for the highest several grades) is intended more as a visual guide rather than a fixed quantity. The percentage of visible mint luster described in the text is the *minimum* allowable amount, and a higher percentage can usually be expected. Luster is not always brilliant and may be evident although sometimes dull or discolored.

A *Choice* coin in any condition is one with an attractive, above average surface relatively free from nicks or bag marks. A *Typical* coin may have more noticeable minor surface blemishes.

In all cases, a coin in lower condition must be assumed to include all the wear features of the next higher grade in addition to its own distinguishing points of wear.

Remarks concerning the visibility of certain features refer to the *maximum* allowable amount of wear for those features.

NOTE: The official ANA Grading System used in this book is with the permission of the American Numismatic Association.

RECORD KEEPING

For your convenience, we suggest you use the following record-keeping system to note condition of your coin in the checklist box.

ABOUT GOOD ☒	FINE ☐	UNCIRCULATED ☒
GOOD ☑	VERY FINE ☐	PROOF ■
VERY GOOD ☒	EXTREMELY FINE ☒	

GRADING ABBREVIATIONS

Corresponding numbers may be used with any of these descriptions.

PROOF-70	Perfect Proof	Perf. Proof	Proof-70
PROOF-65	Choice Proof	Ch. Proof	Proof-65
PROOF-60	Proof	Proof	Proof-60
MS-70	Perfect Uncirculated	Perf. Unc.	Unc.-70
MS-65	Choice Uncirculated	Ch. Unc.	Unc.-65
MS-60	Uncirculated	Unc.	Unc.-60
AU-55	Choice About Uncirculated	Ch. Abt. Unc.	Ch. AU
AU-50	About Uncirculated	Abt. Unc.	AU
EF-45	Choice Extremely Fine	Ch. Ex. Fine	Ch. EF
EF-40	Extremely Fine	Ex. Fine	EF
VF-30	Choice Very Fine	Ch. V. Fine	Ch. VF
VF-20	Very Fine	V. Fine	VF
F-12	Fine	Fine	F
VG-8	Very Good	V. Good	VG
G-4	Good	Good	G
AG-3	About Good	Abt. Good	AG

PROOF COINS

The mirrorlike surface of a brilliant proof coin is much more susceptible to damage than are the surfaces of an Uncirculated coin. For this reason, proof coins which have been cleaned often show a series of fine hairlines or minute striations. Also, careless handling has resulted in certain proofs acquiring marks, nicks and scratches.

Some proofs, particularly nineteenth century issues, have "lintmarks." When a proof die was wiped with an oily rag, sometimes threads, bits of hair, lint, and so on would remain. When a coin was struck from such a die, an incuse or recessed impression of the debris would appear on the piece. Lintmarks visible to the unaided eye should be specifically mentioned in a description.

Proofs are divided into the following classifications:

Proof-70 (Perfect Proof). A Proof-70 or Perfect Proof is a coin with no hairlines, handling marks, or other defects; in other words, a flawless coin. Such a coin may be brilliant or may have natural toning.

Proof-65 (Choice Proof). Proof-65 or Choice Proof refers to a proof which may show some fine hairlines, usually from friction-type cleaning or friction-type drying or rubbing after dipping. To the unaided eye, a Proof-65 or a Choice Proof will appear to be virtually perfect. However, 5x magnification will reveal some minute lines. Such hairlines are best seen under strong incandescent light.

Proof-60 (Proof). Proof-60 refers to a proof with some scattered handling marks and hairlines which will be visible to the unaided eye.

Impaired Proofs; Other Comments. If a proof has been excessively cleaned, has many marks, scratches, dents or other defects, it is described as an impaired proof. If the coin has seen extensive wear then it will be graded one of the lesser grades — Proof-55, Proof-45 or whatever. It is not logical to describe a slightly worn proof as "AU" (Almost Uncirculated) for it never was "Uncirculated" to begin with — in the sense that Uncirculated describes a top grade normal production strike. So, the term "impaired proof" is appropriate. It is best to describe fully such a coin, examples being: "Proof with extensive hairlines and scuffing," or "Proof with numerous nicks and scratches in the field," or "Proof-55, with light wear on the higher surfaces."

UNCIRCULATED COINS

The term "Uncirculated," interchangeable with "Mint State," refers to a coin which has never seen circulation. Such a piece has no wear of any kind. A coin as bright as the time it was minted or with very light natural toning can be described as "Brilliant Uncirculated." A coin which has natural toning can be described as "Toned Uncirculated." Except in the instance of copper coins, the presence or absence of light toning does not affect an Uncirculated coin's grade. Indeed, among silver coins, attractive natural toning often results in the coin bringing a premium.

The quality of luster or "mint bloom" on an Uncirculated coin is an essential element in correctly grading the piece, and has a bearing on its value. Luster may in time become dull, frosty, spotted or discolored. Unattractive luster will normally lower the grade.

With the exception of certain Special Mint Sets made in recent years for collectors, Uncirculated or normal production strike coins were produced on high speed presses, stored in bags together with other coins, run through counting machines, and in other ways handled without regard to numismatic posterity. As a result, it is the rule and not the exception for an Uncirculated coin to have bag marks and evidence of coin-to-coin contact, although the piece might not have seen actual commercial circulation. The amount of such marks will depend upon the coin's size. Differences in criteria in this regard are given in the individual sections under grading descriptions for different denominations and types.

Uncirculated coins can be divided into three major categories:

MS-70 (Perfect Uncirculated). MS-70 or Perfect Uncirculated is the finest quality available. Such a coin under 4x magnification will show no bag marks, lines, or other evidence of handling or contact with other coins.

A brilliant coin may be described as "MS-70, Brilliant" or "Perfect Brilliant Uncirculated." A lightly toned nickel or silver coin may be described as "MS-70, toned" or "Perfect Toned Uncirculated." Or, in the case of particularly attractive or unusual toning, additional adjectives may be in order such as "Perfect Uncirculated with attractive iridescent toning around the borders."

Copper and bronze coins: To qualify as MS-70 or Perfect Uncirculated, a copper or bronze coin must have its full luster and natural surface color, and may not be toned brown, olive, or any other color. (Coins with toned surfaces which are otherwise perfect should be described as MS-65 as the following text indicates.)

MS-65 (Choice Uncirculated). This refers to an above average Uncirculated coin which may be brilliant or tones (and described accordingly) and which has fewer bag marks than usual; scattered occasional bag marks on the surface or perhaps one or two very light rim marks.

MS-60 (Uncirculated). MS-60 or Uncirculated (typical Uncirculated without any other adjectives) refers to a coin which has a moderate number of bag marks on its surface. Also present may be a few minor edge nicks and marks, although not of a serious nature. Unusually deep bag marks, nicks and the like must be described separately. A coin may be either brilliant or toned.

Striking and Minting Peculiarities on Uncirculated Coins

Certain early United States gold and silver coins have mint-caused planchet or adjustment marks, a series of parallel striations. If these are visible to the naked eye they should be described adjectively in addition to the numerical or regular descriptive grade. For example: "MS-60 with adjustment marks," or "MS-65 with adjustment marks," or "Perfect Uncirculated with very light adjustment marks," or something similar.

If an Uncirculated coin exhibits weakness due to striking or die wear, or unusual (for the variety) die wear, this must be adjectivally mentioned in addition to the grade. Examples are: "MS-60, lightly struck," or "Choice Uncirculated, lightly struck," and "MS-70, lightly struck."

CIRCULATED COINS

Once again a coin enters circulation it begins to shows signs of wear. As time goes on the coin becomes more and more worn until; after a period of many decades, only a few features may be left.

Dr. William H. Sheldon devised a numerical scale to indicate degrees of wear. According to this scale, a coin in condition 1 or "Basal State" is barely recognizable. At the opposite end, a coin touched by even the slightest trace of wear (below MS-60) cannot be called Uncirculated.

While numbers from 1 through 59 are continuous, it has been found practical to designate specific intermediate numbers to define grades. Hence, this text uses the following descriptions and their numerical equivalents:

AU-55 (Choice About Uncirculated). Only a small trace of wear is visible on the highest points of the coin. As is the case with the other grades here, specific information is listed in the following text under the various types, for wear often occurs in different spots on different designs.

AU-50 (About Uncirculated). With traces of wear on nearly all of the highest areas. At least half of the original mint luster is present.

EF-45 (Choice Extremely Fine). With light overall wear on the coin's highest points. All design details are very sharp. Mint luster is usually seen only in protected areas of the coin's surface such as between the star points and in the letter spaces.

EF-40 (Extremely Fine). With only slight wear but more extensive than the preceding, still with excellent overall sharpness. Traces of mint luster may still show.

VF-30 (Choice Very Fine). With light even wear on the surface; design details on the highest points lightly worn, but with all lettering and major features sharp.

VF-20 (Very Fine). As preceding but with moderate wear on highest parts.

F-12 (Fine). Moderate to considerable even wear. Entire design is bold. All lettering, including the word LIBERTY (on coins with this feature on the shield or headband), visible, but with some weaknesses.

VG-8 (Very Good). Well worn. Most fine details such as hair strands, leaf details, and so on are worn nearly smooth. The word LIBERTY, if on a shield or headband, is only partially visible.

G-4 (Good). Heavily worn. Major designs visible, but with faintness in areas. Head of Liberty, wreath, and other major features visible in outline form without center detail.

AG-3 (About Good). Very heavily worn with portions of the lettering, date and legends being worn smooth. The date barely readable.

Note: The exact descriptions of circulated grades vary widely from issue to issue. It is essential to refer to the specific text when grading any coin.

SPLIT AND INTERMEDIATE GRADES

It is often the case that because of the peculiarities of striking or a coin's design, one side of the coin will grade differently from the other. When this is the case, a diagonal mark is used to separate the two. For example, a coin with an AU-50 obverse and a Choice Extremely Fine-45 reverse can be described as: AU/EF or, alternately, 50/45.

The ANA standard numerical scale is divided into the following steps: 3, 4, 8, 12, 20, 30, 40, 45, 50, 60, 65 and 70. Most advanced collectors and dealers find that the gradations from AG-3 through Choice AU-55 are sufficient to describe nearly every coin showing wear. The use of intermediate grade levels such as EF-42, EF-43 and so on is not encouraged. Grading is not that precise, and using such finely split intermediate grades is imparting a degree of accuracy which probably will not be able to be verified by other numismatists. As such, it is discouraged.

A split or intermediate grade, such as that between VF-30 and EF-40, should be called Choice VF-35 rather than VF-EF or About EF.

An exception to intermediate grades can be found among Mint State coins, coins grading from MS-60 through MS-70. Among Mint State coins there are fewer variables. Wear is not a factor; the considerations are the amount of bag marks and surface blemishes. While it is good numismatic practice to adhere to the numerical classifications of 60, 65 and 70, it is permissible to use intermediate grades.

In all instances, the adjectival description must be of the next lower grade. For example, a standard grade for a coin is MS-60 or Uncirculated Typical. The next major category is MS-65 or Uncirculated Choice. A coin which is felt to grade, for example, MS-64, must be described as "MS-64, Uncirculated Typical." It may not be described as Choice Uncirculated, for the minimum definition of Choice Uncirculated is MS-65. Likewise, a MS-69 coin must be described as: MS-69, Uncirculated Choice. It is not permissible to use Uncirculated Perfect for any coin which is any degree less than MS-70.

The ANA grading system considers it to be good numismatic practice to adhere to the standard 60, 65 and 70 numerical designations. Experienced numismatists can generally agree on whether a given coin is MS-60 or MS-65. However, not even the most advanced numismatists can necessarily agree on whether a coin is MS-62 or MS-63; the distinction is simply too minute to permit accuracy. In all instances, it is recommended that intermediate grades be avoided, and if there is any doubt, the lowest standard grade should be used. The use of plus or minus signs is also not accepted practice.

SMALL CENTS — INDIAN HEAD 1859-1909

REVERSE
(without shield, 1859)

OBVERSE

REVERSE
(with shield, 1860-1909)

MINT STATE *(Absolutely no trace of wear.)*

MS-70 (Perfect Uncirculated)
A flawless coin exactly as it was minted, with no trace of wear or injury. Must have full mint luster and brilliance of light toning. Any unusual die or planchet traits must be described.

MS-65 (Choice Uncirculated)
No trace of wear; nearly as perfect as MS-70 except for some small blemish. Has full mint luster but may be unevenly toned or lightly fingermarked. A few barely noticeable nicks or marks may be present.

MS-60 (Uncirculated)
A strictly Uncirculated coin with no trace of wear, but with blemishes more obvious than for MS-65. May lack full mint luster, and surface may be dull or spotted. Check points for signs of abrasion: hair above ear; curl to right of ribbon; bow knot.

ABOUT UNCIRCULATED *(Small trace of wear visible on highest points.)*

AU-55 (Choice About Uncirculated)
OBVERSE: Only a trace of wear shows on the hair above the ear.
REVERSE: A trace of wear shows on the bow knot. Three-quarters of the mint luster is still present.

AU-50 (About Uncirculated)
OBVERSE: Traces of wear show on the hair above ear and curl to right of ribbon.
REVERSE: Traces of wear show on the leaves and bow knot. Half of the mint luster is still present.

EXTREMELY FINE *(Very light wear on only the highest points.)*

EF-45 (Choice Extremely Fine)
OBVERSE: Wear shows on hair above ear, curl to right of ribbon and on the ribbon end. All of the diamond design and letters in LIBERTY are very plain.
REVERSE: High points of the leaves and bow are lightly worn. Traces of mint luster still show.

EF-40 (Extremely Fine)
OBVERSE: Feathers well defined and LIBERTY is bold. Wear shows on hair above ear, curl to right of ribbon and on the ribbon end. Most of the diamond design shows plainly.
REVERSE: High points of the leaves and bow are worn.

VERY FINE *(Light to moderate even wear. All major features are sharp.)*

VF-30 (Choice Very Fine)
OBVERSE: Small flat spots of wear on tips of feathers, ribbon and hair ends. Hair still shows half of details. LIBERTY slightly worn but all letters are sharp.
REVERSE: Leaves and bow worn but fully detailed.

VF-20 (Very Fine)
OBVERSE: Headdress shows considerable flatness. Nearly half of the details still show in hair and on ribbon. Head slightly worn but bold. LIBERTY is worn but all letters are complete.
REVERSE: Leaves and bow are almost fully detailed.

FINE *(Moderate to heavy even wear. Entire design clear and bold.)*

F-12 (Fine)
OBVERSE: One-quarter of details show in the hair. Ribbon is worn smooth. LIBERTY shows clearly with no letters missing.
REVERSE: Some details visible in the wreath and bow. Tops of leaves are worn smooth.

VERY GOOD *(Well worn. Design clear but flat and lacking details.)*

VG-8 (Very Good)
OBVERSE: Outline of feather ends shows but some are smooth. Legend and date are visible. At least three letters in LIBERTY show clearly, but any combination of two full letters and parts of two others are sufficient.

REVERSE: Slight detail in wreath shows, but the top is worn smooth. Very little outline showing in the bow.

GOOD *(Heavily worn. Design and legend visible but faint in spots.)*

G-4 (Good)
OBVERSE: Entire design well worn with very little detail remaining. Legend and date are weak but visible.
REVERSE: Wreath is worn flat but completely outlined. Bow merges with wreath.

ABOUT GOOD *(Outlined design. Parts of date and legend worn smooth.)*

AG-3 (About Good)
OBVERSE: Head is outlined with nearly all details worn away. Legend and date readable but very weak and merging into rim.
REVERSE: Entire design partially worn away. Bow is merged with the wreath.

SMALL CENTS — LINCOLN 1909 TO DATE

REVERSE	OBVERSE	REVERSE
(wheatline, 1909-1958)		(memorial, 1959-date)

MINT STATE *(Absolutely no trace of wear.)*

MS-70 (Perfect Uncirculated)
A flawless coin exactly as it was minted, with no trace of wear or injury. Must have full mint luster and brilliance of light toning. Any unusual die or planchet traits must be described.

MS-65 (Choice Uncirculated)
No trace of wear; nearly as perfect as MS-70 except for some small blemish. Has full mint luster but may be unevenly toned or lightly fingermarked. A few barely noticeable nicks or marks may be present.

MS-60 (Uncirculated)
A strictly Uncirculated coin with no trace of wear, but with blemishes more obvious than for MS-65. May lack full mint luster, and surface may be dull or spotted. Check points for signs of abrasion: high points of cheek and jaw; tips of wheat stalks.

ABOUT UNCIRCULATED *(Small trace of wear visible on highest points.)*

AU-55 (Choice About Uncirculated)
OBVERSE: Only a trace of wear shows on the highest point of the jaw.
REVERSE: A trace of wear on the top of wheat stalks. Almost all of the mint luster is still present.

AU-50 (About Uncirculated)
OBVERSE: Traces of wear show on the cheek and jaw.
REVERSE: Traces of wear show on the wheat stalks. Three-quarters of the mint luster is still present.

EXTREMELY FINE *(Very light wear on only the highest points.)*

EF-45 (Choice Extremely Fine)
OBVERSE: Slight wear shows on hair above ear, on the cheek, and at the jaw.
REVERSE: High points of wheat stalks are lightly worn, but each line is clearly defined. Half of the mint luster still shows.

EF-40 (Extremely Fine)
OBVERSE: Wear shows on hair above ear, on the cheek, and on the jaw.
REVERSE: High points of wheat stalks are worn, but each line is clearly defined. Traces of mint luster still show.

VERY FINE *(Light to moderate even wear. All major features are sharp.)*

VF-30 (Choice Very Fine)
OBVERSE: There are small flat spots of wear on cheek and jaw. Hair still shows details. Ear and bow tie slightly worn but show clearly.
REVERSE: Lines in wheat stalks are lightly worn but fully detailed.

VF-20 (Very Fine)
OBVERSE: Head shows considerable flatness. Nearly all the details still show in hair and on the face. Ear and bow tie worn but bold.
REVERSE: Lines in wheat stalks are worn but plain and without weak spots.

FINE *(Moderate to heavy even wear. Entire design clear and bold.)*

F-12 (Fine)
OBVERSE: Some details show in the hair. Cheek and jaw are worn nearly smooth. LIBERTY shows clearly with no letters missing. The ear and bow tie are visible.
REVERSE: Most details are visible in the stalks. Top wheat lines are worn but separated.

VERY GOOD *(Well worn. Design clear but flat and lacking details.)*

VG-8 (Very Good)
OBVERSE: Outline of hair shows but most details are smooth. Cheek and jaw are smooth. More than half of bow tie is visible. Legend and date are clear.
REVERSE: Wheat shows some details and about half of the lines at the top.

GOOD *(Heavily worn. Design and legend visible but faint in spots.)*

G-4 (Good)
OBVERSE: Entire design well worn with very little detail remaining. Legend and date are weak but visible.
REVERSE: Wheat is worn nearly flat but is completely outlined. Some grains are visible.

ABOUT GOOD *(Outlined design. Parts of date and legend worn smooth.)*

AG-3 (About Good)
OBVERSE: Head is outlined with nearly all details worn away. Legend and date readable but very weak and merging into rim.
REVERSE: Entire design partially worn away. Parts of wheat and motto merged with the wreath.

Note: The Memorial cents from 1959 to date can be graded by using the obverse descriptions.

The following characteristic traits will assist in grading but must not be confused with actual wear on the coins:

Matte proof cents of 1909 through 1916 are often spotted or stained.

Branch mint cents of the 1920's are usually not as sharply struck as later dates.

Many of the early dates of Lincoln cents are weakly struck either on the obverse or the reverse, especially the following dates: 1911-D, 1914-D, 1917-D, 1918-D, 1921, 1922-D, 1923, 1924, 1927-D, 1927-S and 1929-D.

1922 "plain" is weakly struck at the head, has a small I and joined RT in LIBERTY. Sometimes the wheat heads are weak on the reverse.

1924-D usually has a weak mint mark.

1931-S is sometimes unevenly struck.

1936 proof cents: early strikes are less brilliant than those made later that year.

1955 doubled die: hair details are less sharp than most cents of the period.

NICKEL FIVE CENTS — LIBERTY HEAD 1883-1912

OBVERSE   "NO CENTS" REVERSE   REVERSE

MINT STATE *(Absolutely no trace of wear.)*

MS-70 (Perfect Uncirculated)
A flawless coin exactly as it was minted, with no trace of wear or injury. Must have full mint luster but this may range from brilliant to frosty. Any unusual die or striking traits must be described.

MS-65 (Choice Uncirculated)
No trace of wear; nearly as perfect as MS-70 except for some small weakness or blemish. Has full mint luster but may be unevenly toned, frosty, or lightly fingermarked. A few barely noticeable nicks or marks may be present.

MS-60 (Uncirculated)
A strictly Uncirculated coin with no trace of wear, but with blemishes more obvious than for MS-65. May lack full mint luster, and surface may be dull or spotted. Check points for signs of abrasion: high points of hair left of ear and at forehead. Corn ears at bottom of wreath.

ABOUT UNCIRCULATED *(Small trace of wear visible on highest points.)*

AU-55 (Choice About Uncirculated)
OBVERSE: Only a trace of wear shows on the highest points of hair left of ear.
REVERSE: A trace of wear shows on corn ears. Half of the mint luster is still present.

AU-50 (About Uncirculated)
OBVERSE: Traces of wear show on hair left of ear and at forehead.
REVERSE: Traces of wear show on the wreath and on corn ears. Part of the mint luster is still present.

EXTREMELY FINE *(Very light wear on only the highest points.)*

EF-45 (Choice Extremely Fine)
OBVERSE: Slight wear shows on high points of hair from forehead to the ear.
REVERSE: High points of wreath are lightly worn. Lines in corn are clearly defined. Traces of mint luster may still show.

EF-40 (Extremely Fine)
OBVERSE: Wear shows on hair from forehead to ear, on the cheek, and on curls.
REVERSE: High points of wreath are worn, but each line is clearly defined. Corn shows wear.

VERY FINE *(Light to moderate even wear. All major features are sharp.)*

VF-30 (Choice Very Fine)
OBVERSE: Three-quarters of hair details show. The coronet has full bold lettering.
REVERSE: Leaves are worn but most of the ribs are visible. Some of the lines in the corn are clear unless weakly struck.

VF-20 (Very Fine)
OBVERSE: Over half the details still show in hair and curls. Head worn but bold. Every letter on coronet is plainly visible.
REVERSE: Leaves are worn but some of the ribs are visible. Most details in the wreath are clear unless weakly struck.

FINE *(Moderate to heavy even wear. Entire design clear and bold.)*

F-12 (Fine)
OBVERSE: Some details show in curls and hair at top of head. All letters of LIBERTY are visible.
REVERSE: Some details visible in wreath. Letters in the motto are worn but clear.

VERY GOOD *(Well worn. Design clear but flat and lacking details.)*

VG-8 (Very Good)
OBVERSE: Bottom edge of coronet, and most hair details, are worn smooth. At least three letters in LIBERTY are clear. Rim is complete.
REVERSE: Wreath shows only bold outline. Some letters in the motto are very weak. Rim is complete.

GOOD *(Heavily worn. Design and legend visible but faint in spots.)*

G-4 (Good)
OBVERSE: Entire design well worn with very little detail remaining. Stars and date are weak but visible.
REVERSE: Wreath is worn flat and not completely outlined. Legend and motto are worn nearly smooth.

ABOUT GOOD *(Outlined design. Parts of date and legend worn smooth.)*

AG-3 (About Good)
OBVERSE: Head is outlined with nearly all details worn away. Date readable but very weak and merging into rim.
REVERSE: Entire design partially worn away.

Note: The 1912-D, 1912-S and 1883 "no cents" variety are often weakly struck.

NICKEL FIVE CENTS — BUFFALO 1913-1938

MINT STATE *(Absolutely no trace of wear.)*

MS-70 (Perfect Uncirculated)
A flawless coin exactly as it was minted, with no trace of wear or injury. Must have full mint luster. Any unusual die or striking traits must be described.

MS-65 (Choice Uncirculated)
No trace of wear; nearly as perfect as MS-70 except for some small weakness or blemish. Has full mint luster but may be unevenly toned or lightly fingermarked. A few barely noticeable nicks or marks may be present.

NICKEL FIVE CENTS — BUFFALO 1913–1938

OBVERSE

REVERSE

MS-60 (Uncirculated)
A strictly uncirculated coin with no trace of wear, but with blemishes more obvious than for MS-65. May lack full mint luster and surface may be dull or spotted. Check points for signs of abrasion: high points of Indian's cheek. Upper front leg, hip, tip of tail. Shallow or weak spots in the relief are usually caused by improper striking and not wear.

ABOUT UNCIRCULATED *(Small trace of wear visible on highest points.)*

AU-55 (Choice About Uncirculated)
OBVERSE: Only a trace of wear shows on high point of cheek.
REVERSE: A trace of wear shows on the hip. Half of the mint luster is still present.

AU-50 (About Uncirculated)
OBVERSE: Traces of wear show on hair above and to left of forehead, and at the cheek bone.
REVERSE: Traces of wear show on tail, hip and hair above and around the horn. Traces of mint luster still show.

EXTREMELY FINE *(Very light wear on only the highest points.)*

EF-45 (Choice Extremely Fine)
OBVERSE: Slight wear shows on the hair above the braid. There is a trace of wear on the temple and hair near cheek bone.
REVERSE: High points of hip and thigh are lightly worn. The horn and tip of tail are sharp and nearly complete.

EF-40 (Extremely Fine)
OBVERSE: Hair and face are lightly worn but well defined and bold. Slight wear shows on lines of hair braid.
REVERSE: Horn and end of tail are worn but all details are visible.

VERY FINE *(Light to moderate even wear. All major features are sharp.)*

VF-30 (Choice Very Fine)
OBVERSE: Hair shows nearly full details. Feathers and braid are worn but sharp.
REVERSE: Head, front leg and hip are worn. Tail shows plainly. Horn is worn but full.

VF-20 (Very Fine)
OBVERSE: Hair and cheek show considerable flatness, but all details are clear. Feathers still show partial detail.
REVERSE: Hair on head is worn. Tail and point of horn are visible.

FINE *(Moderate to considerable even wear. Entire design clear and bold.)*

F-12 (Fine)
OBVERSE: Three-quarters of details show in hair and braid. LIBERTY is plain but merging with rim.
REVERSE: Major details visible along the back. Horn and tail are smooth but three-quarters visible.

VERY GOOD *(Well worn. Design clear but flat and lacking details.)*

VG-8 (Very Good)
OBVERSE: Outline of hair is visible at temple and near cheek bone. LIBERTY merges with rim. Date is clear.
REVERSE: Some detail shows in head. Lettering is all clear. Horn is worn nearly flat but is partially visible.

GOOD *(Heavily worn. Design and legend visible but faint in spots.)*

G-4 (Good)
OBVERSE: Entire design well worn with very little detail remaining in central part. LIBERTY is weak and merged with rim.
REVERSE: Buffalo is nearly flat but is well outlined. Horn does not show. Legend is weak but readable. Rim worn to tops of letters.

ABOUT GOOD *(Outlined design. Parts of date and legend worn smooth.)*

AG-3 (About Good)
OBVERSE: Design is outlined with nearly all details worn away. Date and motto partially readable but very weak and merging into rim.
REVERSE: Entire design partially worn away. Rim is merged with the letters.

Note: Buffalo nickels were often weakly struck, and lack details even on Uncirculated specimens. The following dates are usually unevenly struck with weak spots in the details:

1913-S I and II, 1917-D, 1917-S, 1918-D, 1918-S, 1919-S, 1920-D, 1920-S, 1921-S, 1923-S, 1924-D, 1924-S, 1925-D, 1925-S, 1926-D, 1926-S, 1927-D, 1927-S, 1928-D, 1928-S, 1929-D, 1931-S, 1934-D and 1935-D.

1913 through 1916 matte proof coins are sometimes spotted or stained.

NICKEL FIVE CENTS — JEFFERSON 1938 TO DATE

| OBVERSE | "WARTIME"
REVERSE 1942-1945 | REVERSE |

MINT STATE *(Absolutely no trace of wear.)*

MS-70 (Perfect Uncirculated)
A flawless coin exactly as it was minted, with no trace of wear or injury. Must have full mint luster and brilliance. Any unusual striking or planchet traits must be described.

MS-65 (Choice Uncirculated)
No trace of wear; nearly as perfect as MS-70 except for some small weakness or blemish. Has full mint luster but may be unevenly toned or lightly fingermarked. A few barely noticeable nicks or marks may be present.

MS-60 (Uncirculated)
A strictly Uncirculated coin with no trace of wear, but with weaknesses and blemishes more obvious than for MS-65. May lack full mint luster, and surface may be dull or spotted. Check points for signs of abrasion: cheek bone and high points of hair. Triangular roof above pillars. Shallow or weak spots in the relief, particularly in the steps below pillars, are usually caused by improper striking and not wear.

ABOUT UNCIRCULATED *(Small trace of wear visible on highest points.)*

AU-55 (Choice About Uncirculated)
OBVERSE: Only a trace of wear shows on cheek bone.
REVERSE: A trace of wear shows on the beam above pillars. Three-quarters of the mint luster is still present.

AU-50 (About Uncirculated)
OBVERSE: Traces of wear show on cheek bone and high points of hair.
REVERSE: Traces of wear show on the beam and triangular roof above pillars. Half of the mint luster is still present.

EXTREMELY FINE *(Very light wear on only the highest points.)*

EF-45 (Choice Extremely Fine)
OBVERSE: Slight wear shows on cheek bone, and central portion of hair. There is a trace of wear at bottom of the bust.
REVERSE: High points of the triangular roof and beam are lightly worn. Traces of mint luster still show.

EF-40 (Extremely Fine)
OBVERSE: Hair is lightly worn but well defined and bold. Slight wear shows on cheek bone and bottom of the bust. High points of hair are worn but show all details.
REVERSE: Triangular roof and beam are worn but all details are visible.

VERY FINE *(Light to moderate even wear. All major features are sharp.)*

VF-30 (Choice Very Fine)
OBVERSE: Hair worn but shows nearly full details. Cheek line and bottom of bust are worn but sharp.
REVERSE: Triangular roof and beam worn nearly flat. Most of the pillar lines show plainly.

VF-20 (Very Fine)
OBVERSE: Cheek line shows considerable flatness. Over half the hair lines are clear. Parts of the details still show in collar.
REVERSE: Pillars are worn but clearly defined. Triangular roof is partially visible.

FINE *(Moderate to heavy even wear. Entire design clear and bold.)*

F-12 (Fine)
OBVERSE: Some details show in hair around face. Cheek line and collar plain but very weak.
REVERSE: Some details visible behind pillars. Triangular roof is very smooth and indistinct.

VERY GOOD *(Well worn. Design clear but flat and lacking details.)*

VG-8 (Very Good)
OBVERSE: Cheek line is visible but parts are worn smooth. Collar is weak but visible. Only a few hair lines show separations.
REVERSE: Slight details shows throughout building. The arch is worn away. Pillars are weak but visible.

GOOD *(Heavily worn. Design and legend visible but faint in spots.)*

G-4 (Good)
OBVERSE: Entire design well worn with very little detail remaining. Motto is weak and merged with rim.
REVERSE: Building is nearly flat but is well outlined. Pillars are worn flat. Rim worn to tops of letters.

ABOUT GOOD *(Outlined design. Parts of date and legend worn smooth.)*

AG-3 (About Good)
OBVERSE: Design is outlined with nearly all details worn away. Date and legend readable but very weak and merging into rim.
REVERSE: Entire design partially worn away. Rim is merged with the letters.

Note: Jefferson nickels are frequently seen weakly struck, and with the horizontal step lines joined even on Uncirculated specimens. Many of the 1950 and 1955 nickels are unevenly struck with weak spots in the details.

DIMES — BARBER 1892-1916

OBVERSE

REVERSE

MINT STATE *(Absolutely no trace of wear.)*

MS-70 (Perfect Uncirculated)
A flawless coin exactly as it was minted, with no trace of wear or injury. Must have full mint luster and brilliance or light toning. Any unusual die or striking traits must be described.

MS-65 (Choice Uncirculated)
No trace of wear; nearly as perfect as MS-70 except for some small blemish. Has full mint luster but may be unevenly toned or lightly fingermarked. A few barely noticeable nicks or marks may be present.

MS-60 (Uncirculated)
A strictly Uncirculated coin with no trace of wear, but with blemishes more obvious than for MS-65. May lack full mint luster, and surface may be dull, spotted, or heavily toned. Check points for signs of abrasion: high points of cheek, and hair below LIBERTY. Ribbon bow and tips of leaves.

ABOUT UNCIRCULATED *(Small trace of wear visible on highest points.)*

AU-55 (Choice About Uncirculated)
OBVERSE: Only a trace of wear shows on highest points of hair below LIBERTY.

REVERSE: A trace of wear shows on ribbon bow, wheat grains and leaf near O. Three-quarters of the mint luster is still present.

AU-50 (About Uncirculated)

OBVERSE: Traces of wear show on cheek, top of forehead and hair below LIBERTY.

REVERSE: Traces of wear show on ribbon bow, wheat grains and tips of leaves. Half of the mint luster is still present.

EXTREMELY FINE *(Very light wear on only the highest points.)*

EF-45 (Choice Extremely Fine)

OBVERSE: Slight wear shows on high points of upper leaves, cheek and hair above forehead. LIBERTY is sharp and band edges are bold.

REVERSE: High points of the wreath and bow lightly worn. Lines in leaves are clearly defined. Part of the mint luster is still present.

EF-40 (Extremely Fine)

OBVERSE: Light wear shows on leaves, cheek, cap and hair above forehead. LIBERTY is sharp and band edges are clear.

REVERSE: High points of wreath and bow are worn, but all details are clearly defined. Traces of mint luster may still show.

VERY FINE *(Light to moderate even wear. All major features are sharp.)*

VF-30 (Choice Very Fine)

OBVERSE: Wear spots show on leaves, cap, hair and cheek. Bottom row of leaves is weak but has some visible details. LIBERTY and band are complete.

REVERSE: Wear shows on the two bottom leaves but most details are visible. Nearly all the details in the ribbon bow and corn kernels are clear.

VF-20 (Very Fine)

OBVERSE: Over half the details still show in leaves. Hair worn but bold. Every letter in LIBERTY is visible.

REVERSE: The ribbon is worn, but some details are visible. Half the details in leaves are clear. Bottom leaves and upper stalks show wear spots.

FINE *(Moderate to heavy even wear. Entire design clear and bold.)*

F-12 (Fine)

OBVERSE: Some details show in hair, cap and facial features. All letters in LIBERTY are weak but visible. Upper row of leaves is outlined, but bottom row is worn smooth.

REVERSE: Some details in the lower leaf clusters are plainly visible. Bow is outlined but flat. Letters in legend are worn but clear.

VERY GOOD *(Well worn. Design clear but flat and lacking details.)*

VG-8 (Very Good)

OBVERSE: Entire head weak, and most of the details in the face are worn smooth. Three letters in LIBERTY are clear. Rim is complete.

REVERSE: Wreath shows only a small amount of detail. Corn and grain are flat. Some of the bow is very weak.

GOOD *(Heavily worn. Design and legend visible but faint in spots.)*

G-4 (Good)

OBVERSE: Entire design well worn with very little detail remaining. Legend is weak but visible. LIBERTY is worn away.

REVERSE: Wreath is worn flat but is completely outlined. Corn and grains are worn nearly smooth.

ABOUT GOOD *(Outlined design. Parts of date and legend worn smooth.)*

AG-3 (About Good)
OBVERSE: Head is outlined with nearly all details worn away. Date readable but partially worn away. Legend merging into rim.
REVERSE: Entire wreath partially worn away and merging into rim.

DIMES — MERCURY 1916-1945

OBVERSE

REVERSE

MINT STATE *(Absolutely no trace of wear.)*

MS-70 (Perfect Uncirculated)
A flawless coin exactly as it was minted, with no trace of wear or injury. Must have full mint luster and brilliance or light toning. Any unusual die or striking traits must be described.

MS-65 (Choice Uncirculated)
No trace of wear; nearly as perfect as MS-70 except for some small blemish. Has full mint luster but may be unevenly toned or lightly fingermarked. A few barely noticeable nicks or marks may be present.

MS-60 (Uncirculated)
A strictly Uncirculated coin with no trace of wear, but with blemishes more obvious than for MS-65. May lack full mint luster, and surface may be dull, spotted or heavily toned. Check points for signs of abrasion: high points of hair and in front of ear. Diagonal bands on fasces.

ABOUT UNCIRCULATED *(Small trace of wear visible on highest points.)*

AU-55 (Choice About Uncirculated)
OBVERSE: Only a trace of wear shows on highest points of hair above forehead and in front of ear.
REVERSE: A trace of wear shows on the horizontal and diagonal fasces bands. Three-quarters of the mint luster is still present.

AU-50 (About Uncirculated)
OBVERSE: Traces of wear show on hair along face, above forehead and in front of ear.
REVERSE: Traces of wear show on the fasces bands but edges are sharply defined. Half of the mint luster is still present.

EXTREMELY FINE *(Very light wear on only the highest points.)*

EF-45 (Choice Extremely Fine)
OBVERSE: Slight wear shows on high points of feathers and at hair line. Hair along face is sharp and detailed.
REVERSE: High points of the diagonal fasces bands are lightly worn. Horizontal lines are clearly defined but not fully separated. Part of the mint luster is still present.

EF-40 (Extremely Fine)
OBVERSE: Wear shows on high points of feathers, hair and at neck line.
REVERSE: High points of fasces bands are worn, but all details are clearly defined and partially separated. Traces of mint luster may still show.

VERY FINE *(Light to moderate even wear. All major features are sharp.)*

VF-30 (Choice Very Fine)
OBVERSE: Wear spots on hair along face, cheek and neck line. Feathers are weak but have nearly full details.
REVERSE: Wear shows on the two diagonal bands but most details are visible. All vertical lines are sharp. All details in the branch are clear.

VF-20 (Very Fine)
OBVERSE: Three-quarters of the details still show in feathers. Hair worn but bold. Some details in hair braid are visible.
REVERSE: Wear shows on the two diagonal bands but most details are visible. All vertical lines are sharp. All details in the branch are clear.

FINE *(Moderate to considerable even wear. Entire design clear and bold.)*

F-12 (Fine)
OBVERSE: Some details show in hair. All feathers are weak but partially visible. Hair braid is nearly worn away.
REVERSE: Vertical lines are all visible but lack sharpness. Diagonal bands show on fasces but one is worn smooth at midpoint.

VERY GOOD *(Well worn. Design clear but flat and lacking details.)*

VG-8 (Very Good)
OBVERSE: Entire head is weak, and most details in the wing are worn smooth. All letters and date are clear. Rim is complete.
REVERSE: About half the vertical lines in the fasces are visible. Rim is complete.

GOOD *(Heavily worn. Design and legend visible but faint in spots.)*

G-4 (Good)
OBVERSE: Entire design well worn with very little detail remaining. Legend and date are weak but visible. Rim is visible.
REVERSE: Fasces is worn nearly flat but is completely outlined. Sticks and bands are worn smooth.

ABOUT GOOD *(Outlined design. Parts of date and legend worn smooth.)*

AG-3 (About Good)
OBVERSE: Head is outlined with nearly all details worn away. Date readable but worn. Legend merging into rim.
REVERSE: Entire design partially worn away. Rim worn half way into the legend.

Note: Coins of this design are sometimes weakly struck in spots, particularly in the lines and horizontal bands of the fasces.

The following dates are usually found poorly struck and lacking full details regardless of condition: 1916-D, 1918-S, 1921, 1921-D, 1925-D, 1925-S, 1926-S, 1927-D and 1927-S.

1920 and 1920-D usually show the zero joined to the rim.
1921 usually has a weakly struck date, especially the last two digits.
1923 often has the bottom of the three weakly struck and joined to the rim.
1945 is rarely seen with full cross bands on the fasces.

DIMES — ROOSEVELT 1946 TO DATE

OBVERSE

REVERSE

MINT STATE *(Absolutely no trace of wear.)*

MS-70 (Perfect Uncirculated)
A flawless coin exactly as it was minted, with no trace of wear or injury. Must have full mint luster and brilliance or light toning. Any unusual striking traits must be described.

MS-65 (Choice Uncirculated)
No trace of wear; nearly as perfect as MS-70 except for some small blemish. Has full mint luster but may be unevenly toned or lightly fingermarked. A few barely noticeable nicks or marks may be present.

MS-60 (Uncirculated)
A strictly Uncirculated coin with no trace of wear, but with blemishes more obvious than for MS-65. Has full mint luster, but surface may be dull, spotted, or toned. Check points for signs of abrasion: high points of cheek and hair above ear. Tops of leaves and details in flame.

ABOUT UNCIRCULATED *(Small trace of wear visible on highest points.)*

AU-55 (Choice About Uncirculated)
OBVERSE: Only a trace of wear shows on highest points of hair above ear.
REVERSE: A trace of wear shows on highest spots of the flame. Three-quarters of the mint luster is still present.

AU-50 (About Uncirculated)
OBVERSE: Traces of wear show on hair above ear.
REVERSE: Traces of wear show on flame but details are sharply defined. Half of the mint luster is still present.

EXTREMELY FINE *(Very light wear on only the highest points.)*

EF-45 (Choice Extremely Fine)
OBVERSE: Slight wear shows on high points of hair above ear. Ear is sharp and detailed.
REVERSE: High points of flame are lightly worn. Torch lines are clearly defined and fully separated. Part of the mint luster is still present.

EF-40 (Extremely Fine)
OBVERSE: Wear shows on high points of hair and at cheek line. Ear shows slight wear on the upper tip.
REVERSE: High points of flame, torch and leaves are worn, but all details are clearly defined and partially separated. Traces of mint luster may still show.

VERY FINE *(Light to moderate even wear. All major features are sharp.)*

VF-30 (Choice Very Fine)
OBVERSE: Wear spots show on hair, ear, cheek and chin. Hair lines are weak but have nearly full visible details.
REVERSE: Wear shows on flame but some details are visible. All vertical lines are plain. Most details in the torch and leaves are clear.

VF-20 (Very Fine)
OBVERSE: Three-quarters of the details still show in hair. Face worn but bold. Some details in the ear are visible.
REVERSE: Wear shows on the flame but a few lines are visible. All torch lines are worn but bold. Most details in leaves are clear.

FINE *(Moderate to heavy even wear. Entire design clear and bold.)*

F-12 (Fine)
OBVERSE: Half the details show in hair. All of the face is weak but boldly visible. Half of inner edge of ear is worn away.
REVERSE: Vertical lines are all visible, but horizontal bands are worn smooth. Leaves show some detail. Flame is nearly smooth.

VERY GOOD *(Well worn. Design clear but flat and lacking details.)*

VG-8 (Very Good)
OBVERSE: Entire head is weak, and most of the details in hair and ear are worn smooth. All letters and date are clear. Rim is complete.
REVERSE: About half the outer vertical lines in torch are visible. Flame is only outlined. Leaves show very little detail. Rim is complete.

GOOD *(Heavily worn. Design and legend visible but faint in spots.)*

G-4 (Good)
OBVERSE: Entire design well worn with very little detail remaining. Ear is completely outlined. Legend and date are weak but visible. Rim is visible.
REVERSE: Torch is worn nearly flat but is completely outlined. Leaves are worn smooth. Legend is all visible.

ABOUT GOOD *(Outlined design. Parts of date and legend worn smooth.)*

AG-3 (About Good)
OBVERSE: Head is outlined with nearly all details worn away. Date readable but worn. Legend merging into rim.
REVERSE: Entire design partially worn away. Rim merges into the legend.

QUARTERS — BARBER 1892-1916

OBVERSE

REVERSE

MINT STATE *(Absolutely no trace of wear.)*

MS-70 (Perfect Uncirculated)
A flawless coin exactly as it was minted, with no trace of wear or injury. Must have full mint luster and brilliance or light toning. Any unusual die or striking traits must be described.

MS-65 (Choice Uncirculated)
No trace of wear; nearly as perfect as MS-70 except for some small blemish. Has full mint luster but may be unevenly toned or lightly fingermarked. A few barely noticeable nicks or marks may be present.

MS-60 (Uncirculated)
A strictly Uncirculated coin with no trace of wear, but with blemishes more obvious than for MS-65. May lack full mint luster, and surface may be dull, spotted, or heavily toned. Check points for signs of abrasion: high points of cheek and hair below LIBERTY. Eagle's head and tips of tail and wings.

ABOUT UNCIRCULATED *(Small trace of wear visible on highest points.)*

AU-55 (Choice About Uncirculated)
OBVERSE: Only a trace of wear shows on highest points of hair below BER in LIBERTY.
REVERSE: A trace of wear shows on head, tip of tail and tips of wings. Three-quarters of the mint luster is still present.

AU-50 (About Uncirculated)
OBVERSE: Traces of wear show on cheek, tips of leaves and hair below LIBERTY.
REVERSE: Traces of wear show on head, neck, tail and tips of wings. Half of the mint luster is present.

EXTREMELY FINE *(Very light wear on only the highest points.)*

EF-45 (Choice Extremely Fine)
OBVERSE: Slight wear shows on high points of upper leaves, cheek and hair above forehead. LIBERTY is sharp and band edges are bold.
REVERSE: High points of head, neck, wings and talons lightly worn. Lines in center tail feathers are clearly defined. Part of the mint luster is still present.

EF-40 (Extremely Fine)
OBVERSE: Light wear shows on leaves, cheek, cap and hair above forehead. LIBERTY is sharp and band edges are clear.
REVERSE: High points of head, neck, wings and tail are lightly worn, but all details are clearly defined. Leaves show trace of wear at edges. Traces of mint luster may still show.

VERY FINE *(Light to moderate even wear. All major features are sharp.)*

VF-30 (Choice Very Fine)
OBVERSE: Wear spots show on leaves, cap, hair and cheek. Bottom row of leaves is weak but has some visible details. LIBERTY and band are complete. Folds in cap are distinct.
REVERSE: Wear shows on shield but all details are visible. Most of the details in neck and tail are clear. Motto is complete.

VF-20 (Very Fine)
OBVERSE: Over half the details still show in leaves. Hair and ribbon worn but bold. Every letter in LIBERTY is visible.
REVERSE: The shield is worn, but most details are visible. Half the details in feathers are clear. Wings and legs show wear spots. Motto is clear.

FINE *(Moderate to heavy even wear. Entire design clear and bold.)*

F-12 (Fine)
OBVERSE: Some details show in hair, cap and facial features. All letters in LIBERTY are weak but visible. Upper row of leaves is outlined, but bottom row is worn nearly smooth. Rim is full and bold.
REVERSE: Half of the feathers are plainly visible. Wear spots show in center of neck, motto and arrows. Horizontal shield lines are merged; vertical lines are separated. Letters in legend are worn but clear.

VERY GOOD *(Well worn. Design clear but flat and lacking details.)*

VG-8 (Very Good)
OBVERSE: Entire head weak, and most details in face are worn smooth. Three letters in LIBERTY are clear. Rim is complete.
REVERSE: Eagle shows only a small amount of detail. Arrows and leaves are flat. Most of the shield is very weak. Part of the eye is visible.

GOOD *(Heavily worn. Design and legend visible but faint in spots.)*

G-4 (Good)
OBVERSE: Entire design well worn with very little detail remaining. Legend is weak but visible. LIBERTY is worn away.
REVERSE: Eagle worn flat but is completely outlined. Ribbon worn nearly smooth. Legend weak but visible. Rim worn to tops of letters.

ABOUT GOOD *(Outlined design. Parts of date and legend worn smooth.)*

AG-3 (About Good)
OBVERSE: Head is outlined with nearly all details worn away. Date readable but partially worn away. Legend merging into rim.
REVERSE: Entire design partially worn away and legend merges with rim.

QUARTERS — LIBERTY STANDING, VARIETY I 1916-1917
LIBERTY STANDING, VARIETY II 1917-1924

OBVERSE

TYPE I
REVERSE

TYPE II
REVERSE

MINT STATE *(Absolutely no trace of wear.)*

MS-70 (Perfect Uncirculated)
A flawless coin exactly as it was minted, with no trace of wear or injury. Must have full mint luster and brilliance or light toning. Head details* are an important part of this grade and must be specifically designated. Any other unusual die or striking traits must be described.

MS-65 (Choice Uncirculated)
No trace of wear; nearly as perfect as MS-70 except for some small blemish. Has full mint luster but may be unevenly toned or lightly fingermarked, may be weakly struck in one small spot. A few barely noticeable nicks or marks may be present. Head details* may be incomplete.

MS-60 (Uncirculated)
A strictly Uncirculated coin with no trace of wear, but with blemishes more obvious than for MS-65. May lack full mint luster, and surface may be dull, spotted or heavily toned. One or two small spots may be weakly struck. Head details* may be incomplete. Check points for signs of abrasion: mail covering breast, knee, high points of gown and shield; high points of eagle's breast and wings. Coins of this design frequently show weakly struck spots and usually lack full head details.

ABOUT UNCIRCULATED *(Small trace of wear visible on highest points.)*

AU-55 (Choice About Uncirculated)
OBVERSE: Only a trace of wear shows on highest points of mail covering breast, inner shield and right knee.
REVERSE: A trace of wear shows on breast and edges of wings. Three-quarters of the mint luster is still present.

AU-50 (About Uncirculated)
OBVERSE: Traces of wear show on breast, knee and high points of inner shield.
REVERSE: Traces of wear show on edges of wings and at center of breast. All of the tail feathers are visible. Half of the mint luster is still present.

EXTREMELY FINE *(Very light wear on only the highest points.)*

EF-45 (Choice Extremely Fine)
OBVERSE: Light wear spots show on upper right leg and knee. Nearly all of the gown lines are clearly visible. Shield details are bold. Breast is lightly worn and may show small flat spot.
REVERSE: Small flat spots show on high points of breast and on front wing edges. Tail feathers have nearly full details. Part of the mint luster is still present.

EF-40 (Extremely Fine)
OBVERSE: Wear shows on breast, and right leg above and below knee. Most of the gown lines are visible. Shield details are bold. Breast is well rounded but has small flat spot.
REVERSE: High points of eagle are lightly worn. Central part of edge on right wing is well worn. Traces of mint luster may still show.

VERY FINE *(Light to moderate even wear. All major features are sharp.)*

VF-30 (Choice Very Fine)
OBVERSE: Wear spots show on breast, shield and leg. Right leg is rounded but worn from above knee to ankle. Gown line crossing thigh is partially visible. Half of mail covering breast can be seen. Circle around inner shield is complete.
REVERSE: Breast and leg are worn but clearly separated, with some feathers visible between them. Feather ends and folds are visible in right wing.

VF-20 (Very Fine)
OBVERSE: Right leg is worn flat in central parts. Wear spots show on head, breast, shield and foot. Beads on outer shield are visible, but those next to body are weak. Inner circle of shield is complete.
REVERSE: Entire eagle is lightly worn but most major details are visible. Breast and edge of right wing are worn flat. Top tail feathers are complete.

FINE *(Moderate to considerable even wear. Entire design clear and bold.)*

F-12 (Fine)
OBVERSE: Gown details worn but show clearly across body. Left leg is lightly worn. Right leg nearly flat and toe is worn. Breast worn but some mail is visible. Date may show some weakness at top. Rim is full. Outer edge of shield is complete.
REVERSE: Breast is worn almost smooth. Half of the wing feathers are visible although well worn in spots. The rim is full.

VERY GOOD *(Well worn. Design clear but flat and lacking details.)*

VG-8 (Very Good)
OBVERSE: Entire design is weak, and most details in gown are worn smooth. All letters and date are clear but tops of numerals may be flat. Rim is complete. Drapery across breast is partially outlined.
REVERSE: About one-third of the feathers are visible, and large feathers at ends of wings are well separated. Eye is visible. Rim is full and all letters are clear.

GOOD *(Heavily worn. Design and legend visible but faint in spots.)*

G-4 (Good)
OBVERSE: Entire design well worn with very little detail remaining. Legend and date are weak but visible. Top of date may be worn flat. Rim is complete.
REVERSE: Eagle worn nearly flat but is completely outlined. Lettering and stars worn but clearly visible. Rim worn to tops of legend.

ABOUT GOOD *(Outlined design. Parts of date and legend worn smooth.)*

AG-3 (About Good)
OBVERSE: Figure is outlined with nearly all details worn away. Legend visible but half worn away and may merge with rim. Date weak and readable.
REVERSE: Entire design partially worn away. Some letters merging into rim.

Note: Coins of this design are sometimes weakly struck in spots, particularly at Liberty's head, breast, knee and shield and on the eagle's breast and wings.

*Specimens with "full head" must show the following details: Three well defined leaves in hair; complete hairline along brow and across face; small indentation at ear. Coins of any grade other than MS-70 can be assumed to lack full head details unless the amount of visible features are specifically designated.

QUARTERS — WASHINGTON 1932 TO DATE

OBVERSE

REVERSE

MINT STATE *(Absolutely no trace of wear.)*

MS-70 (Perfect Uncirculated)
A flawless coin exactly as it was minted, with no trace of wear or injury. Must have full mint luster and brilliance or light toning. Any unusual striking traits must be described.

MS-65 (Choice Uncirculated)
No trace of wear; nearly as perfect as MS-70 except for some small blemish. Has full mint luster but may be unevenly toned or lightly fingermarked. A few barely noticeable nicks or marks may be present.

MS-60 (Uncirculated)
A strictly Uncirculated coin with no trace of wear, but with blemishes more obvious than for MS-65. May lack full mint luster, and surface may be dull, spotted or heavily toned. Check points for signs of abrasion: high points of cheek and hair in front and back of ear. Tops of legs and details in breast feathers.

ABOUT UNCIRCULATED *(Small trace of wear visible on highest points.)*

AU-55 (Choice About Uncirculated)
OBVERSE: Only a trace of wear shows on highest points of hair in front and in back of ear.
REVERSE: A trace of wear shows on highest spots of breast feathers. Nearly all of the mint luster is still present.

AU-50 (About Uncirculated)
OBVERSE: Traces of wear show on hair in front and in back of ear.
REVERSE: Traces of wear show on legs and breast feathers. Three-quarters of the mint luster is still present.

EXTREMELY FINE *(Light wear on most of the highest points.)*

EF-45 (Choice Extremely Fine)
OBVERSE: Slight wear shows on high points of hair around ear and along hairline up to crown. Hairlines are sharp and detailed.
REVERSE: High points of legs are lightly worn. Breast feathers are worn but clearly defined and fully separated. Half of the mint luster is still present.

EF-40 (Extremely Fine)
OBVERSE: Wear shows on high points of hair around and at hairline up to crown.
REVERSE: High points of breast, legs and claws are lightly worn, but all details are clearly defined and partially separated. Part of the mint luster is still present.

VERY FINE *(Light to moderate even wear. All major features are sharp.)*

VF-30 (Choice Very Fine)
OBVERSE: Wear spots show on hair at forehead and ear, cheek and jaw. Hair lines are weak but have nearly full visible details.
REVERSE: Wear shows on breast but a few feathers are visible. Legs are worn smooth. Most details in the wings are clear.

FINE *(Moderate to considerable even wear. Entire design clear and bold.)*

F-12 (Fine)
OBVERSE: Details show only at back of hair. Motto is weak but clearly visible. Part of cheek edge is worn away.
REVERSE: Feathers in breast and legs are worn smooth. Leaves show some detail. Parts of wings are nearly smooth.

VERY GOOD *(Well worn. Design clear but flat and lacking details.)*

VG-8 (Very Good)
OBVERSE: Entire head is weak, and most details in hair are worn smooth. All letters and date are clear. Rim is complete.
REVERSE: About half of the wing feathers are visible. Breast and legs only outlined. Leaves show very little detail. Rim is complete.

GOOD *(Heavily worn. Design and legend visible but faint in spots.)*

G-4 (Good)
OBVERSE: Hair is well worn with very little detail remaining. Half of motto is readable. LIBERTY and date are weak but visible. Rim merges with letters.
REVERSE: Eagle is worn nearly flat but is completely outlined. Leaves, breast and legs are worn smooth. Legend is all visible but merges with rim.

ABOUT GOOD *(Outlined design. Parts of date and legend worn smooth.)*

AG-3 (About Good)
OBVERSE: Head is outlined with nearly all details worn away. Date readable but worn. Traces of motto are visible. Legend merging into rim.
REVERSE: Entire design partially worn away. Rim merges into legend.

Note: The obverse motto is always weak on coins of 1932 and early issues of 1934.
The reverse rim and lettering has a tendency to be very weak, particularly on coins dated 1934-D, 1935-D and S, 1936-D and S, 1937-D and S (especially), 1938-D and S, and 1939-D and 1940-D.

HALF DOLLARS — BARBER 1892-1915

OBVERSE   REVERSE

MINT STATE *(Absolutely no trace of wear.)*

MS-70 (Perfect Uncirculated)
A flawless coin exactly as it was minted, with no trace of wear or injury. Must have full mint luster and brilliance or light toning. Any unusual die or striking traits must be described.

MS-65 (Choice Uncirculated)
No trace of wear; nearly as perfect as MS-70 except for some small blemish. Has full mint luster but may be unevenly toned or lightly fingermarked. A few barely noticeable nicks or marks may be present.

MS-60 (Uncirculated)
A strictly Uncirculated coin with no trace of wear, but with blemishes more obvious than for MS-65. May lack full mint luster, and surface may be dull, spotted or heavily toned. Check points for signs of abrasion: high points of cheek and hair below LIBERTY. Eagle's head and tips of tail and wings.

ABOUT UNCIRCULATED *(Small trace of wear visible on highest points.)*

AU-55 (Choice About Uncirculated)
OBVERSE: Only a trace of wear shows on highest points of hair below BER in LIBERTY.
REVERSE: A trace of wear shows on head, tip of tail and tips of wings. Three-quarters of the mint luster is still present.

AU-50 (About Uncirculated)
OBVERSE: Traces of wear show on cheek, tips of leaves and hair below LIBERTY.
REVERSE: Traces of wear show on head, neck, tail and tips of wings. Half of the mint luster is still present.

EXTREMELY FINE *(Very light wear on only the highest points.)*

EF-45 (Choice Extremely Fine)
OBVERSE: Slight wear shows on high points of upper leaves, cheek and hair above forehead. LIBERTY is sharp and band edges are bold.
High points of head, neck, wings and talons lightly worn. Lines in reverse center tail feathers are clearly defined. Part of the mint luster is still present.

EF-40 (Extremely Fine)
OBVERSE: Light wear shows on leaves, cheek, cap and hair above forehead. LIBER-TY is sharp and band edges are clear.
REVERSE: High points of head, neck, wings and tail are lightly worn, but all details are clearly defined. Leaves show trace of wear at edges. Traces of mint luster may still show.

VERY FINE *(Light to moderate even wear. All major features are sharp.)*

VF-30 (Choice Very Fine)
OBVERSE: Wear spots show on leaves, cap, hair and cheek. Bottom row of leaves is weak but has some visible details. LIBERTY and band are complete. Folds in cap are distinct.
REVERSE: Wear shows on shield but all details are visible. Most of the details in neck and tail are clear. Motto is complete.

VF-20 (Very Fine)
OBVERSE: Over half the details still show in leaves. Hair and ribbon worn but bold. Every letter in LIBERTY is visible. Bottom folds in cap are full.
REVERSE: Shield is worn, but all details are visible. Half the details in feathers are clear. Wings, tail and legs show small wear spots. Motto is clear.

FINE *(Moderate to considerable even wear. Entire design clear and bold.)*

F-12 (Fine)
OBVERSE: Some details show in hair, cap and facial features. All letters in LIBERTY are weak but visible. Upper row of leaves is outlined, but bottom row is worn nearly smooth. Rim is full and bold.
REVERSE: Half the feathers are plainly visible. Wear spots show in center of neck, motto and arrows. Horizontal shield lines are merged; vertical lines are separated. Letters in legend are worn but clear.

VERY GOOD *(Well worn. Design clear but flat and lacking details.)*

VG-8 (Very Good)
OBVERSE: Entire head weak, and most details in face are heavily worn. Three letters in LIBERTY are clear. Rim is complete.
REVERSE: Eagle shows only a small amount of detail. Arrows and leaves are flat. Most of shield is very weak. Parts of eye and motto visible.

GOOD *(Heavily worn. Design and legend visible but faint in spots.)*

G-4 (Good)
OBVERSE: Entire design well worn with very little detail remaining. Legend and date weak but visible. LIBERTY is worn away.
REVERSE: Eagle worn flat but is completely outlined. Ribbon worn nearly smooth. Legend weak but visible. Rim worn to tops of letters.

ABOUT GOOD *(Outlined design. Parts of date and legend worn smooth.)*

AG-3 (About Good)
OBVERSE: Head is outlined with nearly all details worn away. Date readable but partially worn away. Legend merging into rim.
REVERSE: Entire design partially worn away and legend merges with rim.

HALF DOLLARS — LIBERTY WALKING 1916-1947

OBVERSE   REVERSE

MINT STATE *(Absolutely no trace of wear.)*

MS-70 (Perfect Uncirculated)
A flawless coin exactly as it was minted, with no trace of wear or injury. Must have full mint luster and brilliance or light toning. Any unusual die or striking traits must be described.

MS-65 (Choice Uncirculated)
No trace of wear; nearly as perfect as MS-70 except for some small blemish. Has full mint luster but may be unevenly toned or lightly fingermarked. May be weakly struck in one of two small spots. A few minute nicks or marks may be present.

MS-60 (Uncirculated)
A strictly Uncirculated coin with no trace of wear, but with blemishes more obvious than for MS-65. May lack full mint luster, and surface may be dull, spotted or heavily toned. A few small spots may be weakly struck. Check points for signs of abrasion: hair above temple, right arm, left breast; high points of eagle's head, breast, legs and wings. Coins of this design frequently show weakly struck spots, and usually lack full head and hand details.

ABOUT UNCIRCULATED *(Small trace of wear visible on highest points.)*

AU-55 (Choice About Uncirculated)
OBVERSE: Only a trace of wear shows on highest points of head, breast and right arm.
REVERSE: A trace of wear shows on left leg between breast and left wing. Three-quarters of the mint luster is still present.

AU-50 (About Uncirculated)
OBVERSE: Traces of wear show on head, breast, arms and left leg.

REVERSE: Traces of wear show on high points of wings and at center of head. All leg feathers are visible. Half of the mint luster is still present.

EXTREMELY FINE *(Very light wear on only the highest points.)*

EF-45 (Choice Extremely Fine)
OBVERSE: Light wear spots show on head, breast, arms, left leg and foot. Nearly all gown lines are clearly visible. Sandal details are bold and complete. Knee is lightly worn but full and rounded.
REVERSE: Small flat spots show on high points of breast and legs. Wing feathers have nearly full details. Part of the mint luster is still present.

EF-40 (Extremely Fine)
OBVERSE: Wear shows on head, breast, arms and left leg. Nearly all gown lines are visible. Sandal details are complete. Breast and knee are nearly flat.
REVERSE: High points of eagle are lightly worn. Half the breast and leg feathers are visible. Central part of feathers below neck is well worn. Traces of mint luster may still show.

VERY FINE *(Light to moderate even wear. All major features are sharp.)*

VF-30 (Choice Very Fine)
OBVERSE: Wear spots on head, breast, arms and legs. Left leg is rounded but worn from above knee to ankle. Gown line crossing body is partially visible. Knee is flat. Outline of breast can be seen.
REVERSE: Breast and legs are moderately worn but clearly separated, with some feathers visible in right wing. Pupil in eye is visible.

VF-20 (Very Fine)
OBVERSE: Left leg is worn nearly flat. Wear spots show on head, breast, arms and foot. Lines on skirt are visible, but may be weak on coins before 1921. Breast is outlined.
REVERSE: Entire eagle is lightly worn but most major details are visible. Breast, central part of legs and top edge of right wing are worn flat.

FINE *(Moderate to considerable even wear. Entire design clear and bold.)*

F-12 (Fine)
OBVERSE: Gown stripes worn but show clearly, except for coins before 1921 where only half are visible. Right leg is lightly worn. Left leg nearly flat and sandal is worn but visible. Center of body worn but some of the gown is visible. Outer edge of rim is complete.
REVERSE: Breast is worn smooth. Half the wing feathers are visible although well worn in spots. Top two layers of feathers are visible in left wing. Rim is full.

VERY GOOD *(Well worn. Design clear but flat and lacking details.)*

VG-8 (Very Good)
OBVERSE: Entire design is weak; most details in gown are worn smooth except for coins after 1921, where half the stripes must show. All letters and date are clear but top of motto may be weak. Rim is complete. Drapery across body is partially visible.
REVERSE: About one-third of the feathers are visible, and large feathers at ends of wings are well separated. Eye is visible. Rim is full and all letters are clear.

GOOD *(Heavily worn. Design and legend visible but faint in spots.)*

G-4 (Good)
OBVERSE: Entire design well worn with very little detail remaining. Legend and date weak but visible. Top of date may be worn flat. Rim is flat but nearly complete.
REVERSE: Eagle worn nearly flat but is completely outlined. Lettering and motto worn but clearly visible.

ABOUT GOOD *(Outlined design. Parts of date and legend worn smooth.)*

AG-3 (About Good)
OBVERSE: Figure is outlined with nearly all details worn away. Legend visible but half worn away. Date weak but readable. Rim merges with lettering.
REVERSE: Entire design partially worn away. Letters merge with rim.

Note: Coins of this design are sometimes weakly struck in spots, particularly at Liberty's head, hand holding branch and drapery lines of dress, and on the eagle's leg feathers.

HALF DOLLARS — FRANKLIN 1948-1963

OBVERSE

REVERSE

MINT STATE *(Absolutely no trace of wear.)*

MS-70 (Perfect Uncirculated)
A flawless coin exactly as it was minted, with no trace of wear or injury. Must have full mint luster and brilliance or light toning. Any unusual striking traits must be described.

MS-65 (Choice Uncirculated)
No trace of wear; nearly as perfect as MS-70 except for some small blemish. Has full mint luster but may be unevenly toned or lightly fingermarked. A few barely noticeable nicks or marks may be present.

MS-60 (Uncirculated)
A strictly Uncirculated coin with no trace of wear, but with blemishes more obvious than for MS-65. May lack full mint luster, and surface may be dull, spotted or heavily toned. Check points for signs of abrasion: high points of cheek, shoulder and hair left of ear. Straps around beam, lines and lettering on bell.

ABOUT UNCIRCULATED *(Small trace of wear visible on highest points.)*

AU-55 (Choice About Uncirculated)
OBVERSE: Only a trace of wear shows on highest spots of cheek and hair left of ear.
REVERSE: A trace of wear shows on highest points of lettering on bell. Nearly all of the mint luster is still present.

AU-50 (About Uncirculated)
OBVERSE: Traces of wear show on cheek and hair on shoulder and left of ear.
REVERSE: Traces of wear show on bell at lettering and along ridges at bottom. Three-quarters of the mint luster is still present.

EXTREMELY FINE *(Very light wear on only the highest points.)*

EF-45 (Choice Extremely Fine)
OBVERSE: Slight wear shows on cheek and high points of hair behind ear and along shoulder. Hair lines at back of head are sharp and detailed.

REVERSE: High points of straps on beam are lightly worn. Lines at bottom of bell are worn but clearly defined and separated. Lettering on bell is very weak at center. Half of the mint luster is still present.

EF-40 (Extremely Fine)
OBVERSE: Wear shows on high points of cheek and hair behind ear and at shoulder.
REVERSE: High points of beam straps, and lines along bottom of bell are lightly worn, but details are clearly defined and partially separated. Lettering on bell is worn away at center. Part of the mint luster is still present.

VERY FINE *(Light to moderate even wear. All major features are sharp.)*

VF-30 (Choice Very Fine)
OBVERSE: Wear spots show on hair at shoulder and behind ear, on cheek and jaw. Hair lines are weak but have nearly full visible details.
REVERSE: Wear shows on bell lettering but some of the details are visible. Straps on beam are plain. Half of line details at bottom of bell are worn smooth.

VF-20 (Very Fine)
OBVERSE: Three-quarters of the lines still show in hair. Cheek lightly worn but bold. Some hair details around the ear are visible.
REVERSE: Wear shows on beam but most details are visible. Bell is worn but bold. Lines across bottom of bell are flat near crack.

FINE *(Moderate to considerable even wear. Entire design clear and bold.)*

F-12 (Very Fine)
OBVERSE: Hair details show only at back and side of head. Designer's initials weak but clearly visible. Part of cheek is worn flat.
REVERSE: Most of lines at bottom of bell are worn smooth. Parts of straps on beam are nearly smooth. Rim is full.

VERY GOOD *(Well worn. Design clear but flat and lacking details.)*

VG-8 (Very Good)
OBVERSE: Entire head is weak, and most details in hair from temple to ear are worn smooth. All letters and date are bold. Ear and designer's initial are visible. Rim is complete.

HALF DOLLARS — KENNEDY 1964 TO DATE

OBVERSE

REVERSE

MINT STATE *(Absolutely no trace of wear.)*

MS-70 (Perfect Uncirculated)
A flawless coin exactly as it was minted, with no trace of wear or injury. Must have full mint luster and brilliance or light toning. Any unusual striking traits must be described.

MS-65 (Choice Uncirculated)
No trace of wear; nearly as perfect as MS-70 except for some small blemish. Has full mint luster but may be unevenly toned or lightly fingermarked. A few barely noticeable nicks or marks may be present.

MS-60 (Uncirculated)
A strictly Uncirculated coin with no trace of wear, but with blemishes more obvious than for MS-65. Has full mint luster, but surface may be dull, spotted or heavily toned. Check points for signs of abrasion: high points of cheek and jawbone, center of neck, hair below part. Bundle of arrows, center tail feather, right wing tip.

ABOUT UNCIRCULATED *(Small trace of wear visible on highest points.)*
AU-55 (Choice About Uncirculated)
OBVERSE: Only a trace of wear shows on highest points of cheek, jawbone and hair below part.
REVERSE: A trace of wear shows on central tail feather. Nearly all of the mint luster is still present.

EXTREMELY FINE *(Very light wear on only the highest points.)*
EF-40 (Extremely Fine)
OBVERSE: Slight wear shows on cheek, along jawbone and on high points of hair below part. Hair lines are sharp and detailed.
REVERSE: High points of arrows and right wing tip are lightly worn. Central tail feathers are worn but clearly defined and fully separated. Three-quarters of the mint luster is still present.

VERY FINE *(Light to moderate even wear. All major features are sharp.)*
VF-30 (Choice Very Fine)
OBVERSE: Wear spots show on hair below part, and along cheek and jaw. Hair lines are weak but have nearly full visible details.
REVERSE: Wear shows on arrow points but some details are visible. All central tail feathers are plain. Wing tips are lightly worn.

DOLLARS — MORGAN 1878-1921

OBVERSE

REVERSE

MINT STATE *(Absolutely no trace of wear.)*
MS-70 (Perfect Uncirculated)
A flawless coin exactly as it was minted, with no trace of wear or injury. Must have full mint luster and brilliance or light toning. Any unusual striking traits must be described.

MS-65 (Choice Uncirculated)
No trace of wear; nearly as perfect as MS-70 except for a few minute bag marks or

surface mars. Has full mint luster but may be unevenly toned. Any unusual striking traits must be described.

MS-60 (Uncirculated)

A strictly Uncirculated coin with no trace of wear, but with bag marks and other abrasions more obvious than for MS-65. May have a few small rim mars and weakly struck spots. Has full mint luster but may lack brilliance, and surface may be spotted or heavily toned. For these coins, bag abrasions and scuff marks are considered different from circulation wear. Full mint luster and lack of any wear are necessary to distinguish MS-60 from AU-55. Check points for signs of wear: hair above eye and ear, edges of cotton leaves and blossoms, high upper fold of cap. High points of eagle's breast and tops of legs. Weakly struck spots are common and should not be confused with actual wear.

ABOUT UNCIRCULATED (*Small trace of wear visible on highest points.*)

AU-55 (Choice About Uncirculated)

OBVERSE: Slight trace of wear shows on hair above ear and eye, edges of cotton leaves, and high upper fold of cap. Luster fading from cheek.
REVERSE: Slight trace of wear shows on breast, tops of legs and talons. Most of the mint luster is still present, although marred by light bag marks and surface abrasions.

AU-50 (About Uncirculated)

OBVERSE: Traces of wear show on hair above eye and ear, edges of cotton leaves, and high upper fold of cap. Partial detail visible on tops of cotton blossoms. Luster gone from cheek.
REVERSE: There are traces of wear on breast, tops of legs, wing tips and talons. Three-quarters of the mint luster is still present. Surface abrasions and bag marks are more noticeable than for AU-55.

EXTREMELY FINE (*Very light wear on only the highest points.*)

EF-45 (Choice Extremely Fine)

OBVERSE: Slight wear on hair above date, forehead and ear. Lines in hair well detailed and sharp. Slight flat spots on edges of cotton leaves. Minute signs of wear on cheek.
REVERSE: High points of breast are lightly worn. Tops of legs and right wing tip show wear. Talons are slightly flat. Half of the mint luster is still present.

EF-40 (Extremely Fine)

OBVERSE: Wear shows on hair above date, forehead and ear. Lines in hair well detailed. Flat spots visible on edges of cotton leaves. Cheek lightly worn.
REVERSE: Almost all feathers gone from breast. Tops of legs, wing tips and feathers on head show wear. Talons are flat. Partial mint luster is visible.

VERY FINE (*Light to moderate even wear. All major features are sharp.*)

VF-30 (Choice Very Fine)

OBVERSE: Wear shows on high points of hair from forehead to ear. Some strands visible in hair above ear. There are smooth areas on cotton leaves and at top of cotton blossoms.
REVERSE: Wear shows on leaves of wreath and tips of wings. Only a few feathers visible on breast and head.

VF-20 (Very Fine)

OBVERSE: Smooth spots visible on hair from forehead to ear. Cotton leaves heavily worn but separated. Wheat grains show wear.
REVERSE: Some leaves on wreath are well worn. Breast is smooth, and only a few feathers show on head. Tips of wings are weak but lines are complete.

FINE *(Moderate to heavy even wear. Entire design clear and bold.)*

F-12 (Fine)
OBVERSE: Hairline along face is clearly defined. Lower two cotton leaves smooth but distinct from cap. Some wheat grains merging. Cotton blossoms flat but the two lines in each show clearly.
REVERSE: One-quarter of eagle's right wing and edge of left wing are smooth. Head, neck and breast are flat and merging. Tail feathers slightly worn. Top leaves in wreath show heavy wear.

VERY GOOD *(Well worn. Design clear but flat and lacking details.)*

VG-8 (Very Good)
OBVERSE: Most details in hair are worn smooth. All letters and date are clear. Cotton blossoms flat and leaves merging in spots. Hair of eagle's right wing and one-third of left wing are smooth. All leaves in wreath are worn. Rim is complete.

GOOD *(Heavily worn. Design and legend visible but faint in spots.)*

G-4 (Good)
OBVERSE: Hair is well worn with very little detail remaining. Date, letters and design clearly outlined. Rim is full.
REVERSE: Eagle is worn nearly flat but is completely outlined. Design elements smooth but visible. Legend is all visible; rim is full.

ABOUT GOOD *(Outlined design. Parts of date and legend worn smooth.)*

AG-3 (About Good)
OBVERSE: Head is outlined with nearly all details worn away. Date readable but worn. Legend merging into rim.
REVERSE: Entire design partially worn away. Rim merges into legend.

Note: Some of these dollars have a prooflike surface; this should be mentioned in any description of such pieces.

Portions of the design are often weakly struck, especially on the hair above the ear and on the eagle's breast.

DOLLARS — PEACE 1921-1935

OBVERSE

REVERSE

MINT STATE *(Absolutely no trace of wear.)*

MS-70 (Perfect Uncirculated)
A flawless coin exactly as it was minted, with no trace of wear or injury. Must have full mint luster or light toning. Any unusual striking traits must be described.

MS-65 (Choice Uncirculated)
No trace of wear; nearly as perfect as MS-70 except for a few minute bag marks or surface mars. Has full mint luster but may be unevenly toned.

MS-60 (Uncirculated)
A strictly Uncirculated coin with no trace of wear, but with bag marks and other abrasions more obvious than for MS-65. May have a few small rim mars, and may be weakly struck. Has full mint luster but may lack brilliance, and surface may be spotted or heavily toned. For these coins, bag abrasions and scuff marks are considered different from circulation wear. Full mint luster and lack of any wear are necessary to distinguish MS-60 from AU-55. Check points for signs of wear: high points of cheek and hair. High points of feathers on right wing and leg. Weakly struck spots are common and should not be confused with actual wear.

ABOUT UNCIRCULATED *(Small trace of wear visible on highest points.)*

AU-55 (Choice About Uncirculated)
OBVERSE: Trace of wear shows on hair over ear and above forehead. Slight wear visible on cheek.
REVERSE: High points of feathers on right wing show a trace of wear. Most of the mint luster is still present, although marred by light bag marks and surface abrasions.

AU-50 (About Uncirculated)
OBVERSE: Traces of wear visible on neck, and hair over ear and above forehead. Cheek shows slight wear.
REVERSE: Traces of wear show on head and high points of feathers on right wing. Three-quarters of the mint luster is still present. Surface abrasions and bag marks are more noticeable than for AU-55.

EXTREMELY FINE *(Very light wear on only the highest points.)*

EF-45 (Choice Extemely Fine)
OBVERSE: Hair around face shows slight wear, but most hair strands are visible. Lower edge of neck lightly worn.
REVERSE: Top of neck and head behind eye show slight wear. Central wing and leg feathers lightly worn. Half of the mint luster is still present.

EF-40 (Extremely Fine)
OBVERSE: Slight flattening visible on high points of hair; most hair strands clearly separated. Entire face and lower edge of neck lightly worn.
REVERSE: Wear shows on head behind eye and top of neck. Some flat spots visible on central wing and leg feathers. Partial mint luster is visible.

DOLLARS — EISENHOWER 1971 TO DATE

OBVERSE

REVERSE

MINT STATE *(Absolutely no trace of wear.)*

MS-70 (Perfect Uncirculated)
A flawless coin exactly as it was minted, with no trace of wear or injury. Must have full mint luster and brilliance or light toning. Any unusual striking traits must be described.

MS-65 (Choice Uncirculated)
No trace of wear; nearly as perfect as MS-70 except for some small blemish. Has full mint luster but may be unevenly toned or lightly fingermarked. A few minute nicks or marks may be present.

MS-60 (Uncirculated)
A strictly Uncirculated coin with no trace of wear, but with blemishes more obvious than for MS-65. Has full mint luster, but surface may be dull, spotted or heavily toned. Check points for signs of abrasion: high points of cheek and jawbone, center of neck, edge of bust. Head, high points of ridges and feathers in wings and legs.

ABOUT UNCIRCULATED (*Small trace of wear visible on highest points.*)

AU-55 (Choice About Uncirculated)
OBVERSE: Only a trace of wear shows on highest points of jawbone and at center of neck.
REVERSE: A trace of wear shows on high points of feathers in wings and legs. Nearly all of the mint luster is still present.

EXTREMELY FINE (*Very light wear on only the highest points.*)

EF-45 (Choice Extremely Fine)
OBVERSE: Slight wear shows on cheek, along jawbone and on high points at edge of bust. Hair lines are sharp and detailed.
REVERSE: High points of head, legs and wing ridges are lightly worn. Central feathers are all clearly defined. Three-quarters of the mint luster is still present.

VERY FINE (*Light to moderate even wear. All major features are sharp.*)

VF-30 (Choice Very Fine)
OBVERSE: Wear spots show on hair below part, and along cheek and jaw. Hair lines are weak but have nearly full visible details. Slight wear shows at center of neck and along edge of bust.
REVERSE: Wear shows on head, and feathers in wings and legs but all details are visible. All central tail feathers are plain. Wing and leg ridges are lightly worn.

GOLD DOLLARS — TYPE I 1849-1854

OBVERSE

REVERSE

MINT STATE (*Absolutely no trace of wear.*)

MS-70 (Perfect Uncirculated)
A flawless coin exactly as it was minted, with no trace of wear or injury. Must have full mint luster and brilliance. Any unusual die or planchet traits must be described.

MS-65 (Choice Uncirculated)
No trace of wear; nearly as perfect as MS-70 except for some small blemish. Has full mint luster and brilliance but may show slight discoloration. A few barely noticeable nicks or marks may be present.

MS-60 (Uncirculated)
A strictly Uncirculated coin with no trace of wear, but with blemishes more obvious than for MS-65. May lack full mint luster and brilliance. Check points for signs of abrasion: hair near coronet; tips of leaves.

ABOUT UNCIRCULATED *(Small trace of wear visible on highest points.)*

AU-55 (Choice About Uncirculated)
OBVERSE: There is a trace of wear at upper hairline below coronet.
REVERE: Trace of wear visible on tips of leaves. Three-quarters of the mint luster is still present.

AU-50 (About Uncirculated)
OBVERSE: There is a trace of wear on hairlines near coronet, and below the ear.
REVERSE: Trace of wear visible on tips of leaves. Half of the mint luster is still present.

EXTREMELY FINE *(Very light wear on only the highest points.)*

EF-45 (Choice Extremely Fine)
OBVERSE: Slight wear shows on highest wave of hair, hairline and below ear. All major details are sharp. Beads at top of coronet are well defined.
REVERSE: Leaves show visible wear at tips, but central details are clearly defined. Part of the mint luster is still present.

EF-40 (Extremely Fine)
OBVERSE: Slight wear shows on highest wave of hair, hairline and below ear. All major details are sharp. Beads at top of coronet are well defined.
REVERSE: Leaves show visible wear at tips but central details are clearly defined. Traces of mint luster will show.

VERY FINE *(Light to moderate even wear. All major features are sharp.)*

VF-30 (Choice Very Fine)
OBVERSE: Beads on top of coronet are well defined. LIBERTY is complete. Hair around face and neck slightly worn but strands fully separated. Star centers show some details.
REVERSE: These is light even wear on legend and date. Some details show in center of leaves.

VF-20 (Very Fine)
OBVERSE: Beads at top of coronet are partially separated. LIBERTY is complete. Hair around face and neck noticeably worn but well outlined. Some star centers show details.
REVERSE: There is light even wear on legend and date. Only traces of leaf ribs are visible. Bow knot is flat on high point.

FINE *(Moderate to heavy even wear. Entire design clear and bold.)*

F-12 (Fine)
OBVERSE: LIBERTY is complete but weak. Ear lobe is visible. Hairlines and beads on coronet, are worn smooth. Stars are clearly outlined, but centers are flat.
REVERSE: Legend within wreath is worn and weak in spots. Leaves and wreath are well outlined. Rim is full and edge beveled.

VERY GOOD *(Well worn. Design clear but flat and lacking details.)*

VG-8 (Very Good)
OBVERSE: Only the outline of hair is visible. Four letters in LIBERTY are clear.
REVERSE: Only the outline of leaves is visible. Legend and numeral are worn and very weak.

GOOD *(Heavily worn. Design and legend visible but faint in spots.)*

G-4 (Good)
OBVERSE: Head is outlined with nearly all details worn away. Stars are weak. Full rim shows.
REVERSE: Date and legend well worn but readable. Leaves are outlined. Full rim shows.
Note: The gold dollars stuck at Charlotte and Dahlonega are crude compared to those of the Philadelphia Mint. Frequently they have rough edges, and the die work appears to be generally inferior. In grading coins from these branch mints, consideration must be made for these factors.

QUARTER EAGLES — CORONET HEAD 1840-1907

OBVERSE

REVERSE

MINT STATE *(Absolutely no trace of wear.)*

MS-70 (Perfect Uncirculated)
A flawless coin exactly as it was minted, with no trace of wear or injury. Must have full mint luster and brilliance. Any unusual die or planchet traits must be described.

MS-65 (Choice Uncirculated)
No trace of wear; nearly as perfect as MS-70 except for some small blemish. Has full mint luster and brilliance but may show slight discoloration. A few barely noticeable nicks or marks may be present.

MS-60 (Uncirculated)
A strictly Uncirculated coin with no trace of wear, but with blemishes more obvious than for MS-65. May lack full mint luster and brilliance. Check points for signs of abrasion: tip of coronet, hair; wings, claws.

ABOUT UNCIRCULATED *(Small trace of wear visible on highest points.)*

AU-55 (Choice About Uncirculated)
OBVERSE: There is a trace of wear on tip of coronet and above eye.
REVERSE: Trace of wear visible on wing tips. Three-quarters of the mint luster is still present.

AU-50 (About Uncirculated)
OBVERSE: There is a trace of wear on coronet and on hair above ear, eye and forehead.
REVERSE: Trace of wear visible on wing tips, below eye and on claw. Half of the mint luster is still present.

EXTREMELY FINE *(Very light wear on only the highest points.)*

EF-45 (Choice Extremely Fine)
OBVERSE: There is light wear on coronet, and on hair above ear, eye, forelocks and top of head.

REVERSE: Light wear shows on edges and tips of wings, on neck, below eye and on claws. Part of the mint luster is still present.

EF-40 (Extremely Fine)
OBVERSE: Light wear shows on coronet, hair above ear and eye, on forelocks, and on cheek. All major details sharp.
REVERSE: Light wear shows on edges and tips of wings, on neck, below eye, on feathers and claws. Shield well defined. Traces of mint luster will show.

VERY FINE *(Light to moderate even wear. All major features are sharp.)*

VF-30 (Choice Very Fine)
OBVERSE: Light wear visible on coronet; hair is worn but shows considerable detail. Most stars show details. LIBERTY bold and clear.
REVERSE: Light wear shows on edges and tips of wings. Some detail shows on head and neck feathers. Vertical shield lines complete but some not separated; horizontal lines worn in center.

VF-20 (Very Fine)
OBVERSE: Hair outlined with very little detail. Only a few stars show any details. LIBERTY clear but not bold.
REVERSE: Half of wing feathers visible. Half of lines in shield are clear.

FINE *(Moderate to heavy even wear. Entire design clear and bold.)*

F-12 (Fine)
OBVERSE: Hair and cheek smooth. Stars outlined with no visible details. LIBERTY worn but visible.
REVERSE: Wings show very little detail. Head and one claw outlined only, with no details visible. Neck almost smooth. Most of shield lines merge.

Note: Coins of this type seldom appear in grades lower than Fine. Pieces made at Charlotte, Dahlonega and New Orleans are frequently found weakly struck. Those from San Francisco often lack feather details.

QUARTER EAGLES — INDIAN HEAD 1908-1929

OBVERSE

REVERSE

MINT STATE *(Absolutely no trace of wear.)*

MS-70 (Perfect Uncirculated)
A flawless coin exactly as it was minted, with no trace of wear or injury. Must have full mint luster and brilliance. Any unusual die or planchet traits must be described.

MS-65 (Choice Uncirculated)
No trace of wear; nearly as perfect as MS-70 except for some small blemish. Has full mint luster and brilliance but may show slight discoloration. A few barely noticeable nicks or marks may be present.

MS-60 (Uncirculated)
A strictly Uncirculated coin with no trace of wear, but with blemishes more obvious than for MS-65. May lack full mint luster and brilliance. Check points for signs of abrasion: cheekbone, headdress, headband feathers; shoulder of eagle's left wing.

ABOUT UNCIRCULATED *(Small trace of wear visible on highest points.)*

AU-55 (Choice About Uncirculated)
OBVERSE: There is a trace of wear on cheekbone.
REVERSE: Trace of wear visible on shoulder of eagle's left wing. Three-quarters of the mint luster is still present.

AU-50 (About Uncirculated)
OBVERSE: There is a trace of wear on cheekbone and headdress.
REVERSE: Trace of wear visible on shoulder of wing, head and breast. Half of the mint luster is still present.

EXTREMELY FINE *(Very light wear on only the highest points.)*

EF-45 (Choice Extremely Fine)
OBVERSE: There is light wear on cheekbone, headdress and headband.
REVERSE: Light wear shows on upper portion of wing, head, neck and breast.

EF-40 (Extremely Fine)
OBVERSE: Light wear shows on cheekbone, jaw and headband. Slight wear visible on feathers of headdress. Stars sharp.
REVERSE: Light wear shows on wing, head, neck and breast. Leg has full feather detail. Traces of mint luster will show.

VERY FINE *(Light to moderate even wear. All major features are sharp.)*

VF-30 (Choice Very Fine)
OBVERSE: Cheekbone shows flat spot. Small feathers clear; large feathers show some detail. Most of headband detail visible.
REVERSE: Wear shows on wing and neck. Some breast feathers show details. Most of leg feathers visible.

VF-20 (Very Fine)
OBVERSE: Cheekbone worn about halfway. Small feathers clear but large feathers show a little detail. Hair cord knot is distinct. Headband shows some detail.
REVERSE: Little detail shows on breast and leg feathers. Top of wing and neck worn. Second layer of wing feathers shows.

FINE *(Moderate to heavy even wear. Entire design clear and bold.)*

HALF EAGLES — CORONET HEAD 1839-1908

OBVERSE

REVERSE

F-12 (Fine)
OBVERSE: Cheekbone worn; all feathers worn with very little detail visible. Stars outlined, with no details visible. Hair cord knot is worn but visible.
REVERSE: Wing worn, with only partial feathers at bottom visible. All lettering worn but visible.

Note: Coins of this type are seldom collected in grades lower than Fine. Mint marks are often weakly struck.

MINT STATE *(Absolutely no trace of wear.)*

MS-70 (Perfect Uncirculated)
A flawless coin exactly as it was minted, with no trace of wear or injury. Must have full mint luster and brilliance. Any unusual die or planchet traits must be described.

MS-65 (Choice Uncirculated)
No trace of wear; nearly as perfect as MS-70 except for some small blemish. Has full mint luster and brilliance but may show slight discoloration. A few barely noticeable bag marks and surface abrasions may be present.

MS-60 (Uncirculated)
A strictly Uncirculated coin with no trace of wear, but with blemishes more obvious than for MS-65. Has full mint luster but may lack brilliance. Surface may be lightly marred by minor bag marks and abrasions. Check points for signs of wear: hair, coronet; wings.

ABOUT UNCIRCULATED *(Small trace of wear visible on highest points.)*

AU-55 (Choice About Uncirculated)
OBVERSE: There is a trace of wear on tip of coronet and hair above eye.
REVERSE: Trace of wear visible on wing tips. Three-quarters of the mint luster is still present.

AU-50 (About Uncirculated)
OBVERSE: There is a trace of wear on coronet, above ear and eye.
REVERSE: Trace of wear visible on wing tips, below eye and on claw. Half of the mint luster is still present.

EXTREMELY FINE *(Light wear on only the highest points.)*

EF-45 (Choice Extremely Fine)
OBVERSE: There is light wear on coronet, and on hair above ear, eye, forelocks and top of head.
REVERSE: Light wear shows on edges and tips of wings, on neck, below eye and on claws. Part of the mint luster is still present.

EF-40 (Extremely Fine)
OBVERSE: Light wear shows on coronet, on hair above ear and eye, on the forelock, on top of head and on cheek. All major details are sharp.
REVERSE: Light wear visible on edges and tips of wings, on neck, below eye, on feathers and claws. Shield is well defined. Traces of mint luster will show.

VERY FINE *(Light to moderate even wear. All major features are sharp.)*

VF-30 (Choice Very Fine)
OBVERSE: Light wear shows on coronet, hair and stars but most details are visible. LIBERTY bold.
REVERSE: Light wear visible on edges and tips of wings. Head and neck feathers show some detail. Vertical lines in shield complete but some not separated; horizontal lines worn in center.

VF-20 (Very Fine)
OBVERSE: Hair worn but major details visible. Top line of coronet broken. Some stars show partial detail. LIBERTY clear but not bold.
REVERSE: Half of wing feathers are visible. Half of lines in shield are clear.

FINE *(Moderate to heavy even wear. Entire design clear and bold.)*

F-12 (Fine)
OBVERSE: Hair and cheekbone smooth. Top line of coronet worn. LIBERTY worn but visible.
REVERSE: Wings show very little detail. Head and one claw outlined only, with no details visible. Neck almost smooth. Most of shield lines merge. (For the 1866 through 1908 group, the motto is half readable.)

Note: Coins of this type are seldom collected in grades lower than Fine.

HALF EAGLES — INDIAN HEAD 1908-1929

OBVERSE · REVERSE

MINT STATE *(Absolutely no trace of wear.)*

MS-70 (Perfect Uncirculated)
A flawless coin exactly as it was minted, with no trace of wear or injury. Must have full mint luster and brilliance. Any unusual die or planchet traits must be described.

MS-65 (Choice Uncirculated)
No trace of wear; nearly as perfect as MS-70 except for some small blemish. Has full mint luster and brilliance but may show slight discoloration. A few barely noticeable bag marks and surface abrasions may be present.

MS-60 (Uncirculated)
A strictly Uncirculated coin with no trace of wear, but with blemishes more obvious than for MS-65. Has full mint luster but may lack brilliance. Surface may be lightly marred by minor bag marks and abrasions. Check points for signs of wear: cheekbone, headdress, headband feathers; shoulder of eagle's left wing.

ABOUT UNCIRCULATED *(Small trace of wear visible on highest points.)*

AU-55 (Choice About Uncirculated)
OBVERSE: There is a trace of wear on cheekbone.
REVERSE: Trace of wear visible on shoulder of eagle's left wing. Three-quarters of the mint luster is still present.

AU-50 (About Uncirculated)
OBVERSE: There is a trace of wear on cheekbone and headdress.
REVERSE: Trace of wear visible on shoulder of wing, head and breast. Half of the mint luster is still present.

EXTREMELY FINE *(Light wear on only the highest points.)*

EF-45 (Choice Extremely Fine)
OBVERSE: There is light wear on cheekbone, headdress and headband.
REVERSE: Light wear shows on upper portion of wing, head, neck and breast. Part of mint luster is still present.

EF-40 (Extremely Fine)
OBVERSE: Light wear shows on cheekbone, jaw and headband. Slight wear visible on feathers of headdress. Stars are sharp.
REVERSE: Light wear shows on wing, head, neck and breast. Leg has full feather detail. Traces of mint luster will show.

VERY FINE *(Light to moderate even wear. All major features are sharp.)*

VF-30 (Choice Very Fine)
OBVERSE: Cheekbone shows flat spot. Small feathers clear; large feathers show some details. Most of headband detail visible.
REVERSE: Wear shows on wing and neck. Some breast feathers show details. Most of leg feathers visible.

VF-20 (Very Fine)
OBVERSE: Cheekbone worn about half-way. Headdress feathers show some details. Hair cord knot is distinct. Headband shows only a little detail.
REVERSE: Little detail shows on breast and leg feathers. Top of wing and neck worn. Second layer of wing feathers shows.

FINE *(Moderate to heavy even wear. Entire design clear and bold.)*

F-12 (Fine)
OBVERSE: Cheekbone worn; all feathers worn with very little detail visible. Stars outlined, with no details visible. Hair cord knot is worn but visible.
REVERSE: Wing worn, with only partial feathers at bottom visible. All lettering worn but visible.

Note: Coins of this type are seldom collected in grades lower than Fine. Mint marks are often very weakly struck.

EAGLES — CORONET HEAD 1838-1907

OBVERSE   REVERSE

MINT STATE *(Absolutely no trace of wear.)*

MS-70 (Perfect Uncirculated)
A flawless coin exactly as it was minted, with no trace of wear or injury. Must have full mint luster and brilliance. Any unusual die or planchet traits must be described.

MS-65 (Choice Uncirculated)
No trace of wear; nearly as perfect as MS-70 except for some small blemish. Has full mint luster and brilliance but may show slight discoloration. A few barely noticeable bag marks and surface abrasions may be present.

MS-60 (Uncirculated)
A strictly Uncirculated coin with no trace of wear, but with blemishes more obvious than for MS-65. Has full mint luster but may lack brilliance. Surface may be lightly marred by minor bag marks and abrasions. Check points for signs of wear: hair, coronet; wings.

ABOUT UNCIRCULATED *(Small trace of wear visible on highest points.)*

AU-55 (Choice About Uncirculated)
OBVERSE: There is a trace of wear on hair above eye and on coronet.
REVERSE: Trace of wear visible on wing tips. Three-quarters of the mint luster is still present.

AU-50 (About Uncirculated)
OBVERSE: There is a trace of wear on hair at ear and above eye, and on coronet.
REVERSE: Trace of wear visible on wing tips, below eye and on claw. Half of the mint luster is still present.

EXTREMELY FINE *(Light wear on only the highest points.)*

EF-45 (Choice Extremely Fine)
OBVERSE: There is light wear on coronet, and on hair above ear, eye, forelocks and top of head.
REVERSE: Light wear shows on edges and tips of wings, on neck, below eye and on claws. Part of the mint luster is still present.

EF-40 (Extremely Fine)
OBVERSE: Light wear shows on coronet, hair, cheek and stars. All major details sharp.
REVERSE: Light wear visible on wings, head, neck and claws. Shield is well defined. Traces of mint luster will show.

VERY FINE *(Light to moderate even wear. All major features are sharp.)*

VF-30 (Choice Very Fine)
OBVERSE: There is light wear on coronet, hair and stars, but most details are visible. There is a break on top line of coronet over two letters in LIBERTY. Cheek worn. LIBERTY bold.
REVERSE: Light wear visible on wings and head but some details show. Vertical lines in shield complete but some are not separated; horizontal lines worn in center.

VF-20 (Very Fine)
OBVERSE: Hair worn but major details visible. Break on top line of coronet extends over at least three letters in LIBERTY. Cheek well worn. Stars worn but show most details. LIBERTY clear but shows wear.
REVERSE: About half of wing feathers are visible. Very little detail shows in head.

FINE *(Moderate to heavy even wear. Entire design clear and bold.)*

F-12 (Fine)
OBVERSE: Hair and cheekbone smooth. Top line of coronet worn. Some details show in stars. LIBERTY worn but visible.
REVERSE: Wings show very little detail. Head and one claw outlined only, with no details visible. Neck is almost smooth. Most of shield lines merge. (In the 1866 through 1907 group, the motto is worn but readable.)

Note: Coins of this type are seldom collected in grades lower than Fine.

EAGLES — INDIAN HEAD 1907-1933

OBVERSE   REVERSE

MINT STATE *(Absolutely no trace of wear.)*

MS-70 (Perfect Uncirculated)
A flawless coin exactly as it was minted, with no trace of wear or injury. Must have full mint luster and brilliance. Any unusual die or planchet traits must be described.

MS-65 (Choice Uncirculated)
No trace of wear; nearly as perfect as MS-70 except for some small blemish. Has full mint luster and brilliance but may show some slight discoloration. A few minute bag marks and surface abrasions may be present.

MS-60 (Uncirculated)
A strictly Uncirculated coin with no trace of wear, but with blemishes more obvious than for MS-65. Has full mint luster but may lack brilliance. Surface may be lightly marred by minor bag marks and abrasions. Check points for signs of wear: above eye, cheek, wing.

ABOUT UNCIRCULATED *(Small trace of wear visible on highest points.)*

AU-55 (Choice About Uncirculated)
OBVERSE: There is a trace of wear above eye.
REVERSE: Trace of wear visible on wing. Three-quarters of the mint luster is still present.

AU-50 (About Uncirculated)
OBVERSE: There is a trace of wear on hair above eye and on forehead.
REVERSE: Trace of wear visible on wing. Half of the mint luster is still present.

EXTREMELY FINE *(Light wear on only the highest points.)*

EF-45 (Choice Extremely Fine)
OBVERSE: There is light wear on hair above eye and on forehead, and on cheekbone.
REVERSE: Light wear shows on wing and head. Part of the mint luster is still present.

EF-40 (Extremely Fine)
OBVERSE: Light wear shows on hair, cheekbone and feathers.
REVERSE: Light wear visible on wing and head. Traces of mint luster will show.

VERY FINE *(Light to moderate even wear. All major features are sharp.)*

VF-30 (Choice Very Fine)
OBVERSE: There is light wear along forehead, but most detail shows. Moderate wear visible on cheekbone. Light wear shows where feathers meet headband.
REVERSE: Left wing shows more than half the details. Some details in head are visible.

VF-20 (Very Fine)
OBVERSE: About half the hair detail is visible. Moderate wear shows on cheekbone. Some feathers do not touch headband.
REVERSE: There is moderate wear on left wing which shows only about one-quarter detail. Head almost smooth. All lettering bold.

FINE *(Moderate to heavy even wear. Entire design clear and bold.)*

F-12 (Fine)
OBVERSE: Hair smooth with no details; cheekbone almost smooth. No feathers touch headband but most feather details visible.
REVERSE: Left wing top and head are worn smooth. Lettering worn but visible.

Note: Coins of this type are seldom collected in grades lower than Fine.

DOUBLE EAGLES — LIBERTY HEAD 1850-1907

OBVERSE   REVERSE

MINT STATE *(Absolutely no trace of wear.)*

MS-70 (Perfect Uncirculated)
A flawless coin exactly as it was minted, with no trace of wear or injury. Must have full mint luster and brilliance. Any unusual die or planchet traits must be described.

MS-65 (Choice Uncirculated)
No trace of wear; nearly as perfect as MS-70 except for some small blemish. Has full mint luster and brilliance but may show slight discoloration. A few minute bag marks and surface abrasions are usually present.

MS-60 (Uncirculated)
A strictly Uncirculated coin with no trace of wear, but with blemishes more obvious than for MS-65. Has full mint luster but may lack brilliance. Surface is usually lightly marred by minor bag marks and abrasions. Check points for signs of wear: hair, coronet; eagle's neck and wing, top of shield.

ABOUT UNCIRCULATED *(Small trace of wear visible on highest points.)*

AU-55 (Choice About Uncirculated)
OBVERSE: There is a trace of wear on hair.
REVERSE: Trace of wear visible on wing tips and neck. Three-quarters of the mint luster is still present.

AU-50 (About Uncirculated)
OBVERSE: There is a trace of wear on hair at top and over eye, and on coronet.
REVERSE: Trace of wear visible on wing tips, neck and at top of shield. Half of the mint luster is still present.

EXTREMELY FINE *(Light wear on only the highest points.)*

EF-45 (Choice Extremely Fine)
OBVERSE: There is light wear on hair and coronet prongs.
REVERSE: Light wear shows on edges and tips of wings, on head and neck, and on horizontal shield lines. Part of the mint luster is still present.

EF-40 (Extremely Fine)
OBVERSE: Light wear shows on hair, coronet prongs and cheek.
REVERSE: Light wear visible on wings, head, neck, horizontal shield lines and tail. Traces of mint luster will show.

VERY FINE *(Light to moderate even wear. All major features are sharp.)*

VF-30 (Choice Very Fine)
OBVERSE: About one-quarter of hair detail below coronet visible; half the detail shows above coronet. Cheek and some coronet prongs worn. Stars show wear but all details visible.
REVERSE: Most of wing details visible. Top part of shield shows moderate wear. About half the detail in tail visible.

VF-20 (Very Fine)
OBVERSE: Less than half the hair detail above coronet visible. About half the coronet prongs are considerably worn. Stars are flat but show most details. LIBERTY shows wear but is very clear.
REVERSE: Some wing details visible. Shield shows very little detail at top. Tail is worn with very little detail.

FINE *(Moderate to heavy even wear. Entire design clear and bold.)*

F-12 (Fine)
OBVERSE: All hairlines are well worn with very little detail visible. About one-quarter of details within coronet visible. Stars show little detail. LIBERTY readable.
REVERSE: Wings show very little detail. Head and neck smooth. Eye visible. Tail and top of shield smooth.

   Note: Coins of this type are seldom collected in grades lower than Fine. The hair curl under the ear is sometimes weakly struck.
   In the group between 1866 and 1876, the reverse motto is sometimes weakly struck.
   Pieces made at the Carson City mint are usually found weakly struck and heavily bag marked.

DOUBLE EAGLES — SAINT-GAUDENS 1907-1932

OBVERSE   REVERSE

MINT STATE *(Absolutely no trace of wear.)*

MS-70 (Perfect Uncirculated)
A flawless coin exactly as it was minted, with no trace of wear or injury. Must have full mint luster and brilliance. Any unusual die or planchet traits must be described.

MS-65 (Choice Uncirculated)
No trace of wear; nearly as perfect as MS-70 except for some small blemish. Has full mint luster and brilliance but may show slight discoloration. A few minute bag marks and surface abrasions are usually present.

MS-60 (Uncirculated)
A strictly Uncirculated coin with no trace of wear, but with blemishes more obvious than for MS-65. Has full mint luster but may lack brilliance. Surface is usually lightly marred by minor bag marks and abrasions. Check points for signs of wear: forehead, breast, knee, nose; eagle's wings and breast.

ABOUT UNCIRCULATED *(Small trace of wear visible on highest points.)*

AU-55 (Choice About Uncirculated)
OBVERSE: There is a trace of wear on left breast and left knee.
REVERSE: Trace of wear visible on high point of wing. Three-quarters of the mint luster is still present.

AU-50 (About Uncirculated)
OBVERSE: There is a trace of wear on nose, breast and knee.
REVERSE: Trace of wear visible on wings. Half of the mint luster is still present.

EXTREMELY FINE *(Light wear on only the highest points.)*

EF-45 (Choice Extremely Fine)
OBVERSE: There is light wear on forehead, nose, breast and knee.
REVERSE: Light wear shows on wings and breast, but all feathers are bold. Part of the mint luster is still present.

EF-40 (Extremely Fine)
OBVERSE: Light wear shows on forehead, nose, breast, knee and just below left knee. Drapery lines on chest visible.
REVERSE: Light wear visible on wings and breast but all feathers bold. Traces of mint luster will show.

VERY FINE *(Light to moderate even wear. All major features are sharp.)*

VF-30 (Choice Very Fine)
OBVERSE: There is light wear on all features, extending above and below left knee and along part of right leg. Some of garment lines on chest are visible.
REVERSE: Light wear visible on left wing and breast; feathers show but some are weak.

VF-20 (Very Fine)
OBVERSE: Forehead moderately worn. Contours of breast worn. Only a few garment lines on chest are visible. Entire right leg shows moderate wear.
REVERSE: Half of feathers are visible in wings and breast.

FINE *(Moderate to heavy even wear. Entire design clear and bold.)*

F-12 (Fine)
OBVERSE: Forehead and garment smooth; breasts flat. Both legs worn with right bottom missing.
REVERSE: Less than half the wing details are visible. Only a little breast detail is visible.

Note: Coins of this type are seldom found in grades lower than Fine.

COLONIAL COINS, PATTERNS AND TOKENS

The most extensively circulated — and faithfully trusted — coin of early colonial America was the Spanish silver dollar or "piece of eight." Introduced to this country by the Spanish explorers and later imported in abundance by traders, it had a value of eight *reals,* each real or "bit" being worth 12½ cents. Thus the quarter or 25 cent piece came to be known as "two bits"

"Two-bits"

"Four-bits"

THE SPANISH MILLED DOLLAR
The "Piece of Eight"

The following pages comprise descriptions and price valuations for most types of monies used in the American colonies, excluding foreign coins intended to serve currency needs abroad. Most can only be classed as tokens as they either had no face value or were struck without government sanction. These include merchant pieces and other speculative issues. However the colonists, being ever-resourceful, attempted from time to time to strike semi-official or official coinage, and these will be found listed as well. Colonial coinage on the whole is not handsome. It was generally produced under conditions inferior to that of governmentally issued money, often designed and struck by persons who had little or no prior experience in such work. It is nevertheless of great interest from both a numismatic and historical point of view and much of it is extremely rare. As a general rule the collector should be wary of counterfeits and reproductions, as the majority of these pieces have at one time or other been facsimilied, either as legitimate souvenirs or fradulently.

SOMMER ISLANDS (BERMUDA)

This so-called "Hog money" is thought to be the first coinage of the American colonies. A hog is pictured on one side and a sailing vessel on the other. The workmanship is English. Hogs were not native to the islands but introduced around 1515 by the Spaniard Juan Bermudez, from whom Bermuda takes its name. They apparently increased and multiplied vastly within the next hundred years, serving as an important article of food for the inhabitants. The suggestion that the coins were intended to represent the market value of a hog, just as early Greek coins were sometimes stamped with a likeness of an animal whose price they equaled, is no longer given serious consideration. It was used merely as an emblem. These coins are of lightly silvered brass, inscribed "SOMMER ISLANDS." The edges are, as to be expected, irregular, having been produced by the hammering technique rather than milling.

SHILLING

TYPE OF COIN	ABP	AG-3 About Good	G-4 Good	F-12 Fine
☐ Shilling	525.00	1000.00	1700.00	6250.00

SIXPENCE

TYPE OF COIN	ABP	AG-3 About Good	G-4 Good	F-12 Fine
☐ Sixpence	325.00	600.00	1100.00	3150.00
☐ Threepence				VERY RARE
☐ Twopence	450.00	800.00	1650.00	3500.00

MASSACHUSETTS-NEW ENGLAND COINAGE

This is the earliest coinage struck on the North American continent. Its history is briefly detailed in the section on Colonial Coins, Patterns and Tokens. This crude coinage may not be appealing aesthetically but its historical significance is as great, or greater, than any coins subsequently issued in this country. It was produced in limited quantities for local circulation in the Boston area and is extremely rare. When the decision was reached to attempt a native currency, the Massachusetts General Court appointed John Hull "mintmaster." The "mint" was an iron works operated by Joseph Jenks at Saugus, just north of Boston. These coins were made of silver by the ancient process of hammering — beating the designs into them by holding the die against the metal blank and striking it with a mallet. There was in fact no design at all. The coins were issued in three denominations — threepence, sixpence and twelvepence (shilling) — and each carried the letters "NE" on one side and the value in roman numerals on the other, most of the surface being blank. Variations in size, shape and placement of the markings are usual. They date to 1652 but no date appears upon them.

NE SHILLING

NE SIXPENCE

NE THREEPENCE

TYPE OF COIN		ABP	G-4 Good	F-12 Fine
☐ NE Shilling		2350.00	4500.00	9250.00
☐ NE Sixpence	Less than 8 known	18000.00	25000.00	50000.00
☐ NE Threepence	Less than 3 known		EXTREMELY RARE	

WILLOW TREE COINS

After about four months of circulation of the Massachusetts-New England coinage (above), it was decided they were unsatisfactory. The legend and numeral of value were so simplistic that anyone possessing smith's tools could reproduce them. There was the further problem — not a new one, as it was faced by English mints in the middle ages — that the large expanses of unstamped metal invited "clipping," a practice in which unscrupulous persons trimmed down the edges and collected quantities of silver while still passing the coins at face value. It was impossible to improve the method of manufacture, there being no milling machines available. But the designs could be improved by the use of more fully engraved dies. This was accomplished with the so-called Willow Tree Coinage, introduced in 1653. On the obverse appears a very abstract rendition of a willow tree, surrounded by the placename, with the date and value designation on the reverse (III stood for threepence, VI for sixpence and XII for shilling). Although struck at odd moments from 1653 to 1660 (there was no regular or continuous production), all specimens are dated 1652.

SHILLING   SIXPENCE

THREEPENCE

TYPE OF COIN	ABP	G-4 Good	F-12 Fine
☐ Willow Tree Shilling	3200.00	6250.00	14000.00
☐ Willow Tree Sixpence	12000.00	17500.00	24500.00
☐ Willow Tree Threepence		EXTREMELY RARE	

OAK TREE COINS

Successors to the Willow Tree Coins, these were likewise of Massachusetts origin and, like them, showed a tree on the obverse with the date and numeral of value on the reverse. They were introduced in 1660, the year of the English Restoration (the return of the Stuarts to the throne), an item of no small significance numismatically. While the previous regime, the Protectorate of Oliver Cromwell, was composed of politicians who supported the pilgrim cause, there was genuine fear that the new king — Charles II — might deal harshly with the colonists for being so bold as to strike coins. They attempted to camouflage this activity by retaining the old date, 1652, during the eight years that Oak Tree Coins were struck; and in fact it remained unaltered for the 16 years of their successors, Pine Tree Coins. In terms of design these Oak Tree Coins were an improvement on their predecessors, being much sharper and bolder. Whether this can be attributed to more deeply engraved dies, more careful hammering, or (usually overlooked possibility) better annealing or heating of the blanks is uncertain. The Mintmaster was still the same: John Hull. But this much is sure, the Oak Tree Coins were turned out in far larger quantities than previous Massachusetts coins.

SHILLING

SIXPENCE

THREEPENCE

TYPE OF COIN	ABP	G-4 Good	F-12 Fine	EF-40 Ex. Fine
☐ Shilling	170.00	310.00	875.00	2750.00
☐ Sixpence	173.00	320.00	975.00	2925.00
☐ Threepence	180.00	345.00	1075.00	2500.00
☐ Twopence	70.00	315.00	950.00	2200.00

PINE TREE COINS

The final version of the Bay Colony *"tree"* coin, it featured a much clearer if not more botanically accurate portrait of a tree. Though struck in the same three denominations as the earlier types, there is a "Large Planchet" and "Small Planchet" version of the shilling, the large being slightly rarer. Both are of the same weight; the metal was simply hammered thinner on the "Large Planchet." It had been demonstrated, by the use of large planchets for the Willow and Oak Tree shillings, that the coin did not stand up well to handling and could be rendered sturdier by reducing its size and thereby increasing the thickness. It was also possible to strike the design more deeply with a thicker planchet. All coins from this series are dated 1652. They were actually struck from 1667 to 1682, during the reign of Britain's Charles II. After 1682 the issuing of coinage was discontinued by the Bay Colony. Many varieties exist in this series.

SHILLING, Large Planchet   SHILLING, Small Planchet

SIXPENCE   THREEPENCE

TYPE OF COIN	ABP	G-4 Good	F-12 Fine	EF-40 Ex. Fine
☐ Shilling, Large Planchet	135.00	230.00	750.00	2100.00
☐ Shilling, Small Planchet	135.00	220.00	700.00	1950.00
☐ Sixpence	135.00	230.00	680.00	1500.00
☐ Threepence	130.00	215.00	620.00	1750.00

MARYLAND

Maryland was the second colony, next to Massachusetts, to have coinage of its own. The origins of these coins bear little relation to those of the Bay Colony. While the Massachusetts pieces had been natively designed and struck, Maryland's coins were entirely a foreign product. They date from 1658. At this time Maryland was very sparsely inhabited, its only residents being small colonies of English immigrants, and could not have suffered too seriously from a shortage of coinage. Though not strictly classified as private issues they might well merit that designation. Maryland's first coins were the brainchild of Cecil Calvert, Lord Baltimore (for whom the colony's chief city was named). Calvert did not, as popularly supposed, "own Maryland." He did however possess large areas of its land and had the title of Lord Proprietor of Maryland. As an English lord with typical lordly pride, Calvert looked with disdain upon the prospect of Englishmen — his subjects, technically — trading with beads or iron or other objects of barter. So he ordered a batch of English-quality coins to be struck in Britain for use in the colony. They comprised a shilling, sixpence, fourpence or groat, and a penny. The first three were of silver, following the British tradition, the penny in copper. As a result of their production in an established, well-equipped mint, these coins are considerably more professional in appearance than those of Massachusetts. Lord Calvert placed his own portrait upon them. There was no need to fear censure from the king for this brazen act as the English Civil War had already swept the king (Charles I) from his throne and Britain was not to again be ruled by a king until 1660. The reverses of the silver pieces carry Calvert's heraldic bearings with the value in roman numerals. The penny's obverse shows a regal crown surmounted by staffs and banners. There is no numeral of value on the penny but instead the word "denarium," the name of an ancient Roman coin from which the British penny evolved. (To this day the symbol for "penny" in Britain is the letter "d," meaning denarium. The cent sign, ¢, is never used.) Lord Calvert's portrait is a shoulder-length bust without crown, wreath of laurel or other symbol of rulership. The penny is the scarcest of the denominations, as this is believed to have been a pattern only, not actually placed in use.

FOURPENCE   SHILLING

TYPE OF COIN	ABP	G-4 Good	F-12 Fine
☐Shilling	520.00	975.00	3375.00
☐Sixpence	500.00	930.00	2400.00
☐Fourpence	550.00	1000.00	3700.00
☐Denarium (Penny)		EXTREMELY RARE	

MARK NEWBY OR ST. PATRICK HALFPENCE

The coinage shortage in the early colonies, and the voraciousness with which anything resembling coinage was seized upon as a medium of exchange, is clearly demonstrated by the Newby or St. Patrick Halfpence. The coins are really misnamed, as they existed not only in halfpence but farthing denomination (in the British currency system a farthing or "fourthling" was equal to one quarter of a penny). Mark Newby was neither an explorer or royal governor but apparently a private Irish citizen who came from Dublin and settled in New Jersey in the year 1681. He brought with him a quantity of tokens — they could only very charitably be called coins — which are thought to have been struck at Dublin about eight years earlier. These were coppers. On the obverse they depict a crowned king kneeling and playing a harp, almost certainly intended as the Biblical king David who is often represented in art as a harpist. St. Patrick, the legendary and patron saint of Ireland, appears on the reverses. On the halfpence he holds a crozier and cross (often mistaken for a clover) while giving benediction to a worshipper; on the farthing he is shown in a similar pose, driving the snakes out of Ireland, one of the many accomplishments with which this saint is credited. The obverse legend is "FLOREAT REX," which can be translated as "PROSPERITY TO THE KING." These are not at all bad-looking pieces and they feature an intriguing detail: the large crown on the obverse was inlaid in brass, to contrast in color with the copper and give the appearance of being golden. It is, however, sometimes lacking. The origin of this St. Patrick Money is not clearly known. The possibility that it was struck for circulation in America seems very remote, as (a) there is no record of supportive legislation on either side of the Atlantic, and (b) the coins were apparently not brought to this country until long after striking, which hardly would have been the case had they been designed for use here. In any event the General Assembly of the New Jersey Province authorized their use as legal tender in May, 1682, and for some while thereafter they served as the common currency of New Jersey. The most logical conclusion to be drawn is that Newby was a commercial trader who sought to profit from the shortage of coinage in America, and that he settled in New Jersey because this area was virtually without money of any kind. If so, he would not have been the only colonist to do this. Silver and gold patterns of the farthing were struck, of which the silver is very rare and the gold unique. There may have been similar patterns of the ½ penny but they have not been discovered. In their normal metal, copper, neither is a coin of extreme scarcity.

ST. PATRICK HALFPENCE   ST. PATRICK FARTHING

TYPE OF COIN	ABP	G-4 Good	F-12 Fine
☐St. Patrick Halfpence	52.00	100.00	325.00
☐St. Patrick Farthing (Brass Insert on Obverse)	36.00	75.00	210.00
☐St. Patrick Farthing (Without Brass Insert)	36.00	75.00	200.00
☐St. Patrick Farthing (Silver Pattern)	320.00	650.00	1700.00
☐St. Patrick Farthing (Gold Pattern)			UNIQUE

COLONIAL PLANTATION TOKEN

The so-called Plantation Token was the first coinage authorized for use in the American colonies by the British government. Its history is of great interest. Throughout the middle 17th century it was well known in England that the American provinces or "plantations" as they were called abroad (largely by persons unaware of the extent of population) suffered from a shortage of coinage. In 1688 an Englishman named John Holt petitioned the king (James II) for a patent or franchise for the striking of coinage for distribution in the colonies. In Britain at this time the system of "patents of exclusivity" was commonplace. Printers would pay a fee to have the exclusive right on putting out Bibles; merchants paid for a franchise to sell a particular product without fear of competition. The fee, which was considerable, had to be paid each year while the franchise was in force. Holt was convinced that the supply of coinage to America would be a very profitable endeavor. The government approved his request for a franchise and shortly thereafter he began to strike his coins, better called tokens. Large in size, they were made of tin and had the face value of 1/24th of a Spanish real or "piece of eight," say about fourpence. On their obverse they pictured an equestrian likeness of James II, regal-looking in this design but soon to be driven out of the country into exile. It is important to note that they were not intended for use in any special region but could be exchanged anywhere in the provinces; thus they carry no placename. The original dies were preserved and restrikes made from them in the late 1820's, whose appearance is quite similar to the original and could well be a cause of confusion to beginners. A very rare variety exists, in which the numeral "4" in the value legend on the reverse is positioned vertically instead of horizontally.

PLANTATION TOKEN

TYPE OF COIN	ABP	G-4 Good	F-12 Fine	EF-40 Ex. Fine	MS-60 Unc.
☐James II Plantation Token ..	75.00	150.00	235.00	525.00	1200.00
☐James II Plantation Token, vertical "4"					RARE

Restrikes exist which are worth slightly less.

ELEPHANT TOKENS

These extremely popular, intriguing pieces have been the subject of much study and debate. Their origins are only sketchily known. There are three specific types: London token, Carolina token and New England token. All have the same obverse, a portrait of an elephant without legend or inscription of any kind. These pieces are coppers and were modeled as halfpennies, though they carry no indication of value. The extent to which they circulated in the American colonies is not established. Based on what little information is available their history may be pieced together as follows.

First in the series was the London token, which on some specimens carries the wording "God Preserve London" on the reverse, on others merely "London," accompanying a heraldic shield. The belief is that they were struck in 1664 when the population of that city was being decimated by an outbreak of bubonic plague, which apparently is the danger from which preservation was sought. So far this theory makes some historical sense though it fails to explain the selection of an elephant as the obverse symbol. Could it be that this was a reference to "stamping out" the plague, and that the elephant, as the largest of creatures, would be best equipped to do so? That elephants were well known at London in the 1660's is well established. There were no zoos for the display of wild beasts but elephants and tigers (both from India) were kept in enclosed dungeons in the Tower of London for the amusement of visitors. Natural history drawing was still in an archaic state at that time, which explains why the elephant on Elephant Tokens looks rather strange. For a long while thereafter there appears to have been no effort to revive the Elephant Token, perhaps because the plague subsided. Then in 1694 it reappeared, in an edition bearing two different reverses: "God Preserve Carolina and the Lord's Proprietors" and "God Preserve New England." Just how these pieces came to be, what their intent was, and how they were circulated, is totally unknown. It may be presumed that "God Preserve" was used merely in the sense of "God Bless," after the fashion of the slogan "God Save the King," not as implication that either Carolina or New England suffered from any specific difficulty. There is little doubt, based on physical evidence, that they were struck in England, as these tokens are handsomely milled (not hammered) and it is doubtful that such work could have been accomplished in the colonies. It has been said that the London variety was intended for circulation in Tangier but even if that were so, there is no evidence of it being an official issue. The Carolina and New England pieces could have been entirely speculative. Their distribution may have been local (in England) with no intention of exporting or using them for actual currency in the colonies. This seems the logical answer, especially in view of the extremely small quantities struck. Of the London token there were considerably larger numbers struck but to classify this as a piece designed for colonial use seems very presumptive. Some specimens undoubtedly reached the colonies at an early date but, if they did, it was only accidentally, in the baggage or pockets of immigrants or traders, just as almost everything else made abroad found its way across the Atlantic.

There are a number of types and varieties. The London token exists in both thin and thick planchet; with interlacing in the central portion of the shield; with sword in the second quarter of the shield (transposed from the first, where it is commonly found); and with the inscription "London" rather than "God Preserve London." Of these the transposed sword is the rarest. The chief variety on the Carolina issue is the alteration from "Proprieters" to the more correct spelling, "Proprietors," accomplished not by the introduction of a fresh die but re-engraving the original. If closely inspected the letter "e," or what remains of it, can be observed.

1694 NEW ENGLAND   1694 PROPRIETORS

1694 PROPRIETERS   1664 GOD PRESERVE LONDON

1664 GOD PRESERVE LONDON (SWORDS)   1664 LON DON

TYPE OF COIN	ABP	G-4 Good	F-12 Fine
☐ 1664 God Preserve London (thin)	35.00	65.00	180.00
☐ 1664 God Preserve London (thick)	27.00	55.00	160.00
☐ 1664 God Preserve London (diag.)	75.00	150.00	275.00
☐ 1664 God Preserve London (swords)		EXTREMELY RARE	
☐ 1664 Lon Don	180.00	325.00	1200.00
☐ 1694 New England			21500.00
☐ 1694 Proprieters (overstrike)	385.00	700.00	2675.00
☐ 1694 Proprieters		EXTREMELY RARE	

NEW YORKE TOKEN

The New York colony (referring to the state, not the city) had no coinage of its own in the 17th century. Though settled somewhat later than Massachusetts, the population of New York came close to equaling it by the century's close and the volume of business transacted was at least comparable. It is curious that tiny Maryland and equally tiny New Jersey had coins during the 17th century while New York did not. The closest it came to having one was the New Yorke Token, but this can hardly be classed with the Massachusetts, Maryland or even the New Jersey coinage as there is no evidence it received official sanction. It was very likely nothing more than a merchant token. This is a smallish piece, roughly equal to our nickel, of which some were struck in brass and others in pewter. On the obverse it carries a rather scrawny eagle with an allegorical design (Cupid is one of the figures) on the reverse. The obverse legend reads "NEW YORKE IN AMERICA." Of its origins practically nothing is known. The belief that this coin was struck in Holland is founded more upon assumption, because of

New York's extensive Dutch population, than evidence. Its date has been the subject of controversy. The spelling of New York as "New Yorke" suggests a dating in the 17th century, but as this spelling lingered on into the 18th century it is quite possible that the coin or token is not so old as commonly presumed. It is very likely that even in the second quarter of the 18th century a European designing such a piece would have used the "New Yorke" spelling, even if it was no longer current in America. The likelihood that the New Yorke Token was struck in Manhattan from dies prepared in Holland is a romantic but not convincing theory.

UNDATED BRASS

TYPE OF COIN	ABP	G-4 Good	F-12 Fine
☐New Yorke Token, undated: Brass	1175.00	2300.00	5125.00
☐New Yorke Token, undated: Tin (Pewter)	3850.00	5650.00	—

GLOUCESTER TOKEN

Very few specimens exist of this early amateur token and information about it is likewise scanty. It is apparently the first private token struck on American soil. The composition is brass, leading to the assumption that it might have been a pattern for a silver shilling that was never produced. Whether the brass pieces were intended to circulate is highly doubtful. The Gloucester Token is thought to have been the work of Richard Dawson of Gloucester, Virginia. On one side appears a five-pointed star, with a building of modest design on the other. Known specimens are so thoroughly worn that the inscription surrounding this building is unreadable. The best guess is that it was intended to represent the Gloucester County Courthouse or some other public structure. It does not appear to be a place of worship. The Gloucester Token dates to 1714.

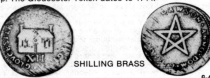

SHILLING BRASS

TYPE OF COIN	ABP	G-4 Good	F-12 Fine
☐Gloucester shilling (brass)			30000.00

ROSA AMERICANA

These extremely handsome coins, thoroughly European in appearance and workmanship, are often referred to as Wood Tokens — not from being made of wood (their composition is copper, zinc and silver) but from William Wood, the Englishman who originated them. Nearly 40 years before their appearance, John Holt, another Englishman, had gained a patent from the then-king, James II, to strike coinage for circulation in the American colonies. Upon expiration of the Holt patent or franchise there had been little enthusiasm for its renewal, as Holt's coins — the so-called Plantation Tokens — had not proved very successful. As time passed and the population of such cities as Boston, New York and Philadelphia increased, the prospects for coinage seemed to brighten. William Wood, of whom there is not very much known, obtained a franchise from George I to supply coinage to America, as well as to Ireland. This resulted in the Rosa Americana tokens. These were struck in small denominations only, from a halfpence to twopence. The earliest, which apparently were struck in 1722, carried no date. Later a date was added and these pieces saw fairly large production in the years 1722, 1723 and 1724. After an interval of nearly ten years in which none were produced a Rosa Americana pattern proof was struck off in 1733. As best as can be ascertained, the Wood patent had fallen into other hands, as Wood died in 1730. His successors probably toyed with the idea of reinstituting the Rosa Americana coins but never got beyond the stage of this single proof. To judge by the relative commonness of the coin (except for certain varieties, which are rare), they must have been turned out at least in the hundreds and possibly the thousands. The obverses are all alike, picturing George I in profile facing the viewer's right (it was switched to the left on the 1733 trial proof). This is not the king against whom America went to war in the Revolution but the first English monarch of that name, a German who could speak but a few words of English. Surrounding the portrait is, generally, a legend giving the names of the countries over which the king ruled: Great Britain, France and Hibernia (Ireland). The claim that he ruled France was a purely speculative one, a reference to the victories of Marlborough over Louis XIV's armies which had ended France's ambition to capture England but in no way gave England rulership over that nation. The reverse shows the Rose, sometimes alone, sometimes surmounted by a crown. There is one variation (on the 1724 penny) where the rose is not pictured symbolically but as an actual flower growing up from the ground. These pieces gain their name from the reverse inscription, not present on all, reading "ROSA AMERICANA UTILE DULCI," or, roughly, "American Rose, utility and pleasure." The rose had been a symbol of the Tudor kings and queens well before colonization of America. In their extent and variety the Rosa Americana coins are unmatched by any others intended for circulation in America. The opinion held of them today was not shared by colonists, however, who protested that the coins were short weighted and refused to accept them.

1722 HALFPENNY "DEI GRATIA REX"   1723 PENNY

TYPE OF COIN	ABP	G-4 Good	F-12 Fine	EF-40 Ex. Fine
☐ Twopence, No Date	40.00	75.00	270.00	725.00
☐ Twopence, No Date, Motto Sans Label				EXTREMELY RARE
☐ 1722 Halfpenny, D. G. REX	35.00	65.00	220.00	630.00
☐ 1722 Halfpenny, DEI GRATIA REX	30.00	55.00	155.00	480.00
☐ 1722 Halfpenny, VTILE DVLCI	450.00	825.00	2450.00	
☐ 1722 Twopence, Period after REX	38.00	72.00	220.00	575.00
☐ 1722 Twopence, No Period after REX	38.00	72.00	220.00	575.00
☐ 1722 Penny, UTILE DULCI	28.00	50.00	145.00	420.00
☐ 1722 Penny, VTILE DVLCI	27.00	50.00	140.00	400.00
☐ 1722 Penny, Georgivs				EXTREMELY RARE
☐ 1723 Twopence	47.00	75.00	225.00	650.00
☐ 1723 Penny	30.00	55.00	140.00	450.00
☐ 1723 Halfpenny	39.00	60.00	170.00	515.00
☐ 1723 Halfpenny, Rose without Crown				EXTREMELY RARE
☐ 1724 Penny (Pattern)				EXTREMELY RARE
☐ 1724 Penny, No Date, ROSA:SINE:SPINA				EXTREMELY RARE
☐ 1724 Twopence (Pattern)				EXTREMELY RARE
☐ 1733 Twopence (Pattern Proof)				EXTREMELY RARE

WOODS COINAGE OR HIBERNIA

These coins, more properly called tokens, were issued under the patent granted to William Wood to strike coinage for American and Ireland (see Rosa Americana). "Hibernia" was the Latin name for Ireland. They are included here because these pieces proved unpopular in Ireland — just as did the Rosa Americanas in America — and Wood sought to recover his investment by circulating them in America. History does not record their fate on this side of the Atlantic but it is doubtful that they received a warm reception. They were struck in such enormous numbers, thanks to excessive over-confidence, that most types can be had inexpensively. George I appears on the obverse. There are two reverse types, both picturing a seated female with a harp representing Hibernia, the Irish equivalent of Britannia. There is no need to speculate on the reason for Type I being changed: the figure is portrayed in so ungainly a manner as to appear comical. Type II is only a slight improvement.

1723 OVER 22 HALFPENNY 1723 HALFPENNY

TYPE OF COIN	ABP	G-4 Good	F-12 Fine	EF-40 Ex. Fine
☐1722 Farthing, D.G.REX	95.00	165.00	260.00	675.00
☐1722 Halfpenny, Harp Facing Left . . .	15.00	28.00	85.00	240.00
☐1722 Halfpenny, Harp Facing Right .	15.00	25.00	75.00	240.00
☐1722 Halfpenny, D.G.REX			EXTREMELY RARE	
☐1723 Halfpenny	9.00	18.00	60.00	190.00
☐1723 Over 22 Halfpenny	20.00	41.00	95.00	250.00
☐1723 Halfpenny, Silver (Pattern)			EXTREMELY RARE	
☐1723 Farthing, Silver (Pattern)	225.00	450.00	1000.00	1950.00
☐1723 Farthing, DEL. GRATIA REX . . .	10.00	20.00	40.00	185.00
☐1723 Farthing, D.G. REX	37.00	70.00	225.00	650.00
☐1724 Halfpenny	17.00	33.00	70.00	230.00
☐1724 Farthing	22.00	40.00	95.00	235.00

HIGLEY COINAGE

The Higley or Granby tokens were entirely private issues. Had they been imported for circulation from abroad they might be of modest interest at best but these are, in fact, **the first privately produced tokens struck on American soil that actually reached circulation.** All are extremely rare. Dr. Samuel Higley, a Connecticut resident and graduate of Yale University, deplored the coinage shortage in his state and took matters into his own hands. Unsupported by legislation and unsponsored by government funds, Higley engraved his own dies and for coin metal used copper from a mine he owned located near Granby, Connecticut (hence the alternate title of these pieces). Considering their amateur origin the designs and workmanship are of higher quality than might be expected. On the obverse appears a deer surrounded by inscription. There are two reverse types, one featuring a trio of small hammers, the other a broad-bladed cleaver. As originally issued in 1737 they carried the value of threepence, stated on the obverse legend. Though well received at first, protest was later raised by persons skeptical of their copper content. This inspired the ever-resourceful Higley to add the inscription "I AM GOOD COPPER." When this failed to silence critics, who persisted in their belief that the face value was too high and that Higley was gaining a profit from circulating them, the statement of value was replaced by the not-too-subtle suggestion to "VALUE ME AS YOU PLEASE." Even so, the Roman numeral III remained. This placed them in the category of bartering pieces which could be exchanged on basis of weight. We are told that the local supply was numerous but this is hardly reflected by their present rarity. It can only be assumed that many individuals hoarded the Higley tokens and melted them. The inscription on the second reverse type (the cleaver) states "I CUT MY WAY THROUGH." The "I" is sometimes stated to be a "J," but in fact was intended merely to represent an ornamental "I" with loop at the base.

The collector is cautioned that reproductions of the Higley Tokens exist, made by electrotyping and casting, and are of sufficient quality to confuse an inexperienced buyer.

1737 THREEPENCE "CONNECTICVT"

1737 VALVE.ME.AS.YOU.PLEASE   1737 VALUE.ME.AS.Y.OU.PLEASE
I.AM.GOOD.COPPER   I.CUT.MY.WAY.THROUGH

TYPE OF COIN	ABP	G-4 Good	VG-8 Very Good
☐ 1737 THE VALVE OF THREEPENCE (3 hammers CONNECTICVT)	2900.00	5200.00	8000.00
☐ 1737 THE VALVE OF THREEPENCE (3 hammers, I AM GOOD COPPER)	3400.00	6000.00	9500.00
☐ 1737 VALUE ME AS YOU PLEASE (3 hammers, I AM GOOD COPPER)	2850.00	5100.00	7500.00
☐ 1737 VALVE ME AS YOU PLEASE (3 hammers, I AM GOOD COPPER)		EXTREMELY RARE	
☐ 1737 VALUE ME AS YOU PLEASE (broad axe, I CUT MY WAY THROUGH)	3675.00	5500.00	9250.00
☐ 1739 VALUE ME AS YOU PLEASE (broad axe, I CUT MY WAY THROUGH)	4500.00	7250.00	14000.00

VOCE POPULI COINAGE

These impressive pieces are exclusively private issues and not of American origin. They were struck in Dublin, Ireland, in 1760 by a firm whose chief occupation was the making of buttons for military uniforms. Its proprietor was named Roche. The 17th and 18th centuries both witnessed an inordinate quantity of private tokens and pseudo-money struck in Ireland, much of which reached America. It could all logically be included within the realm of Americana but the Voce Populi Tokens have become special favorites of collectors, probably on strength of design more than anything else. The obverse features a classical style portrait profile crowned with laurel wreath. It has traditionally been assumed to be George III but no actual evidence exists to support this belief. The inscription makes no reference to the king but merely carries the words "VOCE POPULI," or "Voice of the People." Various interpretations (too lengthy to be discussed here) could be placed upon the use of this common slogan. The reverse pictures a female with harp, a standard Irish symbol, and the word "HIBERNIA." This was the Latin name for Ireland. The date is shown in the exergue beneath the figure. It should always be 1760; however, on one occasion a defective die was used for the halfpenny, causing it to read 1700. That the token was actually struck in 1700 can easily be refuted on stylistic as well as other evidence. There is also a variety in which the inscription reads "VOOE POPULI."

1760 "VOCE POPULI" HALFPENNY   1760 "VOCE POPULI" FARTHING

TYPE OF COIN	ABP	G-4 Good	F-12 Fine
☐ 1700 Halfpenny (diecutters error)	565.00	850.00	1600.00
☐ 1760 Halfpenny	20.00	35.00	95.00
☐ 1760 Halfpenny, P beneath bust	39.00	65.00	160.00
☐ 1760 Halfpenny, P beside face	39.00	65.00	160.00
☐ 1760 Halfpenny, VOOE POPULI (diecutters error) . .	24.00	43.00	135.00
☐ 1760 Farthing	125.00	200.00	500.00
☐ 1760 Farthing, small lettering		EXTREMELY RARE	

PITT TOKENS

William Pitt, for whom Pittsburgh is named, is associated with these tokens only to the extent that his portrait appears on them. He apparently was connected in no way with their issuance. Two denominations were struck, or rather pieces in the **sizes** of two denominations (as they bear no value markings): farthing and halfpenny. They carry the date 1766. Just what their purpose was is not clear. The suggestion has been put forward that they were issued in the nature of medals as an honor to Pitt, who, for his stand against the British stamp tax, was held in high regard by agitators for self-government. The long-held popular belief that Pitt Tokens were designed by Paul Revere would probably be best relegated to the ranks of numismatic folklore until some firm evidence is discovered. Similarly long-held belief that the engraver was Smithers of Philadelphia is more acceptable. The obverse has Pitt's likeness in profile with the legend "NO STAMPS:THE RESTORE OF COMMERCE:1766." The reverse shows a handsomely rendered sailing ship with the inscription "THANKS TO THE FRIENDS OF LIBERTY AND TRADE." Next to the ship is the word "AMERICA," which apparently suggests that the vessel is traveling from some foreign port with cargo for this country. "The Restore of Commerce" was a reference to the fact that British-imposed taxes were periling American commerce by rendering goods so costly that the public could not buy nearly so much as it wished to. The halfpenny is known to have been used briefly as coinage. No such use has been established for the farthing, which is much rarer.

1766 HALFPENNY   1766 FARTHING

TYPE OF COIN	ABP	G-4 Good	F-12 Fine
☐ 1766 Halfpenny	70.00	135.00	275.00
☐ 1766 Farthing	1500.00	2800.00	5000.00

FRENCH COLONIES IN AMERICA

A number of coins were struck in France for use in that nation's colonies during the 18th century. These were non-geographical pieces that could be exchanged in any French province and carried inscriptions in French and Latin rather than in local languages. It is important to remember in collecting these coins that they were **not** expressly struck for use in America, though they did see use in areas such as Louisiana (named for Louis XIV).

1722 SOU   1767 SOU

COUNTERSTAMPED "RF"   1670 5 SOLS SILVER

TYPE OF COIN	ABP	G-4 Good	F-12 Fine
☐ 1670 5 sols	75.00	150.00	400.00
☐ 1670 15 sols	2375.00	4375.00	11250.00
☐ 1709-1713 30 deniers, mint mark AA	32.00	55.00	135.00
☐ 1709-1713 30 deniers, mint mark D	32.00	55.00	135.00
☐ 1710-1713 15 deniers	45.00	80.00	200.00
☐ 1738-1748 ½ sou marque	20.00	33.00	85.00
☐ 1738-1760 sou marque	11.75	19.00	42.00
☐ 1717 6 deniers		EXTREMELY RARE	
☐ 1720 6 deniers		EXTREMELY RARE	
☐ 1717 12 deniers		EXTREMELY RARE	
☐ 1721 SOU, mint mark B for ROUEN	35.00	60.00	190.00
☐ 1721 SOU, mint mark H for ROCHELLE	21.00	32.00	95.00
☐ 1722 SOU, mint mark H	21.00	34.00	95.00
☐ 1722 Over 1721	28.00	60.00	160.00
☐ 1767 SOU	20.00	33.00	110.00
☐ 1767 SOU, counterstamped RF	12.00	20.00	80.00

VIRGINIA

Plagued by a coinage shortage, Virginia's colonists petitioned George III for supplies of trading pieces. He responded by authorizing the striking of a copper halfpenny, with his likeness on the obverse and the Virginia seal on its reverse. Proposals were also made for a penny and shilling, or coins which, to judge by the size of the few specimens struck, were intended for these denominations. They never reached circulation and are very rare. The halfpenny was struck in large quantities.

SHILLING

TYPE OF COIN	ABP	G-4 Good	F-12 Fine	MS-60 Unc.
☐ 1773 Halfpenny, (Period After GEORGIVS)	17.00	29.00	59.00	675.00
☐ 1773 Halfpenny, (No Per. After GEORGIVS)	25.00	40.00	80.00	715.00
☐ 1773 Penny . . . . PROOF				5600.00
☐ 1774 Shilling (SILVER)	PROOF			17750.00

STATE OF NEW HAMPSHIRE

New Hampshire has the distinction of being the first state to attempt a local coinage following the Declaration of Independence. In 1776 it authorized William Moulton to produce an experimental batch of copper pieces. The small numbers that have been traced indicate this coin never attained general circulation, though it probably circulated in a small way. The chief type has a tree on the obverse and a harp on the reverse. Other types are known but their status has not been positively established.

1776 PINE TREE   1776 WM COPPER

TYPE OF COIN	VG-8 Very Good
☐ 1776 New Hampshire Copper	10500.00
☐ 1776 New Hampshire Copper, WM in center (Pattern Piece)	EXTREMELY RARE

STATE OF VERMONT

Vermont's post-revolutionary coinage, probably the best known for its designs of any regional pieces, was struck by Reuben Harmon of Rupert, Vermont, and some by Thomas Machin of Newburgh, New York. This extensive series most often employed portraits of George III but is best known for its "plough money," an obverse design picturing a farm plough in a field against a background of tree-laden mountains. This is sometimes referred to as the most original, creative and authentically American design to be found on our colonial or federal-era coins. William Coley, a New York goldsmith, was the die-cutter for this design.

1785 VERMONTS   1786 VERMONTENSIUM

1787 BRITANNIA

TYPE OF COIN	ABP	G-4 Good	F-12 Fine
☐ 1785 Immune Colombia	550.00	1150.00	2500.00
☐ 1785 VERMONTS	75.00	150.00	475.00
☐ 1785 VERMONTIS	125.00	200.00	550.00
☐ 1786 VERMONTENSIUM	50.00	100.00	385.00
☐ 1786 Baby Head	85.00	165.00	525.00
☐ 1786 Bust faces left	60.00	110.00	475.00
☐ 1787 Bust faces right	40.00	70.00	220.00

TYPE OF COIN	ABP	G-4 Good	F-12 Fine
☐ 1787 BRITANNIA reverse; it is thought that the reverse of the Brittania piece was struck from a worn discarded die for a counterfeit British half-penny	35.00	60.00	200.00
☐ 1788 Cent	40.00	70.00	220.00
☐ 1788 ET LIB INDE	80.00	150.00	435.00
☐ 1788 VERMON AUCTORI; reversed C			VERY RARE
☐ 1788 GEORGIVS III REX	85.00	150.00	500.00

STATE OF CONNECTICUT

Connecticut struck more coins in the period from the Revolution to the establishment of a federal currency than any other state. Or, it might be better put, more varieties, as they represent numerous variations of three basic issues. The mint at which they were struck was established by authority of the state in 1785. It was located at New Haven. The chief die-cutters were Abel Buel and James Atlee.

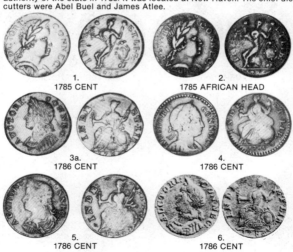

1.
1785 CENT

2.
1785 AFRICAN HEAD

3a.
1786 CENT

4.
1786 CENT

5.
1786 CENT

6.
1786 CENT

7.
1786 CENT

8.
1787 CENT

9.
1787 CENT

10.
1787 CENT

11a.
1787 CENT

12.
1787 CENT

13a.
1787 CENT

14.
1788 CENT

15a.
1788 CENT

16.
1788 CENT

TYPE OF COIN	ABP	G-4 Good	F-12 Fine
☐ 1. 1785 Cent, Bust right	20.00	38.00	90.00
☐ 2. 1785 Cent, Bust right: African head	25.00	40.00	125.00
☐ 3. 1785 Cent, Bust left	75.00	135.00	325.00
☐ 3a. 1786 Cent, ET LIB INDE	30.00	55.00	155.00
☐ 4. 1786 Cent, Large Bust Faces Right	38.00	80.00	275.00
☐ 5. 1786 Cent, Mailed Bust Left	20.00	32.00	100.00
☐ 6. 1786 Cent, Mailed Bust Left (Hercules Head)	40.00	70.00	215.00
☐ 7. 1786 Cent, Draped Bust	35.00	65.00	185.00
☐ 8. 1787 Cent, Mailed Bust, Small Head Faces Right, ET LIB ENDE	40.00	75.00	210.00
☐ 9. 1787 Cent, Mailed Bust Faces Right, INDE ET LIB	45.00	85.00	235.00
☐ 10. 1787 Cent, Muttonhead: INDE ET LIB	35.00	65.00	185.00
☐ 11. 1787 Cent, Mailed Bust Faces Left	15.00	25.00	75.00
☐ 11a. 1787 Cent, Horned Bust	15.00	27.00	85.00
☐ 12. 1787 Cent, CONNECT	35.00	60.00	165.00
☐ 13. 1787 Cent, Draped Bust Faces Left	12.00	20.00	52.00
☐ 13a. 1787 Cent, Bust Left: AUCIORI	15.00	25.00	70.00
☐ 13b. 1787 Cent: AUCTOPI	17.00	30.00	90.00
☐ 13c. 1787 Cent: AUCTOBI	17.00	30.00	120.00
☐ 13d. 1787 Cent: CONNFC	20.00	35.00	80.00
☐ 13e. 1787 Cent: FNDE	17.00	29.00	70.00
☐ 13f. 1787 Cent: ETLIR	17.00	29.00	70.00
☐ 13g. 1787 Cent: ETIIB	15.00	28.00	65.00
☐ 14. 1788 Cent, Mailed Bust Faces Right	18.00	30.00	110.00
☐ 14a. 1788 Cent: Small Head	90.00	165.00	490.00
☐ 15. 1788 Cent, Mailed Bust Faces Left	18.00	30.00	85.00
☐ 15a. 1788 Cent, Mailed Bust Left: CONNLC	20.00	35.00	110.00
☐ 16. 1788 Cent, Draped Bust Faces Left	18.00	32.00	85.00
☐ 16a. Same: CONNLC	33.00	60.00	160.00
☐ 16b. 1788 Same: INDL ET LIB	25.00	45.00	125.00

STATE OF NEW JERSEY

No coinage was struck for New Jersey in the colonial period, but see Mark Newby Halfpence (above). As the state's population increased a serious coin shortage was experienced and on June 1, 1786, its legislature authorized the striking of three million copper pieces, each to weigh "six pennyweight and six grains apiece." The contract for these tokens was awarded to Thomas Goadsby, Walter Mould and Albion Cox. The full quantity was to be delivered by June 1788, with partial deliveries to be made in quarterly installments of 300,000 each. Soon after work had begun, Goadby and Cox requested and were granted permission to divide up the quantities and strike them separately, each operating his own facility. Mould set up at

Morristown, New Jersey, Cox at Rahway. Goadsby's location is not established but is thought to also have been Rahway. The obverses of all these tokens show a horse's head and a plough, symbolic of the state's economy being founded largely on agriculture. The legend "NOVA CAESAREA" is simply New Jersey in Latin. On the reverse is a U.S. shield and "E PLURIBUS UNUM." A number of varieties are to be encountered.

1.
1786

3.
1786

8.
1787

11.
1788

12.
1788

TYPE OF COIN	ABP	G-4 Good	F-12 Fine
☐ 1. 1786 Date Under Plow Handle			VERY RARE
☐ 2. 1786 Normal Legends	25.00	38.00	80.00
☐ 3. 1786 No Coulter	80.00	145.00	425.00
☐ 4. 1786 Bridle Variety (NOT ILLUS.)	18.00	32.00	85.00
☐ 5. 1786 Narrow Shield (NOT ILLUS.)	20.00	35.00	90.00
☐ 6. 1786 Wide Shield (NOT ILLUS.)	23.00	37.00	100.00
☐ 7. 1787 Normal Legends (NOT ILLUS.)	15.00	25.00	60.00
☐ 8. 1787 PLURIBS	25.00	42.00	115.00
☐ 9. 1787 "Serpent Head" (NOT ILLUS.)	30.00	50.00	135.00
☐ 10. 1788 Normal Legends (NOT ILLUS.)	15.00	25.00	75.00
☐ 11. 1788 Horses Head Faces Right, Running Fox	28.00	45.00	130.00
☐ 12. 1788 Horses Head Left	75.00	150.00	375.00

STATE OF NEW YORK

The history of New York's local coinage prior to the Revolution reveals only the supposed Dutch merchant token discussed above and various coins and tokens struck for use elsewhere that, in the ordinary course of trade, found their way to the state. For more than a hundred years it was without locally authorized coinage. This void was filled by Dutch, British, French and, to a lesser extent, Spanish monies, which came to New York through its great port and disseminated throughout the region. Apparently no pressing need was felt for a local coinage because none was officially instituted, even after independence. However, quantities of privately struck money did circulate. Some were the work of Thomas Machin of Newburgh, New York (where Washington had a headquarters during the war), who operated what he surreptitiously called a "hardware manufactory." It was in fact a copper mill, whose chief products were tokens. Other New York coins were produced at Rupert, Vermont, by a team of millers (Reuben Harmon and William Coley) who also made coins for Vermont and Connecticut. There is yet to be learned about New York's federal-era coinage but quite a good deal has already been determined. The theory, once popularly maintained, that coins bearing the inscription "NOVA EBORAC" are of foreign origin, is now known to be false. Nova Eborac is not some sort of mysterious foreign term. It is simply New York in Latin. (If you wonder how there could be a Latin name for New York, when there are none for railroad and television and other things discovered after the Latin language died, the explanation is quite simple. The Romans did not know of New York but they certainly knew of old York in Britain, which they called Eborac. To change this into New York you need only add the Latin word for new — nova — and you have Nova Eborac.)

All the New York coins (or tokens) are coppers. They carry various designs, of which the portrait of George Clinton is most famous. There was also an Indian figure (not too impressively portrayed), a New York coat-of-arms, and profile bust pretty confidently believed to be George Washington. Though the designs are not very well drawn the coins themselves are very professionally struck.

1.
1786

2.
1787

3.
1787

4.
1787

5.
1787

6c.
1787

TYPE OF COIN	ABP	F-12 Fine	VF-20 V.Fine
☐1. 1786 NON VI VIRTUTE VICI; Thought to be the head of George Washington	2175.00	4250.00	7000.00
☐2. 1787 EXCELSIOR; Eagle on Obv. faces left	870.00	1325.00	4150.00
☐3. 1787 EXCELSIOR; Eagle on Obv. faces right	950.00	1510.00	4300.00
☐3a. 1787 EXCELSIOR; Large Eagle on reverse (NOT ILLUS.)			VERY RARE
☐3b. 1787 EXCELSIOR; George Clinton reverse (NOT ILLUS.)	3900.00	8000.00	15000.00
☐3c. 1787 EXCELSIOR; Indian Standing reverse (NOT ILLUS.)	3150.00	6750.00	11000.00
☐3d. 1787 EXCELSIOR; Indian Standing Eagle on globe (NOT ILLUS.)	3400.00	7250.00	13500.00
☐4. 1787 LIBERTATEM; Indian Standing, George III			EXTREMELY RARE
☐5. 1787 NOVA EBORAC; Rev. seated figure faces left	110.00	190.00	425.00
☐5a. 1787 NOVA EBORAC; Rev. seated figure faces right (NOT ILLUS.)	140.00	220.00	500.00
☐5b. 1787 NOVA EBORAC; Small head (NOT ILLUS.)	900.00	1500.00	2750.00
☐6c. 1787 NOVA EBORAC; Large head	325.00	575.00	1350.00

BRASHER DOUBLOONS

Perhaps the most celebrated, at any rate the most glamorized, U.S. colonial coin is the Brasher Doubloon. Though traditionally referred to as colonial it should correctly be termed a federal-era piece, as it was struck after our independence had been gained. This is a private issue. Ephraim Brasher was a goldsmith from New York who became acquainted with George Washington when the latter resided there following the war. To classify this handsome goldpiece as a speculative coin would be mistaken. Brasher, artist and patriot, appears to have manufactured it not for purposes of general circulation but as a memorial to the nation's independence and, possibly, a model from which federal coiners could gain inspiration. It dates to 1787, before the introduction of federal coinage but not before much speculation and debate on the matter. The Brasher Doubloon, as the name suggests, was modeled after the Spanish coin of that name. It contained 408 grains of gold. As a goldsmith Brasher would have encountered no difficulty securing the needed bullion for a small quantity of such pieces, but it is doubtful that he had either the resources or intention to strike this coin in large numbers. The obverse pictures the sun rising over a mountain, with the American eagle emblem on the back. The reverse bears the impressed letters E.B., the initials of Brasher's name. Obviously they were not clandestine issues or their origin would not have been so plainly identified. At the time of its issue the Brasher Doubloon had a value of about $16. There was also a Half Doubloon worth $8. All are extremely rare, the variety in which the initials appear on the eagle's breast being preserved in a single specimen only.

EB Punch on Wing

TYPE OF COIN

□1787 (GOLD) DOUBLOON, EB punch on breast . . . ⎫
□1787 (GOLD) DOUBLOON, EB punch on wing . . . . ⎬ ALL TYPES EXTREMELY RARE
□1787 (GOLD) HALF DOUBLOON . . . . ⎭

Garrett Sale November, 1979 . . . . $725,000.00
Yale University Specimen, 1980 . . . . 600,000.00
Estimated Current Value . . . . Under 500,000.00

STATE OF MASSACHUSETTS

Massachusetts, the first colony to strike its own coins in pre-revolution days, also had its own coinage in the period between independence and the establishment of the U.S. Mint. On October 17, 1786, the General Court of that state authorized the setting up of a mint, "for the coinage of gold, silver and copper." A stipulation was made that the design for coinage should employ the "figure of an Indian with bow and arrow and a star on one side with the word Commonwealth, on the reverse a spread eagle with the words Massachusetts 1787." The ambitiousness of this project was

COLONIAL COINS, PATTERNS AND TOKENS / 109

never fully realized. While coppers were struck in some quantities, a coinage of silver and gold never appeared. In 1789 the mint was abandoned, having proven costly to operate.

1788 CENT   1788 HALF CENT

TYPE OF COIN	ABP	G-4 Good	F-12 Fine
☐ 1787 Cent, Arrows in Left Talon	20.00	35.00	80.00
☐ 1787 Cent, Arrows in Right Talon	1600.00	3000.00	5250.00
☐ 1787 Cent, Horned Eagle (Die Break)	20.00	37.00	85.00
☐ 1787 Half Cent	25.00	45.00	95.00
☐ 1788 Cent	20.00	35.00	85.00
☐ 1788 Half Cent	29.00	55.00	110.00

MASSACHUSETTS PINE TREE COPPER

The origin of this unique coin is undetermined. Only one specimen is known, undoubtedly a pattern piece, and but for the greatest of good luck it would have been undiscovered. It turned up, buried beneath a Boston street, during an excavation in the 1800's, having probably been entombed nearly a century. Only the sharp eyes of a laborer prevented it from being discarded along with rubbish. Despite this imprisonment its condition is surprisingly good. It shows a pine tree on the obverse, obviously inspired by the Pine Tree Coinage of a century earlier, and a figure of Liberty posed as Britannia on the reverse, complete with globe and dog. The date 1776 appears beneath the reverse figure. Whether this was the year of striking or was used merely symbolically to denote our independence from Britain is unknown. The obverse inscription is "MASSACHUSETTS STATE" while the reverse reads "LIBERTY AND VIRTUE." This unique item is owned today by the Massachusetts Historical Society. Reproductions exist.

1776 PINE TREE
(UNIQUE)

MASSACHUSETTS HALFPENNY

This intriguing coin, classical in appearance, is dated 1776 and is often referred to as the Janus Copper or Janus Halfpenny. This is a reference (though not quite historically accurate) to the obverse design, which shows a three-sided head with faces looking forward, left and right. The mythological god Janus had only two faces, looking right and left (the month of January is named for him; one face looks to the old year, one to the new). On the reverse is a seated representation of Liberty. The Massachusetts Halfpenny is a unique pattern piece. The only known specimen sold for $40,000 in 1979.

 MASSACHUSETTS HALFPENNY

KENTUCKY TOKEN

This novel piece was not of American origin but struck in England around the year 1792. It is thought to have been occasioned by admission of Kentucky into the Union. On the obverse is a hand holding a petition reading "OUR CAUSE IS JUST" surrounded by the wording "UNANIMITY IS THE STRENGTH OF SOCIETY." The reverse is composed of a star in which are circular ornaments, each bearing the initial letter of a state. As K for Kentucky appears at the top. This piece is identified with that state. Some specimens have plain edges while others are stamped "Payable at Bedworth," "Payable in Lancaster," etc. It is vital to take note of these markings as they have a great influence on the value.

1792 TOKEN

TYPE OF COIN	ABP	G-4 Good	F-12 Fine	MS-60 Unc.
☐ 1792 Token, plain edge	20.00	40.00	80.00	650.00
☐ 1792 Token, engrailed edge	70.00	120.00	220.00	1500.00
☐ 1792 Token, lettered edge, Payable at I. Fielding, etc.			EXTREMELY RARE	
☐ 1792 Token, lettered edge, Payable at Bedworth, etc.			EXTREMELY RARE	
☐ 1792 Token, lettered edge, Payable at Lancaster, London, or Bristol	28.00	50.00	100.00	700.00

MARYLAND - CHALMERS

The Chalmers tokens were the second group of coins to be struck for circulation in Maryland, preceded by the Lord Baltimore money of a century earlier. Unlike these early pieces, which were of foreign manufacture, the Chalmers coins evolved locally. They were minted at Annapolis in 1783. Apparently they came into being because of the coinage shortage which then existed in Maryland and the hesitency of that state's legislature to take official action. John Chalmers, their maker, was a goldsmith. He struck them in silver in denominations of threepence, sixpence and one shilling (twelve pence). Their odd geometrical designs given them almost a cabbalistic appearance. All are quite scarce but the majority are obtainable.

LONG WORM   DATE

1783 SHILLING   1783 SIXPENCE   1783 THREEPENCE

TYPE OF COIN	ABP	G-4 Good	F-12 Fine
☐ 1783 Shilling, short worm	200.00	350.00	1200.00
☐ 1783 Shilling, long worm	250.00	415.00	1350.00
☐ 1783 Shilling, rings on reverse		EXTREMELY RARE	
☐ 1783 Sixpence, small date	360.00	700.00	1575.00
☐ 1783 Sixpence, large date	300.00	550.00	1350.00
☐ 1783 Threepence	250.00	400.00	1250.00

BALTIMORE, MARYLAND/STANDISH BARRY

Standish Barry was a private citizen of Baltimore who worked at various craft trades including watchmaking and silversmithing. In 1790 he struck, in very limited quantities, a silver threepence token bearing a portrait on one side and the words "THREE PENCE" on the other. Due to the low face value and the fact of its being made of silver the physical size is quite small, about comparable to our dime. Barry's motive is not known with certainty. That he wished to alleviate the shortage of small-denomination coinage in his neighborhood is a possibility, but he produced so few specimens that this goal, if such was his intent, could not have been achieved. A more likely suggestion is that the Barry token was intended chiefly as an advertising piece. This is supported by the appearance of his name, spelled out in full on the reverse, which commonly was done only with tradesmens' tokens. The obverse portrait is thought to have been intended as George Washington, which fails to resemble him only because of artistic inability. Not only the year but the month is stated and the day as well: July 4, 90. The whole appearance is crude and amateurish, but collectors treasure it.

TYPE OF COIN	ABP	G-4 Good	F-12 Fine
☐ 1790 Silver Threepence	1000.00	2000.00	3800.00

RHODE ISLAND TOKEN

The Rhode Island Ship Token has been variously classified as a coin, token and medal, and its status is hardly clearer today than when research first began. Struck in 1778 or 1779 (the obverse carries one date, the reverse another), the piece is known in a variety of base metals: copper, brass, tin and pewter, the composition having little influence on its value. That it was intended as a coin for ordinary circulation and exchange appears remote as it carries no mark of value and would have had to trade on the basis of weight. Being made of different metals, the weight varies and would have resulted in no small measure of confusion. The obverse shows a well-drawn ocean vessel. On the reverse is a complex scene representing the flight of Continental troops from Rhode Island. The inscriptions are in Dutch but the old belief that this production was of Dutch or Dutch-American origin is now given little support. Based upon the reverse theme it could well have been struck in England or by royalists in America. It should be kept in mind that the Revolutionary war had not yet ended in 1778-9 and coins or medals had a certain propaganda value. Reproductions are known to exist.

1778-1779 "VLUGTENDE"   1778-1779 WREATH

TYPE OF COIN	ABP	VF-20 V. Fine	EF-40 Ex. Fine
☐ 1778-1779 "VLUGTENDE" Below Ship			RARE
☐ 1778-1779 "VLUGTENDE" Removed	290.00	525.00	1150.00
☐ 1778-1779 Wreath Below Ship	325.00	600.00	1280.00

1776 CONTINENTAL CURRENCY

The Continental Dollar and its affiliates were struck as pattern pieces only, based upon the latest research, and never reached general circulation. They are believed to represent the first attempt at coinage by the Continental Congress, at any rate the first to achieve physical form. Upon declaring its independence from Britain the United States was cut off from supplies of British currency and anticipated an extreme shortage within the coming months. Actually this shortage did not materialize to the degree feared. Continental Currency is crown-size and struck in silver, pewter and brass. Though the sizes are identical and the coins bear no indication of value it is presumed the silver pieces were intended as dollars and the base metal varieties as divisions thereof. The exact history of their origin is not recorded, the documentation of it having apparently been swept away in the turbulent times of war. We know that the engraver bore the initials E.G. because he signed his work. An exhaustive search of goldsmiths, silversmiths and other metalworkers active at that time, having the initials E.G., has led to the conclusion that the 1776 Continental Currency was the work of Elisha Gallaudet of Philadelphia. If this is the case they would undoubtedly have been struck in that city as well. Which, considering that it was headquarters of the Continental Congress, seems to fit together historically. The legends include "WE ARE ONE" and "MIND YOUR BUSINESS," the latter not, probably, having been directed toward the British but used merely as a piece of sage advice in the spirit of Ben Franklin. Copies exist, struck at the 1876 Centennial exposition.

1776
CURENCY
Brass, Pewter,
Silver

1776
CURRENCY
E. G. FECIT
Pewter, Silver

TYPE OF COIN	ABP	F-12 Fine	EF-40 Ex. Fine
☐ 1776 CURENCY, Brass			VERY RARE
☐ 1776 CURENCY, Pewter	1500.00	2500.00	4250.00
☐ 1776 CURENCY, Silver			VERY RARE
☐ 1776 CURRENCY, Pewter	1700.00	2800.00	6000.00
☐ 1776 CURRENCY, E.G. FECIT, Pewter	1525.00	2600.00	5000.00
☐ 1776 CURRENCY, E.F. FECIT, Silver			UNIQUE
☐ 1776 CURRENCY, Pewter			UNIQUE

NOVA CONSTELLATIO SILVER

These Nova Constellatio silvers are pattern pieces for a federal coinage, the first such pattern pieces of silver struck by the newly born government. They date from 1783, shortly after the war for Independence had been concluded. Supposedly the brainchild of Gouverneur Morris, a signer of the Declaration of Independence and Assistant Financier of the Confederation, their designer was Benjamin Dudley. At this point the system of cents and dollars, later agreed upon, had not yet evolved; but there was no wish to continue use of the British pound standard. Morris evolved a currency system in which the chief denomination was a mark, consisting of 1,000 units. Divisions of this coin — also included among the Nova Constellatio patterns — were the quint, equal to 500 units or half a mark, and the bit, with a value of 100 units or a tenth of a mark. Further divisions could then supposedly be made of base metal, in 50 or 10 units or whatever seemed practical. If we think of Morris' mark as the equivalent of the dollar (which in reality it was), then the 500 unit piece was the counterpart of 50¢ and the 100 unit piece of 10¢. Morris won little support for his currency proposals and the patterns were never approved for general circulation. Just one specimen is known to exist of each example, however there are two types (and consequently two known specimens) of the 500 unit piece, one having an inscription on the obverse and the other bearing no inscription.

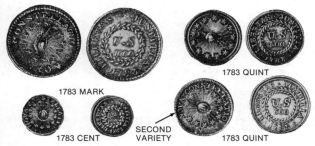

1783 QUINT

1783 MARK

1783 CENT   SECOND VARIETY   1783 QUINT

TYPE OF COIN
- ☐ 1783 MARK — 1000 Mills, Silver . . . .
- ☐ 1783 QUINT — 500 Mills, Silver . . . .
- ☐ 1783 QUINT — Second Variety, Silver . . . . } ALL TYPES EXTREMELY RARE
- ☐ 1783 Cent — 100 Mills, Silver. . . . .
- ☐ 1783 "S" Copper . . . .

NOVA CONSTELLATIO COPPERS

Though their name and design is similar to the Nova Constellatio silvers, it is important to note that these coins had quite different origins and purposes. The concept for both was that of Gouveneur Morris, who, in addition to being a legislator was also a prominent businessman in the late colonial/early federal age. While the silvers were pattern pieces for a proposed federal coinage, these coppers were struck as a personal speculative venture. It is quite likely that their place of origin was not America but Birmingham, England, and that their dies were engraved by an Englishman named Wyon. Upon importation to this country Morris placed them into circulation as best he could. To judge from the fairly large quantities that exist of most types their production must have reached the tens of thousands if not higher.

CONSTELATIO 1783 BLUNT RAYS

1785 CENT

TYPE OF COIN	ABP	G-4 Good	F-12 Fine
☐ 1783 Cent, CONSTELLATIO, Pointed Rays, Large U.S.	19.00	32.00	105.00
☐ 1783 Cent, CONSTELLATIO, Pointed Rays, Small U.S.	15.00	25.00	85.00
☐ 1783 Cent, CONSTELLATIO, Blunt Rays	17.00	28.00	85.00
☐ 1785 Cent, CONSTELATIO, Blunt Rays	19.00	32.00	120.00
☐ 1785 Cent, CONSTELLATIO, Point Rays	18.50	30.00	80.00
☐ 1786 Cent, CONSTALLATIO, Point Rays			VERY RARE

IMMUNE COLUMBIA

It is believed that this token, whose obverse designs are in some instances similar to those of the Nova Constellatio Coppers, were struck from dies engraved by Thomas Wyon of Birmingham, England. Their history is otherwise shrouded in mystery. That they represent pattern pieces which did not actually circulate seems unquestionable as they exist in extremely limited quantities. There are several varieties, chiefly in copper but the piece does exist in silver. A single gold specimen, dated 1785, is included in the government's collection at Washington. It was obtained by trade with the collector Stickney, who accepted a duplicate 1804 silver dollar for it. A later version of the Immune Columbia token, dated 1787, was struck from dies by James Atlee. Justice with scales is the reverse theme with a number of different obverses, including a portrait of the then-not-too-popular George III.

OBVERSE 1785   REVERSE   1787 IMMUNIS COLUMBIA
IMMUNE COLUMBIA   1785 "NOVA"

TYPE OF COIN	ABP	G-4 Good	F-12 Fine
☐ 1785 Cent, Copper			
☐ 1785 Cent, Silver			
☐ 1785 Cent, Copper, Extra Star in Reverse			ALL RARE
☐ 1785 Cent, Copper—CONSTELATIO —Blunt Rays			
☐ 1785 Cent, VERMON AUCTORI	600.00	1100.00	2500.00
☐ 1785 Cent, GEORGE III OBVERSE	750.00	1300.00	3000.00
☐ 1787 Immunis Columbia	98.00	190.00	450.00

CONFEDERATIO

The Confederatio Cent, also known as Confederatio Coppers, is a hybrid coin found with various obverse and reverse designs. Regardless of the designs these are all pattern pieces that never reached circulation and all are extremely rare. Identity of the die cutters is not known but it is believed that at least some were the work of Thomas Wyon of Birmingham, England, and undoubtedly they were struck abroad. One of the obverse motifs features George Washington.

1785 CENT   1785 WASHINGTON

TYPE OF COIN	ABP	G-4 Good	F-12 Fine
☐1785 Cent, Stars in Small Circle		8500.00	13250.00
☐1785 Cent, Stars in Large Circle		8500.00	13250.00
☐1785 Cent, George Washington		EXTREMELY RARE	

SPECIMEN PATTERNS

A number of copper pattern pieces were struck in or about 1786 for possible use as token currency. Their history is not well established and all are extremely rare. The shield design and "E PLURIBUS UNUM" inscription on the reverses of some were subsequently used on New Jersey tokens, but the following patterns cannot be classified as belonging to any given locality.

TYPE OF COIN	ABP	G-4 Good	F-12 Fine
☐1786 IMMUNIS COLUMBIA, shield reverse		EXTREMELY RARE	
☐1786 IMMUNIS COLUMBIA, eagle reverse		EXTREMELY RARE	
☐1786 Eagle on obverse		EXTREMELY RARE	
☐1786 Washington/eagle		EXTREMELY RARE	
☐Undated, Washington obverse		EXTREMELY RARE	

NORTH AMERICAN TOKEN

This is a private piece, one of a number issued following the Revolution that circulated in this country. Its origin is Irish, having been struck in Dublin. Undoubtedly it represented the effort of an Irish merchant or metalsmith to take advantage of America's coin shortage. The date shown is 1781 but belief is strong that it was actually produced at some later time, possibly in the late 1790's or early 1800's. The U.S. was experiencing a coin shortage during the presidency of Thomas Jefferson, so it could well date from that era. This situation was well known abroad as foreigners melting down our coinage were chiefly responsible. On the obverse it pictures a sailing ship with the word "COMMERCE" and a seated likeness of Hibernia (symbol of Ireland) with her harp on the reverse, inscribed "NORTH AMERICAN TOKEN." It may well be that the side of this token traditionally regarded as the obverse was intended as the reverse. Quantities in which the North American Token were distributed in the U.S. are not known. The piece is far from rare. Its size is roughly equivalent to a quarter.

TYPE OF COIN	ABP	G-4 Good	F-12 Fine
☐1781 Token	8.75	16.50	40.00

MACHIN COPPERS

Thomas Machin operated a copper mill at Newburgh, New York. From 1786 to 1789 he was active in the production of tokens, some designed for use in the State of New York (listed under New York) and others that were nothing but counterfeits of the British copper halfpenny. He attempted to profit by placing these counterfeits, of lighter than standard weight, into immense circulation. To avoid suspicion he used a variety of dates, going back as far as 1747. But the majority are dated in the early 1770's. The design is always the same: a portrait of the king on the obverse with Britannia on the reverse. As these pieces are not collected by date, their values are constant irrespective of date. They can easily be distinguished from genuine British halfpennies by their cruder die engraving. However, the Machin fakes were not the only ones made of this coin.

TYPE OF COIN	ABP	G-4 Good	F-12 Fine
☐Halfpenny, various dates	30.00	57.00	160.00

GEORGIUS TRIUMPHO TOKEN

This controversial coin, dating from 1783, is made of copper. On the obverse is a male portrait in profile with the inscription "GEORGIUS TRIUMPHO," which cannot be translated in any other fashion but "George Has Triumphed." Considering that the War for Indpendence had recently ended with an American victory, the triumphal George should be Washington. But the portrait much more closely resembles George III, the British monarch who sought to preserve American colonization. Just how this George could be regarded to have triumphed at that moment is puzzling. Perhaps the explanation is that Washington was intended but the engraver, being unskilled and having no likeness at hand from which to copy, merely fashioned the portrait after that on English money. A similar situation prevailed at the time among illustrators who designed copperplate portraits for books, the likeness often being guessed at. As photography did not exist and few citizens actually saw celebrities in the flesh, it was not really known if such works were accurate. The reverse pictures Liberty holding an olive branch, and thirteen bars representing the confederation. Its inscription is "VOCE POPOLI," an error for Voce Populi or "Voice of the People."

TYPE OF COIN	ABP	G-4 Good	F-12 Fine	VF-20 V. Fine
☐ 1783 GEORGIUS TRIUMPHO	17.00	30.00	110.00	300.00

AUCTORI PLEBIS TOKEN

Not much is known of this copper piece, other than the fact that it closely resembles the early coinage of Connecticut. It is thought to have been struck in England and may never have been intended for American circulation. It has, however, traditionally been included in American colonial and federal-era collections. It bears a date of 1787 and carries a male portrait profile on the obverse with a seated figure of Liberty on the reverse. The workmanship is not especially skilled.

TYPE OF COIN	ABP	G-4 Good	F-12 Fine	VF-20 V. Fine
☐ 1787 AUCTORI PLEBIS Token	29.00	48.00	130.00	265.00

MOTT TOKEN

An early trade token, this piece had no official sanction nor any legal value as money. Its issuers were William and John Mott, who operated a business at Water Street in the downtown area of Manhattan. Mott Street, now the central boulevard of New York's Chinatown, was named for this family. The Mott Token is of copper, picturing on one side the American eagle emblem and (quite unusual) a shelf clock on the other. The clock served an advertising purpose as the Motts dealt in goldware, silverware and fancy goods, including importations. This token dates from 1789. Of too high a quality for local production, it seems evident they were manufactured in England.

TYPE OF COIN	ABP	G-4 Good	F-12 Fine	EF-40 Ex. Fine
☐ 1789 Mott Token, thick planchet	35.00	65.00	160.00	500.00
☐ 1789 Mott Token, thin planchet	50.00	90.00	230.00	650.00
☐ 1789 Mott Token, engrailed edge ...	60.00	105.00	450.00	1100.00

BAR CENT

The Bar Cent is a very simply designed coin whose name derives from the fact that its reverse design is composed of a grid containing thirteen bars (one for each state of the confederation). On the obverse are the letters USA in large size, intertwined. Beyond this there is no further ornament or inscription and the origin of this piece has proven a dilemma. It is almost surely a foreign product, made possibly by Wyon (of Nova Constellatio copper fame) of Birmingham, England. Its first public appearance was made in New York in late 1785. It may be presumed that the date of minting was either that year or possibly 1784. Reproductions were produced during the Civil War, against which collectors are cautioned.

TYPE OF COIN	ABP	G-4 Good	F-12 Fine	EF-40 Ex. Fine
☐Undated, Bar Cent	120.00	195.00	500.00	1000.00

TALBOT, ALLUM AND LEE CENTS

These are trade tokens, circulated by a firm of importers known as Talbot, Allum and Lee, who were headquartered at 241 Pearl Street, New York, in what is now the financial district but then was given over largely to import/export because of its access to the Battery docks. There is no question but that they were struck in England. The corporation's name appears on one side, sometimes with and sometimes without its place of location. The earliest date is 1794 and at this point they carried a value legend of one cent. In 1794 this was removed, possibly out of fear of government protest, and an inscription added to the edge: "WE PROMISE TO PAY THE BEARER ONE CENT." There are, however, specimens of the 1795 edition with unlettered edge, which are considerably scarcer. This practice of issuing tokens redeemable at a certain place of business became widespread in the 19th century, especially during the small-change shortage of the Civil War.

1794 NEW YORK   1795 CENT

TYPE OF COIN	ABP	G-4 Good	F-12 Fine	EF-40 Ex. Fine
☐1794 Cent w/''NEW YORK''	15.00	25.00	75.00	180.00
☐1794 Cent without ''NEW YORK'' . . .	75.00	150.00	400.00	825.00
☐1795 Cent	13.00	24.00	70.00	275.00

GEORGE WASHINGTON PIECES

Following the Revolution, George Washington became a national hero and idol to such degree that he was virtually worshipped. Books were written on his life, engravers published pictures of him, and his likeness was set into snuff boxes, jewelry cases and other fancy goods. It is only natural that Washington would also be the subject of numerous tokens and pseudo-coins. These were issued beginning in 1783 and (for practical purposes) ceasing about 1795, after official federal coinage began circulating. No exact date can be placed on their discontinuance, however, as tokens and medals honoring Washington appeared from time to time thereafter. Those listed below are not strictly classed as commemoratives but might just as well be. They were primarily coppers and contained a cent's worth of that metal. They could therefore be used as money but the extent to which this was done is not known and can be presumed to have been limited, as none was struck in large quantities. The best title for them might be "celebration pieces." Building a complete collection is outside the realm of possibility, because of the extreme scarcity of some issues. A fair assembly of them can, however, be made. Their origins are not well established. Some are believed to have been designed and struck in England. This would seem logical on the basis of workmanship. Those made abroad were surely not designed for circulation there, but for export and distribution within the United States. One of the Washington tokens — in ½ penny value — declares itself a Welsh product; it carries the inscription "NORTH WALES" on the reverse. Another was a London tradesman's token. As for their dates, the presumption is that some, at least, were struck subsequent to the year indicated, perhaps in the first decade of the 19th century or even later. Most have distinctive reverses and are known chiefly by these reverse types. So far as the portraiture is concerned, there is a rich and interesting variety, differing not only in artistic quality but concept. On some, Washington is shown as a Roman-style emperor, wearing a laurel wreath. The majority portray him in military dress. Though a few coins of amateurish design are included in this group there are likewise several of the most skilled and impressive workmanship, which, if executed as sculptures, would be regarded as important works of art. The likelihood that Washington sat for any of the die-cutters is remote, but apparently they either had prior experience drawing or sculpting him or worked from some of the better oil pictures, such as those of Stuart. They could not have achieved such faithful portraiture merely from descriptions of his physical appearance.

1.
1783 CENT

2.
1783 CENT

3.
1783 CENT

4.
1783 CENT (DOUBLE HEAD)

6.
1791 CENT

7.
1791 CENT

8.
1791 HALFPENNY

9.
1792 CENT

10.
1792 CENT

11.
1792 HALF DOLLAR

12.
1792 ROMAN HEAD

13.
1792 EAGLE

14.
1793 HALFPENNY

15.
1795 HALFPENNY

16.
1795 PENNY

17.
1795 HALFPENNY

18.
TOKEN

19.
TOKEN

20.
TOKEN

TYPE OF COIN	ABP	G-4 Good	F-12 Fine
☐ 1. 1783 Cent, Large Military Bust	15.00	25.00	40.00
☐ 1a. 1783 Cent, Small Military Bust	20.00	35.00	55.00
☐ 1b. 1783 Cent, Small Military Bust, engrailed edge	25.00	40.00	60.00
☐ 2. 1783 Cent, Draped Bust	20.00	35.00	60.00
☐ 2a. 1783 Cent, Draped Bust, button on cloak	30.00	45.00	80.00
☐ 2b. 1783 Cent, Draped Bust, silver restrike		PROOF: $550.00	
☐ 3. 1783 Cent, Draped Bust: Unity States	18.00	30.00	90.00
☐ 4. 1783 Cent (Undated) Double Head	15.00	25.00	75.00
☐ 5. 1784 (Ugly Head) (NOT ILLUS.)			RARE
☐ 6. 1791 Cent, Small Eagle	40.00	80.00	160.00
☐ 7. 1791 Cent, Large Eagle	40.00	80.00	160.00
☐ 8. 1791 Liverpool Halfpenny	190.00	300.00	600.00
☐ 9. 1792 Cent, WASHINGTON PRESIDENT	1200.00	2000.00	3500.00
☐10. 1792 Cent, BORN VIRGINIA	500.00	900.00	2100.00
☐11. 1792 Silver		EXTREMELY RARE	
☐11a. 1792 Copper	850.00	1650.00	3900.00
☐11b. 1792 Large Eagle		UNIQUE	
☐12. 1792 Roman Head		PROOF RARE	
☐13. 1792 Eagle, Copper			
☐13a. 1792 Eagle, Silver		EXTREMELY RARE	
☐13b. 1792 Eagle, Gold			
☐14. 1793 Ship Halfpenny	50.00	80.00	125.00
☐15. 1795 Halfpenny, Reeded Edge, "GRATE", small buttons	70.00	120.00	185.00
☐15a. 1795 Halfpenny, Reeded Edge, "GRATE" large buttons	20.00	35.00	60.00
☐15b. 1795 Halfpenny, Lettered Edge, "GRATE" large buttons	100.00	175.00	250.00
☐16. 1795 Penny, Undated, LIBERTY AND SECURITY	60.00	100.00	175.00
☐17. 1795 Halfpenny, Dated LIBERTY AND SECURITY, London	30.00	50.00	90.00
☐17a. 1795 Halfpenny, LIBERTY AND SECURITY, Birmingham	35.00	60.00	115.00
☐17b. 1795 Halfpenny, Dated, LIBERTY AND SECURITY, Asylum	45.00	80.00	175.00
☐17c. 1795 Halfpenny, Dated, LIBERTY AND SECURITY, Plain Edge	35.00	65.00	120.00
☐18. Success Token, Large	65.00	125.00	190.00
☐19. Success Token, Small	65.00	125.00	190.00
☐20. 1795 Halfpenny, NORTH WALES	55.00	100.00	215.00

FRANKLIN PRESS TOKEN

This copper token was struck in England as a merchant piece and its use apparently restricted there. Because of its connection with Benjamin Franklin it has interest for collectors of American coinage. The obverse pictures an old-fashioned screw press (driven by jerking a lever), with the words "PAYABLE AT THE FRANKLIN PRESS LONDON" on the opposite side. It carries a date of 1794. As Franklin died in 1790 he could not have seen this token. Reproductions exist.

TYPE OF COIN	ABP	G-4 Good	F-12 Fine	EF-40 Ex. Fine
☐ 1794 Token	20.00	32.00	100.00	270.00

CASTORLAND

Royalists who fled France following the revolution's outbreak in 1791 scattered to many parts of the globe. A small colony settled in the New York State farmlands (near Carthage) and called the locality Castorland. The Castorland medal or token is said to be a pattern piece struck in France for a proposed currency. It never reached beyond the experimental stage and both varieties, in silver and copper, are extremely rare. They carry a date of 1796.

TYPE OF COIN	ABP	G-4 Good	VG-8 Very Good	F-12 Fine
☐ 1796 Silver Original, Reeded Edge . . ⎱			BOTH TYPES RARE	
☐ 1796 Copper Original, Reeded Edge . ⎰				

FUGIO CENTS

The Fugio Cents, so called because that word is a component in the obverse inscription, were the first officially sanctioned U.S. federal coinage. It was resolved by Congress in 1787 that a contract be put out with a private miller, James Jarvis, for 300 tons of copper coins. The arrangement was for Jarvis to secure the metal himself and pay all expenses, then sell the coins to the government at face value — his profit arising from the difference between his cost and the total face value. It was a venture of enormous proportions, considering that the U.S. had not previously authorized any coins. The matter of designing was not left to the contractor. Congress specifically spelled out what these coins should look like: "thirteen circles linked together, a small circle in the middle with the words United States around it, and in the center the words 'We are one'; on the other side of the same piece the following device, viz: a dial with the hours expressed on the face of it; a meridian sun above on one side of which is the word Fugio." Fugio is Latin for "time flies." As the obverse carries the saying "Mind your Business," often attributed to Benjamin Franklin, this is sometimes called the Franklin Cent; such terminology is, however, misleading and confusing. The dies were produced by Abel Buel of New Haven, Connecticut, and most of the striking was apparently carried out in that city. Jarvis failed to deliver the agreed-on number of coins, was prosecuted for breach of contract and imprisoned.

1787 CENT

TYPE OF COIN	ABP	G-4 Good	F-12 Fine
☐ 1787 Cent, Club Rays, Rounded Ends	40.00	71.00	235.00
☐ 1787 Cent, Club Rays, Concave Ends, FUCIO (NOT ILLUS.)			
☐ 1787 Cent, Club Rays, Concave Ends, FUGIO		ALL VERY RARE	
☐ 1787 Cent, Club Rays, States United			
☐ 1787 Cent, Pointed Rays, UNITED above, STATES below			
☐ 1787 Cent, Pointed Rays, UNITED STATES at side of circle (NOT ILLUS.)	35.00	62.00	145.00
☐ 1787 Cent, Pointed Rays, STATES UNITED at side of circle; Cinquefoils	35.00	62.00	135.00

TYPE OF COIN	ABP	G-4 Good	F-12 Fine
☐ 1787 Cent, Pointed Rays, STATES UNITED at sides, 8 pointed star on reverse band (NOT ILLUS.)	40.00	75.00	185.00
☐ 1787 Cent, Pointed Rays, STATES UNITED, raised edge on reverse band	45.00	90.00	270.00
☐ 1787 Cents, Pointed Ray, UNITED STATES, No Cinquefoils	90.00	160.00	550.00
☐ 1787 Cent, Pointed Rays, STATES UNITED, No Cinquefoils	110.00	190.00	600.00
☐ 1787 Cent, AMERICAN CONGRESS, with Rays (NOT ILLUS.)			VERY RARE

NEW HAVEN RESTRIKES

1787 CENT

In 1858, C. Wyllys Betts found in New Haven 3 sets of dies. Restrikes in various metals were made. The restrikes were not made directly from these dies but copies fashioned from them.

TYPE OF COIN	ABP	MS-60 UNC
☐ Copper	160.00	300.00
☐ Silver	350.00	625.00
☐ Brass	160.00	300.00
☐ Gold		EXTREMELY RARE

FIRST UNITED STATES OF AMERICA MINT ISSUES

1792 BIRCH CENT

The 1792 Birch Cent was the first coin to be struck at the newly established U.S. Mint in Philadelphia and the first governmental issue struck by the government as opposed to private contractors. This coin was not circulated but produced as a trial piece only. Along with it there were also trial or pattern pieces of half disme, disme, and quarter dollar denominations, all of which are extremely rare. A motion is said to have been made for placing George Washington's likeness on these pieces but that Washington, when informed of this plan, declined to be honored in such a manner. It was then decided to use a portrait of the Goddess of Liberty. The better-known version of the Birch Cent is large in size and composed entirely of copper. A smaller cent was also produced, containing a droplet of silver at the center. This was done entirely experimentally, in an effort to determine whether a penny coin in small size might be publicly more acceptable than one made exclusively of base metal. The pattern quarter dollar has more the appearance of a medal than a coin. The Birch Cent derives its name from Robert Birch, its designer. Birch is thought also to have been among the die-cutters for the half disme and disme.

1792 HALF DISME

1792 BIRCH CENT

1792 DISME

TYPE OF COIN

☐ 1792 (Silver), DISME . . . .
☐ 1792 (Copper), DISME . . . .
☐ 1792 (Silver), HALF DISME . . . .
☐ 1792 BIRCH CENT (Copper) . . . .   ALL COINS ARE RARE,
☐ 1792 BIRCH CENT (White Metal) . . . .   VERY RARE, OR UNIQUE

☐ 1792 QUARTER DOLLAR (Pattern, Copper) . . . .   EXTREMELY RARE

☐ 1792 QUARTER DOLLAR (Pattern, White Metal) . . . .   EXTREMELY RARE

EXTREMELY RARE

EXTREMELY RARE

1792 SILVER CENTER CENT

TYPE OF COIN

☐ 1792 Silver Center Cent . . . .
☐ 1792 Cent, No Silver Center . . . .   ALL COINS ARE VERY RARE, OR UNIQUE

HALF CENTS, 1793 - 1857

That the lowly half cent survived into the second half of the 19th century is looked upon as remarkable today by persons not well acquainted with the economic conditions of that time. Despite its minute face value, and the grumblings of many citizens that it did little but clutter their pockets, it served an important function in trade. Many articles in shops were priced fractionally and without the half cent difficulty would have been encountered in making change for such purchases. Their availability was, however, frequently abused. Merchants, anxious to rid themselves of half cents, would often give them instead of pennies. As first introduced in 1793 the coin bore a portrait of Liberty facing left on its obverse and a wreathed reverse with the words "HALF CENT" and "UNITED STATES OF AMERICA." The designer was Adam Eckfeldt. The original weight was 6.74 grams and the composition pure copper. The coin has a diameter of 22 mm. and is stamped along the edge, "TWO HUNDRED FOR A DOLLAR." After being struck for a single year it was decided to redesign the coin (coin redesigning occurred frequently in the Mint's early days of operation), the new design being the work of Robert Scot. Liberty was switched round to face right, her features streamlined, and her cap (the "cap of liberty," a reference to caps worn by freed slaves in Roman times) enlarged. The reverse was restyled but not materially altered. Planchets were of the same weight but slightly larger physically, measuring 23½ mm. Another fresh version was placed into use in 1795, this one the work of John S. Gardner; its specifications were the same as its predecessor's. It was later concluded that the weight had been set too high. This ushered in the so-called "thin planchet" half cent, weighing 5.44 grams and still measuring 23½ mm. "TWO HUNDRED FOR A DOLLAR" was removed from the edge. The varieties of this "Liberty Cap" half cent are numerous, despite the brief period of its manufacture.

The Liberty Cap half cent was followed in 1800 by introduction of the Draped Bust design, after a period of two years in which coins of this denomination were not minted (they could hardly have been in short supply as well over 200,000 had been circulated). Liberty's cap was removed and her hairstyle made somewhat more fashionable. The portrait was lengthened somewhat to include a suggestion of shoulders, over which a classical-style garment is placed. The designer was Robert Scot, who had done the 1794 version. Specifications remained the same as before. It was resolved to get these coins into very extensive circulation, resulting in a mintage quantity of more than one million in the year 1804 alone. By the end of 1808, the last year for this design, more than three million had been struck. The new half cent was the so-called "Classic Head" variety, designed by John Reich. Apparently this title was bestowed in the belief that Reich's Liberty more closely approximated Grecian sculpture than had the other types. The face, if stronger, became less physically attractive and more masculine. Stars were set at either side of the portrait and Liberty was given a band round her head with her name imprinted on it. The next design, and the last, was introduced in 1840 but used for proofs only, as the half cent did not return to general circulation until 1849. Christian Gobrecht was the designer and his rendition of Liberty has come to be known as the "Braided Hair Type." A sharp departure from the Reich approach, it pictured Liberty with Roman nose and considerable loss of bulk. This could well be considered the most attractive design, portrait-wise, of the half cent series.

HALF CENTS—LIBERTY CAP, 1793-1797

1793   1794 Pole to Cap

DATE	MINTAGE	ABP	G-4 Good	F-12 Fine	VF-20 V. Fine
☐ 1793 (Facing Left)	31,534	600.00	1150.00	2250.00	3700.00
☐ 1794 (Facing Right)	81,600	150.00	275.00	700.00	1075.00
☐ 1795 Plain Edge		150.00	240.00	470.00	875.00
☐ 1795 Lettered Edge	25,600	150.00	250.00	500.00	950.00
☐ 1796 With Pole	5,090	1200.00	2500.00	7500.00	11750.00
☐ 1796 No Pole			EXTREMELY RARE		
☐ 1797 Plain Edge		200.00	300.00	600.00	1000.00
☐ 1797 Lettered Edge	119,214	300.00	500.00	1300.00	3300.00
☐ 1797 1 Above 1		150.00	285.00	550.00	950.00

HALF CENTS—DRAPED BUST, 1800-1808

1804   Plain **4**   Crosslet **4**   Spiked Chin Variety

DATE	MINTAGE	ABP	G-4 Good	F-12 Fine	VF-20 V. Fine	EF-40 Ex. Fine
☐ 1800	211,530	24.00	26.00	50.00	95.00	235.00
☐ 1802 with 1800 reverse		200.00	350.00	925.00	3100.00	—
☐ 1802	14,366	80.00	160.00	400.00	1000.00	3275.00
☐ 1803	87,900	14.00	27.00	53.00	85.00	300.00
☐ 1804 Plain 4		14.00	27.00	40.00	76.00	180.00
☐ 1804 Crosslet	1,055,312	14.00	25.00	42.00	79.00	180.00

DATE	MINTAGE	ABP	G-4 Good	F-12 Fine	VF-20 V. Fine	EF-40 Ex. Fine
☐1804 Spiked Chin		13.00	25.00	39.00	75.00	185.00
☐1805	814,464	11.00	24.00	38.00	80.00	210.00
☐1806	356,000	13.00	25.00	39.00	74.00	185.00
☐1806 Small 6, Stems		39.00	70.00	190.00	270.00	650.00
☐1807	476,000	13.00	24.00	43.00	79.00	240.00
☐1808 Normal Date	400,000	11.00	23.00	42.00	82.00	350.00
☐1808 Over 7		38.00	70.00	320.00	730.00	1725.00

HALF CENTS — TURBAN HEAD, 1809 - 1837

1837   1837 TOKEN

DATE	MINTAGE	ABP	G-4 Good	F-12 Fine	VF-20 V. Fine	EF-40 Ex. Fine
☐1809	1,154,572	11.00	21.00	33.00	55.00	82.00
☐1809 over 6		11.00	21.00	33.00	55.00	125.00
☐1809 Circle Inside 0		11.00	28.00	39.00	59.00	110.00
☐1810	215,000	13.00	26.00	49.00	110.00	230.00
☐1811	63,140	55.00	100.00	410.00	980.00	2075.00
☐1811 Restrike with 1802 Reverse			EXTREMELY RARE			
☐1825	63,000	13.00	24.00	36.00	65.00	125.00
☐1826	234,000	12.00	23.00	34.00	55.00	85.00
☐1828 12 Stars	606,000	12.00	24.00	35.00	62.00	115.00
☐1828 13 Stars		11.00	22.00	30.00	40.00	70.00
☐1829	487,000	11.00	21.00	31.00	41.00	65.00
☐1831-8 known	2200		Business	Strikes-	Original	4750.00
☐1831 SMALL BERRIES		7350.00	Proof Only	Restrike		
☐1831 LARGE BERRIES		6200.00	Proof Only	Restrike		
☐1832	154,000	11.00	21.00	30.00	40.00	65.00
☐1833	120,000	11.00	21.00	30.00	40.00	65.00
☐1834	141,000	11.00	21.00	30.00	40.00	65.00
☐1835	398,000	11.00	21.00	30.00	40.00	65.00
☐1836		Proof Only	Original	6150.00	—Restrike	6150.00
☐1837 (Token) pure copper		17.00	32.00	50.00	100.00	165.00

HALF CENTS — BRAIDED HAIR, 1840 · 1857

DATE		ABP			PRF-65 Proof
☐1840		3000.00	Proof Only		4250.00
☐1841		3000.00	Proof Only		3900.00
☐1842	ORIGINAL	3000.00	Proof Only		4250.00
☐1843	AND RESTRIKE	3000.00	Proof Only		4250.00
☐1844	PROOFS ONLY	3000.00	Proof Only		4250.00
☐1845	1840-1849	3000.00	Proof Only		4500.00
☐1846	NO MINTAGE	3000.00	Proof Only		4250.00
☐1847	RECORDS	3000.00	Proof Only		4250.00
☐1848	AVAILABLE	3000.00	Proof Only		4250.00
☐1849		3000.00	Proof Only		4250.00

DATE	MINTAGE	ABP	G-4 Good	F-12 Fine	VF-20 V. Fine	EF-40 Ex. Fine
☐1849	39,864	16.00	31.00	44.00	60.00	85.00
☐1850	39,812	16.00	30.00	43.00	52.00	76.00
☐1851	147,672	13.00	26.00	37.00	47.00	65.00
☐1852		Proofs Only—Original and Restrike 4150.00				
☐1853	129,964	13.00	26.00	38.00	48.00	67.00
☐1854	55,358	13.00	26.00	38.00	48.00	67.00
☐1855	56,500	13.00	26.00	38.00	48.00	67.00
☐1856	40,430	16.00	31.00	42.00	54.00	75.00
☐1857	35,180	21.00	40.00	50.00	65.00	80.00

LARGE CENTS — 1793 · 1857

The shrinkage of the cent from its introduction in 1793 to its present size is ample evidence of inflation; the present Lincoln cent weighs only about one third as much as its distant ancestor. But what the penny has lost in bulk and buying power has been compensated for, at least in part, by its greater convenience. The series began with the Flowering Hair/Chain Reverse type designed by Henry Voight. Its weight was set at 13.48 grams of pure copper, precisely twice that of the half cent. (The government set rigid standards of weight, fearing that without such regulations its coinage would not inspire confidence). There were no long suspensions of production, as with the half cent. A quantity — varying of course in number — was minted each year from the coin's inception until conclusion of the Large Cent in 1857, with the single exception of 1815 because of a metal shortage. The first design, aptly named as Liberty, is shown with billowing hair that appears breeze-blown. Her features are delicate and the overall composition is pleasing. It will be noted that the reverse design bears very close resemblance to the Fugio cent or Franklin cent, struck in 1787. The diameter of this coin varies from 26 to 27 mm. It is consequently not very much smaller than the present 50¢ piece. After three months of striking coins from these dies, during which time more than 36,000 were produced, a new design was introduced. The work of Adam Eckfeldt, designer of the first half cent, it retained the Flowing Hair portrait on the obverse but employed a wreath rather than the chained reverse, enclosing the words "ONE CENT." Its weight was unchanged but the diameter varies from 26 to 28 mm. or slightly larger than its predecessor. Along the edge is stamped the inscription "ONE HUNDRED FOR A DOLLAR."

This design got somewhat further, resulting in a mintage of more than 60,000 pieces, but before the year was out another had taken its place. The Flowing Hair portrait, subjected to criticism in the press (to which the government seems to have been more sensitive than subsequently), was removed in favor of a "Liberty Cap" type, designed by Joseph Wright. Here the bust of Liberty is positioned somewhat to the right of center; over her left shoulder she balances a staff, on the tip of which rests of a conical-shaped cap — the "cap of liberty" symbolic of freedom from slavery in Roman times. This version, too, was assailed, but minters were so weary of making alterations that they continued using it until 1796. The staff and cap looked like an Indian arrow in the opinion of some; others fancied that Liberty was wearing an oversized bow in her hair. The weight was retained but the planchet grew slightly larger, to 29 mm. In 1795, still using the same design, the weight was dropped to 10.89 grams, diameter remained 29 mm., and new dies were engraved. The artist was John S. Gardner. His work is often said to be superior to other efforts. The "Draped Bust Type," first struck in mid 1796, was an effort to render more classicism to the portrait. Designed by Robert Scot, it deleted the much-maligned liberty cap and, while not materially altering Miss Liberty's facial features, gave her the appearance of chubbiness. Specifications remained as previously. In 1808 the so-called "Classic Head" made its bow, designed by John Reich. Here Liberty wears a coronet with the word "LIBERTY" spelled out upon it and the bust is shortened with drapery removed. She grows chubbier still. The reverse is very close to that of a modern "wheat" cent: the words "ONE CENT" encircled in laurel, surrounded by the legend "UNITED STATES OF AMERICA." There are numerous varieties, as enumerated below. The classic head survived until the copper shortage which followed close upon the heels of the War of 1812, when production of large cents was temporarily halted. When resumed in 1816 the design was new. The work of Robert Scot, it was referred to as "Matron Head," as Liberty appears to have taken on added years. She in fact was growing old with her coinage. A youth in 1792 when the series began, she had now advanced into middle age. The bust is shortened even further; stars now totally encircle it (except for the space containing the date); but the reverse remains the same.

In 1837 the last large cent design was put into production. The next two decades yielded many varieties of it, from die re-engravings. This is the

Gobrecht version, basically a handsome portrait which returns the youthful goddess image to Liberty and slims her down. The weight was 10.89 grams (the penny was never to return to its old weight-standard), the diameter 27½ mm. Chief variations are the Silly Head and Booby Head, neither of which really merited such ridicule. There was also a Petite Head and Mature Head and ample differences in letter and numeral sizes.

LARGE CENTS — FLOWING HAIR, 1793

1793 Chain   1793 Wreath

DATE	MINTAGE	ABP	G-4 Good	VG-8 V. Good	F-12 Fine	VF-20 V. Fine
☐ 1793 Chain AMERI	36,103	1100.00	2185.00	2800.00	4075.00	6800.00
☐ 1793 Chain AMERICA		1000.00	2185.00	2800.00	4075.00	6800.00
☐ 1793 Chain type, period after date and Liberty		950.00	2000.00	2500.00	3800.00	6375.00
☐ 1793 Wreath type, edge has vine and bars	63,353	650.00	925.00	1300.00	1675.00	2950.00
☐ 1793 Wreath type, lettered edge, one leaf on edge		650.00	925.00	1300.00	1675.00	2950.00
☐ 1793 Wreath type lettered edge, double leaf on edge		650.00	925.00	1300.00	1675.00	2950.00

LARGE CENTS—LIBERTY CAP, 1793 - 1796

1793 LIBERTY CAP   1795 JEFFERSON HEAD

ONE CENT
in Center of Wreath

ONE CENT
High in Wreath

DATE	MINTAGE	ABP	G-4 Good	VG-8 V. Good	F-12 Fine	VF-20 V. Fine
☐ 1793	11,056	900.00	1650.00	2500.00	3400.00	6450.00
☐ 1794		80.00	160.00	240.00	350.00	820.00
☐ 1794* ALL KINDS		150.00	330.00	500.00	1200.00	2150.00
☐ 1794**		70.00	140.00	210.00	400.00	680.00
☐ 1794***	918,521	70.00	140.00	210.00	400.00	680.00
☐ 1794****		1200.00	2450.00	3885.00	7900.00	18500.00
☐ 1795 Jefferson Head		900.00	1700.00	3125.00	5300.00	13750.00

*Head of 1793 **Head of 1795 ***No Fraction Bar ****Stars on Back

DATE	MINTAGE	ABP	Good	V. Good	Fine	V. Fine
☐ 1795† Lettered Edge*		85.00	175.00	280.00	500.00	1250.00
☐ 1795† Lettered Edge**		100.00	200.00	300.00	600.00	1350.00
☐ 1795†† Plain Edge*		70.00	140.00	230.00	370.00	650.00
☐ 1795†† Plain Edge**		70.00	140.00	230.00	370.00	650.00
☐ 1796††† Liberty Cap		73.00	155.00	240.00	435.00	800.00

†Total Mintage: 82,000 ††Total Mintage: 456,500 †††Total Mintage: 109,825
*''ONE CENT'' in Center of Wreath **''ONE CENT'' High in Wreath

LARGE CENTS—DRAPED BUST, 1796 - 1800

Gripped or
Milled Edge

LIHERTY 1796 (error)

DATE	MINTAGE	ABP	G-4 Good	VG-8 V. Good	F-12 Fine	VF-20 V. Fine
☐ 1796†		43.00	85.00	150.00	260.00	585.00
☐ 1796† ''LIHERTY'' (error)		50.00	90.00	135.00	250.00	525.00
☐ 1796†† Stems on Wreath		40.00	80.00	140.00	240.00	600.00
☐ 1797†† Stemless Wreath		40.00	80.00	140.00	270.00	675.00
☐ 1797†† Stems on Wreath		23.00	46.00	90.00	130.00	275.00
☐ 1797†† Gripped		22.00	43.00	85.00	140.00	285.00
☐ 1797†† Plain Edge		23.00	45.00	95.00	150.00	305.00
☐ 1798††† over 97		45.00	90.00	185.00	280.00	700.00

DATE	MINTAGE	ABP	G-4 Good	VG-8 V. Good	F-12 Fine	VF-20 V. Fine
☐ 1798††† Small. Date		19.00	40.00	75.00	130.00	350.00
☐ 1798††† Large Date		19.00	40.00	75.00	130.00	350.00
☐ 1798†††*		21.00	45.00	90.00	140.00	375.00
☐ 1799** over 98		500.00	1100.00	1950.00	2850.00	5500.00
☐ 1799** Normal Date		450.00	1000.00	1825.00	2700.00	5275.00
☐ 1800*** over 1798		15.00	30.00	45.00	90.00	235.00

†Total Mintage: 363,372 ††Total Mintage: 897,509 †††Total Mintage: 979,700
*Reverse of 96. Single leaf Reverse. Total Mintage: 904,584 ***Part of 2,822,170

LARGE CENTS — DRAPED BUST, 1800 - 1801

Normal Date—Normal Die

1800 over 179

DATE	MINTAGE	ABP	G-4 Good	VG-8 V. Good	F-12 Fine	VF-20 V. Fine
☐ 1800 over 79, Style I Hair		15.00	32.00	49.00	90.00	230.00
☐ 1800† over 79 Style II Hair		15.00	32.00	49.00	90.00	230.00
☐ 1800† Unfinished Cyphers		15.00	32.00	49.00	90.00	230.00
☐ 1800† Normal Date		15.00	32.00	49.00	90.00	230.00
☐ 1801†† Normal Dies, Blunt "1"		21.00	45.00	70.00	100.00	245.00
☐ 1801†† First "1" Pointed		17.00	34.00	53.00	75.00	225.00
☐ 1801†† 3 Errors - 1/1000, one stem, and IINITED		40.00	82.00	150.00	285.00	850.00

†Total Mintage: 2,822,170†† Total Mintage (all 1801 Varieties) 1,362,837

LARGE CENTS — DRAPED BUST, 1801 - 1804

1802- $\frac{1}{100}$

ERROR

$\frac{1}{100}$

OVER

$\frac{1}{000}$

DATE	MINTAGE	ABP	G-4 Good	VG-8 V. Good	F-12 Fine	VF-20 V. Fine
☐ 1801†† 1/000		20.00	41.00	75.00	140.00	265.00
☐ 1801†† 1/100 Over 1/000		24.00	50.00	110.00	180.00	350.00
☐ 1802††† Normal Dies		12.00	24.00	36.00	70.00	235.00
☐ 1802††† Stemless Wreath		12.00	28.00	45.00	90.00	245.00
☐ 1802††† Fraction 1/000		15.00	33.00	55.00	110.00	300.00
☐ 1803* Sm. Date, Sm. Fract.		10.00	23.00	36.00	70.00	225.00
☐ 1803* Sm. Date, Lg. Fract.		10.00	23.00	36.00	70.00	225.00
☐ 1803* Lg. Date, Sm. Fract.				Rare (about 20 Known)		
☐ 1803* Lg. Date, Lg. Fract.		10.00	23.00	36.00	70.00	225.00

Total Mintage: ††1,362,837   †††3,435,100   *2,471,350

LARGE CENTS — DRAPED BUST, 1803 - 1804

"Mumps" Obverse

"Normal" Obverse

DATE	MINTAGE	ABP	G-4 Good	VG-8 V. Good	F-12 Fine	VF-20 V. Fine
☐ 1803† Mumps Obverse		15.00	31.00	60.00	100.00	250.00
☐ 1803† Stemless Wreath		15.00	31.00	60.00	100.00	250.00
☐ 1803† 1/100 over 1/000		15.00	31.00	60.00	100.00	250.00
☐ 1804 Normal Dies	756,837	265.00	535.00	800.00	1375.00	2100.00
☐ 1804 Broken Obverse Die		265.00	535.00	800.00	1375.00	2100.00
☐ 1804 Broken Obverse & Reverse Die		265.00	535.00	800.00	1375.00	2100.00

†Part of 2,471,350

LARGE CENTS — DRAPED BUST, 1804 - 1807

1804 Normal Die

1804 Restruck in 1860

Small Fraction

Large Fraction

COMET VARIETY, 1807

DATE	MINTAGE	ABP	G-4 Good	VG-8 V. Good	F-12 Fine	VF-20 V. Fine
☐ 1804 Restrike of 1860					UNC.	310.00
☐ 1805 Blunt "1" in Date	941,115	15.00	30.00	48.00	80.00	240.00
☐ 1805 Pointed "1" in Date		15.00	30.00	48.00	80.00	240.00
☐ 1806	348,000	21.00	45.00	85.00	175.00	420.00
☐ 1807 over 6 lg. 7		13.00	26.00	42.00	77.00	230.00
☐ 1807 over 6 sm. 7					RARE-ABOUT 21 KNOWN	
☐ 1807 Small Fraction	727,000	13.00	26.00	42.00	77.00	230.00
☐ 1807 Large Fraction		13.00	26.00	42.00	77.00	230.00
☐ 1807 Comet Variety		13.00	26.00	42.00	77.00	230.00

LARGE CENTS — TURBAN HEAD, 1808 - 1814

DATE	MINTAGE	ABP	G-4 Good	VG-8 V. Good	F-12 Fine	VF-20 V. Fine
☐ 1808 13 Stars	1,109,000	15.00	31.00	52.00	90.00	275.00
☐ 1808 12 Stars		15.00	31.00	52.00	90.00	275.00
☐ 1809	222,867	45.00	80.00	150.00	280.00	575.00
☐ 1810 over 9	1,458,400	14.00	27.00	45.00	78.00	260.00
☐ 1810 Normal Date		14.00	27.00	45.00	90.00	260.00
☐ 1811 over 10	218,025	35.00	70.00	110.00	210.00	450.00
☐ 1811 Normal Date		32.00	62.00	105.00	185.00	430.00
☐ 1812 Small Date	1,075,500	14.00	27.00	45.00	78.00	260.00
☐ 1812 Large Date		14.00	27.00	45.00	78.00	260.00

DATE	MINTAGE	ABP	G-4 Good	VG-8 V. Good	F-12 Fine	VF-20 V. Fine
☐ 1813 Close Stars }	418,000	21.00	40.00	70.00	120.00	285.00
☐ 1813 Distant Stars }		21.00	40.00	70.00	120.00	285.00
☐ 1814 Plain 4 }	357,830	14.00	26.00	45.00	78.00	280.00
☐ 1814 Crosslet 4 }		14.00	26.00	45.00	78.00	280.00

LARGE CENTS — CORONET, 1816 - 1838

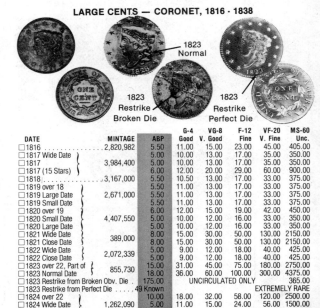

1823 Normal

1823 Restrike Broken Die

1823 Restrike Perfect Die

DATE	MINTAGE	ABP	G-4 Good	VG-8 V. Good	F-12 Fine	VF-20 V. Fine	MS-60 Unc.
☐ 1816	2,820,982	5.50	11.00	15.00	23.00	45.00	405.00
☐ 1817 Wide Date		5.00	10.00	13.00	17.00	35.00	350.00
☐ 1817	3,984,400	5.00	10.00	13.00	17.00	35.00	350.00
☐ 1817 (15 Stars) }		6.00	12.00	20.00	29.00	60.00	900.00
☐ 1818	3,167,000	5.50	10.50	13.00	17.00	33.00	375.00
☐ 1819 over 18		5.50	11.00	13.00	17.00	33.00	375.00
☐ 1819 Large Date }	2,671,000	5.50	11.00	13.00	17.00	33.00	375.00
☐ 1819 Small Date		5.50	11.00	13.00	17.00	33.00	375.00
☐ 1820 over 19		6.00	12.00	15.00	19.00	42.00	450.00
☐ 1820 Small Date }	4,407,550	5.00	10.00	12.00	16.00	33.00	350.00
☐ 1820 Large Date		5.00	10.00	12.00	16.00	33.00	350.00
☐ 1821 Wide Date }	389,000	8.00	15.00	30.00	50.00	130.00	2150.00
☐ 1821 Close Date		8.00	15.00	30.00	50.00	130.00	2150.00
☐ 1822 Wide Date }	2,072,339	5.00	9.00	12.00	18.00	40.00	425.00
☐ 1822 Close Date		5.00	9.00	12.00	18.00	40.00	425.00
☐ 1823 over 22, Part of }	855,730	15.00	31.00	45.00	75.00	180.00	2750.00
☐ 1823 Normal Date		18.00	36.00	60.00	100.00	300.00	4375.00
☐ 1823 Restrike from Broken Obv. Die	175.00	UNCIRCULATED ONLY					365.00
☐ 1823 Restrike from Perfect Die	49 Known	EXTREMELY RARE					
☐ 1824 over 22		10.00	18.00	32.00	58.00	120.00	2500.00
☐ 1824 Wide Date }	1,262,090	5.00	11.00	15.00	24.00	56.00	1500.00
☐ 1824 Close Date		5.00	11.00	15.00	24.00	56.00	1500.00
☐ 1825 Small A's }	1,461,000	4.50	8.00	12.00	20.00	48.00	800.00
☐ 1825 Large A's		4.50	8.00	12.00	20.00	48.00	800.00

DATE	MINTAGE	ABP	G-4 Good	VG-8 V. Good	F-12 Fine	VF-20 V. Fine	MS-60 Unc.
☐ 1826 over 25	}	12.00	25.00	38.00	70.00	130.00	635.00
☐ 1826 Wide Date	1,517,422	4.50	8.00	13.00	20.00	45.00	375.00
☐ 1826 Close Date	}	4.50	8.00	13.00	20.00	45.00	375.00
☐ 1827	2,357,733	4.50	8.00	12.00	15.00	41.00	350.00
☐ 1828 Small Date	2,260,625	6.00	11.00	14.00	23.00	48.00	520.00
☐ 1828 Large Date		4.50	8.00	11.00	15.00	36.00	335.00
☐ 1829 Small Letters	1,414,500	5.50	11.00	16.00	21.00	48.00	375.00
☐ 1829 Large Letters	}	5.00	9.00	12.00	16.50	40.00	355.00
☐ 1830 Small Letters	1,711,500	6.00	12.00	15.00	21.00	50.00	410.00
☐ 1830 Large Letters	}	4.50	8.00	11.00	14.00	33.00	360.00
☐ 1831 Small Letters	3,359,260	4.50	8.00	10.00	12.00	30.00	350.00
☐ 1831 Large Letters	}	4.50	8.00	10.00	12.00	30.00	350.00
☐ 1832 Small Letters	2,362,000	4.50	8.00	10.00	13.00	34.00	375.00
☐ 1832 Large Letters	}	4.50	8.00	10.00	13.00	34.00	375.00
☐ 1833 Small Letters	2,739,000	4.00	7.50	10.00	12.00	29.00	315.00
☐ 1833 Large Letters	}	4.00	7.50	10.00	12.00	29.00	315.00
☐ 1834*	1,855,110	5.00	10.00	12.00	17.00	36.00	340.00
☐ 1834**		4.50	9.00	11.00	15.00	33.00	325.00
☐ 1834***	}	4.50	9.00	11.00	15.00	33.00	325.00
☐ 1835 Sm. Date — Sm. Stars		4.50	9.00	10.75	17.00	35.00	320.00
☐ 1835 Lg. Date Lg. Stars	3,878,397	4.50	9.00	10.75	14.00	31.00	310.00
☐ 1835 Type of 1836		4.00	7.50	9.00	12.00	30.00	320.00
☐ 1836	2,111,000	3.50	7.00	10.00	15.00	31.00	315.00
☐ 1837 Plain Hair Cord Small Letters		4.00	8.00	11.00	14.00	30.00	325.00
☐ 1837 Plain Hair Cord Large Letters	5,558,301	3.50	7.00	9.00	12.00	25.00	315.00
☐ 1837 Beaded Hair Cord — Small Letters	}	4.00	8.00	11.75	14.00	28.00	315.00
☐ 1838	6,370,200	3.50	7.00	9.00	11.00	20.00	300.00

*Large Date — Large Stars — Large Letters Reverse **Small Date — Small Stars — Small Letters Reverse ***Large Date — Small Stars — Small Letters Reverse.

LARGE CENTS — BRAIDED HAIR, 1839 - 1857

Booby Head

1856 Slants

DATE	MINTAGE	ABP	G-4 Good	VG-8 V. Good	F-12 Fine	VF-20 V. Fine	MS-60 Unc.
☐ 1839 over 36		80.00	170.00	230.00	425.00	800.00	3900.00
☐ 1839 Type 1838 Line under Cent		4.50	9.00	11.00	15.00	30.00	350.00
☐ 1839 Silly Head No Center Dot	ALL KINDS	4.50	10.00	13.00	21.00	42.00	560.00
☐ 1839 Booby Head	3,128,662	4.00	8.00	11.00	18.00	39.00	415.00
☐ 1839 Petite Head	....	4.00	8.00	11.00	17.00	30.00	330.00
☐ 1840 Small Date	} 2,462,700	3.50	7.00	9.00	12.00	19.00	250.00
☐ 1840 Large Date		3.50	7.00	9.00	12.00	19.00	250.00
☐ 1841	1,597,366	3.50	7.00	9.00	13.00	21.00	275.00
☐ 1842 Small Date	} 2,383,390	3.50	6.75	8.50	10.00	16.00	245.00
☐ 1842 Large Date		3.50	6.75	8.50	10.00	16.00	245.00
☐ 1843 Obv. and Rev. 1842		3.50	7.00	10.00	13.00	20.00	265.00
☐ 1843 Obv. 1842 Rev. 1844	} 2,428,319	7.75	14.00	22.00	40.00	70.00	570.00
☐ 1843 Obv. and Rev. 1844		3.50	7.00	10.00	13.00	20.00	250.00
☐ 1844	} 2,398,752	3.50	7.00	9.00	11.00	15.00	245.00
☐ 1844 over 81		7.00	16.00	23.00	29.00	65.00	600.00
☐ 1845	3,894,805	3.50	6.75	8.00	10.00	14.00	240.00
☐ 1846 Small Date		3.50	6.75	8.00	10.00	14.00	245.00
☐ 1846 Med. Date	} 4,120,800	3.50	6.75	8.00	10.00	14.00	245.00
☐ 1846 Tall Date		3.50	6.75	8.00	10.00	14.00	245.00
☐ 1847	6,183,669	3.50	6.75	8.00	10.00	14.00	250.00
☐ 1847 7 over Small 7	....	3.50	6.75	8.00	10.00	15.00	260.00
☐ 1848	6,415,799	3.50	6.75	8.00	10.00	14.00	260.00
☐ 1849	4,178,500	3.50	6.75	8.00	10.00	14.00	265.00
☐ 1850	4,426,844	3.50	6.75	8.00	10.00	14.00	260.00
☐ 1851	} 9,899,700	3.50	6.00	8.00	10.00	14.00	260.00
☐ 1851 over 81		6.00	13.00	16.00	19.00	37.00	425.00
☐ 1852	5,063,094	3.50	6.75	8.00	10.00	14.00	255.00
☐ 1853	6,641,131	3.50	6.75	8.00	10.00	14.00	255.00
☐ 1854	4,236,156	3.50	6.75	8.00	10.00	14.00	255.00

DATE	MINTAGE	ABP	G-4 Good	VG-8 V. Good	F-12 Fine	VF-20 V. Fine	MS-60 Unc.
☐ 1855 Upright 5's		3.50	7.00	9.00	11.00	14.00	250.00
☐ 1855 Slanting 5's	1,574,829	3.50	7.00	9.00	11.00	14.00	250.00
☐ 1855 Slanting 5's Knob on Ear		3.50	7.00	9.00	11.00	14.00	250.00
☐ 1856 Upright 5		3.50	7.00	9.00	11.00	15.00	240.00
☐ 1856 Slanting 5	2,690,465	3.50	7.00	9.00	11.00	15.00	240.00
☐ 1857 Small Date		15.00	32.00	42.00	55.00	70.00	375.00
☐ 1857 Large Date	333,456	14.00	29.00	36.00	48.00	59.00	370.00

SMALL CENTS — FLYING EAGLE, 1856 - 1858

It would be hard to find a coin in the standard U.S. series that proved so unpopular as the Flying Eagle cent — unpopular, that is, originally. It has since become a favorite of collectors. During 1856, while the large cent continued in production, plans were underway to replace it with a smaller coin of the same value. A number of patterns of the Flying Eagle were struck that year at the Philadelphia Mint but were not circulated because the large cent was still current. In the early part of the following year the large cent was discontinued and minting switched over to this new piece, with a huge output in that one year of nearly 17,500,000 coins. The public balked. It charged that the government was forcing the small cent on it. Not only didn't the public care much for that idea, it was also not too fond of the coin. Instead of being struck in pure copper and having the substantial appearance that a cent was supposed to have, its composition was 88% copper and 12% nickel, yielding a coin that was sufficiently pale in color to be called white. (If one wonders about the bickerings over coin sizes, designs and compositions in the 18th and 19th centuries, it should be realized that far greater attention was focused upon money in those days, when few persons used checks and credit cards were unknown.) The Flying Eagle Cent was designed by James Longacre. Its weight was 4.67 grams and its diameter 19 mm. As a designer Longacre was not unskilled. He proved his abilities with the Indian Head Cent, which replaced the Flying Eagle in 1859.

DATE	MINTAGE	ABP	G-4 Good	F-12 Fine	EF-40 Ex. Fine	MS-60 Unc.	PRF-65 Proof
☐ 1856	Approx. 1,000	675.00	1300.00	1850.00	2500.00	3275.00	7250.00
☐ 1857	17,450,000	4.00	8.00	13.80	60.00	240.00	6800.00
☐ 1858 Small Letters		4.00	8.00	13.80	62.00	230.00	6800.00
☐ 1858 Large Letters	24,600,000	4.00	8.00	13.80	63.00	230.00	6800.00

SMALL CENTS — INDIAN HEAD, 1859 - 1909

Probably the most famous of all U.S. coins (its only challenger for that honor being the Morgan Dollar), the Indian Head cent remained in production without change in design for half a century. After the disaster of the Flying Eagle Cent, rejected by the public because of its almost white color, the government knew that it must manufacture a cent whose appearance was that of good metal, even if it was not to return to the large cent. The question remained: would a small copper piece be accepted, when large cents, containing a much greater quantity of metal, were still widely circulating? The new cent had the same composition as its predecessor, 88% copper and 12% nickel. The first batch of Indian Heads, released in 1859, amounted to 36,400,000 pieces, more than had ever been coined of a single denomination in one year: $364,000 worth of pennies. Beginning in 1864 the copper content was increased to 95%, the nickel removed entirely and replaced with a 5% alloy of tin and zinc. This was so successfully absorbed into the copper that the resulting coin was hardly different in color than if copper alone were used. Finally the problem was solved, and the Indian Head Cent was on the road to a long successful existence. Its designer was James Longacre. The weight was 4.67 grams and the diameter 19 mm., these specifications being the same as the Flying Eagle Cent. The portrait is that of an Indian maiden. As first designed the reverse carried no shield but this was added in 1860, the second year of issue. The Indian Head became the first U.S. coin struck in a quantity of more than 100 million in a year, when 108 million specimens were turned out in 1907. This exceeded the country's population. It is interesting to note that the 1908 and 1909 editions, representing the last two years of this design, are the only dates to be found with mintmarks. The origin of the portrait has been for many years a matter of discussion. It was at one time thought that Longacre had taken it from life, using an Indian girl as his model. This was dismissed when the suggestion was advanced that the profile resembled Longacre's daughter. It is now generally believed that no live model sat for the likeness but that it was based upon classical statuary, of which Longacre was known to be a collector. The Indian Head Cent portrait is neither as realistic or impressive as that featured on the Buffalo Nickel, but this is nevertheless an important coin whose design represented a bold innovation.

1901   1860-1864 Wreath on Shield

DATE	MINTAGE	ABP	G-4 Good	F-12 Fine	EF-40 Ex. Fine	MS-60 Unc.	PRF-65 Proof
☐ 1859 Copper-Nickel	36,400,000	2.50	4.00	8.50	54.00	280.00	4075.00
☐ 1860 Copper-Nickel	20,566,000	1.75	3.50	7.00	20.00	135.00	2300.00
☐ 1861 Copper-Nickel	10,100,000	4.50	8.50	13.00	42.00	190.00	2300.00
☐ 1862 Copper-Nickel	28,075,000	1.30	2.60	4.00	17.00	120.00	2300.00
☐ 1863 Copper-Nickel	49,840,000	1.20	2.30	3.75	16.00	120.00	2300.00
☐ 1864 Copper-Nickel	13,740,000	4.00	7.50	13.00	28.00	145.00	2300.00
☐ 1864 Bronze	39,233,714	1.50	3.00	7.00	25.00	60.00	1300.00
☐ 1864 L on Ribbon		16.00	37.00	53.00	130.00	330.00	12500.00
☐ 1865	35,429,286	1.25	2.75	7.00	24.00	55.00	1175.00
☐ 1866	9,826,500	10.00	19.00	28.00	80.00	160.00	1175.00
☐ 1867	9,821,000	10.00	19.00	28.00	80.00	160.00	1175.00
☐ 1868	10,266,500	10.00	19.00	28.00	80.00	160.00	1175.00
☐ 1869	6,420,000	12.00	24.00	60.00	140.00	300.00	1350.00
☐ 1869 over 8		42.00	85.00	190.00	450.00	800.00	
☐ 1870	5,275,000	9.50	19.00	52.00	110.00	220.00	1175.00
☐ 1871	3,929,500	13.00	25.00	65.00	125.00	240.00	1175.00
☐ 1872	4,042,000	18.00	35.00	80.00	160.00	330.00	1175.00
☐ 1873	11,676,500	3.50	8.50	16.00	45.00	120.00	1100.00
☐ 1873 Doubled Liberty						EXTREMELY RARE	
☐ 1874	14,187,500	3.50	8.00	15.00	55.00	115.00	1125.00
☐ 1875	13,528,000	3.50	8.00	15.00	55.00	115.00	1125.00
☐ 1876	7,944,000	6.00	13.00	23.00	52.00	140.00	1125.00
☐ 1877	852,500	90.00	180.00	320.00	700.00	1400.00	4375.00
☐ 1878	5,799,850	6.00	13.00	24.00	58.00	140.00	1100.00
☐ 1879	16,231,000	1.10	2.50	5.50	20.00	55.00	925.00
☐ 1880	38,964,955	.50	1.45	2.75	11.00	50.00	925.00
☐ 1881	39,211,575	.50	1.45	2.75	11.00	50.00	925.00
☐ 1882	38,581,100	.50	1.45	2.75	11.00	50.00	925.00
☐ 1883	45,598,109	.50	1.45	2.75	17.00	50.00	925.00
☐ 1884	23,261,742	.75	1.75	5.00	33.00	52.00	925.00
☐ 1885	11,765,384	1.25	3.25	8.00	38.00	68.00	925.00
☐ 1886	17,654,290	.75	1.60	5.00	25.00	60.00	925.00
☐ 1887	45,226,483	.40	.90	1.75	9.00	50.00	925.00
☐ 1888	37,494,414	.40	.90	1.75	9.00	50.00	925.00
☐ 1889	48,868,361	.40	.90	1.75	9.00	38.00	925.00
☐ 1890	57,182,854	.40	.85	1.75	9.00	34.00	925.00
☐ 1891	47,072,350	.40	.85	1.75	9.00	34.00	925.00
☐ 1892	37,649,832	.40	.85	1.75	9.00	34.00	925.00
☐ 1893	46,642,195	.40	.85	1.75	9.00	34.00	925.00
☐ 1894	16,752,132	.65	1.20	5.00	20.00	72.00	925.00
☐ 1895	38,343,636	.40	.80	1.30	7.25	34.00	925.00
☐ 1896	39,057,293	.40	.80	1.30	7.25	34.00	925.00
☐ 1897	50,466,330	.40	.80	1.30	7.25	34.00	925.00
☐ 1898	49,923,079	.40	.80	1.30	7.25	34.00	925.00
☐ 1899	53,600,031	.40	.80	1.30	7.25	34.00	925.00
☐ 1900	66,833,764	.40	.80	1.30	6.00	34.00	925.00
☐ 1901	79,611,143	.40	.75	1.30	6.00	34.00	925.00
☐ 1902	87,376,722	.40	.70	1.30	6.00	34.00	925.00
☐ 1903	85,094,493	.40	.70	1.30	6.00	34.00	925.00

			G-4	F-12	EF-40	MS-60	PRF-65
DATE	MINTAGE	ABP	Good	Fine	Ex. Fine	Unc.	Proof
☐ 1904	61,328,015	.40	.70	1.10	6.00	34.00	925.00
☐ 1905	80,719,163	.40	.70	1.10	6.00	34.00	925.00
☐ 1906	96,022,255	.40	.70	1.10	6.00	34.00	925.00
☐ 1907	108,138,618	.40	.70	1.10	6.00	34.00	925.00
☐ 1908	32,327,987	.40	.70	1.10	6.00	34.00	925.00
☐ 1908S	1,115,000	10.00	19.00	25.00	43.00	140.00	
☐ 1909	14,370,645	.50	1.10	2.00	8.00	45.00	925.00
☐ 1909S	309,000	45.00	90.00	125.00	200.00	350.00	

SMALL CENTS — LINCOLN HEAD, 1909 to Date

It is quite likely that, despite having remained in use for 50 years, the Indian Head design would have been retained for the cent beyond 1909, had not President Roosevelt pressed for its removal. The year 1909 marked the 100th anniversary of Abraham Lincoln's birth and Roosevelt (who, not coincidentally, was a member of the same political party) wanted to memorialize the anniversary by placing a likeness of Lincoln on the penny. His suggestion was adopted, the result being a design that has survived in continuous use longer than any other in the Mint's history: 76 years, with no indication that it will soon be replaced. The Indian Head Cents were so popular that criticism was risked by their removal. Had they been abandoned in favor of any other design a public outcry might have ensued. But for Lincoln, allowances could be made. This was incidentally the first time an American citizen appeared on coinage of the Mint, as George Washington, though depicted on numerous coins and tokens, was never portrayed on an issue of the federal Mint. Designer of the Lincoln Cent was Victor D. Brenner. Rather than using a close-up profile Brenner showed Lincoln in quarter-length, with beard, as he appeared in the last few years of his life. It is not known whether the likeness was adapted from a specific photograph, from statuary, or merely from a study of various photos and other artworks. As first struck the coin carried Brenner's initials and this variety is known as the VDB Cent. They were removed midway through production of the 1909 issue and not reinstated until 1918, when they were switched from the reverse to the obverse. Specimens of the 1909 coin with initials, especially those struck at San Francisco, where less than half a million were produced, eventually became favorite collectors' items. At the time little notice was taken of them.

Originally the reverse was composed of the wording "ONE CENT - UNITED STATES OF AMERICA" enshrouded by wheat sheaves. In 1959 a new reverse was introduced, on the occasion of the 150th anniversary of Lincoln's birth and the 50th of the coin's use. Designed by Frank Gasparro, it pictures the Lincoln Memorial building in Washington, D.C. From 1909 to 1942 the Lincoln Cent had a composition of 95% copper and 5% tin and zinc with a weight of 3.11 grams and a diameter of 19 mm.

In 1943 it was made of steel coated zinc. From 1944 to 1946 what are known as "Shell Case Cents" were made from spent shell casings, their content was 95% copper and 5% TIN and ZINC, until September of 1962 when the tin was removed from the cent for the last time. The content of the cent from 1962 until 1981 was 95% copper and 5% zinc. Beginning in 1982, the cent has been made of a zinc core with copper coating. Thus it is now another "clad" coin, leaving only the nickel as the lone non-clad U.S. coin.

| | 1909 | | | No V.D.B. | V.D.B. Restored | | |

DATE	MINTAGE	ABP	G-4 Good	F-12 Fine	VF-20 V. Fine	EF-40 Ex. Fine	MS-60 Unc.	PRF-65 Proof
(1909-1942 COMPOSITIDN-95% COPPER WITH 5% TIN AND ZINC)
1909 72,702,618	.22	.55	.80	1.00	2.00	14.00	1000.00
1909 V.D.B. . . 27,995,000	1.15	2.00	2.75	3.10	3.60	13.00	3000.00
1909S 1,825,000	20.00	42.00	55.00	65.00	90.00	190.00	
1909S V.D.B. . . .484,000	105.00	210.00	260.00	300.00	350.00	500.00	
1910 146,801,218	.08	.15	.35	.60	2.00	15.00	975.00
1910S 6,045,000	2.50	6.00	9.00	11.00	20.00	85.00	
1911 101,177,787	.08	.17	.50	1.10	3.00	17.00	825.00
1911D 12,672,000	1.50	3.50	6.00	10.00	24.00	90.00	
1911S 4,026,000	6.00	11.00	15.00	18.00	30.00	120.00	
1912 68,153,060	.15	.30	1.50	3.25	6.00	25.00	900.00
1912D 10,411,000	1.65	3.75	7.00	12.00	27.00	115.00	
1912S 4,431,000	4.50	10.00	14.00	17.50	30.00	110.00	
1913 76,532,352	.15	.30	1.25	2.75	5.00	22.00	900.00
1913D 15,804,000	1.00	2.00	4.00	6.00	18.00	70.00	
1913S 6,101,000	3.00	7.00	10.00	13.00	23.00	100.00	
1914 75,238,432	.20	.40	1.00	3.00	6.75	58.00	975.00
1914D 1,193,000	28.00	55.00	100.00	150.00	350.00	800.00	
1914S 4,137,000	4.00	8.00	13.00	18.00	31.00	165.00	
1915 29,092,120	.40	1.00	3.50	7.00	26.00	90.00	1150.00
1915D 22,050,000	.30	.70	1.25	3.75	8.00	40.00	
1915S 4,833,677	3.25	7.00	10.00	11.50	21.00	90.00	
1916 131,838,677	.07	.20	.25	.75	2.50	9.00	1450.00
1916D 35,956,000	.09	.17	1.15	1.75	6.00	45.00	
1916S 22,510,000	.35	.85	1.50	2.50	6.20	52.00	
1917 196,429,785	.07	.20	.30	.60	2.00	10.00	
1917D 55,120,000	.10	.23	.65	1.75	4.50	47.00	
1917S 32,620,000	.18	.37	.70	2.00	4.50	52.00	
1918 288,104,634	.06	.12	.40	.70	2.00	10.00	
1918D 47,830,000	.10	.20	.75	2.00	6.00	47.00	
1918S 34,680,000	.10	.20	.55	1.75	5.00	52.00	
1919 392,021,000	.06	.12	.25	.45	1.50	9.00	
1919D 57,154,000	.10	.20	.55	2.00	4.00	42.00	
1919S 139,760,000	.06	.12	.30	.65	2.50	35.00	
1920 310,165,000	.05	.09	.25	.45	1.50	9.00	

DATE	MINTAGE	ABP	G-4 Good	F-12 Fine	VF-20 V. Fine	EF-40 Ex. Fine	MS-60 Unc.	PRF-65 Proof
☐ 1920D 49,280,000		.07	.13	.50	1.50	3.50	45.00	
☐ 1920S 46,220,000		.07	.13	.35	1.50	3.25	56.00	
☐ 1921 39,157,000		.10	.17	.80	3.80	39.00		
☐ 1921S 15,274,000		.20	.55	1.60	2.50	10.00	120.00	
☐ 1922 Plain (No Mint Mark)*		75.00	155.00	270.00	375.00	800.00	2750.00	
☐ 1922D 7,160,000		2.10	4.00	7.00	9.00	19.00	70.00	
☐ 1923 74,723,000		.07	.11	.30	.50	2.00	10.00	
☐ 1923S 8,700,000		.65	1.50	2.50	4.00	13.00	170.00	
☐ 1924 75,178,000		.07	.08	.30	.50	2.25	21.00	
☐ 1924D 2,520,000		5.00	10.00	15.00	18.00	40.00	215.00	
☐ 1924S 11,696,000		.25	.60	1.15	1.75	6.00	100.00	
☐ 1925 139,949,000		.07	.08	.30	.50	2.00	9.00	
☐ 1925D 22,580,000		.12	.19	.50	1.10	3.75	45.00	
☐ 1925S 26,380,000		.07	.11	.30	.80	4.00	56.00	
☐ 1926 157,088,000		.07	.11	.20	.35	2.00	7.00	
☐ 1926D 28,022,022		.10	.17	.55	1.85	4.00	45.00	
☐ 1926S 4,550,000		1.50	2.50	3.75	5.00	10.00	85.00	
☐ 1927 144,440,000		.07	.15	.30	.45	2.00	7.00	
☐ 1927D 27,170,000		.07	.15	.30	.45	2.75	26.00	
☐ 1927S 14,276,000		.25	.60	1.15	2.25	5.50	60.00	
☐ 1928 134,116,000		.07	.15	.30	.50	1.50	7.00	
☐ 1928D 31,170,000		.10	.17	.25	.40	2.00	21.00	
☐ 1928S 17,266,000		.12	.25	.40	.85	3.50	45.00	
☐ 1929 185,262,000		.06	.12	.20	.35	1.15	6.00	
☐ 1929D 41,730,000		.09	.20	.35	.50	1.10	15.00	
☐ 1929S 50,148,000		.06	.15	.23	.35	1.10	9.00	
☐ 1930 157,415,000		.06	.13	.23	.30	1.10	6.00	
☐ 1930D 40,100,000		.06	.13	.23	.35	1.10	11.00	
☐ 1930S 24,286,000		.06	.13	.23	.35	1.10	7.00	
☐ 1931 19,396,000		.14	.30	.75	1.00	2.00	16.00	
☐ 1931D 4,480,000		1.50	2.35	3.00	4.00	5.00	45.00	
☐ 1931S 866,000		13.00	25.00	30.00	36.00	45.00	72.00	
☐ 1932 9,062,000		.55	1.20	2.00	2.50	3.00	17.00	
☐ 1932D** 10,500,000		.25	.45	.90	1.20	1.80	15.00	
☐ 1933 14,360,000		.30	.60	1.15	1.70	2.50	16.00	
☐ 1933D 6,200,000		.80	1.75	2.30	2.90	4.00	22.00	
☐ 1934 219,080,000		.05	.11	.16	.28	.30	4.00	
☐ 1934D 28,446,000		.06	.11	.19	.28	.70	24.00	
☐ 1935 245,388,000		.06	.10	.15	.20	.30	2.00	
☐ 1935D 47,000,000		.06	.11	.19	.28	.50	5.50	
☐ 1935S 38,702,000		.06	.11	.19	.28	.50	11.00	
☐ 1936 309,637,569		.06	.10	.15	.20	.30	1.25	
☐ 1936D 40,620,000		.06	.12	.21	.30	.50	2.50	
☐ 1936S 29,130,000		.06	.12	.21	.30	.60	3.00	
☐ 1937 309,179,320		.03	.07	.12	.19	.30	1.50	160.00
☐ 1937D 50,430,000		.04	.08	.15	.22	.30	2.00	
☐ 1937S 35,500,000		.05	.10	.15	.22	.30	2.50	
☐ 1938 156,696,734		.03	.06	.13	.20	.28	1.75	100.00
☐ 1938D 20,010,000		.04	.10	.25	.45	.50	2.75	
☐ 1938S 15,180,000		.07	.20	.40	.55	.60	3.00	

*Beware of Removed Mintmark
**NOTE: More than 15,000 specimens of the 1932D cent were included in the Dr. Jerry Buss Collection, sold in 1985. This was the largest quantity ever sold at one time.

DATE	MINTAGE	ABP	G-4 Good	F-12 Fine	VF-20 V. Fine	EF-40 Ex. Fine	MS-60 Unc.	PRF-65 Proof
☐ 1939	316,479,520	.03	.06	.11	.15	.20	.75	85.00
☐ 1939D	15,160,000	.15	.30	.45	.55	.75	4.00	
☐ 1939S	52,070,000	.04	.10	.18	.25	.35	2.00	
☐ 1940	586,825,872	.03	.06	.11	.15	.20	.60	75.00
☐ 1940D	81,390,000	.03	.06	.11	.15	.20	1.50	
☐ 1940S	112,940,000	.03	.06	.11	.15	.20	2.00	
☐ 1941	887,039,100	.03	.06	.11	.15	.20	1.00	72.00
☐ 1941D	128,700,000	.03	.06	.11	.15	.20	3.00	
☐ 1941S	92,360,000	.04	.08	.11	.15	.20	3.90	
☐ 1942	657,828,600	.04	.06	.11	.15	.20	.70	72.00
☐ 1942D	206,698,000	.03	.06	.11	.15	.20	.90	
☐ 1942S	85,590,000	.03	.06	.11	.20	.30	4.50	
(1943 WARTIME STEEL COMPOSITION-STEEL COATED WITH ZINC)								
☐ 1943	684,628,670	.03	.06	.10	.15	.25	1.10	
☐ 1943D	217,660,000	.04	.10	.15	.20	.35	2.00	
☐ 1943S	191,550,000	.04	.10	.20	.30	.40	3.75	
(1944-1946 ''SHELL CASE'' COPPER COMPOSITION-95% COPPER AND 5% ZINC)								
☐ 1944	1,435,400,000	.05			.10	.15	.35	
☐ 1944D	430,578,000	.05			.10	.25	.70	
☐ 1944S	282,760,000	.06			.12	.20	.60	
☐ 1945	1,040,515,000	.03			.08	.10	.35	
☐ 1945D	226,268,000	.03			.08	.15	.60	
☐ 1945S	181,770,000	.03			.08	.15	.65	
☐ 1946	991,655,000	.03			.08	.10	.35	
☐ 1946D	315,690,000	.03			.08	.10	.40	
☐ 1946S	198,100,000	.03			.08	.15	.55	
(1947-1962 COMPOSITION-95% COPPER AND 5% TIN AND ZINC)								
☐ 1947	190,555,000	.02			.08	.15	.70	
☐ 1947D	194,750,000	.02			.08	.10	.50	
☐ 1947S	99,000,000	.02			.10	.15	.60	
☐ 1948	317,570,000	.02			.08	.10	.50	
☐ 1948D	172,637,500	.02			.12	.20	.65	
☐ 1948S	81,735,000	.02			.15	.25	.90	
☐ 1949	217,490,000	.02			.08	.15	1.10	
☐ 1949D	154,370,500	.02			.08	.15	.90	
☐ 1949S	64,290,000	.02			.10	.35	1.85	
☐ 1950	272,686,386	.02				.10	1.00	85.00
☐ 1950D	334,950,000	.02				.10	.75	
☐ 1950S	118,505,000	.02			.10	.15	.60	
☐ 1951	294,633,500	.02				.10	.80	50.00
☐ 1951D	625,355,000	.02				.10	.40	
☐ 1951S	100,890,000	.02			.10	.25	1.20	
☐ 1952	186,856,980	.02				.10	.70	35.00
☐ 1952D	746,130,000	.02				.10	.30	
☐ 1952S	137,800,004	.02			.10	.20	.85	
☐ 1953	256,883,800	.02				.10	.22	20.00
☐ 1953D	700,515,000	.02				.10	.20	
☐ 1953S	181,835,000	.02				.15	.48	
☐ 1954	71,873,350	.02			.12	.20	.48	10.00

DATE	MINTAGE	ABP	G-4 Good	F-12 Fine	VF-20 V. Fine	EF-40 Ex. Fine	MS-60 Unc.	PRF-65 Proof
☐ 1954D 251,552,500	.02					.10	.25	
☐ 1954S 96,190,000	.02				.08	.15	.40	
☐ 1955 330,958,200	.02					.10	.20	6.00
☐ 1955 Double Die	110.00			175.00	350.00	405.00	665.00	
☐ 1955D 563,257,500	.02					.07	.20	
☐ 1955S 44,610,000	.10			.15	.20	.25	.50	
☐ 1956 421,414,384	.02					.06	.15	3.00
☐ 1956D 1,098,201,100	.02					.06	.15	
☐ 1957 283,787,952	.02					.06	.15	2.00
☐ 1957D 1,051,342,000	.02					.06	.15	
☐ 1958 253,400,652	.02					.06	.15	3.00
☐ 1958D 800,953,000	.02					.06	.15	

LINCOLN MEMORIAL DESIGN

LINCOLN MEMORIAL — 1955 DOUBLE DIE — SMALL DATE — LARGE DATE

DATE	MINTAGE	ABP	EF-40 Ex. Fine	MS-60 Unc.	PRF-65 Proof
☐ 1959 610,864,291				.03	1.50
☐ 1959D 1,279,760,000				.03	
☐ 1960 Small Date	588,096,602	.25	1.00	2.20	18.00
☐ 1960 Large Date				.10	
☐ 1960D Small Date	1,580,884,000			.35	
☐ 1960D Large Date				.15	
☐ 1961 756,373,244				.04	1.25
☐ 1961D 1,753,266,700				.04	
(SEPTEMBER 1962-1981 COMPOSITION-95% COPPER AND 5% ZINC)					
☐ 1962 609,263,019				.04	1.25
☐ 1962D 1,793,148,400				.04	
☐ 1963 757,185,645				.04	1.25
☐ 1963D 1,744,020,400				.04	
☐ 1964 2,652,525,762				.04	1.25
☐ 1964D 3,799,071,500				.04	
☐ 1965 1,497,224,900				.04	
☐ 1966 2,188,147,783				.04	
☐ 1967 3,048,667,077				.04	
☐ 1968 1,707,880,965				.20	
☐ 1968D 2,886,269,590				.03	
☐ 1968S 261,311,500				.03	1.25
☐ 1969 1,136,910,000				.35	
☐ 1969D 4,002,832,200				.03	
☐ 1969S 547,309,631				.03	1.25
☐ 1970 1,898,315,000				.26	

DATE	MINTAGE	ABP	EF-40 Ex. Fine	MS-60 Unc.	PRF-65 Proof
☐ 1970D	2,891,438,900			.03	
☐ 1970S	693,192,814			.03	1.25
☐ 1970S Small Date		.25	.60	11.00	
☐ 1971	1,919,490,000			.16	
☐ 1971D	2,911,045,600			.08	
☐ 1971S	528,354,192			.16	1.25
☐ 1972	2,933,255,000			.03	
☐ 1972 Double Die		65.00	140.00	190.00	
☐ 1972D	2,665,071,400			.06	
☐ 1972S	380,200,104			.03	1.25
☐ 1973	3,728,245,000			.03	
☐ 1973D	3,549,576,588			.03	
☐ 1973S	319,937,634			.03	1.25
☐ 1974	4,232,140,523			.03	
☐ 1974D	4,235,098,000			.03	
☐ 1974S	412,039,228			.07	1.25
☐ 1975	4,505,275,300			.02	
☐ 1975D	5,505,275,300			.05	
☐ 1975S Proof Only	2,909,369				6.00
☐ 1976	4,674,292,426			.02	
☐ 1976D	4,221,595,455			.04	
☐ 1976S Proof Only	4,149,945				2.25
☐ 1977	4,469,972,000			.02	
☐ 1977D	4,149,055,800			.02	
☐ 1977S Proof Only	3,250,895				2.25
☐ 1978	5,266,905,000			.03	
☐ 1978D	4,280,233,400			.03	
☐ 1978S Proof	3,127,781				3.00
☐ 1979P	6,018,515,201			.02	
☐ 1979D	4,139,357,000			.02	
☐ 1979S Proof	3,677,200				3.10
☐ 1979S Proof (II)					3.35
☐ 1980	7,414,705,002			.02	
☐ 1980D	5,140,098,675			.02	
☐ 1980S Proof Only	3,547,130				1.60
☐ 1981	7,491,750,500			.02	
☐ 1981D	5,373,235,000			.02	
☐ 1981S Proof (I)	4,065,000				2.00
☐ 1981S Proof (II)					4.00
☐ 1982, Introduction of zinc cent	10,712,520,000			.02	
☐ 1982D	6,013,000			.02	
☐ 1982S Proof Only	3,857,480				3.25
☐ 1983*	7,752,354,900			.02	
☐ 1983D	6,468,000,000			.02	
☐ 1983S Proof Only	3,228,650				5.00
☐ 1984				.02	
☐ 1984D				.02	
☐ 1984S Proof Only				.02	5.00

NOTE: The 1982 cent was the first U.S. coin struck in a quantity of more than ten billion.
*Double die reverses occurred on some 1983 cents struck at Philadelphia. As yet these coins

have not established a clear market value. The doubling is very slight and for this reason the variety may not become popular with collectors.

TWO-CENT PIECES — TWO-CENT (BRONZE), 1864-1873

The two cent piece was a short-lived coin whose impact upon the world fell far short of its impact on modern numismatists. Small change was growing increasingly scarce during the Civil War, to the point where postage stamps, encased in holders, were being used for money. The government sought to alleviate this by increased production of the penny and introduced the two cent piece to take the penny's place in areas where it might not be in sufficient supply. Enormous quantities were struck at the outset, approaching 20 million per year, the composition being the same as that of the penny, 95% copper to 5% of tin and zinc. The diameter was 23 mm. Designer of the two cent piece was James Longacre, who did most of the Mint's designing at that time. There is no portrait on the coin; it carries a U.S. shield on one side and a value statement on the other. The lack of portraiture was undoubtedly an effort to prevent this coin from being confused with the penny. Though larger by 4 mm. in diameter than the penny, it must be remembered that large cents were still found in circulation in 1864 — they had been discontinued less than ten years earlier — and one almost needed a scoreboard to keep track of the denominations of coins passing through his hands. Production totals of the two cent piece decreased each year of its minting, until only 65,000 were turned out in 1872 and nothing but proofs and restrikes the following year. It died a very silent death.

1864 Small Motto

First Coin to Bear the Motto "In God We Trust"

1864 Large Motto

DATE	MINTAGE	ABP	G-4 Good	F-12 Fine	EF-40 Ex. Fine	MS-60 Unc.	PRF-65 Proof
☐ 1864 Small Motto }	19,847,500	27.00	55.00	90.00	230.00	460.00	12500.00
☐ 1864 Large Motto }		2.50	4.00	6.00	28.00	150.00	3250.00
☐ 1865	13,640,000	2.00	3.75	6.00	26.00	155.00	2875.00
☐ 1866	3,177,000	2.50	4.00	7.00	29.00	160.00	2875.00
☐ 1867	3,915,000	2.00	3.75	6.00	30.00	165.00	2875.00
☐ 1867 Double Die						EXTREMELY RARE	
☐ 1868	3,252,000	2.75	4.50	8.00	33.00	180.00	2875.00
☐ 1869	1,546,500	3.00	5.00	9.00	37.00	190.00	2875.00
☐ 1870	861,250	4.00	9.00	17.00	62.00	280.00	2875.00
☐ 1871	721,250	5.00	10.00	20.00	80.00	330.00	2875.00
☐ 1872	65,000	38.00	80.00	150.00	325.00	835.00	3000.00
☐ 1873 Closed 3	600	1250.00				PROOFS ONLY	3500.00
☐ 1873 Open 3 (Restrike)	480	1250.00				PROOFS ONLY	3750.00

THREE-CENT PIECES — THREE CENT (SILVER), 1851 - 1873

America's burgeoning population, plus conditions brought about by the California gold strike, resulted in a shortage of small change during the middle 19th century. The decision was made to strike a coin in three cents denomination and to have its composition of silver, alloyed with 25% copper. Because of its low face value and precious metal content the coin was extremely small physically. Its designer was James Longacre. Rather than portraiture, a symbolic obverse was used, consisting of a six-pointed star and shield. This was done to avoid confusion with the half dime, whose size and color were similar. On the reverse was the Roman numeral III enclosed within an ornamental letter C (for "cents") and surrounded by small stars. The weight was only 4/5th of a gram — the lightest coin ever struck by the Mint — with a diameter of just 14 mm. It was tiny indeed. Undoubtedly the government expected that this coin, despite serving an important purpose, would not prove popular. It didn't. After striking about 35 million in the first three years of its production, quantities were sharply reduced thereafter. It was subsequently replaced by the "nickel" 3¢ piece following the Civil War, which contained no silver whatever. Though the basic design of the silver three cent piece was maintained throughout its lifetime — they continued being struck until 1873, though rarely circulated after 1862 — some minor changes were introduced. In 1854 the obverse star was redrawn with a triple border. The final version, put into use in 1859, has a double border. As there are no great rarities among the circulating dates of this series, a complete collection is well within the realm of possibility. In 1854 there was a change of composition to 90% silver/10% copper and the weight was brought down to 3/4ths of a gram. From then until conclusion of the series all minting was carried out in Philadelphia. Previously the manufacture of this coin had been divided between Philadelphia and New Orleans.

The Mint Mark "O" is on the Reverse to the right of the III

DATE	MINTAGE	ABP	G-4 Good	F-12 Fine	EF-40 Ex. Fine	MS-60 Unc.	PRF-65 Proof
☐ 1851	5,447,400	5.00	10.00	15.00	50.00	235.00	
☐ 1851 0	720,000	7.00	15.00	29.00	110.00	500.00	
☐ 1852	18,663,500	4.50	9.00	14.00	50.00	235.00	
☐ 1853	11,400,000	4.50	9.00	14.00	50.00	235.00	
☐ 1854	671,000	5.00	10.00	18.00	80.00	400.00	
☐ 1855	139,000	9.00	19.00	39.00	140.00	550.00	6000.00
☐ 1856	1,458,000	5.00	10.00	16.00	80.00	400.00	5800.00
☐ 1857	1,042,000	4.75	9.00	16.00	83.00	415.00	5800.00

DATE	MINTAGE	ABP	G-4 Good	F-12 Fine	EF-40 Ex. Fine	MS-60 Unc.	PRF-65 Proof
☐ 1858	1,604,000	5.00	9.00	16.00	100.00	400.00	5600.00
☐ 1859	365,000	5.00	9.00	16.00	53.00	235.00	2525.00
☐ 1860	287,000	5.00	9.00	16.00	53.00	235.00	2525.00
☐ 1861	498,000	5.00	9.00	16.00	53.00	235.00	2525.00
☐ 1862	363,550	5.00	9.00	16.00	53.00	235.00	2525.00
☐ 1862, 2 over 1		5.50	11.00	18.00	135.00	375.00	2775.00
☐ 1863	21,460	375.00				575.00	2775.00
☐ 1863, 3 over 2		375.00				650.00	2900.00
☐ 1864	470	375.00				600.00	2825.00
☐ 1865	8,500	375.00				600.00	3000.00
☐ 1866	22,725	375.00				600.00	2800.00
☐ 1867	4,625	375.00				600.00	3100.00
☐ 1868	4,100	375.00				650.00	3100.00
☐ 1869	5,100	375.00				650.00	3100.00
☐ 1870	4,000	375.00				600.00	2900.00
☐ 1871	4,260	375.00				600.00	3000.00
☐ 1872	1,950	375.00				650.00	3200.00
☐ 1873	600	1650.00		PROOF ONLY			3500.00

THREE-CENT PIECES — THREE CENT (NICKEL), 1865 - 1889

For all practical purposes the three cent piece had been out of circulation during most of the Civil War. Upon the war's conclusion its manufacture was resumed, but no longer was the composition chiefly of silver. In fact the new version contained no precious metal at all. It was composed of 75% copper and 25% nickel. What the three cent piece lost metallically it gained physically: its weight more than doubled, rising to 1.94 grams, and its diameter increased to 17.0 mm. It may be wondered why a coin containing 75% copper would be referred to as a "nickel" rather than a "copper." The explanation is that the term "copper" was already in use for the cent. Americans picked up this nickname from the British, who had long been calling their pennies "coppers." As the new three cent coin represented the greatest use made of nickel by the Mint up to that time, the name "nickel" seemed appropriate. The coin was somewhat better received than its predecessor, as there was not so much danger of confusing it with another denomination. The fact that its life was not particularly long (it was discontinued in 1889) can be attributed more to inflation than any fault of its own. By 1889 there was simply no longer a pressing need for three cent pieces. At least 20 million were in circulation at that time and this was deemed more than enough to meet whatever demand might exist. The five cent piece, which began in 1866 to be composed of the same copper-nickel ratio as the three cent, was adequately filling whatever need the three cent had earlier satisfied.

The three cent Nickel carried a Liberty head on its obverse and a large Roman numeral III on the reverse. Like the silver version it was designed by James Longacre. All were struck at Philadelphia. Throughout the quarter-century of production no changes occured in its design.

DATE	MINTAGE	ABP	G-4 Good Fine	F-12 Fine	EF-40 Ex. Fine	MS-60 Unc.	PRF-65 Proof
☐ 1865	11,382,000	2.00	3.50	5.00	14.00	120.00	3450.00
☐ 1866	4,801,000	2.00	3.50	5.00	14.00	115.00	1500.00
☐ 1867	3,915,000	2.00	3.50	5.00	14.00	115.00	1425.00
☐ 1868	3,252,000	2.00	3.50	5.00	14.00	115.00	1425.00
☐ 1869	1,604,000	2.25	4.00	6.00	14.00	115.00	1425.00
☐ 1870	1,335,000	2.25	4.00	6.50	14.00	140.00	1425.00
☐ 1871	604,000	2.25	4.00	7.00	19.00	150.00	1425.00
☐ 1872	862,000	2.25	4.00	6.50	18.00	140.00	1425.00
☐ 1873 Closed 3 }	1,173,000	2.25	4.00	6.00	17.00	130.00	1425.00
☐ 1873 Open 3 }		2.25	4.00	6.00	17.00	130.00	1425.00
☐ 1874	790,000	2.25	4.00	6.00	17.00	140.00	1425.00
☐ 1875	228,000	3.00	7.00	11.00	30.00	180.00	1425.00
☐ 1876	162,000	4.50	10.00	15.00	32.00	180.00	1425.00
☐ 1877	510	1800.00		PROOF			3500.00
☐ 1878	2,350	800.00		PROOF			2500.00
☐ 1879	41,200	17.00	35.00	60.00	90.00	240.00	1675.00
☐ 1880	24,955	22.00	45.00	80.00	115.00	300.00	1775.00
☐ 1881	1,080,575	2.50	4.00	5.00	17.00	120.00	1500.00
☐ 1882	25,300	21.00	40.00	75.00	110.00	275.00	1735.00
☐ 1883	10,609	45.00	95.00	175.00	230.00	400.00	1735.00
☐ 1884	5,642	115.00	250.00	350.00	400.00	600.00	1735.00
☐ 1885	4,790	150.00	300.00	410.00	550.00	750.00	1850.00
☐ 1886	4,290	1150.00		PROOF			2250.00
☐ 1887	7,961	80.00	175.00	275.00	350.00	500.00	1850.00
☐ 1887 over 86		1150.00		PROOF			2350.00
☐ 1888	41,083	19.00	38.00	60.00	75.00	300.00	1850.00
☐ 1889	21,561	21.00	45.00	75.00	110.00	310.00	1850.00

A.B.P. is for coins in fine condition or better. Superbly struck uncirculated coins bring proportionately more than price listed.

NICKELS — SHIELD, 1866 - 1883

Though the silver half dime was still being struck in 1866 its production was too limited to serve as a general circulating coin. This noble old soldier, its origins dating back to the Mint's beginnings, was suffering the effects of general inflation and the bullion shortage of the Civil War, caused in part by a scarcity of laborers for the silver mines. Not knowing what the future might hold, the government had no wish to terminate the silver half dime but it wanted, at the same time, to introduce a coin of proportionate value made of base metal and attempt to popularize it. Thus was born the five cent piece Nickel or "true nickel," as opposed to the three cent coin that was also called a nickel. The five cent Nickel was authorized by Congress on May 16, 1866. It was to have a weight of 5 grams and be composed of three parts copper and one part nickel. The diameter was 20½ mm. James Longacre, chief engraver of the Mint, was called upon to design it and produced a portraitless coin consisting of a shielded obverse with arabic numeral "5" on the reverse surrounded by stars and rays (or bars). "IN GOD WE TRUST" appears on the obverse above the shield. Nearly 15,000,000 pieces were struck in the first year of issue. In the following year, 1867, after production had continued briefly, the rays were removed from the reverse, resulting in a rarity of moderate proportions for the "with rays" type. This is not, however, an expensive coin except in uncirculated condition. It may be asked why the 1867 variety with rays and the standard 1866 date are valued almost equally, when only 2,019,000 of the former and 14,742,500 of the latter were struck, yielding a scarcity ratio of 7-to-1. The answer is simply that the 1866 would *not* be worth so much, if it wasn't the first date of its series. There are many collectors buying "first dates" who buy no other coins of the series. For this reason the first year of minting of *any* U.S. coin carries a premium over and above the quantity struck or available in the market. (Compare the 1866 value with that of the 1872, of which fewer than half as many were struck; the former is more common but worth more.)

1866-83

1866-67
with rays

1867-83
without rays

DATE	MINTAGE	ABP	G-4 Good	F-12 Fine	EF-40 Ex. Fine	MS-60 Unc.	PRF-65 Proof
☐ 1866 w/rays	14,742,500	6.00	13.00	19.00	75.00	300.00	5750.00
☐ 1867 w/rays	30,909,500	6.00	13.00	21.00	85.00	350.00	10000.00
☐ 1867 no rays		3.50	7.00	9.00	29.00	160.00	2000.00
☐ 1868	28,817,000	3.00	5.50	9.00	28.00	155.00	1975.00
☐ 1869	16,395,000	2.75	5.00	9.00	28.00	155.00	1975.00
☐ 1870	4,806,000	2.75	5.00	11.00	35.00	170.00	1975.00
☐ 1871	561,000	11.00	21.00	40.00	95.00	300.00	2150.00
☐ 1872	6,036,000	3.50	6.00	11.00	40.00	190.00	1975.00
☐ 1873 closed 3	4,550,000	3.50	6.00	12.00	40.00	200.00	1975.00
☐ 1873 open 3		3.50	6.00	13.00	40.00	200.00	1975.00
☐ 1874	3,538,000	4.00	8.00	13.00	43.00	200.00	2000.00
☐ 1875	2,097,000	4.00	8.00	16.00	50.00	200.00	2000.00
☐ 1876	2,530,000	4.00	8.00	15.00	45.00	200.00	2000.00
☐ 1877	500	1300.00		PROOF			3250.00
☐ 1878	2,350	1000.00		PROOF			2750.00

DATE	MINTAGE	ABP	G-4 Good	F-12 Fine	EF-40 Ex. Fine	MS-60 Unc.	PRF-65 Proof
☐ 1879	29,100	100.00	200.00	320.00	475.00	600.00	2000.00
☐ 1879 9 over 8						EXTREMELY RARE	
☐ 1880	19,955	110.00	230.00	350.00	500.00	650.00	1950.00
☐ 1881	72,375	85.00	170.00	260.00	400.00	550.00	1950.00
☐ 1882	11,476,600	2.50	5.00	10.00	30.00	170.00	1925.00
☐ 1883	1,456,919	4.00	10.00	18.00	30.00	170.00	1900.00
☐ 1883 over 2		18.00	36.00	85.00	160.00	310.00	2500.00

NICKEL — LIBERTY HEAD, 1883 - 1912

When production of the silver half dime picturing Liberty ceased in the 1870's, designers were free to transfer the likeness of this goddess to our nickel five cent piece. This, however, was not immediately done and when finally undertaken in 1883 the portrait was not the full figure used for half dimes but a profile bust. The new design was created by Charles E. Barber and gained for this piece the name "Barber Nickel," which was once used commonly but seems to have lost popularity. Like its predecessor it was made of 75% copper and 25% nickel and had a weight of 5 grams. The diameter was slightly larger, measuring 21.2 mm., and striking was done at Philadelphia, Denver and San Francisco. An embarrassing difficulty occurred with this coin at the outset of production. As first designed the reverse carried the Roman numeral V (for 5) without the word "cents" or any sign indicating that cents was intended. Very shortly, unscrupulous persons began gilding the coin with gold wash and passing it to foreigners and other uninformed individuals as a $5 gold piece. The government put a halt to this acitivity by having the die re-engraved and the word "Cents" added. From then until 1913, when a new design was introduced (the famous Buffalo/Indian), no changes were made in designing. The Liberty Head was struck in great quantities throughout almost its entire run of production, with the total output reaching well into the hundreds of millions. It could still be found in general circulation, though not with much frequency, as late as the 1940's. The 1913 Liberty Head, America's most valuable base-metal coin, has long proved an enigma. The Mint claims not to have struck any Liberty Heads that year, asserting that its production consisted entirely of the Buffalo/Indian. It is certainly believable that no regular production occurred, otherwise the total in existence would not be as small as just five specimens. Even assuming that minting for the year was started with the Liberty Head design and was switched off to the new type after a few days, thousands of coins would by that time have been struck. There seems no logical way in which just five pieces could have been manufactured. The likelihood — though it may slightly tarnish this rarity's appeal — is that 1913 dies were produced, then put aside when the change of design was authorized and used (possibly clandestinely) to strike just a few specimens by a person or persons unknown. This theory is supported by the fact that originally, when first brought to public light, *all five* were owned by the same individual: Colonel Edward H. R. Green of New York, a noted collector of coins, stamps and art in the World War I era. If struck by the Mint and dispersed, it is almost beyond the realm of possibility that they could have been acquired by one collector within so short a period of time. (Colonel Green, incidentally, is equally noted for being the purchaser of the sheet of 24¢ inverted-center airmail stamps issued in 1918, which he *broke up and sold;* his approach to collecting was rather like that of a dealer or speculator, and one can only wonder at the reason for his association with the 1913 Liberty Head five cent piece.)

1883

Without "CENTS"

1887 Cents

DATE	MINTAGE	ABP	G-4 Good	F-12 Fine	EF-40 Ex. Fine	MS-60 Unc.	PRF-65 Proof
☐ 1883 no cents	5,479,519	1.00	2.20	3.50	7.00	40.00	1850.00
☐ 1883 w/cents	16,032,983	2.50	5.00	9.00	30.00	160.00	1350.00
☐ 1884	11,273,942	3.00	6.00	11.00	35.00	170.00	1350.00
☐ 1885	1,476,490	100.00	200.00	400.00	650.00	1100.00	2475.00
☐ 1886	3,330,290	20.00	40.00	100.00	200.00	450.00	1900.00
☐ 1887	15,263,652	2.25	4.50	10.00	32.00	175.00	1325.00
☐ 1888	10,720,483	3.00	6.00	12.00	39.00	175.00	1325.00
☐ 1889	15,881,361	2.00	4.00	9.00	31.00	175.00	1325.00
☐ 1890	16,259,272	2.00	4.00	10.00	31.00	175.00	1325.00
☐ 1891	16,834,350	1.75	3.50	8.00	31.00	175.00	1475.00
☐ 1892	11,699,642	2.00	4.00	9.00	31.00	175.00	1475.00
☐ 1893	13,370,195	1.75	3.50	8.00	31.00	175.00	1475.00
☐ 1894	5,413,132	2.50	5.00	11.00	45.00	180.00	1475.00
☐ 1895	9,979,884	1.75	3.50	8.00	28.00	175.00	1475.00
☐ 1896	8,842,920	2.00	4.00	9.00	32.00	180.00	1475.00
☐ 1897	20,428,735	.50	1.10	3.00	20.00	140.00	1475.00
☐ 1898	12,532,087	.50	1.15	3.00	18.00	150.00	1475.00
☐ 1899	26,029,031	.25	.50	1.75	18.00	123.00	1475.00
☐ 1900	27,255,995	.25	.50	1.75	18.00	123.00	1475.00
☐ 1901	26,480,213	.25	.50	1.75	18.00	123.00	1475.00
☐ 1902	31,480,579	.25	.50	1.75	18.00	123.00	1375.00
☐ 1903	28,006,725	.25	.50	1.75	18.00	123.00	1375.00
☐ 1904	21,404,984	.25	.50	1.75	18.00	123.00	1375.00
☐ 1905	29,827,276	.25	.50	1.75	18.00	123.00	1375.00
☐ 1906	38,613,725	.25	.50	1.75	18.00	123.00	1375.00
☐ 1907	39,214,800	.25	.50	1.75	18.00	123.00	1375.00
☐ 1908	22,686,177	.25	.50	1.75	18.00	123.00	1375.00
☐ 1909	11,590,526	.25	.50	1.75	18.00	123.00	1375.00

DATE	MINTAGE	ABP	G-4 Good	F-12 Fine	EF-40 Ex. Fine	MS-60 Unc.	PRF-65 Proof
☐ 1910	30,169,353	.25	.50	1.75	18.00	123.00	1400.00
☐ 1911	39,559,372	.25	.50	1.75	18.00	123.00	1400.00
☐ 1912	26,236,714	.25	.50	1.75	18.00	123.00	1400.00
☐ 1912D	8,474,000	.50	1.00	2.50	40.00	230.00	
☐ 1912S	238,000	23.00	45.00	65.00	330.00	600.00	
☐ 1913* Not a Regular Mint Issue—5 Known—BUSS SALE 1985							350,000.00

NICKELS — BUFFALO OR INDIAN HEAD, 1913 - 1938

Undoubtedly the most dramatic, artistic and original set of designs employed for a U.S. coin, the Buffalo/Indian Head Nickel went into production in 1913. The composition was 75% copper and 25% nickel, with a weight of five grams. Its diameter was 21.2 mm. James E. Fraser, the designer, was not one to go half way. He hired an Indian to sit for the obverse portrait and took his sketching gear to the Bronx Zoo to get a likeness of a buffalo in the flesh. The artwork of this coin is little short of superb: each motif fully fills the planchet ground and is unencumbered by large inscriptions or miscellaneous symbols. Unfortunately the rate of wear in handling was such that few individuals aside from collectors had the opportunity to see the coin at its best. Just like the noble animal it pictured, the American bison, this coin proved to be a rapidly disappearing species. Within only 20 years after its discontinuation in 1938 it had all but vanished from circulation, despite enormous production output. Critics of the Buffalo/Indian Head Nickel were few. Those who spoke against it raised the objection that the buffalo was endangered by extinction because of its hunting by the Indians, and that to place both on the same coin was similar to picturing a woolly mastodon and a caveman. However, the intent, very well accomplished, was to use the medium of coinage to portray a subject genuinely Amercan rather than endlessly repeating such symbols of foreign origin as Liberty. So popular did the bison likeness become that the coin, unlike most others, came to be popularly known by its reverse rather than its obverse. In 1916 a Double Die error resulted on some specimens, producing a twin or ghost impression of the date. Of regularly struck pieces, those from the San Francisco mint in the early and middle 1920's are scarcest.

1913-1938

1913-
Type I
Buffalo on high mound

Mint Mark
is on the
Reverse, under
"Five Cents"

1913
Type 2
Buffalo on Level Ground

DATE	MINTAGE	ABP	G-4 Good	F-12 Fine	EF-40 Ex. Fine	MS-60 Unc.	PRF-65 Proof
☐ 1913 Type-1	30,993,520	1.15	2.50	4.00	12.00	30.00	3000.00
☐ 1913D Type-1	5,337,000	2.00	4.00	8.00	21.00	65.00	
☐ 1913S Type-1	2,105,000	4.00	8.00	15.00	38.00	95.00	
☐ 1913 Type-2	29,858,700	1.50	3.00	4.50	10.00	31.00	2800.00
☐ 1913D Type-2	4,156,000	15.00	30.00	45.00	80.00	185.00	
☐ 1913S Type-2	1,209,000	30.00	60.00	110.00	180.00	315.00	
☐ 1914	20,665,738	1.50	3.00	5.00	13.00	55.00	2750.00
☐ 1914D	3,912,000	10.00	20.00	40.00	90.00	235.00	
☐ 1914S	3,470,000	2.50	5.00	9.00	32.00	100.00	
☐ 1915	20,987,270	1.00	2.00	4.00	11.00	50.00	2900.00
☐ 1915D	7,569,500	2.50	5.00	12.50	45.00	130.00	
☐ 1915S	1,505,000	5.00	10.00	20.00	90.00	240.00	
☐ 1916 Double Die Obverse		90.00	170.00	420.00	900.00	2500.00	
☐ 1916	63,498,000	.35	.75	1.50	4.50	35.00	3100.00
☐ 1916D	13,333,000	2.00	4.00	8.00	42.00	140.00	
☐ 1916S	11,860,000	1.50	3.00	6.00	42.00	135.00	
☐ 1917	51,424,029	.40	.80	1.85	8.00	42.00	
☐ 1917D	9,910,800	2.50	5.00	10.00	70.00	200.00	
☐ 1917S	4,193,000	3.00	6.00	11.00	65.00	225.00	
☐ 1918	32,086,314	.65	1.00	2.00	14.00	70.00	
☐ 1918D	8,362,000	2.00	4.50	19.00	80.00	280.00	
☐ 1918D over 17		190.00	375.00	800.00	2375.00	7500.00	
☐ 1918S	4,882,000	2.00	4.50	9.00	75.00	240.00	
☐ 1919	60,868,000	.30	.60	1.00	6.00	37.00	
☐ 1919D	8,006,000	2.00	5.00	12.00	95.00	330.00	
☐ 1919S	7,521,000	1.75	2.50	7.00	72.00	270.00	
☐ 1920	63,093,000	.25	.50	1.00	7.00	39.00	
☐ 1920D	9,418,000	2.00	4.00	8.00	85.00	300.00	
☐ 1920S	9,689,000	1.00	2.00	5.00	75.00	185.00	
☐ 1921	10,683,000	.50	1.00	2.00	16.00	78.00	
☐ 1921S	1,557,000	6.00	13.00	30.00	275.00	625.00	
☐ 1923	35,715,000	.25	.50	1.00	6.00	37.00	
☐ 1923S	6,142,000	1.00	2.00	4.00	45.00	125.00	
☐ 1924	21,620,000	.25	.50	1.30	8.00	50.00	
☐ 1924D	5,258,000	1.00	2.00	6.00	70.00	185.00	
☐ 1924S	1,437,000	3.00	5.00	12.00	300.00	700.00	
☐ 1925	35,565,100	.25	.50	1.00	6.00	35.00	
☐ 1925D	4,450,000	2.00	4.50	9.00	75.00	275.00	
☐ 1925S	6,256,000	1.25	2.50	5.00	45.00	195.00	
☐ 1926	44,693,000	.20	.40	.80	4.00	32.00	
☐ 1926D	5,638,000	1.50	3.00	8.00	80.00	140.00	
☐ 1926S	970,000	2.50	5.00	11.00	250.00	600.00	
☐ 1927	37,981,000	.25	.50	.75	4.00	32.00	
☐ 1927D	5,730,000	.60	1.20	2.50	35.00	90.00	
☐ 1927S	3,430,000	.50	1.00	2.00	45.00	160.00	
☐ 1928	23,411,000	.25	.50	.85	4.00	35.00	
☐ 1928D	6,436,000	.40	.80	2.00	11.00	50.00	
☐ 1928S	6,936,000	.30	.60	1.50	9.00	65.00	
☐ 1929	36,446,000	.25	.50	.85	4.00	28.00	

DATE	MINTAGE	ABP	G-4 Good	F-12 Fine	EF-40 Ex. Fine	MS-60 Unc.	PRF-65 Proof
☐ 1929D	8,370,000	.40	.75	1.30	9.75	50.00	
☐ 1929S	7,754,000	.25	.50	.75	8.00	40.00	
☐ 1930	22,849,000	.25	.50	.75	3.00	28.00	
☐ 1930S	5,435,000	.30	.60	1.00	6.00	46.00	
☐ 1931S	1,200,000	1.00	2.50	3.60	10.00	53.00	
☐ 1934	20,313,000	.25	.50	.75	4.00	27.00	
☐ 1934D	7,480,000	.25	.50	.80	7.00	50.00	
☐ 1935	58,264,000	.15	.30	.50	2.00	18.00	
☐ 1935D	12,092,000	.30	.60	1.00	6.00	45.00	
☐ 1935S	10,300,000	.25	.50	.75	4.00	25.00	
☐ 1936	119,001,420	.20	.35	.60	2.00	15.00	2500.00
☐ 1936D	24,418,000	.20	.45	.65	4.00	18.00	
☐ 1936S	14,390,000	.20	.40	.55	2.75	18.00	
☐ 1937	79,485,769	.20	.30	.50	2.00	12.00	2400.00
☐ 1937D	17,826,000	.20	.30	.55	2.00	15.00	
☐ 1937D—3 Legged Buffalo*		35.00	70.00	125.00	200.00	500.00	
☐ 1937S	5,635,000	.20	.35	.65	2.25	14.00	
☐ 1938D	7,020,000	.20	.35	.60	2.00	12.00	
☐ 1938D over S		1.25	2.50	6.00	9.00	22.00	

*Beware of altered coins

NICKELS — JEFFERSON, 1938 to Date

In 1938 Thomas Jefferson became the third President to be pictured on an American coin (preceded by Lincoln and Washington), when his likeness was installed on the five cent piece replacing the Buffalo/Indian Head. When the decision was made to use Jefferson's portrait on this coin a public competition was instituted to select the best design, accompanied by an award of $1,000. A total of 390 entries was received, the winning one being that of Felix Schlag. Jefferson is shown in profile facing left on the obverse with his home at Monticello pictured on the reverse. No alteration has ever been made in the design of this coin but some changes occurred in composition and modeling of the dies. In 1966 Schlag's initials were added, the feeling being that he deserved this honor as much as the designer of the Lincoln Cent, whose initials were incorporated into the design. The coin has always weighed five grams and measured 21.1 mm. Originally its content was 75% copper and 25% nickel. Due to a shortage of nickel during World War II, because of its use in military production, this metal was entirely removed from the coin in 1942 and substituted by a composition of 56% copper, 35% silver and 9% manganese. Wartime nickels consequently carry a premium value because of their silver content, though the silver additive was so small that the premium is only minimal. In 1946 the pre-war composition was resumed, and has since remained constant. Prior to 1968 the mint mark was on the reverse, to the right of the design. On wartime specimens (1942-45) it is considerably enlarged and placed above Monticello's dome. From 1968 on it appears on the obverse between the date and portrait.

Mint Mark
from 1968

Felix
Schlag
(after 1966)

1938-1942,
1946 to 1968

1942-1945
Silver Content Type with
Large Mint Mark over Dome

DATE	MINTAGE	ABP	G-4 Good	F-12 Fine	EF-40 Ex. Fine	MS-60 Unc.	PRF-65 Proof
☐ 1938	19,515,365	.07	.15	.30	.60	2.00	75.00
☐ 1938D	5,376,000	.35	.75	1.10	2.00	5.00	
☐ 1938S	4,105,000	.60	1.25	1.75	3.00	6.50	
☐ 1939	120,627,535	.10	.18	.20	.40	1.75	70.00
☐ 1939D	3,514,000	1.75	3.50	4.50	7.50	35.00	
☐ 1939S	6,630,000	.25	.50	.75	3.00	20.00	
☐ 1940	176,499,158				.30	1.00	55.00
☐ 1940D	43,540,000				.45	2.00	
☐ 1940S	39,690,000				.50	2.00	
☐ 1941	203,283,730				.20	1.00	50.00
☐ 1941D	53,432,000				.40	3.00	
☐ 1941S	43,445,000				.40	3.50	
☐ 1942	49,818,600				.30	1.40	50.00
☐ 1942D	13,938,000	.10	.20	.40	2.00	21.00	
WARTIME SILVER NICKELS							
☐ 1942P	57,900,600	.20	.25	.45	2.25	9.00	265.00
☐ 1942S	32,900,000	.20	.25	.45	1.70	8.00	
☐ 1943P	271,165,000	.20	.25	.45	1.35	3.50	
☐ 1943D	15,294,000	.20	.25	.45	1.70	3.75	
☐ 1943S	104,060,000	.20	.25	.45	1.70	4.00	
☐ 1944P	119,150,000	.20	.25	.45	1.70	4.50	
☐ 1944D	32,309,000	.20	.25	.45	1.70	8.00	
☐ 1944S	21,640,000	.20	.25	.45	1.70	7.50	
☐ 1945P	119,408,100	.20	.25	.45	1.70	6.00	
☐ 1945D	37,158,000	.20	.25	.45	1.70	5.00	
☐ 1945S	58,939,000	.20	.25	.45	1.70	3.75	
REGULAR PRE-WAR TYPE							
☐ 1946	161,116,000				.22	.50	
☐ 1946D	45,292,200				.27	.70	
☐ 1946S	13,560,000				.45	.70	
☐ 1947	95,000,000				.20	.45	
☐ 1947D	37,882,000				.30	.65	
☐ 1947S	24,720,000			.12	.25	.65	
☐ 1948	89,348,000				.20	.40	
☐ 1948D	44,734,000			.15	.40	1.00	

DATE	MINTAGE	ABP	G-4 Good	F-12 Fine	EF-40 Ex. Fine	MS-60 Unc.	PRF-65 Proof
☐ 1948S	11,300,000			.25	.50	1.00	
☐ 1949	60,652,000				.25	.90	
☐ 1949D	36,498,000			.20	.30	1.00	
☐ 1949, "D" over "S"				22.00	80.00	350.00	
☐ 1949S	9,716,000	.10	.20	.30	.70	1.75	
☐ 1950	9,847,386	.15	.30	.45	.80	1.50	60.00
☐ 1950D	2,530,000	3.00	4.50	5.50	6.50	8.00	
☐ 1951	28,689,500				.30	.90	45.00
☐ 1951D	20,460,000				.30	.90	
☐ 1951S	7,776,000	.10	.25	.50	.80	2.20	
☐ 1952	64,069,980				.15	.60	30.00
☐ 1952D	30,638,000			.20	.30	1.50	
☐ 1952S	20,572,000			.10	.25	.85	
☐ 1953	46,772,800				.15	.40	19.00
☐ 1953D	59,878,600				.20	.30	
☐ 1953S	19,210,900			.15	.25	.45	
☐ 1954	47,917,350					.20	9.00
☐ 1954D	117,183,060					.30	
☐ 1954S	29,834,000			.10	.20	.35	
☐ 1954, S over D				6.00	16.00	32.00	
☐ 1955	8,266,200	.10	.30	.45	.60	1.00	6.00
☐ 1955D	74,464,100					.25	
☐ 1955, D over S				5.00	14.00	24.00	
☐ 1956	35,885,384					.25	2.50
☐ 1956D	67,222,940					.25	
☐ 1957	39,655,952					.25	1.80
☐ 1957D	136,828,900					.25	
☐ 1958	17,963,653					.32	2.75
☐ 1958D	168,249,120					.23	
☐ 1959	28,397,291					.23	1.15
☐ 1959D	160,738,240		Circulated			.23	
☐ 1960	57,107,602		Coins			.23	.85
☐ 1960D	192,582,180		of			.23	
☐ 1961	76,668,344		these			.23	.85
☐ 1961D	229,342,760		Dates			.23	
☐ 1962	100,602,019		are			.23	.85
☐ 1962D	280,195,720		not			.23	
☐ 1963	178,851,645		Bought			.23	.85
☐ 1963D	276,829,460		by			.23	
☐ 1964	1,028,622,762		Dealers			.23	.85
☐ 1964D	1,787,297,160					.23	
☐ 1965	136,131,380					.16	
☐ 1966	156,208,283					.16	
☐ 1967	107,324,750					.16	
☐ 1968D	91,227,800					.16	
☐ 1968S	103,437,510					.16	.85
☐ 1969D	202,807,500					.16	
☐ 1969S	128,099,631					.16	.85

DATE	MINTAGE	ABP	G-4 Good	F-12 Fine	EF-40 Ex. Fine	MS-60 Unc.	PRF-65 Proof
☐1970D	515,485,380					.16	
☐1970S	241,464,814					.16	1.15
☐1971	108,884,000					.20	
☐1971D	316,144,800					.16	
☐1971S	3,224,138					1.50	
☐1972	202,036,000					.16	
☐1972D	351,694,600					.16	
☐1972S	3,267,667						1.15
☐1973	384,396,000					.15	
☐1973D	261,405,400					.15	
☐1973S Proof Only	2,769,624						1.15
☐1974	601,752,000					.15	
☐1974D	277,373,000			Circulated		.15	
☐1974S Proof Only	2,617,350			Coins			1.35
☐1975	181,772,000			of		.15	
☐1975D	401,875,300			these		.15	
☐1975S Proof Only	2,909,369			Dates			1.00
☐1976	376,124,000			are		.15	
☐1976D	563,964,147			not		.15	
☐1976S Proof Only	4,149,945			Bought			.65
☐1977	585,175,250			by		.15	
☐1977D	297,325,618			Dealers		.15	
☐1977S Proof Only	3,250,095						.75
☐1978	391,308,000					.15	
☐1978D	313,092,780					.15	
☐1978S Proof Only	3,127,781						1.00
☐1979	463,188,123					.12	
☐1979D	325,867,600					.12	
☐1979S Proof (I)	3,677,200						1.20
☐1979S Proof (II)							2.50
☐1980P	593,004,060					.12	
☐1980D	502,324,000					.12	
☐1980S Proof Only	3,554,800						.90
☐1981P	657,503,295					.12	
☐1981D	364,802,000					.12	
☐1981S Proof (I)	4,000,000						.90
☐1981S Proof (II)							2.00
☐1982P	292,350,000					.12	
☐1982D	373,725,500					.12	
☐1982S Proof (I)	3,856,995						2.25
☐1982S Proof (II)							3.25
☐1983P	560,750,000					.12	
☐1983D						.12	
☐1983S Proof	3,228,537						.80

HALF DIMES, 1794 - 1873

The first half dimes did not technically reach manufacture until 1795 but carried a 1794 date as the dies had been engraved that year and there was no desire to redo this work. The weight was 1.35 grams, the composition consisting of .8924 silver and .1076 copper; or, to speak in rounded figures, nine parts silver to one part copper. After more than 40 years of being unchanged compositionally the silver content was raised to a full nine parts in 1837, which necessitated a weight reduction to 1.34 grams. The original obverse type was the Flowing Hair Liberty, similar to that of other silver coinage of the time. Its designer was Robert Scot. On the reverse appeared the standing eagle and legend "UNITED STATES OF AMERICA." This was replaced by the Draped Bust type with similar reverse in 1796, and the shield eagle reverse in 1800. Beginning in 1829 the Capped Bust was introduced, along with a modified version of the shield eagle (wings downward instead of upturned). The sharpest departure occured in 1837, with the introduction of a design that was to remain — with modifications — until the series closed out in 1873. This was the Seated Liberty, an attractive bit of classical portraiture but one to which some objection was voiced, on grounds that it closely resembled the figure of Britannia on British coins. The reverse carried the wording "HALF DIME" within an open wreath, encircled by "UNITED STATES OF AMERICA." There was initially no decoration of the obverse beyond the figure of Liberty. In 1838 a series of stars was added as a half-frame to the portrait. Arrows were placed by the date in 1853. The chief revision came in 1860 when the words "UNITED STATES OF AMERICA" were removed from the reverse and placed on the obverse, supplanting the stars. The reverse wreath was redesigned and made larger and frillier to fill the vacancy.

1794-1795 HALF DIMES, LIBERTY WITH FLOWING HAIR

DATE	MINTAGE	ABP	G-4 Good	F-12 Fine	VF-20 V. Fine
☐1794 ⎰	86,416	450.00	750.00	1500.00	2275.00
☐1795 ⎱		375.00	650.00	1075.00	1700.00

(Both the 1794 and 1795 were struck in 1795)

HALF DIMES — DRAPED BUST, SMALL EAGLE, 1796 - 1797

DATE	MINTAGE	ABP	G-4 Good	F-12 Fine	VF-20 V. Fine
☐ 1796 over 5 ⎫		425.00	800.00	1275.00	2000.00
☐ 1796 ⎬	10,230	385.00	750.00	1250.00	1925.00
☐ 1796 LIKERTY ⎭		425.00	800.00	1300.00	2100.00
☐ 1797 (13 stars) ⎫		430.00	800.00	1325.00	1925.00
☐ 1797 (15 stars) ⎬	44,527	385.00	750.00	1225.00	1825.00
☐ 1797 (16 stars) ⎭		385.00	750.00	1275.00	1825.00

HALF DIMES — DRAPED BUST, LARGE EAGLE, 1800 - 1805

DATE	MINTAGE	ABP	G-4 Good	F-12 Fine	VF-20 V. Fine
☐ 1800 ⎫		300.00	600.00	800.00	1225.00
☐ 1800 LIBEKTY ⎬	24,000	300.00	600.00	850.00	1300.00
☐ 1801	33,910	300.00	600.00	900.00	1500.00
☐ 1802 (Very Rare)	13,010	1550.00	3375.00	8000.00	12500.00
☐ 1803	37,850	275.00	550.00	950.00	1350.00
☐ 1805	15,600	325.00	700.00	1000.00	1900.00

HALF DIMES — LIBERTY CAP, 1829 - 1837

DATE	MINTAGE	ABP	G-4 Good	F-12 Fine	EF-40 Ex. Fine	MS-60 Unc.
☐ 1829	1,230,000	6.00	12.00	22.50	95.00	475.00
☐ 1830	1,240,000	6.00	12.00	22.50	95.00	475.00
☐ 1831	1,242,700	6.00	12.00	22.50	95.00	475.00
☐ 1832	965,000	6.00	12.00	22.50	95.00	475.00
☐ 1833	1,370,000	6.00	12.00	22.50	95.00	475.00
☐ 1834	1,480,000	6.00	12.00	22.50	95.00	475.00
☐ 1835*	2,760,000	6.00	12.00	22.50	95.00	475.00
☐ 1836	1,900,000	6.00	12.00	22.50	95.00	475.00
☐ 1837 large $.05	2,276,000	6.00	12.00	22.50	95.00	475.00
☐ 1837 small $.05		13.00	25.00	60.00	300.00	1625.00

*1835 Large Date — Large $.05, Large Date — Small $.05, Same prices.
 Small Date — Small $.05, Small Date — Large $.05, Same prices.

HALF DIMES — LIBERTY SEATED, 1837 - 1859

1837-1839O
no Stars

1838-1859
with Stars

1837-1859

Mint Mark is on the Reverse under the Value

DATE	MINTAGE	ABP	G-4 Good	F-12 Fine	EF-40 Ex. Fine	MS-60 Unc.	PRF-65 Proof
☐ 1837 Small Date, No Stars	} 2,250,000	14.00	28.00	58.00	210.00	575.00	
☐ 1837 Large Date, No Stars		13.00	25.00	52.00	200.00	535.00	
☐ 1838O No Stars	70,000	45.00	85.00	160.00	700.00	2175.00	
☐ 1838 w/Stars	2,255,000	3.00	5.50	10.00	60.00	450.00	
☐ 1839	1,069,150	3.00	5.50	10.00	60.00	365.00	
☐ 1839O	1,096,550	5.00	10.00	19.00	70.00	500.00	
☐ 1840 No Drapery	1,344,085	3.00	6.00	11.00	55.00	490.00	
☐ 1840 Drapery		10.00	25.00	55.00	210.00	900.00	
☐ 1840O Drapery		20.00	35.00	90.00	390.00	2150.00	
☐ 1840O No Drapery		5.00	10.00	22.00	75.00	650.00	
☐ 1841	1,500,000	3.00	6.00	11.00	50.00	250.00	
☐ 1841O	815,000	4.00	8.00	21.00	70.00	650.00	
☐ 1842	815,000	3.00	6.00	10.00	50.00	265.00	
☐ 1842O	350,000	15.00	29.00	60.00	370.00		
☐ 1843	1,165,000	3.00	6.00	11.00	50.00	245.00	
☐ 1844	430,000	3.00	6.00	11.00	53.00	335.00	
☐ 1844O	220,000	35.00	85.00	200.00	800.00		
☐ 1845	1,564,000	3.00	6.00	11.00	50.00	245.00	
☐ 1846	27,000	65.00	130.00	290.00	700.00		
☐ 1847	1,274,000	3.00	6.00	11.00	50.00	245.00	
☐ 1848 (Medium Date)	} 668,000	3.00	6.00	12.00	55.00	245.00	
☐ 1848 (Large Date)		11.00	21.00	45.00	110.00	375.00	
☐ 1848D	600,000	6.50	12.00	28.00	90.00	650.00	
☐ 1849	1,309,000	3.00	6.00	11.00	50.00	600.00	
☐ 1849 over 46	1,309,000	6.00	12.00	15.00	75.00	450.00	
☐ 1849 over 48	1,309,000	7.00	14.00	27.00	100.00	550.00	
☐ 1849O	140,000	16.00	30.00	65.00	400.00		
☐ 1850	955,000	3.00	6.00	11.00	50.00	300.00	
☐ 1850O	690,000	7.00	14.00	27.00	150.00	820.00	
☐ 1851	781,000	3.00	6.00	11.00	50.00	300.00	
☐ 1851O	860,000	5.00	9.00	25.00	100.00	700.00	
☐ 1852	1,000,000	3.00	6.00	11.00	50.00	275.00	
☐ 1852O	260,000	14.00	29.00	72.00	275.00		

DATE	MINTAGE	ABP	G-4 Good	F-12 Fine	EF-40 Ex. Fine	MS-60 Unc.	PRF-65 Proof
☐ 1853 w/arrows	13,210,020	3.00	5.00	8.00	45.00	310.00	4750.00
☐ 1853 no arrows	135,000	11.00	25.00	53.00	170.00	675.00	
☐ 1853O w/arrows	2,360,000	4.00	7.00	10.00	50.00	425.00	
☐ 1853O no arrows	160,000	80.00	150.00	275.00	750.00		
☐ 1854 w/arrows	5,740,000	3.00	5.00	8.00	45.00	4750.00	4750.00
☐ 1854O w/arrows	1,560,000	4.50	8.00	11.00	85.00	650.00	
☐ 1855 w/arrows	1,750,000	3.00	5.00	8.00	50.00	280.00	4750.00
☐ 1855O w/arrows	600,000	7.00	14.00	25.00	90.00	750.00	
☐ 1856	4,880,000	3.00	5.00	8.00	35.00	250.00	6500.00
☐ 1856O	1,100,000	6.00	13.00	28.00	110.00	900.00	
☐ 1857	7,280,000	3.00	5.00	8.00	40.00	250.00	3800.00
☐ 1857O	1,380,000	5.00	10.00	15.00	75.00	675.00	
☐ 1858	3,500,000	3.00	5.00	8.00	45.00	250.00	3800.0C
☐ 1858 over inverted date		17.00	36.00	75.00	215.00	700.00	
☐ 1858O	1,660,000	4.50	9.00	15.00	75.00	600.00	
☐ 1859 +	340,000	5.00	11.00	30.00	260.00	3800.00	3800.00
☐ 1859O	560,000	7.00	16.00	25.00	85.00	650.00	

+ There are two recognized patterns in this series, the transitional pieces of 1859 and 1860:
1859 — proof: $8,750.00   1860 — unc: $3,250

HALF DIMES — LIBERTY SEATED, 1860-1873
with "UNITED STATES OF AMERICA" on Obverse

Mint Marks are Under or Within Wreath on Reverse

DATE	MINTAGE	ABP	G-4 Good	F-12 Fine	EF-40 Ex. Fine	MS-60 Unc.	PRF-65 Proof
☐ 1860 Legend	799,000	2.75	5.00	10.00	35.00	250.00	850.00
☐ 1860O	1,060,000	2.75	5.00	18.00	50.00	310.00	
☐ 1861	3,361,000	2.75	5.00	9.50	32.00	220.00	850.00
☐ 1862	1,492,550	2.75	5.00	9.50	32.00	220.00	850.00
☐ 1863	18,460	50.00	100.00	170.00	350.00	400.00	850.00
☐ 1863S	100,000	7.00	15.00	35.00	140.00	750.00	
☐ 1864	48,470	120.00	230.00	300.00	500.00	1475.00	850.00
☐ 1864S	90,000	12.00	27.00	70.00	260.00		
☐ 1865	13,500	85.00	170.00	260.00	510.00	1075.00	850.00
☐ 1865S	120,000	6.00	13.00	30.00	130.00	850.00	
☐ 1866	10,725	80.00	160.00	250.00	420.00	700.00	850.00

DATE	MINTAGE	ABP	G-4 Good	F-12 Fine	EF-40 Ex. Fine	MS-60 Unc.	PRF-65 Proof
☐ 1866S	120,000	6.50	12.00	30.00	130.00	800.00	
☐ 1867	8,625	115.00	280.00	375.00	500.00	900.00	850.00
☐ 1867S	120,000	7.00	15.00	30.00	140.00	750.00	
☐ 1868	89,200	13.00	25.00	70.00	200.00	650.00	850.00
☐ 1868S	280,000	3.00	6.00	10.00	70.00	675.00	
☐ 1869	280,000	3.00	6.00	20.00	65.00	380.00	850.00
☐ 1869S	230,000	3.00	6.00	10.00	70.00	500.00	
☐ 1870*	536,000	2.50	5.50	11.00	40.00	250.00	850.00
☐ 1871	1,873,960	2.50	5.50	9.00	40.00	230.00	850.00
☐ 1871S	161,000	6.00	12.00	35.00	75.00	400.00	
☐ 1872	2,947,950	2.50	5.00	8.00	40.00	235.00	850.00
☐ 1872S in wreath	837,000	3.00	6.00	10.00	36.00	235.00	
☐ 1872S below wreath		3.00	6.00	10.00	40.00	235.00	
☐ 1873	712,600	2.50	5.00	8.00	42.00	235.00	850.00
☐ 1873S	324,000	3.00	6.00	10.00	40.00	290.00	

*1870S is unique — only one known. Private Sale 1980 — $425,000.00

DIMES — EARLY DIMES, 1796 - 1891

A coin valued at 1/10th of a dollar was among the first to be authorized by the U.S. Mint, though production did not begin until 1796. Had the dime made its debut even just a year sooner there is every likelihood it would have carried the Flowing Hair design, but by 1796 there was no longer much enthusiasm for this rendition of Liberty and so the coin got its start with the Draped Bust portrait. This version of Liberty, familiar on other silver pieces, lacks the "cap of liberty" and shows the goddess with a somewhat more fashionable hairdo. On the reverse was the standing eagle, encircled by branches and the inscription "UNITED STATES OF AMERICA." Stars were placed in circular pattern on the obverse, ranging in number from 13 to 16. The designer was Robert Scot. The weight of this coin was 2.70 grams and its original composition was .8924 silver and .1076 copper, the same as that of the Half Dime (or, approximately, nine parts of silver to one part of copper). Its diameter was generally 19 mm. but slight variations are observed. In 1798 the standing eagle was replaced by the heraldic or shield eagle on the reverse, over which is a series of stars. Just like the stars on the original obverse, these too can vary in quantity from 13 to 16. In 1809 the portrait was changed to the Capped Bust, whose chief characteristic (aside from Liberty's headgear) is that the profile is switched round to face left instead of right. The reverse type is now the eagle-on-branch, still bearing a shield but with its wings down instead of opened wide. The year 1837 witnessed the most significant alteration up to the time; a likeness of Liberty seated replaced the bust type and the eagle's place on the reverse was taken by the wording "ONE DIME" within a wreath, surrounded by "UNITED STATES OF AMERICA." At first there were no stars on the obverse but these were added in 1838 and arrows were placed at the date in 1853. These, however, were of little duration as they disappeared in 1856.

DIMES — DRAPED BUST, 1796 - 1807
Eagle on Reverse

1798-1807

1796-1797
Small Eagle

1798-1807
Large Eagle

DATE	MINTAGE	ABP	G-4 Good	F-12 Fine	VF-20 V. Fine
☐ 1796	22,135	500.00	950.00	1580.00	2300.00
☐ 1797 (13 stars)		425.00	800.00	1450.00	1900.00
☐ 1797 (16 stars)	25,261	425.00	800.00	1450.00	1900.00
☐ 1798		275.00	475.00	800.00	1000.00
☐ 1798 over 97 w/13 stars on reverse					VERY RARE
☐ 1798 small 8	27,500				VERY RARE
☐ 1798 over 97 w/16 stars on reverse		285.00	525.00	1000.00	1625.00
☐ 1800	21,760	275.00	475.00	800.00	1000.00
☐ 1801	34,640	275.00	475.00	800.00	1075.00
☐ 1802	10,975	350.00	700.00	1550.00	2400.00
☐ 1803	33,040	280.00	500.00	1200.00	1075.00
☐ 1804 w/13 stars on reverse	8,265	485.00	900.00	2175.00	3250.00
☐ 1804 w/14 stars on reverse	8,265	485.00	900.00	2175.00	3250.00
☐ 1805 w/4 berries	120,780	250.00	450.00	750.00	1050.00
☐ 1805 w/5 berries	120,780	250.00	450.00	750.00	1050.00
☐ 1807	165,000	250.00	450.00	750.00	1100.00

DIMES — LIBERTY CAP, 1809 - 1837

DATE	MINTAGE	ABP	G-4 Good	F-12 Fine	EF-40 Ex. Fine	MS-60 Unc.
☐ 1809	44,710	40.00	80.00	300.00	650.00	2850.00
☐ 1811 over 9	65,180	20.00	40.00	100.00	400.00	2375.00
☐ 1814 (Small Date)	421,500	14.00	28.00	90.00	410.00	980.00
☐ 1814 STATESOFAMERICA (No Breaks Between Words: Large Date)		8.00	16.00	40.00	300.00	980.00
☐ 1820	942,587	8.00	16.00	32.00	280.00	980.00
☐ 1821	1,186,512	8.00	16.00	32.00	280.00	980.00
☐ 1822	100,000	85.00	180.00	600.00	1250.00	4000.00
☐ 1823 over 22	440,000	11.00	22.00	30.00	275.00	980.00
☐ 1824 over 22		11.00	22.00	40.00	275.00	980.00

DATE	MINTAGE	ABP	G-4 Good	F-12 Fine	EF-40 Ex. Fine	MS-60 Unc.
☐ 1825 (Mintage includes 1824)	510,000	6.00	12.00	25.00	260.00	1075.00
☐ 1827	1,215,000	5.50	11.00	23.00	260.00	1075.00
☐ 1828 Large Date	125,000	12.00	25.00	60.00	320.00	3100.00
☐ 1828 Small Date	125,000	13.00	28.00	75.00	280.00	1600.00
☐ 1829 Small $.10	770,000	8.00	17.00	32.00	240.00	1075.00
☐ 1829 Large $.10	770,000	17.00	35.00	80.00	350.00	1200.00
☐ 1830*	510,000	10.00	18.00	180.00	800.00	
☐ 1830, 30 over 29		20.00	35.00	90.00	275.00	2000.00
☐ 1831	771,350	5.00	10.00	18.00	180.00	800.00
☐ 1832	522,500	5.00	10.00	18.00	180.00	825.00
☐ 1833	485,000	5.00	10.00	18.00	180.00	800.00
☐ 1834**	635,000	5.00	10.00	18.00	180.00	800.00
☐ 1835	1,410,000	5.00	10.00	18.00	180.00	715.00
☐ 1836	1,190,000	5.00	10.00	18.00	180.00	715.00
☐ 1837 ALL KINDS	359,500	5.00	10.00	20.00	185.00	715.00

*1830 — Small $.10, 1830 — Large $.10: Same Price
**1834 Small 4, 1834 — Large 4: Same Price

DIMES — LIBERTY SEATED, 1837 - 1860

1837-38O
no stars

1837-91
with stars

1838-60
with stars

DATE	MINTAGE	ABP	G-4 Good	F-12 Fine	EF-40 Ex. Fine	MS-60 Unc.
☐ 1837 No Stars*	682,500	11.00	23.00	55.00	300.00	1100.00
☐ 1838O No Stars	402,404	18.00	35.00	90.00	380.00	2400.00
☐ 1838 Small Stars		12.00	25.00	55.00	200.00	1300.00
☐ 1838 Large Stars	1,992,500	4.00	8.00	17.00	65.00	500.00
☐ 1838 Partial Drapery		14.00	28.00	70.00	300.00	675.00
☐ 1839	1,053,115	4.00	8.00	17.00	55.00	310.00
☐ 1839O	1,243,272	5.00	9.00	22.00	80.00	550.00
☐ 1840 No Drape	1,358,580	3.00	6.00	12.00	52.00	315.00
☐ 1840O No Drape	1,175,000	5.00	9.00	25.00	95.00	1100.00
☐ 1840 Drapery added	377,541	18.00	38.00	100.00	300.00	
☐ 1841	1,622,500	2.50	5.00	12.00	40.00	290.00
☐ 1841O	2,007,500	5.00	9.00	22.00	95.00	1000.00
☐ 1842	1,887,500	2.50	5.00	11.00	40.00	290.00
☐ 1842O	2,020,000	5.00	9.00	21.00	105.00	

*Small and Large date same price.

DATE	MINTAGE	ABP	G-4 Good	F-12 Fine	EF-40 Ex. Fine	MS-60 Unc.	PRF-65 Proof
☐ 1843	1,370,000	2.50	5.00	10.00	40.00	280.00	
☐ 1843O	150,000	20.00	40.00	100.00	500.00		
☐ 1844	72,500	12.00	25.00	85.00	280.00	2000.00	
☐ 1845	1,755,000	2.50	5.00	10.00	45.00	285.00	
☐ 1845O	230,000	9.00	18.00	60.00	400.00		
☐ 1846	31,300	25.00	50.00	115.00	425.00		
☐ 1847	245,000	7.00	13.00	35.00	130.00	1100.00	
☐ 1848	451,000	5.00	10.00	21.00	80.00	850.00	
☐ 1849	839,000	3.50	7.00	16.00	55.00	530.00	
☐ 1849O	300,000	4.50	9.00	50.00	200.00		
☐ 1850	1,931,500	2.50	5.00	13.00	50.00	285.00	
☐ 1850O	510,000	4.50	9.00	28.00	110.00	1050.00	
☐ 1851	1,026,500	2.50	5.00	13.00	50.00	285.00	
☐ 1851O	400,000	5.00	10.00	28.00	120.00	1575.00	
☐ 1852	1,535,500	2.50	5.00	13.00	50.00	285.00	
☐ 1852O	430,000	6.00	12.00	38.00	200.00	1750.00	
☐ 1853 No arrows	95,000	15.00	30.00	75.00	220.00	550.00	
☐ 1853 w/arrows	12,173,010	2.00	4.00	7.00	45.00	310.00	4500.00
☐ 1853O	1,100,000	3.00	7.00	25.00	100.00	900.00	
☐ 1854	4,470,000	2.00	4.00	10.00	45.00	600.00	9750.00
☐ 1854O	1,770,000	2.00	4.00	7.00	50.00	450.00	
☐ 1855	2,075,000	2.00	4.00	10.00	47.00	425.00	9750.00
☐ 1856 (Small Date)	5,780,000	2.00	4.00	13.00	45.00	350.00	7000.00
☐ 1856 (Large Date)		4.50	9.00	17.00	62.00	400.00	
☐ 1856O	1,180,000	4.00	7.00	17.00	75.00	750.00	
☐ 1856S	70,000	30.00	65.00	150.00	290.00		
☐ 1857	5,580,000	2.00	4.00	8.00	40.00	280.00	6850.00
☐ 1857O	1,540,000	2.50	5.00	10.00	60.00	500.00	
☐ 1858	1,540,000	2.00	4.00	8.00	45.00	275.00	6650.00
☐ 1858O	290,000	7.00	14.00	53.00	130.00	850.00	
☐ 1858S	60,000	29.00	60.00	130.00	350.00		
☐ 1859†	430,000	2.00	4.00	9.00	60.00	500.00	5175.00
☐ 1859O	480,000	4.00	8.00	20.00	65.00	550.00	
☐ 1859S	60,000	24.00	50.00	150.00	350.00		
☐ 1860S	140,000	10.00	20.00	50.00	230.00		

†There is a recognized pattern in this series - 1859 Transitional Pattern Proof: $26,000

DIMES — LIBERTY SEATED, 1860-1891
with "UNITED STATES OF AMERICA" on Obverse

Mint Marks under or within Wreath on Reverse

DATE	MINTAGE	ABP	G-4 Good	F-12 Fine	EF-40 Ex. Fine	MS-60 Unc.	PRF-65 Proof
☐ 1860	607,000	2.50	5.00	11.00	40.00	275.00	3075.00
☐ 1860O	40,000	140.00	270.00	500.00	1875.00		
☐ 1861	1,924,000	2.50	5.00	10.00	34.00	250.00	3075.00
☐ 1861S	172,500	9.00	19.00	60.00	135.00		
☐ 1862	847,550	2.50	5.00	10.00	34.00	250.00	3075.00
☐ 1862S	180,750	9.00	19.00	50.00	130.00		
☐ 1863	14,460	80.00	175.00	400.00	550.00	950.00	3075.00
☐ 1863S	157,000	9.00	18.00	40.00	120.00	1275.00	
☐ 1864	39,070	65.00	170.00	430.00	630.00	1200.00	
☐ 1864S	230,000	7.00	14.00	30.00	105.00	1275.00	
☐ 1865	10,500	90.00	200.00	500.00	700.00	1375.00	3075.00
☐ 1865S	175,000	7.00	15.00	32.00	180.00		
☐ 1866	8,725	115.00	250.00	600.00	850.00	1450.00	3150.00
☐ 1866S	135,000	8.00	17.00	32.00	120.00	1300.00	
☐ 1867	6,625	160.00	330.00	700.00	900.00	1850.00	3100.00
☐ 1867S	140,000	10.00	20.00	35.00	140.00	1275.00	
☐ 1868	466,250	3.50	7.00	18.00	80.00	400.00	3075.00
☐ 1868S	260,000	6.00	11.00	25.00	90.00	450.00	
☐ 1869	256,600	6.00	12.00	27.00	95.00	400.00	3075.00
☐ 1869S	450,000	4.00	7.50	15.00	80.00	500.00	
☐ 1870	471,500	3.00	6.00	10.00	55.00	320.00	3075.00
☐ 1870S	50,000	36.00	70.00	150.00	330.00	1200.00	
☐ 1871	753,610	2.50	5.00	9.00	45.00	350.00	3075.00
☐ 1871CC	20,100	250.00	500.00	900.00	2475.00		
☐ 1871S	320,000	4.00	8.00	27.00	80.00	700.00	
☐ 1872	2,396,450	2.50	5.00	8.00	35.00	310.00	3075.00
☐ 1872CC	24,000	130.00	275.00	620.00	1400.00		
☐ 1872S	190,000	8.00	16.00	55.00	200.00	900.00	
☐ 1873*	2,378,500	4.50	9.00	24.00	90.00	600.00	4250.00
☐ 1873** Open "3"	1,508,600	7.00	15.00	40.00	110.00	300.00	
☐ 1873** Close "3"	60,000	4.50	9.00	20.00	40.00	250.00	3175.00
☐ 1873CC**	12,400				UNIQUE—ONLY ONE KNOWN		
☐ 1873CC*	18,791	300.00	650.00	1100.00	2950.00		11000.00
☐ 1873S*	455,000	6.00	13.00	30.00	100.00	1000.00	
☐ 1874 w/arrows	2,940,000	5.00	10.00	25.00	95.00	675.00	4175.00
☐ 1874CC w/arrows	10,817	500.00	925.00	2000.00	3800.00		
☐ 1874S w/arrows	240,000	9.00	18.00	50.00	130.00	700.00	
☐ 1875	10,350,000	2.00	4.00	6.00	21.00	210.00	2900.00
☐ 1875CC in Wreath } below Wreath	4,645,000	2.50 2.50	5.00 5.00	16.00 20.00	45.00 55.00	210.00 210.00	
☐ 1875S in Wreath } below Wreath	9,070,000	3.00 1.75	6.00 3.50	18.00 6.00	70.00 25.00	500.00 195.00	
☐ 1876	11,461,150	1.75	3.50	6.00	24.00	195.00	2900.00
☐ 1876CC	8,270,000	1.75	3.50	6.00	24.00	195.00	
☐ 1876S	10,420,000	1.75	3.50	6.00	24.00	195.00	
☐ 1877	7,310,510	1.75	3.50	6.00	24.00	195.00	2900.00
☐ 1877CC	7,700,000	1.75	3.50	6.00	24.00	195.00	
☐ 1877S	2,340,000	1.75	3.50	6.00	24.00	195.00	
☐ 1878	1,678,300	1.75	3.50	6.00	24.00	195.00	2900.00

*With Arrows   **No Arrows

DATE	MINTAGE	ABP	G-4 Good	F-12 Fine	EF-40 Ex. Fine	MS-60 Unc.	PRF-65 Proof
☐ 1878CC	200,000	15.00	30.00	75.00	140.00	600.00	
☐ 1879	15,100	75.00	150.00	230.00	360.00	650.00	3150.00
☐ 1880	37,355	45.00	90.00	180.00	270.00	550.00	3150.00
☐ 1881	24,975	50.00	100.00	190.00	300.00	600.00	3150.00
☐ 1882	3,911,100	1.50	4.00	6.00	21.00	200.00	3075.00
☐ 1883	7,675,712	1.50	4.00	6.00	21.00	200.00	3075.00
☐ 1884	3,366,380	1.50	4.00	6.00	21.00	200.00	3075.00
☐ 1884S	564,969	4.00	8.00	22.00	60.00	370.00	
☐ 1885	2,533,427	2.00	4.00	6.00	21.00	200.00	3075.00
☐ 1885S	43,690	65.00	130.00	250.00	450.00	1400.00	
☐ 1886	6,377,570	2.50	4.00	6.00	21.00	190.00	3075.00
☐ 1886S	206,524	8.00	18.00	33.00	80.00	500.00	
☐ 1887	11,283,939	1.50	4.00	6.00	21.00	180.00	3075.00
☐ 1887S	4,454,450	1.50	4.00	6.00	21.00	180.00	
☐ 1888	5,496,487	1.50	4.00	7.00	21.00	180.00	3075.00
☐ 1888S	1,720,000	2.00	4.50	7.00	21.00	180.00	
☐ 1889	7,380,711	1.50	4.00	6.00	21.00	180.00	3075.00
☐ 1889S	972,678	4.25	10.00	20.00	55.00	300.00	
☐ 1890	9,911,541	2.00	4.00	6.00	21.00	180.00	3075.00
☐ 1890S	1,423,076	3.00	7.00	20.00	40.00	270.00	
☐ 1891	15,310,600	1.50	3.00	6.00	21.00	210.00	3075.00
☐ 18910	4,540,000	1.50	3.00	6.00	21.00	270.00	
☐ 1891S	3,196,116	1.50	4.00	6.00	21.00	280.00	

DIMES — LIBERTY HEAD OR BARBER, 1892 - 1916

After many years of using a seated figure of Liberty on the dime, it was decided in 1892 to return to a facial portrait. The designer was Charles E. Barber, resulting in the coin coming to be popularly known among collectors as the "Barber Dime." Liberty wears a wreath and is encircled by the inscription "UNITED STATES OF AMERICA," with the date appearing below the portrait. The reverse is unchanged from that used earlier, the words "ONE DIME" enclosed in a wreath. This coin's weight was set at 2½ grams. Its composition was nine parts silver to one part copper and its diameter 17.9 mm. It was struck at Philadelphia, Denver, San Francisco and New Orleans. The very rare 1894 San Francisco minting, of which only 24 were produced, is the stellar item of this series. In 1916 the Liberty Head design was replaced by the so-called Mercury Head.

DATE	MINTAGE	ABP	G-4 Good	F-12 Fine	EF-40 Ex. Fine	MS-60 Unc.	PRF-65 Proof
☐ 1892	12,121,245	1.25	2.20	6.00	20.00	150.00	2800.00
☐ 18920	3,841,700	2.00	4.50	8.00	25.00	170.00	
☐ 1892S	990,710	12.00	25.00	40.00	85.00	230.00	
☐ 1893	3,340,792	1.75	4.00	9.00	22.00	150.00	2800.00
☐ 1893, 3 over 2						EXTREMELY RARE	
☐ 18930	1,760,000	4.50	11.00	22.00	45.00	220.00	

Mint Mark is under Wreath on the Reverse

DATE	MINTAGE	ABP	G-4 Good	F-12 Fine	EF-40 Ex. Fine	MS-60 Unc.	PRF-65 Proof
☐1893S	2,491,401	2.25	5.00	12.00	30.00	195.00	
☐1894	1,330,972	2.75	6.00	13.00	50.00	200.00	2800.00
☐1894O	720,000	12.00	30.00	65.00	200.00	800.00	
☐1894S		EXTREMELY RARE BUSS SALE 1985 MS-60 46,000.00					
☐1895	690,880	25.00	47.00	75.00	175.00	500.00	2800.00
☐1895O	440,000	80.00	130.00	180.00	350.00	800.00	
☐1895S	1,120,000	6.00	13.00	28.00	50.00	220.00	
☐1896	2,000,672	2.50	5.00	11.00	35.00	160.00	2800.00
☐1896O	610,000	18.00	39.00	65.00	160.00	550.00	
☐1896S	575,056	16.00	31.00	55.00	120.00	280.00	
☐1897	10,869,264	.80	2.00	5.00	20.00	150.00	2800.00
☐1897O	666,000	15.00	32.00	60.00	170.00	575.00	
☐1897S	1,342,844	3.25	7.00	18.00	55.00	220.00	
☐1898	16,320,735	.60	1.50	3.00	18.00	150.00	2800.00
☐1898O	2,130,000	2.00	3.50	11.00	45.00	250.00	
☐1898S	1,702,507	1.75	3.00	9.00	35.00	210.00	
☐1899	19,580,846	.60	1.50	3.00	18.00	150.00	2800.00
☐1899O	2,650,000	1.75	3.00	10.00	45.00	250.00	
☐1899S	1,867,493	1.50	3.00	9.00	28.00	185.00	
☐1900	17,600,912	.60	1.50	3.00	18.00	150.00	2800.00
☐1900O	2,010,000	2.00	4.50	11.00	50.00	275.00	
☐1900S	5,168,270	.60	2.00	5.00	23.00	180.00	
☐1901	18,860,478	.60	1.50	3.00	18.00	140.00	2800.00
☐1901O	5,620,000	.60	2.00	6.00	45.00	275.00	
☐1901S	593,022	15.00	32.00	70.00	200.00	650.00	
☐1902	21,380,777	.60	1.50	3.00	18.00	140.00	2800.00
☐1902O	4,500,000	.60	2.00	5.00	30.00	225.00	
☐1902S	2,070,000	1.50	3.20	10.00	55.00	250.00	
☐1903	19,500,755	.60	1.50	3.00	18.00	140.00	2800.00
☐1903O	8,180,000	.60	2.00	4.00	25.00	220.00	
☐1903S	613,300	15.00	28.00	50.00	140.00	515.00	
☐1904	14,601,027	.60	1.50	3.00	18.00	140.00	2800.00
☐1904S	800,000	10.00	20.00	40.00	115.00	500.00	
☐1905	14,552,350	.50	1.50	3.00	18.00	140.00	2800.00
☐1905O	3,400,000	.50	2.25	5.00	30.00	185.00	
☐1905S	6,855,199	.50	1.75	4.00	25.00	195.00	
☐1906	19,958,406	.50	1.50	3.00	18.00	140.00	2800.00
☐1906D	4,060,000	.50	2.00	5.00	23.00	175.00	
☐1906O	2,610,000	.50	2.15	9.00	30.00	185.00	

DATE	MINTAGE	ABP	G-4 Good	F-12 Fine	EF-40 Ex. Fine	MS-60 Unc.	PRF-65 Proof
☐ 1906S	3,136,640	.50	2.00	6.00	27.00	180.00	
☐ 1907	22,220,575	.50	1.30	3.00	17.00	140.00	2800.00
☐ 1907D	4,080,000	.50	1.75	5.00	25.00	170.00	
☐ 1907O	5,058,000	.50	1.75	5.00	20.00	150.00	
☐ 1907S	3,178,470	.50	1.75	5.50	29.00	200.00	
☐ 1908	10,600,545	.50	1.25	3.00	18.00	140.00	2800.00
☐ 1908D	7,490,000	.50	1.65	4.00	19.00	145.00	
☐ 1908O	1,789,000	.90	2.00	9.00	35.00	210.00	
☐ 1908S	3,220,000	.50	2.00	5.00	24.00	185.00	
☐ 1909	10,240,650	.50	1.50	3.00	17.00	140.00	2800.00
☐ 1909D	954,000	1.10	3.00	11.00	35.00	205.00	
☐ 1909O	2,287,000	.50	2.00	6.00	25.00	175.00	
☐ 1909S	2,000,000	1.10	3.00	12.00	40.00	215.00	
☐ 1910	11,520,551	.50	1.75	3.00	17.00	140.00	2800.00
☐ 1910D	3,490,000	.50	1.90	5.00	28.00	205.00	
☐ 1910S	1,240,000	.90	2.00	7.00	26.00	175.00	
☐ 1911	18,870,543	.50	1.65	2.50	16.00	140.00	2800.00
☐ 1911D	11,209,000	.50	1.65	3.50	17.00	140.00	
☐ 1911S	3,530,000	.50	1.90	5.00	20.00	165.00	
☐ 1912	19,350,700	.50	1.30	2.50	15.00	140.00	2800.00
☐ 1912D	11,760,000	.50	1.30	3.50	15.00	140.00	
☐ 1912S	3,420,000	.50	1.85	4.00	19.00	165.00	
☐ 1913	19,760,000	.50	1.65	3.00	15.00	140.00	2800.00
☐ 1913S	510,000	3.00	6.00	21.00	95.00	265.00	
☐ 1914	17,360,655	.50	1.30	2.00	15.00	140.00	3200.00
☐ 1914D	11,908,000	.50	1.30	3.00	15.00	140.00	
☐ 1914S	2,100,000	.50	1.90	5.00	25.00	160.00	
☐ 1915	5,620,450	.50	1.90	3.00	15.00	150.00	3275.00
☐ 1915S	960,000	.50	2.00	6.00	26.00	170.00	
☐ 1916	18,490,000	.50	1.30	2.50	15.00	140.00	
☐ 1916S	5,820,000	.50	1.30	3.00	16.00	155.00	

DIMES — MERCURY DIMES, 1916 - 1945

The Mercury Dime is misnamed. The likeness on its obverse is not that of Mercury (a male god) but Liberty, the same mythological figure who had graced dimes since their introduction in 1796. Confusion resulted from the attachment of small wings to Liberty's headdress, which to students of Greek and Roman folklore could only represent Mercury, the "quick messenger," whom the gods equipped with wings to better execute his duties. To give Liberty wings was a bit of poetic license; the intended meaning was "liberty of thought," but so vague was this concept that its purpose remained unserved. On the reverse was an object that caused only slightly less confusion, a vertical column of some kind that only the most astute observers could identify. This was designed as a bundle of fasces or sticks with axe protruding. In Roman times, an imperial or senatorial procession was often accompanied by "fasces bearers" who carried these bundles of wood sticks throughout the streets. Their meaning was supposedly symbolic but they likewise served a practical function: when dusk fell they could be lighted to illuminate the path. Designer of the Mercury Dime was Adolph Weinman. Its specifications are the same as those of the Barber Dime. The mintmark appears on the reverse, between the words "ONE" and "DIME," to the left of the fasces. The Mercury Dime was composed of 90% silver and 10% copper. It has a weight of 2½ grams and diameter of 17.9 mm.

Mint Mark is on Reverse
at Bottom to Left of Branches

Enlargement Showing
1942 over 41 Dime

DATE	MINTAGE	ABP	G-4 Good	F-12 Fine	VF-20 V. Fine	EF-40 Ex. Fine	MS-60 Unc.
☐ 1916	22,180,000	.50	2.00	4.00	6.00	8.00	23.00
☐ 1916D	264,000	175.00	350.00	700.00	1000.00	1300.00	2000.00
☐ 1916S	10,450,000	.50	2.50	5.00	8.00	13.00	35.00
☐ 1917	55,230,000	.50	1.25	2.50	5.00	7.00	20.00
☐ 1917D	9,402,000	.50	2.50	6.00	12.00	30.00	90.00
☐ 1917S	27,330,000	.50	1.25	2.75	5.00	8.00	32.00
☐ 1918	26,680,000	.50	1.25	3.00	9.00	20.00	50.00
☐ 1918D	22,674,800	.50	1.25	3.75	8.00	18.00	60.00
☐ 1918S	19,300,000	.50	1.25	2.75	6.00	11.00	40.00
☐ 1919	35,740,000	.50	1.00	2.50	5.00	6.00	25.00
☐ 1919D	9,939,000	.50	1.80	5.00	12.00	28.00	110.00
☐ 1919S	8,850,000	.50	1.50	4.00	10.00	24.00	120.00
☐ 1920	59,030,000	.50	.80	2.00	4.00	6.00	20.00
☐ 1920D	19,171,000	.50	1.50	3.00	6.00	12.00	60.00
☐ 1920S	13,820,000	.50	1.50	3.00	6.00	11.00	55.00
☐ 1921	1,230,000	11.00	20.00	60.00	100.00	310.00	700.00
☐ 1921D	1,080,000	14.00	28.00	80.00	150.00	330.00	700.00
☐ 1923*	50,130,000	.50	.80	3.00	3.50	5.00	19.00
☐ 1923S	6,440,000	.50	1.50	4.00	7.00	16.00	70.00
☐ 1924	24,010,000	.50	1.50	3.00	4.00	7.00	35.00
☐ 1924D	6,810,000	.50	1.50	3.50	7.00	15.00	80.00
☐ 1924S	7,120,000	.50	1.25	3.00	6.00	13.00	75.00
☐ 1925	25,610,000	.50	1.00	2.00	4.00	6.00	32.00
☐ 1925D	5,117,000	1.10	3.00	7.00	19.00	60.00	210.00
☐ 1925S	5,850,000	.50	1.25	3.00	6.00	15.00	95.00
☐ 1926	32,160,000	.50	.80	1.50	3.75	5.00	15.00
☐ 1926D	6,828,000	.50	1.25	3.00	6.00	12.00	57.00
☐ 1926S	1,520,000	3.00	6.00	13.00	25.00	70.00	335.00
☐ 1927	28,080,000	.50	.80	1.50	4.00	5.00	15.00
☐ 1927D	4,812,000	.50	1.75	4.00	10.00	28.00	150.00

*All dimes with 23D date are counterfeit.

DATE	MINTAGE	ABP	G-4 Good	F-12 Fine	VF-20 V. Fine	EF-40 Ex. Fine	MS-60 Unc.	PRF-65 Proof
☐ 1927S	4,770,000	.50	1.35	2.30	5.00	11.00	65.00	
☐ 1928	19,480,000	.50	1.00	1.50	3.75	5.00	15.00	
☐ 1928D	4,161,000	.50	2.00	5.00	12.00	27.00	110.00	
☐ 1928S	7,400,000	.50	1.35	2.50	4.00	9.00	45.00	
☐ 1929	25,970,000	.50	.90	1.50	3.00	4.00	12.00	
☐ 1929D	5,034,000	.50	2.00	4.00	6.00	8.00	35.00	
☐ 1929S	4,730,000	.50	1.00	1.75	4.00	5.00	37.00	
☐ 1930	6,770,000	.50	1.00	1.75	3.75	5.00	19.00	
☐ 1930S	1,843,000	.50	2.25	4.00	5.00	10.00	60.00	
☐ 1931	3,150,000	.50	1.20	2.50	4.00	8.00	30.00	
☐ 1931D	1,260,000	2.50	5.50	9.00	14.00	25.00	85.00	
☐ 1931S	1,800,000	.50	2.25	4.00	5.00	10.00	60.00	
☐ 1934	24,080,000	.50	.70	.95	1.20	2.75	14.00	
☐ 1934D	6,772,000	.50	1.30	2.00	2.50	3.75	28.00	
☐ 1935	58,830,000	.50	.70	.95	1.20	2.25	10.00	
☐ 1935D	10,477,000	.50	1.00	1.50	2.00	4.00	35.00	
☐ 1935S	15,840,000	.50	1.00	1.50	2.00	3.50	18.00	
☐ 1936	87,504,130	.50	.70	.95	1.20	2.00	10.00	850.00
☐ 1936D	16,132,000	.50	.70	1.50	2.00	3.00	24.00	
☐ 1936S	9,210,000	.50	.70	1.50	2.00	2.50	16.00	
☐ 1937	56,865,756	.50	.70	.95	1.20	2.00	9.00	650.00
☐ 1937D	14,146,000	.50	.70	1.50	2.00	2.80	21.00	
☐ 1937S	9,740,000	.50	.70	1.50	2.00	2.80	15.00	
☐ 1938	22,198,728	.50	.70	.95	1.20	1.90	11.00	475.00
☐ 1938D	5,537,000	.50	.70	1.50	2.00	2.80	20.00	
☐ 1938S	8,090,000	.50	.70	1.50	2.00	2.80	16.00	
☐ 1939	67,749,321	.50	.70	.95	1.20	1.90	7.00	425.00
☐ 1939D	24,394,000	.50	.70	.95	1.20	2.40	8.00	
☐ 1939S	10,540,000	.50	.70	1.50	2.00	2.50	14.00	
☐ 1940	65,361,827	.50	.70	.95	1.20	1.45	5.00	385.00
☐ 1940D	21,560,000	.50	.70	.95	1.20	1.45	12.00	
☐ 1940S	21,560,000	.50	.70	.95	1.20	1.45	6.00	
☐ 1941	175,106,557	.50	.70	.95	1.20	1.45	5.00	350.00
☐ 1941D	45,634,000	.50	.70	.95	1.20	1.45	8.00	
☐ 1941S	43,090,000	.50	.70	.95	1.20	1.45	9.00	
☐ 1942	205,432,329	.50	.70	.95	1.20	1.45	7.00	350.00
☐ 1942 Part of Above over 41		85.00	150.00	190.00	210.00	250.00	850.00	
☐ 1942/41-D		85.00	160.00	200.00	220.00	280.00	975.00	
☐ 1942D	60,740,000	.50	.70	.95	1.20	1.45	8.00	
☐ 1942S	49,300,000	.50	.70	.95	1.20	1.45	11.00	
☐ 1943	191,710,000	.50	.70	.95	1.20	1.45	6.00	
☐ 1943D	71,949,000	.50	.70	.95	1.20	1.45	7.00	
☐ 1943S	60,400,000	.50	.70	.95	1.20	1.45	9.00	
☐ 1944	231,410,000	.50	.70	.95	1.20	1.45	6.00	
☐ 1944D	62,224,000	.50	.70	.95	1.20	1.45	7.00	
☐ 1944S	49,490,000	.50	.70	.95	1.20	1.45	7.00	
☐ 1945	159,130,000	.50	.70	.95	1.20	1.45	6.00	
☐ 1945D	40,245,000	.50	.70	.95	1.20	1.45	7.00	
☐ 1945S	41,920,000	.50	.70	.95	1.20	1.45	7.00	
☐ 1945S (Micros)		.50	.70	.95	1.20	1.45	13.00	

DIMES — ROOSEVELT, 1946 TO DATE

The Roosevelt Dime series is significant for the change made to clad composition in 1965. Upon the death of President Roosevelt in 1945 there was considerable public sentiment to install his likeness on a coin. The penny, nickel and quarter were not seriously considered as they already carried portraits of former Presidents. As no dollars were being struck this left only the dime and half dollar, which both carried representations of Liberty, as suitable choices. The dime was selected, probably because of the much wider distribution of this coin. The designer was John Sinnock. Roosevelt is shown in profile facing left, with the word "LIBERTY" and the inscription "IN GOD WE TRUST." The bundle of fasces was retained as the central element for the reverse type, which was redrawn. Originally the mint mark appeared on the reverse, as it had on the Mercury Dime, then was switched to the obverse on clad pieces. The weight was 2½ grams. The composition of this coin, originally 90% silver and 10% copper, was altered in 1965 to three parts copper/one part nickel outer covering with an interior of pure copper, yielding a weight of 2.27 grams. The diameter remained 17.9 mm. In the first year of striking the clad dime, more pieces were manufactured than had ever been turned out of a ten cent piece in the Mint's history, more than 1.6 billion. A serious shortage of dimes that resulted from spectators hoarding the silver coins and this abundant new supply was intended to replace those lost from circulation. A mintage figure of more than two billion was achieved in 1967, or more than $1 worth of dimes for every U.S. citizen.

Mint Mark is on Reverse of Left, Bottom of Torch.

From 1968 Mint Mark at Base of Neck.

DATE	MINTAGE	ABP	MS-60 Unc.	PRF-65 Proof
☐ 1946	255,250,000	.50	1.60	
☐ 1946D	61,043,500	.50	3.00	
☐ 1946S	27,900,000	.50	4.00	
☐ 1947	121,500,000	.50	3.00	
☐ 1947D	46,835,000	.50	5.00	
☐ 1947S	34,840,000	.50	4.00	
☐ 1948	74,950,000	.50	3.00	
☐ 1948D	52,841,000	.50	6.00	
☐ 1948S	35,520,000	.50	5.00	
☐ 1949	30,940,000	.50	12.00	
☐ 1949D	26,034,000	.50	8.00	
☐ 1949S	13,510,000	.50	32.00	
☐ 1950	50,181,500	.50	3.50	55.00
☐ 1950D	46,803,000	.50	3.50	
☐ 1950S	20,440,000	.50	12.00	
☐ 1951	103,937,602	.50	2.40	
☐ 1951D	52,191,800	.50	2.00	45.00
☐ 1951S	31,630,000	.50	10.00	
☐ 1952	99,122,073	.50	2.50	30.00

DATE	MINTAGE	ABP	MS-60 Unc.	PRF-65 Proof
☐ 1952D	122,100,000	.50	2.50	
☐ 1952S	44,419,500	.50	4.50	
☐ 1953	53,618,920	.50	2.00	18.00
☐ 1953D	156,433,000	.50	1.75	
☐ 1953S	39,180,000	.50	1.50	
☐ 1954	114,243,503	.50	1.40	6.00
☐ 1954D	106,397,000	.50	1.40	
☐ 1954S	22,860,000	.50	1.40	
☐ 1955	12,828,381	.50	2.00	5.50
☐ 1955D	13,959,000	.50	1.75	
☐ 1955S	18,510,000	.50	1.75	
☐ 1956	109,309,384	.50	1.35	3.00
☐ 1956D	108,015,100	.50	1.35	
☐ 1957	161,407,952	.50	1.35	2.50
☐ 1957D	113,354,330	.50	1.50	
☐ 1958	32,785,652	.50	1.50	3.00
☐ 1958D	136,564,600	.50	1.15	
☐ 1959	86,929,291	.50	1.15	2.00
☐ 1959D	164,919,790	.50	1.15	
☐ 1960	72,081,602	.50	1.15	1.65
☐ 1960D	200,160,400	.50	1.15	
☐ 1961	96,756,244	.50	1.15	1.65
☐ 1961D	209,146,550	.50	1.15	
☐ 1962	75,668,019	.50	1.15	1.65
☐ 1962D	334,948,380	.50	1.15	
☐ 1963	126,725,645	.50	1.15	1.65
☐ 1963D	421,476,530	.50	1.15	
☐ 1964	933,310,762	.50	1.15	1.65
☐ 1964D	1,357,517,180	.50	1.15	
☐ 1965 Clad Coinage Begins	1,652,140,570		.30	
☐ 1966	1,382,734,540		.30	
☐ 1967	2,244,077,300		.30	
☐ 1968	424,470,400		.30	
☐ 1968D	480,748,280		.30	
☐ 1968S Proof Only	3,041,508			.75
☐ 1969	145,790,000		.30	
☐ 1969D	563,323,870		.30	
☐ 1969S Proof Only	2,934,631			.75
☐ 1970	345,570,000		.30	
☐ 1970D	754,942,000		.30	
☐ 1970S Proof Only	2,632,810			.75
☐ 1971	162,690,000		.30	
☐ 1971D	377,914,240		.30	
☐ 1971S Proof Only	3,244,138			.75
☐ 1972	431,540,000		.30	
☐ 1972D	330,290,000		.30	
☐ 1972S Proof Only	3,267,667			.75
☐ 1973	315,670,000		.30	
☐ 1973D	455,032,426		.30	
☐ 1973 Proof Only	2,769,624			.75
☐ 1974	470,248,000		.30	
☐ 1974D	571,083,000		.30	

DATE	MINTAGE	ABP	MS-60 Unc.	PRF-65 Proof
☐ 1974S Proof Only	2,617,350			.75
☐ 1975	585,673,900		.30	
☐ 1975D	313,705,250		.30	
☐ 1975S Proof Only	2,909,369			.75
☐ 1976	568,760,000		.30	
☐ 1976D	695,222,774		.30	
☐ 1976S Proof Only	4,149,945			.75
☐ 1977	796,900,480		.30	
☐ 1977D	376,610,420		.30	
☐ 1977S Proof Only	3,250,895			.75
☐ 1978	663,908,000		.30	
☐ 1978D	282,847,540		.30	
☐ 1978S Proof Only	3,127,781			.75
☐ 1979	315,440,007		.30	
☐ 1979D	390,921,285		.30	
☐ 1979S Proof (I)	3,677,200			.75
☐ 1979 Proof (II)				3.00
☐ 1980P	735,170,079		.25	
☐ 1980D	719,354,382		.25	
☐ 1980S Proof Only	3,547,130			.75
☐ 1981P	676,000,000		.25	
☐ 1981D	712,285,000		.25	
☐ 1981S Proof (I)	4,063,080			.75
☐ 1982P*	519,474,983		.25	
☐ 1982S Proof (I)	3,857,000			.75
☐ 1983D	730,130,000		.25	
☐ 1983S Proof	3,228.650			.75
☐ 1984P			.25	
☐ 1984D			.25	
☐ 1984S Proof				.75

*NOTE. In 1983, dimes dated 1982 and bearing no mintmark began to be discovered. At first they caused a furor as it was believed they might be great rarities (largely because a whole year had passed before any were noticed). During the first month ot two of trading, prices on MS-60 specimens reached as high as $600. At that time it was thought that as few as 300 or 400 might exist. Later it was revealed that a midwest source owned 4,000, and the existing total is now estimated at around 8,000. At the time of going to press, prices on MS-65 specimens were in the $225 range. Beware of removed mintmark.

TWENTY-CENT PIECES — LIBERTY SEATED, 1875 - 1878

The 20¢ piece has the unenviable distinction of being the shortest-lived of any U.S. coin. Authorized by a Congressional Act on March 3, 1875, it was placed into production immediately thereafter, with manufacture divided up between the Philadelphia, San Francisco and Carson City mints (mints on the east and west coasts being employed in hopes the coin would distribute more evenly in circulation than if released exclusively from a single source of production). Designed by William Barber, it pictured a figure of the goddess Liberty seated on the obverse, framed by stars, with an eagle on the reverse. It was composed of nine-tenths silver and one-tenth copper, with a weight of five grams and a diameter of 22 mm. Despite high hopes the 20¢ piece never achieved popularity, the chief reason for its rejection being the physical similarity to the quarter. Production was greatly cut back in 1876 and discontinued two years thereafter. All told, less than a million and a half were struck.

DATE	MINTAGE	ABP	G-4 Good	F-12 Fine	EF-40 Ex. Fine	MS-60 Unc.	PRF-65 Proof
☐ 1875	39,700	25.00	50.00	85.00	235.00	875.00	6000.00
☐ 1875CC	133,290	25.00	50.00	85.00	235.00	1100.00	
☐ 1875S	1,155,000	12.00	25.00	55.00	150.00	700.00	
☐ 1876	15,900	50.00	100.00	170.00	370.00	1425.00	6000.00
☐ 1876CC	10,000		(EXTREMELY RARE) 75,000.00				
☐ 1877	510	3250.00	PROOFS ONLY				6750.00
☐ 1878	600	3250.00	PROOFS ONLY				6325.00

QUARTERS — EARLY QUARTERS, 1796 - 1866

It became evident from a very early period that the quarter or 25¢ piece would be the most significant division of the dollar in everyday commerce. However, the effect was not fully felt until the 19th century. Striking of the quarter dollar was authorized in 1792 along with other denominations, upon establishment of a national currency. No actual specimens came into circulation until 1796. The earliest design was the Draped Bust portrait of Liberty, common to other silver coinage, with eagle reverse and the legend "UNITED STATES OF AMERICA." Stars appeared alongside Liberty on the obverse and her name was affixed above the portrait, with the date below. The designer was Robert Scot. The original quarter dollar was composed of .8924 silver alloyed with .1076 copper, or roughly a nine-to-one ratio. Its weight was 6.74 grams and the diameter generally 27½ mm. with slight variations to be observed according to the flatness of the planchet. Only 6,146 pieces were struck in 1796 as a trial issue (influenced in some measure by a shortage of silver) and this date has become scarce, even in less than the best condition. Production of quarters was not resumed until 1804, when discontinuation of dollar coins increased the need for them. The Draped Bust type was retained but the reverse changed to the Heraldic or Shield Eagle design. John Reich designed a new quarter dollar in 1815, identical in composition to its predecessors but having a slightly smaller diameter, 27 mm. This was the Capped Bust type, with naturalistic shielded eagle on the reverse. Production got off to a small start but was rapidly expanded. No further change occurred until 1831 when the coin was brought down in size to 24.3 mm. but was made a bit thicker, retaining the old weight of 6.74 grams. The designer of this new 25¢ piece was William Kneass (pronounced Niece) and all striking was done at Philadelphia. There is a "small letters" and "large letters" variety of this design, with little influence on value. The portrait is a somewhat streamlined Capped Liberty who appears more noble than previously. This design was of short duration, replaced by the Seated Liberty type in 1838. On the reverse was the shield eagle, beneath which appeared the words "QUAR. DOL." (The use of abbreviations did not fully meet the approval of artistic-minded persons.) There was an accompanying change in specifications as well. The silver content was slightly raised, to an even 90%; the copper dropped to an even 10%; and the weight went down to 6.68 grams. The diameter was the same as previously. Designer of this coin was Christian Gobrecht. It was stuck at both Philadelphia and New Orleans. A further reduction in weight was made to 6.22 grams in 1853; arrows were placed at the dates to remind users of the coin that it contained less silver than previously. Compositionally it was unaltered, with nine parts silver to one of copper. On the reverse, sunrays sprang from behind the eagle, an area of the design which previously had been blank. This addition was made for the same reason as the arrows.

QUARTERS — DRAPED BUST, 1796 - 1807

1796-1807

1796
Small Eagle

1804-1807
Large Eagle

DATE	MINTAGE	ABP	G-4 Good	F-12 Fine	VF-20 V. Fine	MS-60 Unc.
☐1796	5,894	1300.00	2450.00	3900.00	6500.00	19500.00
☐1804	6,738	350.00	700.00	1800.00	3700.00	20000.00
☐1805	121,394	110.00	210.00	500.00	900.00	5750.00
☐1806	206,124	110.00	210.00	500.00	900.00	5500.00
☐1806 over 5		110.00	210.00	500.00	900.00	8500.00
☐1807	220,643	110.00	210.00	500.00	900.00	5300.00

QUARTERS — LIBERTY CAP, 1815 - 1838

1815-1838

1815-1828
Motto over Eagle

1831-1838
Without Motto

DATE	MINTAGE	ABP	G-4 Good	F-12 Fine	VF-20 V. Fine	MS-60 Unc.	PRF-65 Proof
☐1815	89,235	22.00	42.00	95.00	230.00	1900.00	
☐1818	361,174	22.00	42.00	95.00	230.00	1800.00	
☐1818 over 15	361,174	22.00	42.00	95.00	250.00	2150.00	
☐1819*	144,000	22.00	42.00	75.00	210.00	1800.00	
☐1820**	127,440	22.00	42.00	80.00	190.00	1775.00	
☐1821	216,850	22.00	42.00	80.00	190.00	1775.00	
☐1822	64,084	39.00	80.00	150.00	310.00	1950.00	

*1819 — Small 9, 1819 — Large 9. **1820 — Small o, 1820 — Large 0; Same Price.

DATE	MINTAGE	ABP	G-4 Good	F-12 Fine	VF-20 V. Fine	MS-60 Unc.	PRF-65 Proof
☐1822 (25 over $.50)		145.00	250.00	475.00	950.00	2750.00	
☐1823 over 22†	17,801	1500.00	3500.00	11000.00	13000.00		28500.00
☐1824		23.00	42.00	90.00	225.00	1900.00	
☐1825 over dates	168,000	23.00	42.00	80.00	200.00	1900.00	
☐1827 (original)††	4,000		few pieces known — RARE				250000.00
☐1828	102,000	23.00	42.00	80.00	210.00	1900.00	
☐1828 (25 over $.50)	102,000	35.00	70.00	185.00	270.00	2400.00	

REDUCED SIZE — NO MOTTO ON REVERSE

DATE	MINTAGE	ABP	G-4 Good	F-12 Fine	VF-20 V. Fine	MS-60 Unc.	PRF-65 Proof
☐1831***	398,000	15.00	28.00	45.00	90.00	1100.00	
☐1832	320,000	15.00	28.00	45.00	90.00	1100.00	
☐1833	156,000	15.00	28.00	57.00	143.00	1450.00	
☐1834	286,000	15.00	28.00	45.00	90.00	1100.00	
☐1835	1,952,000	15.00	28.00	45.00	90.00	1100.00	
☐1836	472,000	15.00	28.00	45.00	90.00	1100.00	
☐1837	252,000	15.00	28.00	45.00	90.00	1100.00	
☐1838	832,000	15.00	28.00	45.00	90.00	1100.00	

***1831 — Small Letters, 1831 — Large Letters: Same Price. †Stack's Auction, March 1977. ††Stack's Auction, 1977: also 1827 restrike proof 12,500.00.

QUARTERS — LIBERTY SEATED, 1838 - 1865
No Motto Above Eagle

1838-1865

1853
With Rays

Mint Mark is Below Eagle on Reverse
1838-1852
1854-1865
Without Rays

DATE	MINTAGE	ABP	G-4 Good	F-12 Fine	EF-40 Ex. Fine	MS-60 Unc.	PRF-65 Proof
☐1838*	832,000	4.00	8.00	19.00	150.00	1550.00	
☐1839*	491,146	4.00	8.00	19.00	150.00	1400.00	
☐1840**	188,127	10.00	20.00	60.00	200.00	1775.00	
☐1840O* }	425,200	4.00	8.00	19.00	140.00	1400.00	
☐1840O** }		11.00	22.00	75.00	225.00	1400.00	
☐1841	120,000	17.00	35.00	90.00	220.00	950.00	
☐1841O	452,000	9.00	18.00	50.00	180.00	1300.00	
☐1842	88,000	42.00	85.00	150.00	350.00	2750.00	
☐1842O Small Date }	769,000	180.00	300.00	800.00	2450.00		
☐1842O Large Date }		6.00	13.00	30.00	85.00		
☐1843	645,000	5.00	8.50	17.00	65.00	600.00	
☐1843O Small "O"	968,000	8.00	15.00	50.00	180.00		
☐1843O Large "O"		8.00	15.00	50.00	180.00		
☐1844	421,000	4.00	8.00	17.00	75.00	650.00	
☐1844O	740,000	4.00	8.00	17.00	85.00	1100.00	

*No Drapery   **Drapery

DATE	MINTAGE	ABP	G-4 Good	F-12 Fine	EF-40 Ex. Fine	MS-60 Unc.	PRF-65 Proof
☐ 1845	922,000	4.00	8.00	17.00	72.00	645.00	
☐ 1846	510,000	4.00	8.00	17.00	72.00	645.00	
☐ 1847	734,000	4.00	8.00	17.00	72.00	645.00	
☐ 1847O	368,000	10.00	20.00	65.00	160.00	735.00	
☐ 1848	146,000	11.00	23.00	70.00	150.00	735.00	
☐ 1849	340,000	6.00	15.00	45.00	95.00	900.00	
☐ 1849O	16,000	225.00	400.00	850.00	2750.00		
☐ 1850	190,800	9.00	18.00	60.00	130.00	1000.00	
☐ 1850O	412,000	8.00	16.00	50.00	100.00	975.00	
☐ 1851	160,000	9.00	19.00	60.00	130.00	700.00	
☐ 1851O	88,000	85.00	150.00	400.00	1300.00		
☐ 1852	177,060	15.00	31.00	80.00	160.00	650.00	
☐ 1852O	96,000	100.00	200.00	370.00	1200.00		
☐ 1853***	15,210,020	3.50	7.00	18.00	100.00	775.00	
☐ 1853/4		25.00	50.00	120.00	600.00	2100.00	
☐ 1853††	44,200	65.00	130.00	300.00	630.00	2300.00	
☐ 1853O***	1,332,000	6.00	11.00	30.00	150.00	1500.00	
☐ 1854†	12,380,000	3.00	6.00	15.00	75.00	600.00	
☐ 1854†O Large "O"	1,484,000	5.00	10.00	28.00	90.00	1250.00	
☐ 1854O Huge "O"		20.00	40.00	160.00	425.00		
☐ 1855†	2,857,000	3.00	6.00	15.00	75.00	600.00	6250.00
☐ 1855O†	176,000	20.00	40.00	80.00	330.00	1400.00	
☐ 1855S†	396,400	15.00	32.00	75.00	300.00	1100.00	
☐ 1856	7,264,000	3.00	6.00	13.00	55.00	400.00	5000.00
☐ 1856O	968,000	5.00	10.00	25.00	90.00	1000.00	
☐ 1856S	} 286,000	15.00	30.00	70.00	250.00		
☐ 1856S over S		45.00	100.00	415.00	1550.00		
☐ 1857	9,644,000	3.50	7.00	15.00	50.00	385.00	5000.00
☐ 1857O	1,180,000	4.00	8.00	17.00	60.00	925.00	
☐ 1857S	82,000	21.00	42.00	120.00	600.00		
☐ 1858	7,368,000	3.50	7.00	15.00	50.00	385.00	4500.00
☐ 1858O	520,000	5.00	10.00	25.00	100.00	1075.00	
☐ 1858S	121,000	14.00	33.00	120.00	430.00		
☐ 1859	1,344,000	4.00	8.00	15.00	55.00	750.00	4750.00
☐ 1859O	260,000	9.00	18.00	45.00	115.00	1100.00	
☐ 1859S	80,000	30.00	75.00	150.00	500.00		
☐ 1860	805,400	3.50	7.00	14.00	50.00	500.00	4000.00
☐ 1860O	388,000	5.00	11.00	35.00	90.00	975.00	
☐ 1860S	56,000	35.00	85.00	250.00	700.00		
☐ 1861	4,854,000	3.50	7.00	14.00	50.00	385.00	3875.00
☐ 1861S	96,000	19.00	45.00	140.00	350.00	2700.00	
☐ 1862	932,550	3.50	7.00	14.00	60.00	450.00	3875.00
☐ 1862S	67,000	23.00	50.00	135.00	370.00		
☐ 1863	192,060	9.00	19.00	40.00	115.00	600.00	3875.00
☐ 1864	94,070	24.00	50.00	95.00	210.00	650.00	3875.00
☐ 1864S	20,000	70.00	140.00	350.00	900.00		
☐ 1865	59,300	24.00	50.00	85.00	210.00	900.00	3875.00
☐ 1865S	41,000	26.00	55.00	120.00	430.00	1600.00	

☐ 1866 Only One Known — Hydeman Sale 1961 Proof — $24,500.00
***W/Arrows and Rays †W/Arrows and no Rays ††Over 52, No Arrows

QUARTERS — LIBERTY SEATED, 1866 · 1891
Motto Above Eagle

In 1866 the words "IN GOD WE TRUST" were added to the reverse, on a banner between the eagle and the inscription "UNITED STATES OF AMERI-CA." When the weight was changed slightly to 6.25 grams in 1873 the arrows were returned but no further use was made of sunrays on the reverse. The arrows were removed in 1875.

Motto Above Eagle

DATE	MINTAGE	ABP	G-4 Good	F-12 Fine	EF-40 Ex. Fine	MS-60 Unc.	PRF-65 Proof
☐1866	17,525	100.00	200.00	375.00	700.00	950.00	3700.00
☐1866S	28,000	85.00	190.00	350.00	780.00	1700.00	
☐1867	20,625	60.00	120.00	225.00	470.00	800.00	3650.00
☐1867S	48,000	43.00	90.00	210.00	500.00	3000.00	
☐1868	30,000	50.00	100.00	200.00	400.00	825.00	3650.00
☐1868S	96,000	30.00	65.00	100.00	225.00	1600.00	
☐1869	16,600	90.00	200.00	350.00	600.00	1100.00	3650.00
☐1869S	76,000	43.00	90.00	200.00	400.00		
☐1870	87,400	19.00	40.00	90.00	200.00	900.00	3500.00
☐1870CC	8,340	650.00	1300.00	2500.00	4300.00		
☐1871	171,232	7.00	16.00	43.00	115.00	700.00	3500.00
☐1871CC	10,890	300.00	600.00	1175.00	3000.00		
☐1871S	30,900	110.00	230.00	450.00	800.00	1800.00	
☐1872	182,950	7.00	15.00	43.00	110.00	650.00	3500.00
☐1872CC	9,100	140.00	300.00	600.00	1950.00		
☐1872S	103,000	110.00	230.00	470.00	900.00	4000.00	
☐1873*	1,263,700	5.00	11.00	25.00	140.00	800.00	5500.00
☐1873** Open "3"	220,600	15.00	30.00	60.00	190.00	500.00	
☐1873** Closed "3"		30.00	60.00	110.00	250.00		3750.00
☐1873CC*	12,462	310.00	700.00	1175.00	2500.00		
☐1873CC**	4,000	RARE—Auction 1980 -$200,000.00					
☐1873S*	15,600	9.00	20.00	45.00	200.00	1150.00	
☐1874*	471,900	5.00	11.00	27.00	140.00	800.00	5600.00
☐1874S**	392,000	8.00	16.00	40.00	170.00	915.00	
☐1875	4,293,500	3.00	6.50	12.00	60.00	350.00	3575.00
☐1875CC	140,000	24.00	50.00	130.00	450.00	1350.00	

Arrows Removed Starting 1875
*W/Arrows   **No Arrows

DATE	MINTAGE	ABP	G-4 Good	F-12 Fine	EF-40 Ex. Fine	MS-60 Unc.	PRF-65 Proof
☐1875S	680,000	5.00	11.00	30.00	75.00	375.00	
☐1876	17,817,150	3.50	7.00	11.50	60.00	375.00	3575.00
☐1876CC	4,944,000	4.00	8.00	25.00	80.00	375.00	
☐1876S	8,596,000	3.50	7.00	11.50	60.00	375.00	
☐1877	10,911,710	3.50	7.00	11.50	60.00	375.00	3575.00
☐1877CC	4,192,000	4.00	8.00	25.00	90.00	450.00	
☐1877S	8,996,000	4.00	8.00	25.00	60.00	375.00	
☐1878	2,260,000	3.50	7.00	15.00	60.00	375.00	3575.00
☐1878CC	996,000	11.00	22.00	60.00	130.00	420.00	
☐1878S	140,000	15.00	32.00	90.00	270.00	1275.00	
☐1879	14,700	55.00	115.00	160.00	350.00	600.00	3650.00
☐1880	14,955	55.00	115.00	165.00	370.00	600.00	3650.00
☐1881	12,975	60.00	130.00	180.00	360.00	600.00	3650.00
☐1882	16,300	60.00	130.00	180.00	360.00	600.00	3650.00
☐1883	15,439	60.00	130.00	180.00	360.00	600.00	3650.00
☐1884	8,875	70.00	150.00	200.00	430.00	700.00	3650.00
☐1885	14,530	60.00	130.00	180.00	360.00	620.00	3650.00
☐1886	5,886	130.00	250.00	330.00	500.00	700.00	3650.00
☐1887	10,710	70.00	150.00	190.00	370.00	600.00	3650.00
☐1888	10,833	70.00	150.00	190.00	370.00	600.00	3650.00
☐1888S	1,216,000	4.00	8.00	16.00	55.00	400.00	
☐1889	12,711	65.00	135.00	180.00	370.00	600.00	3650.00
☐1890	80,590	29.00	60.00	85.00	260.00	600.00	3650.00
☐1891	3,920,600	3.50	7.00	15.00	55.00	350.00	3650.00
☐18910	68,000	65.00	140.00	210.00	610.00		
☐1891S	2,216,000	4.50	9.00	20.00	65.00	350.00	

QUARTERS — BARBER OR LIBERTY HEAD, 1892 - 1916

The Barber or Liberty Head Quarter with its classical portrait bust was introduced in 1892 after a design by Charles E. Barber. Liberty faces right and wears a cap and laurel wreath. On the reverse is a shield eagle holding arrows and branch, with (at long last) the words "QUARTER DOLLAR" spelled out without abbreviation. This was without doubt the handsomest design in the quarter dollar series and has become extremely popular with collectors. It was struck at Philadelphia, Denver, New Orleans and San Francisco. The Barber quarter has a composition of 90% silver and 10% copper with a weight of 6¼ grams and a diameter of 24.3 mm.

Mint Mark is below
the Eagle on Reverse

DATE	MINTAGE	ABP	G-4 Good	F-12 Fine	EF-40 Ex. Fine	MS-60 Unc.	PRF-65 Proof
☐ 1892	8,237,245	1.50	3.75	9.00	45.00	275.00	3575.00
☐ 1892O	2,640,000	1.50	5.00	11.00	60.00	280.00	
☐ 1892S	964,079	5.00	12.00	26.00	80.00	340.00	
☐ 1893	5,444,815	2.00	4.00	9.00	45.00	275.00	3575.00
☐ 1893O	3,396,000	2.00	4.00	12.00	55.00	290.00	
☐ 1893S	1,454,535	2.00	5.00	13.00	60.00	300.00	
☐ 1894	3,432,972	2.00	4.00	9.00	45.00	275.00	3575.00
☐ 1894O	2,852,000	2.00	4.00	12.00	55.00	290.00	
☐ 1894S	2,648,821	2.00	4.00	11.00	60.00	300.00	
☐ 1895	4,440,880	2.00	3.75	9.00	45.00	275.00	3575.00
☐ 1895O	2,816,000	2.00	4.25	13.00	55.00	350.00	
☐ 1895S	1,764,681	2.00	5.00	14.00	70.00	330.00	
☐ 1896	3,874,762	2.00	3.75	9.00	45.00	270.00	3575.00
☐ 1896O	1,484,000	2.00	5.00	15.00	90.00	650.00	
☐ 1896S	188,039	100.00	225.00	470.00	1375.00	2900.00	
☐ 1897	8,140,731	2.00	3.00	8.00	40.00	250.00	3575.00
☐ 1897O	1,414,800	3.00	6.00	17.00	100.00	700.00	
☐ 1897S	542,229	4.00	9.00	20.00	90.00	340.00	
☐ 1898	11,100,735	2.00	3.00	8.00	40.00	250.00	3575.00
☐ 1898O	1,868,000	2.00	4.50	12.00	67.00	385.00	
☐ 1898S	1,020,592	2.00	4.00	11.00	50.00	330.00	
☐ 1899	12,624,846	1.50	3.00	8.00	40.00	250.00	3575.00
☐ 1899O	2,644,000	2.00	4.50	12.00	60.00	350.00	
☐ 1899S	708,000	3.50	7.00	15.00	65.00	330.00	
☐ 1900	10,016,912	2.00	3.00	7.00	40.00	250.00	3575.00
☐ 1900O	3,416,000	2.00	5.00	13.00	70.00	340.00	
☐ 1900S	1,858,585	2.00	4.50	11.00	50.00	310.00	
☐ 1901	8,892,813	2.00	3.00	7.00	40.00	250.00	3575.00
☐ 1901O	1,612,000	4.50	10.00	30.00	120.00	675.00	
☐ 1901S	72,664	450.00	950.00	1700.00	3350.00	7750.00	
☐ 1902	12,197,744	1.50	3.00	7.00	40.00	240.00	3575.00
☐ 1902O	4,748,000	2.00	4.25	11.00	55.00	340.00	
☐ 1902S	1,524,612	2.00	7.00	14.00	70.00	350.00	
☐ 1903	9,670,064	1.50	3.00	7.00	40.00	240.00	3575.00
☐ 1903O	3,500,000	2.00	4.50	11.00	60.00	295.00	
☐ 1903S	1,036,000	2.00	7.00	14.00	80.00	350.00	
☐ 1904	9,588,813	2.00	3.00	7.00	40.00	240.00	3575.00
☐ 1904O	2,456,000	2.00	4.50	14.00	85.00	630.00	
☐ 1905	4,968,250	1.50	3.00	7.00	40.00	240.00	3575.00
☐ 1905O	1,230,000	2.00	5.00	14.00	60.00	310.00	
☐ 1905S	1,884,000	2.00	5.20	15.00	50.00	300.00	
☐ 1906	3,656,435	1.50	3.00	7.00	40.00	240.00	3575.00
☐ 1906D	3,280,000	2.00	4.75	9.00	45.00	285.00	
☐ 1906O	2,056,000	2.00	5.50	13.00	50.00	270.00	
☐ 1907	7,192,575	1.50	3.00	7.00	40.00	240.00	3575.00
☐ 1907D	2,484,000	2.00	4.25	9.00	45.00	270.00	
☐ 1907O	4,560,000	2.00	4.50	8.00	42.00	270.00	
☐ 1907S	1,360,000	2.00	5.00	11.00	50.00	325.00	
☐ 1908	4,232,545	1.50	3.00	7.00	40.00	240.00	3575.00
☐ 1908D	5,788,000	2.00	3.50	8.00	45.00	270.00	
☐ 1908O	6,244,000	1.50	3.00	8.00	45.00	275.00	

DATE	MINTAGE	ABP	G-4 Good	F-12 Fine	EF-40 Ex. Fine	MS-60 Unc.	PRF-65 Proof
☐ 1908S	784,000	3.00	6.00	16.00	70.00	330.00	
☐ 1909	9,268,650	1.25	3.00	7.00	40.00	240.00	3575.00
☐ 1909D	5,114,000	1.25	3.00	7.00	45.00	245.00	
☐ 1909O	712,000	4.00	8.00	28.00	140.00	500.00	
☐ 1909S	1,348,000	1.25	4.00	8.00	50.00	335.00	
☐ 1910	2,244,551	1.25	3.00	7.00	40.00	240.00	3575.00
☐ 1910D	1,500,000	1.25	4.00	9.00	50.00	290.00	
☐ 1911	3,270,543	1.25	3.00	7.00	40.00	240.00	3575.00
☐ 1911D	933,600	1.25	4.00	11.00	50.00	260.00	
☐ 1911S	988,000	1.25	4.00	9.00	45.00	300.00	
☐ 1912	4,400,700	1.25	3.00	7.00	40.00	250.00	3575.00
☐ 1912S	708,000	1.25	3.00	9.00	50.00	320.00	
☐ 1913	484,613	4.00	10.00	40.00	350.00	1100.00	3750.00
☐ 1913D	1,450,800	1.25	3.00	8.00	50.00	285.00	
☐ 1913S	40,000	160.00	280.00	550.00	1500.00	3000.00	
☐ 1914	6,244,610	1.25	3.00	7.00	40.00	250.00	3750.00
☐ 1914D	3,046,000	1.25	3.00	8.00	40.00	275.00	
☐ 1914S	264,000	6.00	13.00	33.00	190.00	700.00	
☐ 1915	3,480,450	1.25	3.00	7.00	40.00	260.00	3750.00
☐ 1915D	3,694,000	1.25	3.00	8.00	40.00	250.00	
☐ 1915S	704,000	1.25	4.00	12.00	50.00	270.00	
☐ 1916	1,788,000	1.25	3.00	7.00	40.00	250.00	
☐ 1916D	6,540,000	1.25	3.00	8.00	45.00	260.00	

QUARTERS — STANDING LIBERTY, 1916 - 1930

The Standing Liberty Quarter was introduced in 1916 during World War I and its theme was intended to reflect the nation's sentiments at that time. The goddess is portrayed in full length holding a shield with which she, presumably, fends off the defilers of liberty. An eagle in flight is pictured on the obverse, with the words "UNITED STATES OF AMERICA" and "E PLUR-IBUS UNUM." The designer was Herman A. MacNeil. Specifications are the same as for the Barber Quarter. This design carried so much fine detailing that very moderate handling resulted in obvious wear, making uncirculated specimens more valuable, proportionately, than in the case of most other coins. The chief point of vulnerability was the date, so small in size, and positioned in such a way as to receive heavy wear, that many specimens lost their date after only a few years of circulation. The government wished to correct this fault without totally redesigning the obverse and in 1925 hit upon the plan of showing the date in incuse — that is, pressed into the coin rather than raised from its surface. While this did not totally prevent wear it helped keep the dates readable for a longer time. A series of minor altera- tions was made in 1917, the second year of issue, including a dressing up of Liberty to satisfy public criticism that the figure was displaying a scan- dalous amount of flesh. Three stars were added beneath the eagle on the reverse.

NOTE: Prices listed for MS-60 specimens of Standing Liberty Quarters are for ordinary strikes. Exceptional strikes with full head of Liberty in detail are scarcer and sell for higher sums. This is not a question of *wear,* but simply the quality of the coin as originally struck.

1916-30
Mint Mark is to
left of Date of Obverse

1916-1917
Type I
No Stars under Eagle

1917-1930
Type II
3 Stars under Eagle

DATE	MINTAGE	ABP	G-4 Good	VG-8 V. Good	F-12 Fine	EF-40 Ex. Fine	MS-60 Unc.
☐1916	52,000	600.00	1000.00	1250.00	1400.00	1975.00	3000.00
☐1917	8,792,000	3.00	7.00	9.00	12.00	55.00	145.00
☐1917D	1,509,200	6.00	12.00	16.00	21.00	85.00	175.00
☐1917S	1,952,000	5.50	11.00	15.00	19.00	80.00	185.00
STARS UNDER EAGLE							
☐1917	13,880,000	5.00	10.00	13.00	16.00	37.00	110.00
☐1917D	6,224,400	9.00	18.00	26.00	40.00	85.00	165.00
☐1917S	5,552,000	8.00	17.00	23.00	30.00	70.00	145.00
☐1918	12,240,000	7.00	13.00	16.00	20.00	45.00	135.00
☐1918D	7,380,000	10.00	19.00	25.00	37.00	85.00	180.00
☐1918S	11,072,000	5.50	11.00	15.00	20.00	45.00	140.00
☐1918S over 7		500.00	1000.00	1350.00	1600.00	3000.00	7000.00
☐1919	11,324,000	11.00	21.00	27.00	35.00	60.00	130.00
☐1919D	1,944,000	21.00	40.00	65.00	95.00	200.00	450.00
☐1919S	1,836,000	21.00	40.00	57.00	80.00	180.00	400.00
☐1920	27,860,000	5.00	10.00	14.00	16.00	35.00	120.00
☐1920D	3,586,400	11.00	23.00	40.00	50.00	95.00	210.00
☐1920S	6,380,000	7.00	13.00	17.00	21.00	45.00	135.00
☐1921	1,916,000	25.00	53.00	80.00	115.00	200.00	395.00
☐1923	9,716,000	4.00	11.00	13.00	18.00	37.00	120.00
☐1923S*	1,360,000	42.00	90.00	130.00	175.00	350.00	530.00
☐1924	10,920,000	5.00	12.00	12.00	17.00	35.00	135.00
☐1924D	3,112,000	10.00	22.00	30.00	40.00	85.00	145.00
☐1924S	2,860,000	6.00	14.00	17.00	20.00	40.00	145.00
☐1925	12,280,000	1.25	2.50	3.50	6.50	25.00	110.00
☐1926	11,316,000	1.25	2.50	3.50	6.50	25.00	110.00
☐1926D	1,716,000	1.25	5.00	8.00	12.00	40.00	110.00
☐1926S	2,700,000	1.25	3.00	6.00	9.00	50.00	185.00
☐1927	11,912,000	1.00	2.50	3.00	7.00	25.00	110.00
☐1927D	976,400	3.50	7.50	10.00	13.00	60.00	140.00
☐1927S	396,000	5.00	10.00	17.00	45.00	450.00	1250.00
☐1928	6,336,000	1.25	2.50	3.50	7.00	23.00	110.00
☐1928D	1,627,600	1.50	5.00	7.00	10.00	30.00	120.00
☐1928S	2,644,000	1.25	2.50	4.00	7.00	30.00	110.00
☐1929	11,140,000	1.10	2.00	3.50	7.00	23.00	100.00

*Check for altered Date.

DATE	MINTAGE	ABP	G-4 Good	VG-8 V. Good	F-12 Fine	EF-40 Ex. Fine	MS-60 Unc.
☐ 1929D	1,358,000	1.50	4.00	6.50	10.00	28.00	115.00
☐ 1929S	1,764,000	1.00	2.50	4.00	7.00	25.00	100.00
☐ 1930	5,632,000	1.00	2.50	4.00	7.00	23.00	100.00
☐ 1930S	1,556,000	1.00	2.50	4.00	7.00	25.00	105.00

QUARTERS — WASHINGTON, 1932 TO DATE

1932-1967
Mint Mark is
on Reverse
Below Eagle

1968 on —
Mint Mark
to Right of
Hair Ribbon

DATE	MINTAGE	ABP	G-4 Good	F-12 Fine	EF-40 Ex. Fine	MS-60 Unc.	PRF-65 Proof
☐ 1932	5,404,000	1.25	3.00	5.00	9.00	25.00	
☐ 1932D	436,800	18.00	38.00	65.00	155.00	480.00	
☐ 1932S	408,000	16.00	33.00	45.00	70.00	250.00	
☐ 1934	31,912,052	1.25	3.00	4.00	7.00	35.00	
☐ 1934 Double Die			35.00	45.00	100.00	250.00	
☐ 1934D	3,527,200	1.25	3.00	8.00	16.00	85.00	
☐ 1935	32,484,000	1.25		4.00	7.00	30.00	
☐ 1935D	5,780,000	1.25		5.00	16.00	85.00	
☐ 1935S	5,550,000	1.25		6.00	12.00	70.00	
☐ 1936	41,303,837	1.25		4.00	8.00	27.00	850.00
☐ 1936D	5,374,000	1.25		7.00	30.00	220.00	
☐ 1936S	3,828,000	1.25		6.00	10.00	70.00	
☐ 1937	19,701,542	1.25		5.00	8.00	30.00	285.00
☐ 1937D	7,189,600	1.25		4.00	9.00	40.00	
☐ 1937S	1,652,000	1.25		8.00	18.00	95.00	
☐ 1938	9,480,045	1.25		5.00	14.00	60.00	235.00
☐ 1938S	2,832,000	1.25		7.00	11.00	55.00	
☐ 1939	33,548,795	1.25		3.50	7.00	16.00	150.00
☐ 1939D	7,092,000	1.25		4.00	9.00	28.00	
☐ 1939S	2,628,000	1.25		6.00	12.00	55.00	
☐ 1940	35,715,246	1.25		3.00	6.00	15.00	100.00
☐ 1940D	2,797,600	1.25		7.00	13.00	65.00	
☐ 1940S	8,244,000	1.25		3.00	7.00	20.00	
☐ 1941	79,047,287	1.25		2.25	5.00	8.00	85.00
☐ 1941D	16,714,800	1.25		2.25	4.00	20.00	
☐ 1941S	16,080,000	1.25		2.25	3.75	20.00	
☐ 1942	102,117,123	1.25		2.25	3.50	8.00	85.00
☐ 1942D	17,487,200	1.25		2.25	3.50	13.00	
☐ 1942S	19,384,000	1.25		2.25	5.00	65.00	
☐ 1943	99,700,000	1.25		2.25	3.50	8.00	
☐ 1943D	16,095,600	1.25		2.25	3.50	16.00	

DATE	MINTAGE	ABP	G-4 Good	F-12 Fine	EF-40 Ex. Fine	MS-60 Unc.	PRF-65 Proof
☐ 1943S	21,700,000	1.25		2.25	4.00	35.00	
☐ 1943S Double Die						EXTREMELY RARE	
☐ 1944	104,956,000	1.25		2.00	2.75	6.00	
☐ 1944D	14,600,000	1.25		2.00	2.75	14.00	
☐ 1944S	12,560,000	1.25		2.00	2.75	15.00	
☐ 1945	74,372,000	1.25		2.00	2.75	7.00	
☐ 1945D	12,341,600	1.25		2.00	2.75	8.75	
☐ 1945S	17,004,001	1.25		2.00	2.75	7.50	
☐ 1946	53,436,000	1.25		2.00	2.75	6.50	
☐ 1946D	9,072,800	1.25		2.00	2.75	7.50	
☐ 1946S	4,204,000	1.25		2.00	2.75	8.00	
☐ 1947	22,556,000	1.25		2.00	2.75	7.50	
☐ 1947D	15,338,400	1.25		2.00	2.75	7.50	
☐ 1947S	5,532,000	1.25		2.00	2.75	7.00	
☐ 1948	35,196,000	1.25		2.00	2.75	7.50	
☐ 1948D	16,768,800	1.25		2.00	2.75	7.00	
☐ 1948S	15,960,000	1.25		2.00	2.75	7.00	
☐ 1949	9,312,000	1.25		2.00	2.75	22.00	
☐ 1949D	10,068,400	1.25		2.00	2.75	8.00	
☐ 1950	24,971,512	1.25		2.00	2.75	6.00	95.00
☐ 1950D	21,075,600	1.25		2.00	2.75	6.00	
☐ 1950S	10,284,004	1.25		2.00	2.75	8.00	
☐ 1951	43,505,602	1.25		2.00	2.75	6.00	50.00
☐ 1951D	35,354,800	1.25		2.00	2.75	7.00	
☐ 1951S	8,948,000	1.25		2.00	2.75	10.00	
☐ 1952	38,862,073	1.25		2.00	2.75	5.00	40.00
☐ 1952D	49,795,200	1.25		2.00	2.75	5.00	
☐ 1952S	13,707,800	1.25		2.00	2.75	7.00	
☐ 1953	18,664,920	1.25		2.00	2.75	5.00	21.00
☐ 1953D	56,112,400	1.25		2.00	2.75	4.50	
☐ 1953S	14,016,000	1.25		2.00	2.75	5.00	
☐ 1954	54,654,503	1.25		2.00	2.75	4.00	9.00
☐ 1954D	46,305,500	1.25		2.00	2.75	4.50	
☐ 1954S	11,834,722	1.25		2.00	2.75	5.00	
☐ 1955	18,558,381	1.25		2.00	2.75	5.00	8.00
☐ 1955D	3,182,400	1.25		2.00	2.75	5.50	
☐ 1956	44,813,384	1.25		2.00	2.75	3.50	6.00
☐ 1956D	32,334,500	1.25		2.00	2.75	3.50	
☐ 1957	47,779,952	1.25		2.00	2.75	3.50	4.50
☐ 1957D	77,924,160	1.25		2.00	2.75	3.50	
☐ 1958	7,235,652	1.25		2.00	2.75	3.75	6.00
☐ 1958D	78,124,900	1.25		2.00	2.75	3.75	
☐ 1959	25,533,291	1.25		1.75	2.00	2.50	4.25
☐ 1959D	62,054,232	1.25		1.75	2.00	2.50	
☐ 1960	30,855,602	1.25		1.75	2.00	2.50	4.00
☐ 1960D	63,000,324	1.25		1.75	2.00	2.50	
☐ 1961	40,064,244	1.25		1.75	2.00	2.50	4.00
☐ 1961D	83,656,928	1.25		1.75	2.00	2.50	
☐ 1962	39,374,019	1.25		1.75	2.00	2.50	4.00

DATE	MINTAGE	ABP	G-4 Good	F-12 Fine	EF-40 Ex. Fine	MS-60 Unc.	PRF-65 Proof
☐ 1962D	127,554,756	1.25		1.75	2.00	2.50	
☐ 1963	77,391,645	1.25		1.75	2.00	2.50	4.00
☐ 1963D	135,288,184	1.25		1.75	2.00	2.50	
☐ 1964	564,341,347	1.25		1.75	2.00	2.50	4.00
☐ 1964D	704,135,528	1.25		1.75	2.00	2.50	
☐ 1965	1,819,717,540					.40	
☐ 1966	821,101,500					.40	
☐ 1967	1,524,031,840					.40	
☐ 1968	220,731,500					.45	
☐ 1968D	101,534,000					.50	
☐ 1968S PROOF ONLY	3,041,500						.85
☐ 1969	176,212,000					.35	
☐ 1969D	114,372,000					.65	
☐ 1969S PROOF ONLY	2,934,631						.85
☐ 1970	136,420,000					.35	
☐ 1970D	417,341,364					.35	
☐ 1970S PROOF ONLY	2,632,810						.85
☐ 1971	109,284,000					.35	
☐ 1971D	258,634,428					.35	
☐ 1971S PROOF ONLY	3,224,138						.85
☐ 1972	215,048,000					.35	
☐ 1972D	311,067,732					.35	
☐ 1972S	3,267,667						.85
☐ 1973	346,924,000					.35	
☐ 1973D	232,977,400					.35	
☐ 1973S PROOF ONLY	2,796,624						.85
☐ 1974	801,456,000					.35	
☐ 1974D	363,160,300					.35	
☐ 1974S PROOF ONLY	2,612,568						1.10
☐ 1976 Copper-Nickel Clad	809,780,016					.35	
☐ 1976D Copper-Nickel Clad	860,108,836					.35	
☐ 1976S Copper-Nickel Clad Proof	7,055,099						.80
☐ 1976S Silver Clad						2.00	
☐ 1976 Silver Clad Proof							3.00
☐ 1977	468,556,900					.32	
☐ 1977D	256,524,078					.32	
☐ 1977S PROOF ONLY	2,909,269						.75
☐ 1978	521,452,000					.32	
☐ 1978D	287,373,152					.32	
☐ 1978S PROOF ONLY	3,127,781						1.00
☐ 1979P	515,709,000					.32	
☐ 1979D	489,790,020					.32	
☐ 1979S PROOF (I)	3,677,200						.80
☐ 1979S PROOF (II)							2.00
☐ 1980P	635,832,101					.32	
☐ 1980D	518,327,444					.32	
☐ 1980S PROOF	3,547,130						.95

DATE	MINTAGE	ABP	G-4 Good	F-12 Fine	EF-40 Ex. Fine	MS-60 Unc.	PRF-65 Proof
☐ 1981P	602,000,000					.30	
☐ 1981D	575,841,732					.30	
☐ 1981S PROOF (I)	4,064,789						.80
☐ 1981S PROOF (II)							2.00
☐ 1982P	500,000,000					.30	
☐ 1982S PROOF (I)	3,856,941						.75
☐ 1983P	674,000,000					.30	
☐ 1983D	617,800,000					.30	

HALF DOLLARS — EARLY HALF DOLLARS, 1794 - 1838

As originally conceived the Half Dollar was to contain precisely — to the grain — half as much metal as the Dollar and was to be struck from metal of the same composition, .8924 silver alloyed with .1076 copper. It weighed 13.48 grams and was slightly larger in diameter than it subsequently became: 32½ mm. Its designer was Robert Scot and its obverse featured a profile portrait of Liberty facing right, the so-called Flowing Hair likeness used on other coins as well, backed by an eagle. Along the edge was stamped its value, as no statement of value appeared within the design: "FIFTY CENTS OR HALF A DOLLAR," the words set apart with small ornamental flourishes. Apparently the initial issue in 1794 was struck from just a single set of dies, but in the following year several dies were employed, resulting in a number of minor varieties. This was the final appearance of the Flowing Hair 50¢ piece. The design was replaced in 1796 by the Draped Bust version, to which the shielded eagle reverse was added in 1801. Because of the trading significance of this coin an effort was made to place as many half dollars as possible into circulation during its early years. It was temporarily discontinued in 1804 as a result of speculation, along with the silver dollar; but unlike the latter, which did not return for more than 30 years, production of the half dollar was resumed in 1805. In that year more than 200,000 were struck, followed by a striking exceeding 800,000 in 1806. The Capped Bust design was installed on the dollar in 1807, as it was on other coins. Its designer was a German-American named John Reich. The Capped Bust is sometimes referred to as "Turban Head." The word "LIBERTY" appears on the cap or turban band. On either side of the portrait is a series of stars, with the date positioned beneath it. The reverse has a modified shielded eagle (or heraldic eagle) with the motto "E PLURIBUS UNUM" on a banner and "50 C." This coin weighs 13.48 grams and has the same metallic composition as its predecessors. Varieties of the Capped Bust half dollar are so numerous, despite being in use for only about 30 years, that a large collection can be built around this coin. And it is, indeed, an ideal target for specialization, as nearly all specimens fall within the low to moderate range of price. Christian Gobrecht redesigned the coin in 1836, retaining the same types but modifying them somewhat. The composition was changed to provide a slightly higher content of silver and a slightly lower content of copper, the ratio now being nine parts silver/one part copper. Its weight was 13.36 grams and the diameter reduced to 30 mm. This design was replaced by Liberty Seated in 1839, which remained in use more than 50 years.

HALF DOLLARS — FLOWING HAIR, 1794 · 1795

DATE	MINTAGE	ABP	G-4 Good	F-12 Fine	VF-20 V. Fine
☐ 1794 5,300		675.00	1325.00	2500.00	3870.00
☐ 1795		210.00	400.00	700.00	1200.00
☐ 1795 Recut Date 317,844		240.00	500.00	850.00	1350.00
☐ 1795*		320.00	600.00	1350.00	2500.00

*3 leaves under each wing

HALF DOLLARS — DRAPED BUST, SMALL EAGLE 1796 · 1797

DATE	MINTAGE	ABP	G-4 Good	F-12 Fine	VF-20 V. Fine
☐ 1796 (15 stars)		4675.00	9250.00	16750.00	21750.00
☐ 1796 (16 stars)		4675.00	9250.00	16750.00	21750.00
☐ 1797 3,918		4675.00	9250.00	16750.00	21750.00

HALF DOLLARS — DRAPED BUST, 1801 · 1807
Eagle on Reverse

DATE	MINTAGE	ABP	G-4 Good	F-12 Fine	VF-20 V. Fine	MS-60 Unc.
☐1801	30,289	75.00	145.00	500.00	780.00	7650.00
☐1802	29,890	60.00	120.00	475.00	700.00	7000.00
☐1803 Large 3	188,234	40.00	80.00	190.00	450.00	6100.00
☐1803 Small 3		50.00	100.00	230.00	550.00	4000.00
☐1805		35.00	70.00	165.00	360.00	3900.00
☐1805 over 4	211,722	55.00	110.00	400.00	650.00	5750.00
☐1806		40.00	75.00	170.00	350.00	3900.00
☐1806 over 5	839,576	40.00	80.00	170.00	380.00	3900.00
☐1806 inverted (over 6)		40.00	80.00	210.00	475.00	5800.00
☐1806 Knobbed 6, Lg. Stars		40.00	75.00	160.00	350.00	3900.00
☐1806 Knobbed 6, Stem not through Claw						EXTREMELY RARE
☐1807	301,076	38.00	75.00	160.00	350.00	3900.00

HALF DOLLARS — TURBAN HEAD or "CAPPED BUST", 1807 - 1836

Motto Above Eagle, Lettered Edge, Large Size

DATE	MINTAGE	ABP	G-4 Good	F-12 Fine	VF-20 V. Fine	MS-60 Unc.
☐1807 Sm./Stars		22.00	45.00	120.00	250.00	2000.00
☐1807 Lg./Stars	750,500	22.00	43.00	100.00	180.00	1975.00
☐1807 .50 over .20		22.00	41.00	70.00	130.00	1800.00
☐1808	1,368,600	20.00	37.00	50.00	70.00	750.00
☐1808 over 7		20.00	37.00	50.00	100.00	1075.00
☐1809	1,405,810	20.00	37.00	55.00	75.00	750.00
☐1810	1,276,276	20.00	37.00	46.00	65.00	750.00
☐1811	1,203,644	20.00	37.00	46.00	65.00	750.00
☐1812	1,628,059	20.00	37.00	46.00	65.00	750.00
☐1812 over 11		22.00	41.00	70.00	100.00	750.00
☐1813	1,241,903	20.00	35.00	45.00	62.00	750.00
☐1814	1,039,075	20.00	35.00	45.00	70.00	1000.00
☐1814 over 13		23.00	45.00	65.00	100.00	1100.00
☐1815 over 12	47,150	325.00	650.00	1375.00	1550.00	5175.00
☐1817	1,215,567	18.00	33.00	45.00	65.00	730.00
☐1817 over 13		45.00	80.00	300.00	400.00	2000.00
☐1818	1,960,322	15.00	30.00	40.00	55.00	700.00
☐1818 over 17		15.00	30.00	45.00	65.00	750.00
☐1819	2,208,000	15.00	30.00	40.00	60.00	725.00

DATE	MINTAGE	ABP	G-4 Good	F-12 Fine	VF-20 V. Fine	MS-60 Unc.
☐ 1819 over 18 Large 9		14.00	28.00	40.00	60.00	725.00
☐ 1820	751,122	14.00	28.00	55.00	75.00	750.00
☐ 1820 over 19		15.00	30.00	55.00	120.00	750.00
☐ 1821	1,305,797	14.00	28.00	42.00	65.00	715.00
☐ 1822	1,559,573	14.00	28.00	42.00	65.00	715.00
☐ 1822 over 21		23.00	48.00	100.00	180.00	1275.00
☐ 1823	1,694,200	14.00	28.00	40.00	60.00	700.00
☐ 1823 Ugly 3		15.00	30.00	50.00	80.00	750.00
☐ 1824	3,504,954	12.00	24.00	32.00	50.00	700.00
☐ 1824 over 21 & others		19.00	35.00	55.00	80.00	750.00
☐ 1825	2,943,166	12.00	24.00	32.00	50.00	700.00
☐ 1826	4,044,180	12.00	24.00	32.00	55.00	700.00
☐ 1827*	5,493,400	12.00	24.00	32.00	50.00	680.00
☐ 1827 over 6 curled 2		16.00	33.00	45.00	65.00	700.00
☐ 1828	3,075,200	12.00	25.00	32.00	50.00	670.00
☐ 1829	3,712,156	12.00	25.00	32.00	50.00	670.00
☐ 1829 over 27		12.00	25.00	32.00	50.00	775.00
☐ 1830**	4,764,800	12.00	25.00	32.00	50.00	675.00
☐ 1831	5,873,660	12.00	25.00	32.00	50.00	675.00
☐ 1832***	4,797,000	12.00	25.00	32.00	50.00	675.00
☐ 1833	5,206,000	12.00	25.00	32.00	50.00	665.00
☐ 1834	6,412,000	12.00	25.00	32.00	50.00	665.00
☐ 1835	5,352,006	12.00	25.00	32.00	50.00	665.00
☐ 1836 ALL KINDS	6,546,200	12.00	25.00	32.00	50.00	665.00

*Square—Based 2.   **Small O, in Date, Large O, in Date: Same Price.
***Small Letters, Large Letters: Same Price.

HALF DOLLARS — TURBAN HEAD or "CAPPED BUST", 1836 - 1839
No Motto Above Eagle, Reeded Edge, Reduced Size

1836-
1837
"50 cents"

1838-
1839
"HALF DOL."

DATE*	MINTAGE	ABP	G-4 Good	F-12 Fine	EX-40 Ex. Fine	MS-60 Unc.	PRF-65 Proof
☐ 1836*		12.00	25.00	32.00	100.00	665.00	
☐ 1836 Reeded Edge		190.00	390.00	700.00	1675.00	4150.00	
☐ 1837	3,629,820	15.00	31.00	42.00	130.00	760.00	
☐ 1838	3,546,000	15.00	31.00	42.00	130.00	760.00	
☐ 18380	Approx. 20	EXTREMELY RARE-Stack's Sale 1975					50000.00
☐ 1839	3,334,500	15.00	31.00	42.00	130.00	760.00	
☐ 18390	179,000	60.00	125.00	250.00	650.00	3000.00	

*Lettered edge 50 over 00

HALF DOLLAR — LIBERTY SEATED, 1839 - 1866
Without Motto Above Eagle

The Seated Liberty half dollar was based on the now-celebrated design of Christian Gobrecht. The goddess sits looking left, holding a shield on which the word "LIBERTY" appears and, in the other hand, a staff. The upper portion of the design is encircled by stars. On the reverse is a shield or heraldic eagle holding arrows and branch. Beneath the eagle are the words "HALF DOL." After some minor modification of both the obverse and reverse design, the numerals used for giving the date were enlarged in 1846 and a major change occurred in 1853. Because the California gold strikes of 1849 had brought great quantities of this metal into circulation, public confidence in silver was gradually eroding. To inspire greater acceptance of silver coinage their composition was revised to include a higher proportion of bullion. The new ratio — not just for half dollars but silver pieces in general — was nine parts silver to one of copper, the one part of copper being necessary to give this undurable metal a fair stability. The weight was 12.44 grams and the diameter 30.6 mm. A pair of arrows was placed on the obverse beside the date, as warning that the metal content had changed, and — in the event this was overlooked — sunrays were installed on the reverse, radiating from behind the eagle. These were discontinued in 1856. Beginning in 1866, and probably not coincidentally because the Civil War had recently ended, the motto "IN GOD WE TRUST" was incorporated into the reverse design, on a banner that flies above the eagle's head. When the weight was increased 6/10th of a gram in 1873, resort was again made to arrows at the date, but no sunrays adorned the reverse. The arrows were removed in 1875. The Seated Liberty Half Dollar continued to be struck until 1891, though throughout the 1880's its output was very limited.

Mint Mark is
Below Eagle
on Reverse

DATE	MINTAGE	ABP	G-4 Good	F-12 Fine	Ex-40 Ex. Fine	MS-60 Unc.
☐ 1839 no drapery from elbow		15.00	30.00	70.00	550.00	5500.00
☐ 1839	3,334,560	9.00	18.00	40.00	85.00	550.00
☐ 1840	1,435,008	8.00	18.00	50.00	95.00	580.00
☐ 1840O	855,100	9.00	20.00	50.00	110.00	675.00
☐ 1841	310,000	15.00	30.00	100.00	270.00	1100.00
☐ 1841O	401,000	8.00	17.00	35.00	115.00	875.00
☐ 1842	2,012,764	13.00	27.00	70.00	130.00	1000.00
☐ 1842O small date		300.00	600.00	1300.00	4675.00	
☐ large date		8.00	17.00	33.00	120.00	630.00
☐ 1843	3,844,000	8.00	17.00	35.00	110.00	560.00
☐ 1843O	2,268,000	8.00	17.00	40.00	110.00	635.00
☐ 1844	1,766,000	8.00	17.00	32.00	110.00	560.00
☐ 1844O	2,005,000	8.00	17.00	30.00	115.00	625.00
☐ 1845	589,000	11.00	22.00	60.00	180.00	950.00
☐ 1845O	2,094,000	8.00	17.00	35.00	110.00	650.00
☐ 1846	2,110,000	8.00	17.00	35.00	85.00	625.00
☐ 1846 over horizontal 6		35.00	70.00	150.00	350.00	1425.00
☐ 1846O	2,304,000	7.00	16.00	33.00	110.00	650.00
☐ 1847	1,156,000	7.00	16.00	30.00	75.00	615.00
☐ 1847 over 6		475.00	800.00	2250.00	4200.00	
☐ 1847O	2,584,000	7.00	16.00	32.00	80.00	775.00
☐ 1848	580,000	11.00	21.00	50.00	190.00	1250.00
☐ 1848O	3,180,000	8.00	16.00	35.00	100.00	825.00
☐ 1849	1,252,000	8.00	16.00	35.00	100.00	1200.00
☐ 1849O	2,310,000	8.00	16.00	35.00	85.00	775.00
☐ 1850	227,000	12.00	25.00	90.00	300.00	1450.00
☐ 1850O	2,456,000	7.00	16.00	32.00	85.00	800.00
☐ 1851	200,750	15.00	30.00	80.00	370.00	1400.00
☐ 1851O	402,000	9.00	18.00	50.00	140.00	775.00
☐ 1852	77,130	32.00	60.00	230.00	550.00	1675.00
☐ 1852O	144,000	15.00	30.00	110.00	290.00	1500.00
☐ 1853**	3,532,708	8.00	16.00	40.00	220.00	1800.00
☐ 1853O**	1,328,000	9.00	19.00	55.00	600.00	2400.00
☐ 1853O NO ARROWS — EXTREMELY RARE				AUCTION SALE 1979 $40,000.00		
☐ 1854***	2,982,000	8.00	15.00	30.00	110.00	875.00
☐ 1854O***	5,240,000	8.00	15.00	30.00	100.00	750.00
☐ 1855***	759,500	8.00	16.00	35.00	140.00	1075.00 10000.00
☐ 1855O	3,688,000	8.00	15.00	30.00	110.00	750.00
☐ 1855S***	129,950	145.00	310.00	570.00	2375.00	5150.00
☐ 1856	938,000	7.00	13.00	26.00	65.00	550.00 7500.00
☐ 1856O	2,658,000	7.00	13.00	26.00	65.00	625.00
☐ 1856S	211,000	17.00	35.00	65.00	350.00	1400.00
☐ 1857	1,988,000	6.00	12.00	26.00	65.00	550.00 7150.00
☐ 1857O	818,000	5.00	13.00	28.00	85.00	1000.00
☐ 1857S	158,000	16.00	34.00	70.00	370.00	1375.00
☐ 1858	4,226,000	6.00	13.00	25.00	65.00	550.00 5850.00
☐ 1858O	7,294,000	6.00	13.00	25.00	70.00	675.00
☐ 1858S	476,000	7.50	16.00	40.00	350.00	830.00

**With Arrows and Rays   ***With Arrows.

DATE	MINTAGE	ABP	G-4 Good	F-12 Fine	Ex-40 Ex. Fine	MS-60 Unc.	PRF-65 Proof
☐ 1859	748,000	6.00	12.00	28.00	70.00	595.00	7750.00
☐ 18590	2,834,000	6.00	12.00	27.00	65.00	630.00	
☐ 1859S	566,000	9.00	18.00	41.00	210.00	850.00	
☐ 1860	303,700	7.00	14.00	30.00	160.00	850.00	5150.00
☐ 18600	1,290,000	6.00	12.00	27.00	65.00	630.00	
☐ 1860S	472,000	11.00	23.00	50.00	140.00	630.00	
☐ 1861	2,888,400	6.00	12.00	30.00	65.00	550.00	5150.00
☐ 18610	330,000	6.00	12.00	30.00	65.00	575.00	
☐ 1861S	939,500	6.00	13.00	30.00	68.00	650.00	
☐ 1862	252,350	10.00	21.00	55.00	180.00	750.00	5150.00
☐ 1862S	1,352,000	6.00	13.00	27.00	60.00	630.00	
☐ 1863	503,660	7.00	14.00	30.00	80.00	670.00	5150.00
☐ 1863S	916,000	6.00	13.00	27.00	60.00	650.00	
☐ 1864	379,570	7.00	14.00	32.00	140.00	680.00	5150.00
☐ 1864S	658,000	6.00	13.00	20.00	75.00	650.00	
☐ 1865	511,900	7.00	14.00	50.00	120.00	750.00	5150.00
☐ 1865S	675,000	6.00	13.00	27.00	70.00	650.00	
☐ 1866S†		25.00	50.00	150.00	575.00	4000.00	

†Part of Total Mintage: 1,054,000

HALF DOLLARS — LIBERTY SEATED, 1866 - 1891
With Motto on Reverse

Arrows at Date

No Arrows at Date

Mint Mark is Below Eagle on Reverse

DATE	MINTAGE	ABP	G-4 Good	F-12 Fine	EF-40 Ex. Fine	MS-60 Unc.	PRF-65 Proof
☐ 1866	745,625	6.00	12.00	25.00	120.00	530.00	4875.00
☐ 1866S***		6.00	13.00	30.00	85.00	575.00	
☐ 1867	424,325	7.00	15.00	32.00	150.00	550.00	4875.00
☐ 1867S	1,196,000	6.00	13.00	30.00	80.00	585.00	
☐ 1868	378,000	9.00	19.00	40.00	250.00	700.00	4875.00
☐ 1868S	1,160,000	6.00	14.00	35.00	140.00	585.00	
☐ 1869	795,900	6.00	13.00	27.00	90.00	500.00	4875.00

***Part of Total Mintage: 1,054,000

DATE	MINTAGE	ABP	G-4 Good	F-12 Fine	EF-40 Ex. Fine	MS-60 Unc.	PRF-65 Proof
☐ 1869S	656,000	7.00	15.00	32.00	160.00	625.00	
☐ 1870	600,900	7.00	14.00	29.00	145.00	500.00	4875.00
☐ 1870CC	54,617	230.00	470.00	1200.00	3850.00	Unknown in BU	
☐ 1870S	1,004,000	7.00	15.00	33.00	150.00	620.00	
☐ 1871	1,165,360	6.00	12.00	25.00	85.00	500.00	4875.00
☐ 1871CC	139,950	32.00	70.00	150.00	700.00	4000.00	
☐ 1871S	2,178,000	7.00	13.00	27.00	65.00	750.00	
☐ 1872	881,550	6.00	12.00	27.00	60.00	500.00	4875.00
☐ 1872CC	272,000	26.00	55.00	100.00	310.00	1500.00	
☐ 1872S	580,000	7.00	18.00	35.00	220.00	1050.00	
☐ 1873 w/arrows	1,815,700	7.00	15.50	30.00	200.00	700.00	7000.00
☐ 1873 no arrows	801,800	7.00	16.00	45.00	180.00	600.00	4875.00
☐ 1873CC w/arrows	214,560	15.00	32.00	95.00	350.00	1400.00	
☐ 1873CC no arrows	122,500	35.00	75.00	160.00	490.00	2500.00	
☐ 1873S w/arrows	288,000	12.00	25.00	50.00	270.00	1150.00	
☐ 1873S no arrows	5,000		NONE KNOWN TO EXIST				
☐ 1874	2,360,300	7.00	15.50	30.00	170.00	750.00	6950.00
☐ 1874CC	59,000	49.00	100.00	350.00	1000.00	4500.00	
☐ 1874S	394,000	13.00	25.00	50.00	270.00	1700.00	
☐ 1875	6,027,500	6.00	13.00	28.00	60.00	520.00	4925.00
☐ 1875CC	1,008,000	6.00	13.00	28.00	130.00	520.00	
☐ 1875S	3,200,000	6.00	13.00	28.00	90.00	520.00	
☐ 1876	8,419,150	6.00	13.00	28.00	60.00	520.00	4925.00
☐ 1876CC	1,956,000	6.00	13.00	28.00	110.00	600.00	
☐ 1876S	4,528,000	6.00	13.00	28.00	60.00	520.00	
☐ 1877	8,304,510	6.00	13.00	28.00	60.00	520.00	4925.00
☐ 1877CC	1,420,000	6.00	13.00	28.00	70.00	520.00	
☐ 1877S	5,356,000	6.00	13.00	28.00	60.00	520.00	
☐ 1878	1,378,400	6.00	13.00	28.00	60.00	520.00	4925.00
☐ 1878CC	62,000	85.00	190.00	400.00	1270.00	2275.00	
☐ 1878S	12,000	1150.00	2000.00	3500.00	7150.00	18000.00	
☐ 1879	5,900	100.00	200.00	260.00	400.00	900.00	5100.00
☐ 1880	1,355	90.00	180.00	230.00	400.00	900.00	5100.00
☐ 1881	10,975	90.00	180.00	230.00	400.00	900.00	5100.00
☐ 1882	5,500	120.00	210.00	270.00	450.00	900.00	5100.00
☐ 1883	9,039	90.00	180.00	230.00	435.00	900.00	5100.00
☐ 1884	5,275	100.00	225.00	270.00	435.00	900.00	5100.00
☐ 1885	6,130	100.00	215.00	300.00	435.00	900.00	5100.00
☐ 1886	5,886	110.00	240.00	330.00	435.00	900.00	5100.00
☐ 1887	5,710	110.00	245.00	320.00	435.00	900.00	5100.00
☐ 1888	12,833	80.00	170.00	215.00	435.00	850.00	5100.00
☐ 1889	12,711	80.00	170.00	215.00	435.00	850.00	5100.00
☐ 1890	12,590	80.00	170.00	215.00	435.00	850.00	5100.00
☐ 1891	200,600	10.00	20.00	55.00	195.00	820.00	5100.00

HALF DOLLARS — LIBERTY HEAD or BARBER, 1892 · 1915

These coins, which resemble the Morgan Dollar in portraiture, were prepared from designs by Charles E. Barber and really have no connection with the Morgan Dollar aside from the possibility that Barber may have been inspired by it. The face of Liberty, which faces right, is strong and classical, suggesting the portraiture of Greek coins of ancient time. The weight is somewhat greater than the final version of the Seated Liberty half, 12½ grams, but its composition is the same, 90% silver and an alloy of 10% copper. The reverse has an attractive eagle with shield and wings spread wide; it holds the traditional arrows and branch. The mintmark appears directly beneath the eagle's tail feathers. Without question this was artistically the finest coin of the half dollar series. It was struck at Philadelphia, New Orleans, Denver and San Francisco. Not a single rarity is to be found among the Barber halves, with the result that it offers splendid opportunities for completion — even if one wishes to include all the mintmarks.

Mint Mark is Below Eagle on Reverse

DATE	MINTAGE	ABP	G-4 Good	F-12 Fine	EF-40 Ex. Fine	MS-60 Unc.	PRF-65 Proof
☐ 1892	935,245	5.00	11.00	25.00	150.00	500.00	5175.00
☐ 1892O	390,000	32.00	75.00	150.00	350.00	850.00	
☐ 1892S	1,029,028	39.00	80.00	160.00	340.00	900.00	
☐ 1893	1,826,792	3.00	9.00	25.00	150.00	550.00	5175.00
☐ 1893O	1,389,000	7.00	14.00	36.00	230.00	685.00	
☐ 1893S	740,000	21.00	45.00	85.00	310.00	850.00	
☐ 1894	1,148,972	3.00	8.00	25.00	150.00	570.00	5175.00
☐ 1894O	2,138,000	3.00	7.00	27.00	200.00	600.00	
☐ 1894S	4,048,690	2.75	6.00	24.00	170.00	580.00	
☐ 1895	1,835,218	2.50	7.00	23.00	145.00	560.00	5175.00
☐ 1895O	1,766,000	3.00	8.00	24.00	170.00	650.00	
☐ 1895S	1,108,086	5.00	13.00	33.00	190.00	600.00	
☐ 1896	950,762	3.00	8.00	27.00	150.00	570.00	5175.00
☐ 1896O	924,000	5.00	12.00	40.00	270.00	900.00	
☐ 1896S	1,140,948	20.00	45.00	80.00	310.00	950.00	
☐ 1897	2,480,731	2.50	5.00	18.00	120.00	550.00	5175.00
☐ 1897O	632,000	21.00	40.00	75.00	350.00	1250.00	
☐ 1897S	933,900	33.00	70.00	130.00	340.00	1050.00	
☐ 1898	2,956,735	2.50	5.00	17.00	120.00	550.00	5175.00

DATE	MINTAGE	ABP	G-4 Good	F-12 Fine	EF-40 Ex. Fine	MS-60 Unc.	PRF-65 Proof
☐ 18980	874,000	5.00	12.00	30.00	250.00	650.00	
☐ 1898S	2,358,550	2.50	7.00	23.00	150.00	595.00	
☐ 1899	5,538,846	2.30	5.00	16.00	120.00	500.00	5175.00
☐ 18990	1,724,000	2.50	7.50	22.00	195.00	650.00	
☐ 1899S	1,686,411	2.50	7.00	21.00	160.00	600.00	
☐ 1900	4,762,912	2.50	6.00	16.00	120.00	500.00	5175.00
☐ 19000	2,744,000	2.50	6.00	23.00	210.00	660.00	
☐ 1900S	2,560,322	2.50	6.00	21.00	160.00	600.00	
☐ 1901	4,268,813	2.50	6.00	16.00	120.00	530.00	5175.00
☐ 19010	1,124,000	2.50	6.00	26.00	250.00	975.00	
☐ 1901S	847,044	2.50	6.00	40.00	350.00	1100.00	
☐ 1902	4,922,777	2.50	6.00	17.00	120.00	540.00	5175.00
☐ 19020	2,526,000	2.50	6.00	21.00	160.00	675.00	
☐ 1902S	1,460,670	2.50	6.00	22.00	180.00	640.00	
☐ 1903	2,278,755	2.50	6.00	16.00	120.00	540.00	5175.00
☐ 19030	2,100,000	2.50	6.00	21.00	165.00	615.00	
☐ 1903S	1,920,772	2.50	6.00	22.00	175.00	615.00	
☐ 1904	2,992,670	2.50	6.00	16.00	120.00	550.00	5175.00
☐ 19040	1,117,600	3.00	8.00	26.00	260.00	1000.00	
☐ 1904S	553,038	3.50	9.50	39.00	310.00	975.00	
☐ 1905	662,727	3.00	8.00	28.00	220.00	630.00	5175.00
☐ 19050	505,000	3.00	9.00	35.00	240.00	660.00	
☐ 1905S	2,494,000	2.50	6.00	21.00	165.00	620.00	
☐ 1906	1,638,675	2.50	6.00	16.00	120.00	550.00	5175.00
☐ 1906D	4,028,000	2.50	6.00	21.00	135.00	565.00	
☐ 19060	2,446,000	2.50	6.00	22.00	140.00	600.00	
☐ 1906S	1,740,154	2.50	6.00	23.00	160.00	620.00	
☐ 1907	2,598,575	2.00	6.00	16.00	120.00	550.00	5175.00
☐ 1907D	3,856,000	2.50	6.00	21.00	140.00	600.00	
☐ 19070	3,946,600	2.50	6.00	22.00	140.00	585.00	
☐ 1907S	1,250,000	2.50	6.00	23.00	175.00	625.00	
☐ 1908	1,354,545	2.30	5.00	16.00	130.00	550.00	5175.00
☐ 1908D	3,280,000	2.50	6.00	19.00	130.00	565.00	
☐ 19080	5,360,000	2.50	6.00	19.00	135.00	565.00	
☐ 1908S	1,644,828	2.50	6.00	21.00	165.00	600.00	
☐ 1909	2,368,650	2.30	5.00	18.00	120.00	550.00	5175.00
☐ 19090	925,400	3.00	8.00	23.00	210.00	700.00	
☐ 1909S	1,764,000	2.50	6.00	20.00	160.00	610.00	
☐ 1910	418,551	2.50	8.00	25.00	250.00	650.00	5175.00
☐ 1910S	1,948,000	2.50	6.00	20.00	145.00	590.00	
☐ 1911	1,406,543	2.30	5.00	16.00	120.00	550.00	5175.00
☐ 1911D	696,080	2.50	6.00	21.00	150.00	570.00	
☐ 1911S	1,272,000	2.50	6.00	20.00	150.00	585.00	
☐ 1912	1,550,700	2.50	6.00	16.00	120.00	550.00	5175.00
☐ 1912D	2,300,800	2.50	6.00	19.00	130.00	530.00	
☐ 1912S	1,370,000	2.50	6.00	19.00	145.00	585.00	
☐ 1913	188,627	5.00	15.00	35.00	230.00	800.00	5175.00
☐ 1913D	534,000	3.00	6.00	20.00	160.00	570.00	
☐ 1913S	604,000	3.00	6.00	23.00	175.00	620.00	

DATE	MINTAGE	ABP	G-4 Good	F-12 Fine	EF-40 Ex. Fine	MS-60 Unc.	PRF-65 Proof
☐ 1914	124,610	9.00	18.00	55.00	290.00	750.00	5375.00
☐ 1914S	992,000	2.50	6.00	21.00	160.00	580.00	
☐ 1915	138,450	7.00	16.00	35.00	250.00	800.00	5325.00
☐ 1915D	1,170,400	2.30	5.00	16.00	120.00	500.00	
☐ 1915S	1,604,000	2.50	6.00	18.00	135.00	565.00	

HALF DOLLARS — LIBERTY WALKING, 1916 - 1947

This attractive design, introduced in 1916, pictured a full-length representation of Liberty on the obverse, dressed in a diaphonous gown and strolling along a field, her right arm upraised as if in acknowledgment of the splendors of nature. In the distance the sun rises (or sets). The designer was A. Weinman, whose initials may be observed — if one has a coin with virtually no wear — on the reverse. His rendition of the eagle on the coin's reverse, a naturalistic type bearing little resemblance to the previously employed shield or heraldic eagle, is a noteworthy piece of art. Sadly the Liberty Walking half dollar suffered a great deal from rubbing in circulation and much of its delicate linework wore down rapidly, resulting in a shortage of presentable specimens. The collector who wishes to build up a set would be well advised to seek the finest condition obtainable, and be prepared to give a slight premium for coins of the best quality, rather than collect "average" specimens which are, truly, mere shadows of their original selves. The Liberty Walking 50¢ piece was struck at Philadelphia, San Francisco and Denver. Its composition is 90% silver and 10% copper with a weight of 12½ grams and diameter of 30.6 mm.

NOTE: The sale of Liberty Walking halves as silver bullion should be approached with care. While the majority of common dates in average condition are of no special numismatic value, this series, though modern, does include scarce dates and mintmarks which deserve a better fate than the smelter's pot. The silver in these coins amounts to .36169 ounce, or slightly more than one-third of an ounce.

DATE	MINTAGE	ABP	G-4 Good	F-12 Fine	EF-40 Ex. Fine	MS-60 Unc.	PRF-65
☐ 1916	608,000	8.00	17.00	52.00	170.00	385.00	
☐ 1916D on obverse	1,014,400	5.00	12.00	30.00	125.00	330.00	
☐ 1916S on obverse	508,000	10.00	21.00	105.00	330.00	750.00	2400.00
☐ 1917	12,292,000	2.25	4.00	10.00	32.00	140.00	
☐ 1917D on obverse	765,400	3.00	9.00	25.00	150.00	500.00	
☐ 1917D on reverse	1,940,000	2.25	6.00	18.00	120.00	530.00	
☐ 1917S on obverse	952,000	7.00	11.00	30.00	300.00	850.00	2400.00
☐ 1917S on reverse	6,554,000	2.25	4.00	12.00	45.00	250.00	
☐ 1918	6,634,000	2.25	5.00	16.00	105.00	335.00	
☐ 1918D	3,853,040	2.25	6.00	17.00	115.00	660.00	
☐ 1918S	10,282,000	2.25	4.00	12.00	42.00	275.00	
☐ 1919	962,000	2.25	9.50	27.00	310.00	950.00	
☐ 1919D	1,165,000	2.25	8.00	26.00	350.00	1700.00	

Mint Mark is Under "In
God We Trust" on 1916
and Early 1917. Later Left of "H"
on Reverse

DATE	MINTAGE	ABP	G-4 Good	F-12 Fine	EF-40 Ex. Fine	MS-60 Unc.	PRF-65
☐1919S	1,552,000	2.25	7.00	20.00	300.00	1575.00	
☐1920	6,372,000	2.25	5.00	9.00	45.00	250.00	
☐1920D	1,551,000	2.25	5.00	20.00	200.00	850.00	
☐1920S	4,624,000	2.25	5.00	12.00	105.00	750.00	
☐1921	246,000	28.00	60.00	140.00	800.00	2000.00	
☐1921D	208,000	32.00	70.00	210.00	900.00	2200.00	
☐1921S	548,000	6.00	13.00	39.00	900.00	5375.00	
☐1923S	2,178,000	2.25	5.00	15.00	130.00	820.00	
☐1927S	2,393,000	2.25	4.75	11.00	70.00	650.00	
☐1928S	1,940,000	2.25	4.75	11.00	80.00	750.00	
☐1929D	1,001,200	2.25	4.75	11.00	55.00	360.00	
☐1929S	1,902,000	2.25	4.75	10.00	50.00	360.00	
☐1933S	1,786,000	2.25	4.75	10.00	35.00	330.00	
☐1934	6,964,000	2.25	4.25	6.00	12.00	75.00	
☐1934D	2,361,400	2.25	4.25	6.00	26.00	160.00	
☐1934S	3,652,000	2.25	4.25	6.00	20.00	320.00	
☐1935	9,162,000	2.25	4.25	6.00	11.00	60.00	
☐1935D	3,003,800	2.25	4.25	6.00	30.00	160.00	
☐1935S	2,854,000	2.25	4.25	6.00	22.00	185.00	
☐1936	12,617,901	2.25	4.25	6.00	11.00	55.00	1800.00
☐1936D	4,252,400	2.25	4.25	6.00	18.00	110.00	
☐1936S	3,884,000	2.25	4.25	6.00	18.00	130.00	
☐1937	9,527,728	2.25	4.25	6.00	11.00	55.00	1225.00
☐1937D	1,760,001	2.25	4.25	6.00	29.00	200.00	
☐1937S	2,090,000	2.25	4.25	6.00	20.00	145.00	
☐1938	4,118,152	2.25	4.25	6.00	13.00	95.00	1125.00
☐1938D	491,600	6.00	14.00	27.00	85.00	400.00	
☐1939	6,820,808	2.25	3.25	5.75	12.00	75.00	925.00
☐1939D	4,267,800	2.25	3.25	5.75	13.00	70.00	
☐1939S	2,552,000	2.25	3.25	5.75	15.00	100.00	
☐1940	9,167,279	2.25	3.25	5.75	10.00	40.00	850.00
☐1940S	4,550,000	2.25	3.25	5.75	13.00	75.00	
☐1941	24,207,412	2.25	3.25	5.75	8.00	35.00	825.00
☐1941D	11,248,400	2.25	3.25	5.75	9.00	55.00	
☐1941S	8,098,000	2.25	3.25	5.75	12.00	160.00	
☐1942	47,839,120	2.25	3.25	5.75	8.00	35.00	825.00
☐1942D	10,973,800	2.25	3.25	5.75	8.00	70.00	
☐1942S	12,708,000	2.25	3.25	5.75	8.00	95.00	
☐1943	53,190,000	2.25	3.25	5.75	8.00	35.00	
☐1943D	11,346,000	2.25	3.25	5.75	8.00	65.00	

DATE	MINTAGE	ABP	G-4 Good	F-12 Fine	EF-40 Ex. Fine	MS-60 Unc.	PRF-65
☐ 1943S	13,450,000	2.25	3.25	5.75	8.00	100.00	
☐ 1944	28,206,000	2.25	3.25	5.75	8.00	32.00	
☐ 1944D	9,769,000	2.25	3.25	5.75	8.00	55.00	
☐ 1944S	8,904,000	2.25	3.25	5.75	9.00	50.00	
☐ 1945	31,502,000	2.25	3.25	5.75	8.00	32.00	
☐ 1945D	9,966,500	2.25	3.25	5.75	8.00	50.00	
☐ 1945S	10,156,000	2.25	3.25	5.75	9.00	65.00	
☐ 1946	12,118,000	2.25	3.25	5.75	7.50	40.00	
☐ 1946D	2,151,000	2.25	3.25	6.00	10.00	55.00	
☐ 1946S	3,724,000	2.25	3.25	5.75	9.00	70.00	
☐ 1947	4,094,000	2.25	3.25	5.75	11.00	73.00	
☐ 1947D	3,900,000	2.25	3.25	5.75	10.00	70.00	

HALF DOLLARS — FRANKLIN or "LIBERTY BELL", 1948 - 1963

The likeness of Benjamin Franklin, which had not previously appeared on a U.S. coin, was installed on the half dollar in 1948. Franklin was — and to this date is — the only non-President to be depicted on our coins, not counting colonial issues and tokens. That he was not President can be accounted for by mere circumstance. Had the federal government been formed ten or twenty years sooner, before Franklin had advanced into old age, there is little doubt but that he would have attained the office. Like the Roosevelt dime, introduced two years earlier, this coin was designed by John R. Sinnock. On the reverse is a large representation of the Liberty Bell, adapted from the artwork on the 1926 Sesquicentennial medal celebrating the 150th anniversary of our Declaration of Independence. Franklin is shown in profile facing right. The mintmark is atop the Liberty Bell on the reverse, directly below the words "UNITED STATES OF AMERICA." Composition is 90% silver, 10% copper, with a weight of 12½ grams. The diameter is 30.6 mm. It contains .36169 ounce of pure silver, or slightly more than one-third of an ounce.

DATE	MINTAGE	ABP	F-12 Fine	EF-40 Ex. Fine	MS-60 Unc.	PFR-65 Proof
☐ 1948	3,006,814	2.25	5.00	8.00	20.00	
☐ 1948D	4,028,600	2.25	5.00	8.00	17.00	
☐ 1949	5,714,000	2.25	5.50	8.50	50.00	
☐ 1949D	4,120,600	2.25	5.00	9.00	47.00	
☐ 1949S	3,744,000	2.25	7.00	18.00	100.00	
☐ 1950	7,793,509	2.25	5.00	9.00	25.00	475.00
☐ 1950D	8,031,600	2.25	5.00	8.00	28.00	
☐ 1951	16,859,602	2.25	2.75	6.00	14.00	275.00
☐ 1951D	9,475,200	2.25	2.75	5.00	40.00	
☐ 1951S	13,696,000	2.25	2.75	5.00	32.00	
☐ 1952	21,274,074	2.25	2.75	5.00	14.00	150.00
☐ 1952D	25,394,600	2.25	2.75	5.00	15.00	
☐ 1952S	5,526,000	2.25	2.75	5.00	35.00	

Mint Mark
is Above
Liberty Bell
on Reverse

DATE	MINTAGE	ABP	F-12 Fine	EF-40 Ex. Fine	MS-60 Unc.	PFR-65 Proof
☐ 1953	2,796,920	2.25	4.25	6.50	20.00	125.00
☐ 1953D	20,900,400	2.25	2.75	4.85	13.00	
☐ 1953S	4,148,000	2.25	2.75	4.85	21.00	
☐ 1954	13,421,503	2.25	2.75	4.85	13.00	60.00
☐ 1954D	25,445,580	2.25	2.75	4.85	10.00	
☐ 1954S	4,993,400	2.25	2.75	4.85	15.00	
☐ 1955	2,876,381	2.25	6.00	9.00	16.00	55.00
☐ 1956	4,701,384	2.25	5.00	7.00	16.00	32.00
☐ 1957	6,361,952	2.25	2.75	4.85	12.00	25.00
☐ 1957D	19,996,850	2.25	2.75	4.85	11.00	
☐ 1958	4,917,652	2.25	4.10	6.00	12.00	32.00
☐ 1958D	23,962,412	2.25	2.75	4.85	9.00	
☐ 1959	7,349,291	2.25	2.75	4.85	9.50	23.00
☐ 1959D	13,053,750	2.25	2.75	4.85	12.00	
☐ 1960	7,715,602	2.25	2.75	4.85	8.00	19.00
☐ 1960D	18,215,812	2.25	2.75	4.85	9.00	
☐ 1961	11,318,244	2.25	2.75	4.85	8.00	17.50
☐ 1961D	20,276,442	2.25	2.75	4.85	8.00	
☐ 1962	12,932,019	2.25	2.75	4.85	8.00	17.50
☐ 1962D	35,473,281	2.25	2.75	4.85	8.00	
☐ 1963	25,239,645	2.25	2.75	4.85	8.00	17.50
☐ 1963D	67,069,292	2.25	2.75	4.85	8.00	

HALF DOLLARS — JOHN F. KENNEDY, 1964 TO DATE

Following the death of President Kennedy in 1963 there was considerable public sentiment for honoring his memory on coinage. As all coins except the half dollar already carried portraits of Presidents it was decided to install his likeness on this coin, even though its design had been changed as recently as 1948. the portrait was designed by Gilroy Roberts and Frank Gasparro, the reverse featuring a shield eagle surrounded by stars. As introduced in 1964 the coin was of regular silver composition (90% silver, 10% copper, .36169 ounces of silver by weight) but was altered in 1965 to the clad standard, consisting of a 21% silver/79% copper interior covered with 80% silver/20% copper, total weight of silver being .14792 ounces. Its weight was 11½ grams, down from 12½. In 1971 the silver was removed from its core and a new composition used for the exterior, comprising three parts copper to one of nickel. The silver had been entirely replaced and the weight fell to 11.34 grams. The only alteration in design occurred in 1976 when a figure of Independence Hall in Philadelphia was added to the reverse, supplanting the eagle, as part of the Bicentennial program. On the obverse the date appeared as "1775-1976." In the following year the normal reverse was readopted. A quantity of silver-clad pieces were struck in 1976, the first (and last) in this series since 1970. This has been termed a difficult coin on which to find the mintmark. As first issued it may be observed on the reverse, above the "L" and "F" in the world "HALF." In 1968 it was brought to the obverse, beneath the portrait and above the date. Scarcest Kennedy half dollar is the 1970D, not minted for general circulation. The Kennedy half dollar has a diameter of 30.6 mm.

Mint Mark 1964-1967

Mint Mark 1968 on.

DATE	MINTAGE	ABP	EF-40 Ex. Fine	MS-60 Unc.	PRF-65 Proof
☐ 1964	277,254,766	2.25	2.75	3.75	14.00
☐ 1964D	156,205,446	2.25	2.75	3.75	
CLAD COINAGE					
☐ 1965	65,879,366	.95		2.50	
☐ 1966	108,984,933	.95		2.00	
☐ 1967	295,045,968	.95		1.80	
☐ 1968D	246,951,930	.95		1.80	
☐ 1968S PROOF	3,041,508				3.25
☐ 1969D	129,881,800	.95		1.80	
☐ 1969S PROOF	2,934,631				3.25
☐ 1970D	2,150,000			20.00	
☐ 1970S PROOF	2,632,810				8.00
☐ 1971	155,164,000			1.00	
☐ 1971D	302,097,424			1.00	
☐ 1971S PROOF	3,224,138				2.25
☐ 1972	153,180,000			.95	
☐ 1972D	141,890,000			.95	
☐ 1972S PROOF	3,224,138				2.35
☐ 1973	64,964,000			.90	
☐ 1973D	83,171,400			.90	
☐ 1973S PROOF	2,769,624				2.25
☐ 1974	201,588,250			.85	
☐ 1974D	79,088,210			.85	
☐ 1974S PROOF	2,617,350				2.25
☐ 1976 Copper-nickel clad	234,318,200			.80	
☐ 1976D Copper-nickel clad	287,565,290			.80	
☐ 1976S Copper-nickel clad	7,123,300				1.75

DATE	MINTAGE	ABP	EF-40 Ex. Fine	MS-60 Unc.	PRF-65 Proof
☐ 1976S Silver clad	4,250,000			2.50	
☐ 1976S Silver clad PROOF	3,215,730				4.00
☐ 1977	43,569,000			.95	
☐ 1977D	31,450,250			.95	
☐ 1977S PROOF	3,450,895				2.00
☐ 1978	14,350,000			1.35	
☐ 1978D	13,765,799			1.35	
☐ 1978S PROOF	3,127,781				2.50
☐ 1979	68,311,400			.85	
☐ 1979D	15,815,400			.85	
☐ 1979S PROOF (I)	3,677,200				2.00
☐ 1979S PROOF (II)					25.00
☐ 1980P	29,500,000			.85	
☐ 1980D	33,456,450			.85	
☐ 1980S PROOF	3,555,000				2.00
☐ 1981P	29,544,206			.85	
☐ 1981D	27,839,525			.85	
☐ 1981S PROOF (I)	4,063,000				2.00
☐ 1981S PROOF (II)					25.00
☐ 1982D	13,150,000			.85	
☐ 1982S PROOF (I)	3,229,000				7.50
☐ 1983P	34,100,000			.85	
☐ 1983D	32,475,000			.85	
☐ 1983S PROOF	3,228,621				7.50
☐ 1984P				.85	
☐ 1984D				.85	
☐ 1984S PROOF					6.50

SILVER DOLLARS — EARLY, 1794 - 1804; Patterns, 1836 - 1839; Regular Issue, 1840 - 1873

The silver dollar, probably the most significant U.S. coin of the 19th century, was authorized on April 2, 1792 and intended as the chief currency piece or standard for other silver coinage. Striking was not however begun until 1794. The word 'dollar' is a corruption of Taler or Thaler, a large silver coin widely distributed in Europe and well known to Colonial America. Prior to use of this term in domestic coinage it had become common to refer to Spain's "pieces of eight" as dollars, so it was natural that this crown-like silver piece should likewise be called a dollar. The first design, the Flowing Hair variety, was executed by Robert Scot and may be observed on other coinage of that era. Its reverse was an eagle surrounded by the words "UNITED STATES OF AMERICA." The composition was .8924 silver and .1076 copper, the addition of this roughly one-tenth part of base-metal being needed to provide ruggedness. It weighed 26.96 grams and was the heaviest U.S. silver coin excepting the Trade Dollar of much later vintage. Its diameter varies between 39 and 40 mm. Along the edge is impressed the words "HUNDRED CENTS ONE DOLLAR OR UNIT," interspersed with typographical ornament. There was very limited striking of dollars in the initial year of their appearance, less than 2,000 being turned out. The following year, 1795, witnessed greatly increased production, but because of the surface softness of these coins and the extensive handling to which they were subjected it is not easy finding specimens in the best grades of condition. "Average" examples can be had rather easily. There are two reverse varieties of the 1795 Flowing Hair dollar, one in which three leaves appear beneath the eagle's wings on either side, another with two leaves. Toward the end of 1795 the Flowing Hair obverse was replaced by the Draped Bust, with the so-called "Small Eagle" reverse (the eagle's wings and body in general being scaled smaller than previously). The Draped Bust obverse is found with dates in small or large numerals, and with the legend "UNITED STATES OF AMERICA" in small or large letters on the reverse. There are also differences in the number of stars on the obverse. In 1798 the shield eagle reverse was introduced, still with the Draped Bust portrait. These types were continued until 1803 when the striking of silver dollars was suspended. It was at one time believed that the Mint coined a few dollars in 1804 but it has now been established beyond reasonable doubt that silver dollars dated 1804 were struck in the 1830's for inclusion in proof sets. Apparently the die for an 1804 coin was prepared before any decision was reached to discontinue production and it was stored away at the Mint for those 30 years. In any case the 1804 dollar is an extremely rare piece whose popularity (and price) has not suffered in the least by results of research into its origins. A handful of restrikes were made later, in 1859. There is scarcely any difference in rarity or value between the 1830's proofs and the 1859 restrikes. Of all 1804 silver dollars (both types), 15 exist.

In 1836 Christian Gobrecht prepared designs for a new silver dollar, which at first was struck in limited numbers to test public response. A seated figure of Liberty appeared on the obverse with a flying eagle reverse. The obverse carried no wording whatever. On the reverse were the words "UNITED STATES OF AMERICA" and "ONE DOLLAR," the eagle set within a ground of stars. There are some varieties of this reverse containing no stars. Full-scale output of silver dollars was not resumed until 1840. For this issue, and for many years following, the shield or heraldic eagle was used for the reverse and the face value was abbreviated into "ONE DOL." In 1866 the motto "IN GOD WE TRUST" was added to the reverse, on a banner flowing above the eagle. The mintmark is located below the eagle and above the statement of value. Striking of dollars in this design ceased in 1873.

SILVER DOLLARS — LIBERTY WITH FLOWING HAIR, 1794 - 1795

DATE	MINTAGE	ABP	G-4 Good	F-12 Fine	VF-20 V. Fine	MS-60 Unc.
☐ 1794	1,758	4250.00	6500.00	13750.00	23000.00	58000.00
☐ 1795*	160,295	550.00	875.00	1550.00	2275.00	41000.00

*Includes both 2 Leaf and 3 Leaf Varieties

SILVER DOLLARS — DRAPED BUST, 1795 - 1798
Small Eagle on Reverse

DATE	MINTAGE	ABP	G-4 Good	F-12 Fine	VF-20 V. Fine	MS-60 Unc.
☐1795	42,738	450.00	850.00	1325.00	1900.00	15500.00
☐1796	72,920	450.00	850.00	1200.00	1800.00	11875.00
☐1797 sm. letters		450.00	850.00	1200.00	1800.00	11875.00
☐1797 lg. letters	7,776	450.00	850.00	1200.00	1800.00	11875.00
☐1797 9 stars left, 7 right, sm. letters		700.00	1250.00	2300.00	4000.00	22500.00
☐1798 (Small eagle)	327,536	650.00	1175.00	2650.00	3450.00	18250.00

SILVER DOLLARS — DRAPED BUST, 1798 - 1804
Large Eagle on Reverse

DATE	MINTAGE	ABP	G-4 Good	F-12 Fine	VF-20 V. Fine	MS-60 Unc.
☐1798**		160.00	315.00	570.00	800.00	7175.00
☐1799***	423,515	160.00	315.00	570.00	800.00	7175.00
☐1800***	220,920	160.00	315.00	570.00	800.00	7175.00
☐1801***	54,454	180.00	345.00	650.00	1000.00	7350.00
☐1802***	41,650	160.00	315.00	570.00	800.00	7175.00
☐1802 over 1***		160.00	315.00	570.00	800.00	7175.00
☐1803***	66,064	160.00	315.00	570.00	800.00	7175.00

☐1804 One of the most valued coins in the world — Less than 15 known. In March, 1980, THE GARRETT SPECIMEN was sold for $400,000.00. In 1982 another specimen brought $190,000. In 1985 the Dr. Jerry Buss specimen was sold for $280,000.
** Includes both 13 star and 15 star varieties
*** Includes all types

SILVER DOLLARS — LIBERTY SEATED (GOBRECHT), 1836 - 1839
With Flying Eagle on Reverse

DATE	MINTAGE	ABP	VF-20 V. Fine	EF-40 Ex. Fine	PRF-65 Proof
☐ 1836	approx. 1,025	800.00	3100.00	4500.00	9000.00
☐ 1838	approx. 31	7500.00	PROOF ONLY		13000.00
☐ 1839	approx. 303	5000.00	PROOF ONLY		10000.00

SILVER DOLLARS — LIBERTY SEATED, 1840 - 1865
No Motto Over Eagle

Mint Mark is Below Eagle on Reverse

DATE	MINTAGE	ABP	VG-8 V. Good	F-12 Fine	VF-20 V. Fine	MS-60 Unc.	PRF-65 Proof
☐ 1840	61,005	90.00	180.00	235.00	280.00	925.00	
☐ 1841	173,000	63.00	120.00	200.00	250.00	850.00	
☐ 1842	184,618	59.00	115.00	180.00	230.00	850.00	
☐ 1843	165,100	59.00	115.00	180.00	230.00	850.00	
☐ 1844	20,000	95.00	190.00	270.00	400.00	1600.00	
☐ 1845	24,500	115.00	230.00	280.00	400.00	1600.00	
☐ 1846	110,600	59.00	115.00	180.00	230.00	950.00	
☐ 1846O	59,000	85.00	170.00	250.00	320.00	2975.00	
☐ 1847	140,750	59.00	115.00	180.00	230.00	1150.00	
☐ 1848	15,000	140.00	280.00	390.00	475.00	1900.00	
☐ 1849	62,600	75.00	150.00	210.00	275.00	1300.00	
☐ 1850	7,500	190.00	370.00	500.00	700.00	3575.00	
☐ 1850O	40,000	160.00	315.00	450.00	620.00	3800.00	
☐ 1851	1,300	950.00	900.00	2600.00	4150.00	11750.00	

DATE	MINTAGE	ABP	VG-8 V. Good	F-12 Fine	VF-20 V. Fine	MS-60 Unc.	PRF-65 Proof
☐1852	1,100	1400.00	2600.00	4250.00	5475.00	9000.00	
☐1853	46,110	85.00	160.00	220.00	300.00	1000.00	
☐1854	33,140	300.00	575.00	800.00	1125.00	3500.00	
☐1855	26,000	290.00	550.00	750.00	1025.00	3750.00	12500.00
☐1856	63,500	110.00	190.00	250.00	325.00	1900.00	10000.00
☐1857	94,000	110.00	190.00	250.00	325.00	1750.00	10000.00
☐1858 PROOFS ONLY	80						12500.00
☐1859	256,500	135.00	260.00	340.00	480.00	1800.00	8175.00
☐1859O	360,000	55.00	100.00	160.00	210.00	800.00	
☐1859S	20,000	140.00	270.00	350.00	480.00	3800.00	
☐1860	218,930	145.00	280.00	400.00	520.00	1775.00	7675.00
☐1860O	515,000	55.00	110.00	170.00	220.00	900.00	
☐1861	78,500	170.00	340.00	470.00	600.00	2000.00	7675.00
☐1862	12,090	160.00	310.00	430.00	550.00	2100.00	7675.00
☐1863	27,660	105.00	190.00	270.00	360.00	1800.00	7675.00
☐1864	31,170	85.00	175.00	250.00	350.00	1725.00	7675.00
☐1865	47,000	83.00	170.00	240.00	320.00	1725.00	7675.00
☐1866 No Motto — 2 Known — PROOF — 150,000.00							

SILVER DOLLARS — LIBERTY SEATED, 1866 - 1873
Motto "IN GOD WE TRUST" Added

DATE	MINTAGE	ABP	VG-8 V. Good	F-12 Fine	VF-20 V. Fine	MS-60 Unc.	PRF-65 Proof
☐1866	49,625	75.00	150.00	210.00	300.00	1575.00	7400.00
☐1867	47,525	75.00	150.00	210.00	300.00	1575.00	7400.00
☐1868	162,700	70.00	140.00	200.00	290.00	1400.00	7400.00
☐1869	424,300	65.00	125.00	185.00	260.00	1000.00	7400.00
☐1870	416,000	65.00	125.00	185.00	240.00	1000.00	7400.00
☐1870CC	12,462	160.00	300.00	450.00	570.00	2575.00	
☐1870S			RARE — $62,500.00: 1973 Sale				
☐1871	1,074,760	55.00	110.00	160.00	210.00	1100.00	7400.00
☐1871CC	1,376	700.00	1375.00	2000.00	3000.00	7500.00	
☐1872	1,106,450	55.00	110.00	160.00	210.00	950.00	7400.00
☐1872CC	3,150	510.00	1000.00	1375.00	1650.00	6500.00	

DATE	MINTAGE	ABP	VG-8 V. Good	F-12 Fine	VF-20 V. Fine	MS-60 Unc.	PRF-65 Proof
☐1872S	9,000	115.00	230.00	360.00	570.00	3300.00	
☐1873	193,600	65.00	130.00	190.00	250.00	1575.00	7500.00
☐1873CC	2,300	900.00	1800.00	2400.00	3450.00	9500.00	
☐1873S	700					UNKNOWN IN ANY COLLECTION	

SILVER DOLLARS — TRADE, 1873 - 1885

In the early 1870's there was mounting pressure to increase the silver dollar's weight, as American commerce with Japan was being hindered by the fact that our silver dollar was somewhat smaller than European crowns. It was decided to strike a special coin, known as the "Trade Dollar," to weigh 27.22 grains and be composed of nine parts silver to one part copper. Much agitation to retain the silver dollar as a domestic circulating coin resulted in the government authorizing this new enlarged version to pass as legal tender (for its $1 face value) in transactions of $5 or less. This caused confusion and dissatisfaction, and in 1878 striking of a separate domestic silver dollar, based upon the pre-Trade Dollar standard, was resumed. For a while they were issued simultaneously until the Trade Dollar died a gradual death, its final year of striking being 1885. 1878 was the last year in which they were struck in numbers that could be termed sufficient for free circulation. The Trade Dollar has sometimes been called one of the handsomest U.S. coins of that denomination. True enough, the design is well drawn, but striking of circulating specimens was in such low relief that the slightest handling all but obliterated the more attractive detailing. Only when seen in proof state can the Trade Dollar's beauty be recognized. The designer was William Barber. On the obverse is a seated figure of Liberty, with an eagle reverse. The wording "TRADE DOLLAR" appears at the foot of the reverse. This is the only U.S. coin to proclaim its composition; the reverse is inscribed "420 GRAINS, 900 FINE." Meaning, of course, .900 silver to .100 base metal. Beginning in 1876 the Trade Dollar was no longer legal for domestic use. The Treasury Department (assailed from all sides in those days) left itself open to sharp criticism by not offering to redeem Trade Dollars until 1887, 11 years later. In diameter the Trade Dollar was no larger than the normal issues, 38.1 mm., but somewhat thicker. It was the heaviest U.S. silver coin ever minted. Only recently has it come into what might be termed popularity among collectors. In terms of mintage totals vs. regular dollars it is still rather underpriced.

Mint Mark
is Below Eagle
in Reverse

DATE	MINTAGE	ABP	F-12 Fine	EF-40 Ex. Fine	MS-60 Unc.**	PRF-65 Proof
☐ 1873	397,500	45.00	90.00	200.00	750.00	6950.00
☐ 1873CC	124,500	80.00	160.00	375.00	1300.00	
☐ 1873S	703,000	49.00	95.00	230.00	1050.00	
☐ 1874	987,800	52.00	105.00	235.00	700.00	6950.00
☐ 1874CC	1,373,200	40.00	80.00	200.00	775.00	
☐ 1874S	2,549,000	36.00	70.00	170.00	680.00	
☐ 1875	218,000	125.00	260.00	550.00	1475.00	6950.00
☐ 1875CC	1,573,700	38.00	75.00	180.00	750.00	
☐ 1875S	4,487,000	36.00	70.00	155.00	675.00	
☐ 1875S over CC		165.00	325.00	650.00	1525.00	
☐ 1876	456,150	38.00	75.00	170.00	700.00	6950.00
☐ 1876CC	509,000	43.00	85.00	215.00	750.00	
☐ 1876S	5,227,000	36.00	70.00	170.00	700.00	
☐ 1877	3,039,710	38.00	75.00	160.00	800.00	6950.00
☐ 1877CC	534,000	52.00	100.00	235.00	850.00	
☐ 1877S	9,519,000	35.00	70.00	160.00	700.00	
☐ 1878	900	4000.00	PROOFS ONLY			7675.00
☐ 1878CC	97,000	170.00	350.00	975.00	9500.00	
☐ 1878S	4,162,000	37.00	70.00	175.00	700.00	
☐ 1879	1,541	3000.00	PROOFS ONLY			7800.00
☐ 1880	1,987	3000.00	PROOFS ONLY			7800.00
☐ 1881	960	3000.00	PROOFS ONLY			7800.00
☐ 1882	1,097	3000.00	PROOFS ONLY			7800.00
☐ 1883	979	3000.00	PROOFS ONLY			7800.00
☐ 1884	10	25000.00	PROOFS ONLY	*		52500.00
☐ 1885	5		PROOFS ONLY—EXTREMELY RARE $125,000.00			

*KREISBERG AUCTION 1976
**Superbly struck pieces bring proportionately more than prices shown.

SILVER DOLLARS — LIBERTY HEAD or "MORGAN", 1878 - 1904, and 1921

For the resumption of the standard silver dollar series a new design was chosen. The work of George T. Morgan, and thereby popularly called Morgan Dollar, it showed a profile head of Liberty backed with an eagle holding arrows and branch. The motto "IN GOD WE TRUST" was installed above the eagle in Old English Gothic lettering. On the obverse appeared the slogan "E PLURIBUS UNUM." For many years the Morgan dollar was the best known and probably most respected silver "crown" in the world. Artistically the work is superb, rendered all the more impressive by the fact that its detailing did not become easily effaced with use. Morgan's goal was to fashion for this country a coin which, if it did not carry the financial power of ancient Greek silver pieces, might be regarded as their equal in design. The Morgan dollar remained unchanged in weight and composition throughout its history. It was comprised of nine parts silver to one part copper and weighed 412.5 grains. The diameter is 38.1 mm. After having been struck in large quantities for two and a half decades, production sometimes exceeding 30 million pieces annually, it was suspended in 1904 because of a shortage of silver. Striking was resumed in 1921, but only briefly, as the new Peace Dollar was introduced that some year. However there were more Morgan dollars coined in 1921 — over 80 million — than in any previous year. The mintmark is placed below the eagle on the reverse. The Morgan dollar contains .77344 ounce of silver, or slightly more than three-quarters of an ounce.

Mint Mark is Below Eagle on Reverse

DATE	MINTAGE	ABP	F-12 Fine	EX-40 Ex. Fine	MS-60 Unc.	PRF-65 Proof
☐ 1878 7 Tail Feathers	416,000	8.50	16.00	21.00	60.00	8350.00
☐ 1878 8 Tail Feathers	750,000	8.50	18.00	25.00	67.00	7000.00
☐ 1878 7 over 8 Tail Feathers		8.50	20.00	30.00	75.00	
☐ 1878CC	2,212,000	8.50	25.00	39.00	125.00	
☐ 1878S	9,774,000	8.50	15.00	20.00	65.00	
☐ 1879	14,807,100	8.50	14.00	19.00	55.00	6000.00
☐ 1879CC	756,000	30.00	50.00	210.00	800.00	
☐ 18790	2,887,000	8.50	14.00	18.00	57.00	
☐ 1879S	9,110,000	8.50	14.00	18.00	56.00	
☐ 1880	12,601,355	8.50	14.00	18.00	54.00	5650.00
☐ 1880CC	591,000	22.00	40.00	82.00	200.00	

DATE	MINTAGE	ABP	F-12 Fine	EX-40 Ex. Fine	MS-60 Unc.	PRF-65 Proof
☐ 1880 over 79CC		23.00	50.00	85.00	205.00	
☐ 18800	5,305,000	8.50	14.00	18.00	75.00	
☐ 1880S	8,900,000	8.50	15.00	19.00	65.00	
☐ 1881	9,163,975	8.50	14.00	18.00	56.00	5700.00
☐ 1881CC	206,000	40.00	70.00	103.00	205.00	
☐ 18810	5,708,000	8.50	15.00	19.00	49.00	
☐ 1881S	12,760,000	8.50	15.00	19.00	60.00	
☐ 1882	11,101,000	8.50	15.00	19.00	57.00	5700.00
☐ 1882CC	1,133,000	15.00	28.00	50.00	105.00	
☐ 18820	6,090,000	8.50	14.00	18.50	50.00	
☐ 18820, O over S		10.00	17.00	20.00	52.00	5700.00
☐ 1882S	9,250,000	8.50	16.00	21.00	70.00	
☐ 1883	12,191,039	8.50	14.50	19.00	55.00	5700.00
☐ 1883CC	1,204,000	14.00	27.00	48.00	105.00	
☐ 18830	8,725,000	8.50	14.00	19.00	48.00	
☐ 1883S	6,250,000	8.50	18.00	27.00	520.00	
☐ 1884	14,070,875	8.50	14.00	19.50	58.00	5700.00
☐ 1884CC	1,136,000	20.00	35.00	55.00	105.00	
☐ 18840	9,730,000	8.50	14.00	19.00	46.00	
☐ 1884S	3,200,000	8.50	17.50	33.00	1175.00	
☐ 1885	17,787,767	8.50	14.00	19.00	45.00	5700.00
☐ 1885CC	228,000	80.00	145.00	180.00	225.00	
☐ 18850	9,185,000	8.50	14.00	19.00	45.00	
☐ 1885S	1,497,000	8.50	16.00	23.00	120.00	
☐ 1886	19,963,886	8.50	14.00	19.00	45.00	5700.00
☐ 18860	10,710,000	8.50	14.00	20.00	360.00	
☐ 1886S	750,000	8.50	23.00	32.00	150.00	
☐ 1887	20,290,710	8.50	14.00	19.00	45.00	5700.00
☐ 18870	11,550,000	8.50	14.00	20.00	57.00	
☐ 1887S	1,771,000	8.50	17.00	21.00	70.00	
☐ 1888	19,183,833	8.50	14.00	18.00	45.00	5700.00
☐ 18880	12,150,000	8.50	15.50	20.00	45.00	
☐ 1888S	657,000	12.00	21.00	35.00	140.00	
☐ 1889	21,726,811	8.50	14.00	20.00	45.00	5700.00
☐ 1889CC	350,000	115.00	220.00	675.00	4575.00	
☐ 18890	11,875,000	8.50	14.00	19.00	85.00	
☐ 1889S	700,000	8.50	26.00	37.00	75.00	
☐ 1890	16,802,590	8.50	14.00	21.00	50.00	5700.00
☐ 1890CC	2,309,041	14.00	27.00	48.00	230.00	
☐ 18900	10,701,000	8.50	14.00	20.00	65.00	
☐ 1890S	8,230,373	8.50	16.00	20.00	60.00	
☐ 1891	8,694,206	8.50	16.00	21.00	85.00	5700.00
☐ 1891CC	1,618,000	14.00	27.00	48.00	215.00	
☐ 18910	7,954,529	8.50	14.00	21.00	90.00	
☐ 1891S	5,296,000	8.50	16.00	22.00	60.00	
☐ 1892	1,037,245	8.50	17.00	23.00	170.00	5700.00
☐ 1892CC	1,352,000	19.00	35.00	80.00	350.00	
☐ 18920	2,744,000	8.50	16.00	23.00	145.00	
☐ 1892S	1,200,000	16.00	30.00	165.00	4150.00	

DATE	MINTAGE	ABP	F-12 Fine	EX-40 Ex. Fine	MS-60 Unc.	PRF-65 Proof
☐ 1893	378,792	27.00	45.00	88.00	330.00	6150.00
☐ 1893CC	667,000	42.00	70.00	325.00	800.00	
☐ 1893O	300,000	30.00	55.00	215.00	1000.00	
☐ 1893S	100,000	590.00	1150.00	2975.00	17500.00	
☐ 1894	110,972	115.00	235.00	380.00	950.00	6100.00
☐ 1894O	1,723,000	8.50	17.00	31.00	465.00	
☐ 1894S	1,260,000	12.00	25.00	85.00	350.00	
☐ 1895*	12,880				125000	32500.00
☐ 1895O	450,000	32.00	60.00	210.00	2025.00	
☐ 1895S	400,000	46.00	85.00	350.00	950.00	
☐ 1896	9,976,762	8.50	14.00	19.00	45.00	5750.00
☐ 1896O	4,900,000	8.50	15.00	21.00	750.00	
☐ 1896S	5,000,000	8.50	22.00	100.00	435.00	
☐ 1897	2,822,731	8.50	14.00	19.00	50.00	5750.00
☐ 1897O	4,004,000	8.50	15.00	21.00	415.00	
☐ 1897S	5,825,000	8.50	15.00	19.00	65.00	
☐ 1898	5,884,725	8.50	14.00	19.00	48.00	5750.00
☐ 1898O	4,440,000	8.50	15.00	20.00	48.00	
☐ 1898S	4,102,000	8.50	16.00	23.00	165.00	
☐ 1899	330,846	16.00	30.00	53.00	100.00	5825.00
☐ 1899O	12,290,000	8.50	15.00	20.00	50.00	
☐ 1899S	2,562,000	8.50	19.50	25.00	170.00	
☐ 1900	8,830,912	8.50	15.00	19.00	47.00	5750.00
☐ 1900O	12,590,000	8.50	15.00	19.00	49.00	
☐ 1900S	3,540,000	8.50	17.00	24.00	145.00	
☐ 1901	6,962,813	13.00	26.00	47.00	875.00	7000.00
☐ 1901O	13,320,000	8.50	17.00	20.00	49.00	
☐ 1901S	2,284,000	8.50	18.00	34.00	310.00	
☐ 1902	7,994,777	8.50	15.00	20.00	60.00	5950.00
☐ 1902O	8,636,000	8.50	15.00	19.50	45.00	
☐ 1902S	1,530,000	18.00	35.00	85.00	250.00	
☐ 1903	4,652,755	8.50	15.00	20.00	57.00	5825.00
☐ 1903O	4,450,000	85.00	150.00	190.00	275.00	
☐ 1903S	1,241,000	11.00	21.00	165.00	1580.00	
☐ 1904	2,788,650	8.50	14.00	20.00	105.00	5825.00
☐ 1904O	3,720,000	8.50	15.00	19.50	45.00	
☐ 1904S	2,304,000	19.00	37.00	110.00	900.00	
☐ 1921	44,690,000	8.50	13.00	16.00	38.00	
☐ 1921D	20,345,000	8.50	13.00	17.00	40.00	
☐ 1921S	21,695,000	8.50	13.00	16.00	42.00	

*Check carefully for removed Mint Mark.
NOTE: Superbly struck specimens with few bag marks bring substantially more than the prices listed.

SILVER DOLLARS — PEACE, 1921 - 1935

It was decided, following the Armistice of 1918, to issue a coin commemorating world peace, and to make this a circulating coin rather than a limited issue. As production of silver dollars was being resumed in 1921 this was the logical denomination. This coin, known as the Peace Dollar, was designed by Anthony DeFrancisci, who had some reputation as a designer of medals. Its obverse pictured a profile head of Liberty, quite different in character from those on other coins, and a standing eagle (perched on a mound) on its reverse. The word "Peace" was incorporated into the reverse. As originally engraved the dies were similar in nature to those of a medal, intended to strike in high relief. The following year modified dies were introduced. Coining of silver dollars was halted in 1935 and never resumed, the subsequent Ike and Anthony dollars being of a different metallic composition. Mintmark appears beneath the word "ONE" in "ONE DOLLAR" on the reverse. The Peace dollar is composed of 90% silver and 10% copper and has a weight of 412½ grains. The diamter is 38.1 mm. and the silver content is .77344 of an ounce.

Mint Mark — Below "One" and to Left of Wingtip

DATE	MINTAGE	ABP	F-12 Fine	EX-40 Ex. Fine	MS-60 Unc.
☐ 1921	1,006,473	11.00	26.00	40.00	215.00
☐ 1922	51,737,000	8.50	13.00	15.00	35.00
☐ 1922D	15,063,000	8.50	13.00	15.00	43.00
☐ 1922S	17,475,000	8.50	13.00	15.00	43.00
☐ 1923	30,800,000	8.50	13.00	15.00	35.00
☐ 1923D	6,811,000	8.50	13.00	15.00	43.00
☐ 1923S	19,020,000	8.50	13.00	15.00	43.00
☐ 1924	11,811,000	8.50	13.00	15.00	40.00
☐ 1924S	1,728,000	8.50	15.00	20.00	180.00
☐ 1925	10,198,000	8.50	13.00	15.00	40.00
☐ 1925S	1,610,000	8.50	14.00	18.00	125.00
☐ 1926	1,939,000	8.50	13.00	15.00	57.00
☐ 1926D	2,348,700	8.50	13.00	15.00	70.00
☐ 1926S	6,980,000	8.50	13.00	15.00	55.00
☐ 1927	848,000	9.00	19.00	25.00	115.00
☐ 1927D	1,268,900	8.50	15.00	21.00	230.00
☐ 1927S	866,000	8.50	15.00	22.00	195.00

DATE	MINTAGE	ABP	F-12 Fine	EX-40 Ex. Fine	MS-60 Unc.
☐ 1928	360,649	42.00	75.00	115.00	235.00
☐ 1928S	1,632,000	8.50	14.00	21.00	160.00
☐ 1934	954,057	8.50	17.00	25.00	115.00
☐ 1934D	1,569,500	8.50	14.00	22.00	130.00
☐ 1934S	1,011,000	8.50	21.00	150.00	1200.00
☐ 1935	1,576,000	8.50	14.00	17.00	75.00
☐ 1935S	1,964,000	8.50	14.50	20.00	200.00
☐ 1964D	316,000	NONE KNOWN TO EXIST			

NOTE: In 1964 it was decided to resume striking silver dollars after a nearly 30 year lapse. The Peace design was used and production was at the Denver Mint. Before the coins reached circulation, the "silver controversy" of the year culminated in the Mint's decision to switch to clad coinage. Production of the 1964D silver dollar was halted and the unreleased total of 316,000 was ordered melted. In the intervening years a number of rumors have circulated about specimens which escaped melting, but there is no proven evidence of any in existence. Technically this coin if it did exist, would be illegal to own and subject to confiscation.

DOLLARS — EISENHOWER, 1971 - 1978

In 1971, following the death of President Eisenhower, a dollar piece with his likeness on the obverse, backed by an adaption of the Apollo 11 insignia, was placed into circulation. Our astronauts had landed on the moon just two years earlier and this was commemorated by the reverse. Frank Gasparro, chief engraver of the Mint, was its designer. Due to the greatly increased price of silver bullion it was not possible to mint this coin as a 'silver dollar." Its size was equivalent to that of earlier silver dollars but the composition bore little resemblance to the old standard. Two versions were struck, a collector's edition with an 80% silver content and ordinary circulating coins with an outer layer of three parts copper and one part nickel enclosing an interior of pure copper. The former had a weight of 24.68 grams. Both have a 38.1 mm. diameter. In 1976 a special reverse design was applied, featuring a representation of the Liberty Bell superimposed against the moon, in connection with the Bicentennial. The obverse carried a double date, 1776-1976. Some silver-clad specimens were struck, their specifications the same as stated above. In the following year the original reverse was reinstated. The final year of production was 1978.

Mint Mark Below
Head of Obverse

Bicentennial
1776-1976 Reverse

DATE	MINTAGE	MS-60 Unc.	PRF-65 Proof
☐ 1971 Copper-nickel clad	47,799,000	2.15	
☐ 1971D Copper-nickel clad	68,587,424	2.15	
☐ 1971S Silver clad	11,133,764	5.00	6.25
☐ 1972 Copper-nickel clad	75,390,000	2.15	
☐ 1972D Copper-nickel clad	92,548,511	2.00	
☐ 1972S Silver clad	4,004,657	8.00	10.50
☐ 1973 Copper-nickel clad	2,000,056	8.75	
☐ 1973D Copper-nickel clad	2,000,000	9.00	
☐ 1973S Copper-nickel clad	2,760,339	1.85	4.50
☐ 1973S Silver clad	1,883,140		70.00
☐ 1974 Copper-nickel clad	27,366,000	1.85	
☐ 1974D Copper-nickel clad	45,520,175	1.85	
☐ 1974S Copper-nickel clad	2,617,350	1.95	4.00
☐ 1974S Silver clad	3,216,420		19.00
☐ 1976 Copper-nickel clad Variety I	4,021,250	3.00	
☐ 1976 Copper-nickel clad Variety II	113,325,000	2.50	
☐ 1976D Copper-nickel clad Variety I	21,048,650	2.85	
☐ 1976D Copper-nickel clad Variety II	82,179,355	2.50	
☐ 1976S Copper-nickel clad Variety I	2,845,390		4.75
☐ 1976S Copper-nickel clad Variety II	4,149,675		3.25
☐ 1976S Silver clad (40%)	4,239,460	7.50	10.00
☐ 1977 Copper-nickel clad	12,598,220	2.25	
☐ 1977D Copper-nickel clad	32,985,000	2.00	
☐ 1977S Copper-nickel clad	3,250,895		3.25
☐ 1978 Copper-nickel clad	25,702,000	1.50	
☐ 1978D Copper-nickel clad	33,012,890	1.50	
☐ 1978S Copper-nickel clad	3,127,731		6.00

DOLLARS — SUSAN B. ANTHONY, 1979 TO DATE

In 1979 the Eisenhower dollar was replaced by one picturing Susan B. Anthony, agitator for female suffrage in the earlier part of this century. The new coin, the target of much controversy, had the distinction of a number of "firsts":

  *First U.S. coin to picture a female (excluding mythological and symbolic types)
  *First non-gold dollar coin of small size.
  *First U.S. coin with non-circular edge.

The Anthony dollar measures 26½ mm., or about the size of a quarter. To avoid its confusion with coins of that denomination, the edge was not made circular but squared out into sections. Its composition is: exterior, three parts copper to one part nickel; interior, pure copper. The weight is eight and 1/10th grams. On the reverse appears the Apollo 11 insignia used for the Eisenhower dollar. Public dissatisfaction with the coin has placed its future in doubt. The designer was Frank Gasparro.

DATE	MINTAGE	MS-60 Unc.	PRF-65 Proof
☐ 1979 Copper-nickel clad	360,200,000	1.80	
☐ 1979D Copper-nickel clad	287,000,000	1.80	
☐ 1979S Copper-nickel clad Proof	110,000,000	2.00	9.50
☐ 1979S Copper-nickel clad (II) Proof	3,677,000		92.00
☐ 1980P	27,600,000	1.90	
☐ 1980D	41,595,000	1.90	
☐ 1980S	20,425,000	3.00	5.75
☐ 1981P	2,995,000	5.75	
☐ 1981D	3,237,631	5.75	
☐ 1981S	3,500,000	5.75	7.75

GOLD DOLLARS, 1849 - 1889

No gold dollars were struck in the Mint's early years. It was felt (logically enough, based upon conditions that existed then) that silver would serve adequately for this denomination, and that gold should be restricted to coins of a higher face value. However a series of events occurred, following the California gold strikes of 1849, which rendered gold dollars a necessity. Chief among them was the growing practice of citizens, especially in the West, to trade with bullion rather than coinage. So in 1849 a gold dollar was introduced. Designed by James Longacre, it carried a Liberty head on the obverse and was backed by a simple reverse featuring a wreath and the numeral one in arabic. A series of stars encircled the obverse portrait. As this coin was by necessity of diminutive size, elaborate designing was not possible. The Liberty Gold Dollar weighed 1.672 grams and was composed of 90% gold and 10% copper. It had a diameter of 13 mm. The mintmark appears below the wreath. In 1854 the obverse was given over to an Indian Head and the coin made flatter, its diameter increased to 15 mm. The weight was unaltered. There was a further change in 1856 when a new die was cast for the obverse, showing the Indian Head a bit larger. This was the final variety for the gold dollar, whose last year of coining was 1889. The gold content by weight for all three types was .04837 of an ounce.

GOLD DOLLARS — LIBERTY HEAD WITH CORONET, SMALL SIZE
1849 - 1854

DATE	MINTAGE	ABP in F-12	F-12 Fine	EF-40 Ex. Fine	MS-60 Unc.
☐ 1849	688,600	105.00	175.00	220.00	750.00
☐ 1849C Closed Wreath	11,634	225.00	300.00	800.00	3250.00
☐ 1849C Open Wreath	4 Known			EXTREMELY RARE	
☐ 1849D	21,588	215.00	290.00	900.00	3000.00
☐ 1849O	215,000	105.00	180.00	350.00	1750.00
☐ 1850	481,953	105.00	180.00	235.00	680.00
☐ 1850C	6,966	240.00	350.00	1150.00	4000.00
☐ 1850D	8,382	250.00	350.00	1100.00	3950.00
☐ 1850O	14,000	195.00	275.00	650.00	1750.00
☐ 1851	3,317,671	105.00	185.00	235.00	680.00
☐ 1851C	41,267	105.00	250.00	525.00	1675.00
☐ 1851D	9,832	200.00	285.00	1000.00	2800.00
☐ 1851O	290,000	110.00	225.00	300.00	900.00
☐ 1852	2,045,351	105.00	180.00	235.00	680.00
☐ 1852C	9,434	195.00	270.00	800.00	2100.00
☐ 1852D	6,360	230.00	335.00	1150.00	3750.00
☐ 1852O	140,000	105.00	175.00	325.00	1075.00
☐ 1853	4,076,051	105.00	175.00	225.00	680.00
☐ 1853C	11,515	180.00	265.00	900.00	4000.00
☐ 1853D	6,583	230.00	335.00	1600.00	4500.00
☐ 1853O	290,000	105.00	175.00	335.00	750.00
☐ 1854*	1,639,445	105.00	175.00	220.00	680.00
☐ 1854D	2,935	400.00	600.00	1750.00	7250.00
☐ 1854S	14,635	220.00	325.00	600.00	2400.00

*Includes Indian Headress Dollars of 1854 Type II

GOLD DOLLARS — SMALL INDIAN HEAD,
FEATHER HEADDRESS, LARGE SIZE, 1854 - 1856

Mint Mark Below Wreath on Reverse

DATE	MINTAGE	ABP in F-12	F-12 Fine	EF-40 Ex. Fine	MS-60 Unc.
☐ *1854**	1,639,445	110.00	235.00	600.00	2850.00
☐ 1854C	4				UNKNOWN
☐ 1855	758,269	110.00	235.00	600.00	2850.00
☐ 1855C	8,903	425.00	850.00	2300.00	6500.00
☐ 1855D	1,811	1250.00	1800.00	5500.00	9250.00
☐ 1855O	55,000	240.00	450.00	910.00	5325.00
☐ 1856S	24,600	240.00	475.00	1000.00	4900.00

*Includes Indian Headdress Dollars of 1854 Type II
**Includes Mintage of Liberty Head of 1854 Type I

GOLD DOLLARS — LARGE LIBERTY HEAD, FEATHER HEADDRESS, LARGE SIZE, 1856 - 1889

Mint Mark is Below Wreath on Reverse

DATE	MINTAGE	ABP in F-12	F-12 Fine	EF-40 Ex. Fine	MS-60 Unc.	PRF-65
☐ 1856 Slant 5	1,762,936	100.00	155.00	230.00	650.00	
☐ 1856D	1,460	2000.00	2650.00	6500.00	16750.00	
☐ 1857	774,789	100.00	155.00	215.00	650.00	
☐ 1857C	13,280	160.00	310.00	975.00	3500.00	
☐ 1857D	3,533	210.00	400.00	1450.00	5000.00	
☐ 1857S	10,000	160.00	320.00	900.00	2250.00	
☐ 1858	117,995	100.00	155.00	230.00	675.00	13500.00
☐ 1858D	3,477	230.00	430.00	1475.00	5000.00	
☐ 1858S	10,000	110.00	320.00	750.00	1900.00	
☐ 1859	168,244	100.00	165.00	300.00	700.00	12000.00
☐ 1859C	5,235	175.00	350.00	975.00	3100.00	
☐ 1859D	4,952	275.00	510.00	1600.00	4400.00	
☐ 1859S	15,000	110.00	330.00	520.00	2275.00	
☐ 1860	36,688	100.00	175.00	250.00	650.00	10000.00
☐ 1860D	1,566	1800.00	2300.00	5200.00	16250.00	
☐ 1860S	13,000	130.00	300.00	600.00	1350.00	
☐ 1861	527,499	100.00	155.00	230.00	675.00	8380.00
☐ 1861D		3000.00	4500.00	11000.00	23500.00	
☐ 1862	1,326,865	100.00	155.00	215.00	650.00	8380.00
☐ 1863	6,250	200.00	350.00	750.00	2000.00	8380.00
☐ 1864	5,950	200.00	340.00	600.00	1500.00	8380.00
☐ 1865	3,725	160.00	325.00	650.00	2000.00	9175.00
☐ 1866	7,180	140.00	310.00	500.00	1300.00	8650.00
☐ 1867	5,250	140.00	310.00	625.00	1300.00	8380.00
☐ 1868	10,525	140.00	280.00	410.00	1100.00	9000.00
☐ 1869	5,925	160.00	325.00	625.00	1400.00	9000.00
☐ 1870	6,335	140.00	280.00	410.00	1150.00	8380.00
☐ 1870S	3,000	250.00	450.00	950.00	2175.00	
☐ 1871	3,930	140.00	275.00	470.00	1100.00	9000.00
☐ 1872	3,530	140.00	280.00	470.00	1300.00	9000.00
☐ 1873 open 3	125,125	100.00	160.00	215.00	650.00	
☐ 1873 closed 3		100.00	170.00	625.00	2100.00	9000.00
☐ 1874	198,820	100.00	160.00	215.00	640.00	11500.00
☐ 1875	420	1700.00	2000.00	3100.00	8575.00	14850.00
☐ 1876	3,245	130.00	240.00	360.00	1400.00	8500.00
☐ 1877	3,920	140.00	230.00	370.00	1100.00	9375.00
☐ 1878	3,020	140.00	250.00	410.00	1225.00	9375.00

DATE	MINTAGE	ABP in F-12	F-12 Fine	EF-40 Ex. Fine	MS-60 Unc.	PRF-65
☐ 1879	3,030	105.00	220.00	375.00	900.00	8700.00
☐ 1880	1,636	105.00	200.00	310.00	800.00	8300.00
☐ 1881	7,660	100.00	190.00	290.00	750.00	8100.00
☐ 1882	5,040	100.00	200.00	310.00	750.00	8100.00
☐ 1883	10,840	100.00	190.00	290.00	750.00	8100.00
☐ 1884	6,206	100.00	190.00	290.00	750.00	7800.00
☐ 1885	12,205	100.00	190.00	290.00	750.00	7800.00
☐ 1886	6,016	100.00	190.00	290.00	750.00	7800.00
☐ 1887	8,543	100.00	190.00	290.00	750.00	7800.00
☐ 1888	16,080	100.00	190.00	290.00	750.00	7800.00
☐ 1889	30,729	100.00	190.00	290.00	750.00	7800.00

Many gold dollars in the 1880's were hoarded and appear in gem prooflike condition. Beware of these pieces being sold as proofs.

QUARTER EAGLES — $2.50 GOLD PIECES

The $2.50 gold piece, authorized on April 2, 1792, was known as a "Quarter Eagle" (i.e., the quarter part of an Eagle or $10 gold piece). Striking was not begun until 1796. As early production was extremely limited — in no year were as many as 10,000 struck until 1834 — these are scarce and valuable coins. Designed by Robert Scot, the original type featured a capped Liberty on the obverse and shield eagle reverse. The portrait is quite different than that used on silver coinage and in general the engraving may be said to be somewhat superior. No wording other than "LIBERTY" adorns the obverse, with "UNITED STATES OF AMERICA" on the obverse. The composition was .9167 gold to .0833 copper, or more than 9/10ths gold, with a weight of 4.37 grams and a diameter which varied slightly but normally was about 20 mm. There are two obverse types, one with and one without a circular border of stars. In 1808 the portrait, while retaining the cap, was entirely redesigned. It was shifted around to face left instead of right, the cap was de-emphasized, Liberty's features were redrawn in an effort at greater femininity, her hair was made curlier, and the eagle was likewise refurbished. John Reish was the designer. From 1809 to 1820 no quarter eagles were minted. When the series was resumed in 1821 it was with modified obverse and reverse types and the diameter had shrank to 18½ mm. However, the coin contained fully as much gold as previously and the decreased diameter was compensated for by a slight increase in thickness. The obverse was changed in 1834 to the so-called "Classic Head" type, a more stylish rendition of Liberty, designed by the Mint's chief designer, William Kneass (pronounced Niece). The weight was reduced to 4.18 grams and the composition altered to contain less than 9/10ths gold: .8992 to .1008 copper. The diameter was 18.2 mm. Christian Gobrecht made some alterations to this design in 1840 but it was not materially changed. However, the gold content was increased to an even .900 and the diameter brought down to 18 mm. Total gold content by weight was .12094. This design remained in use for 67 years, surpassed for longevity only by the Lincoln Penny (1909-present). An interesting variation occurred in 1848, the so-called "California Quarter Eagle." In that year Colonel Mason, the Military Governor of California, shipped about 230 ounces of gold to Secretary of War Marcy in Washington, D.C. March had the bullion melted down and struck into quarter eagles, distinguished by the abbreviation, "CAL.", above the eagle's head on the reverse. This was not an integral part of the design but was stamped separately. As little more than 1,000 specimens were struck it became a choice collector's item. Purchasers should be on guard against fakes. The Gobrecht Quarter Eagle was discontinued in 1907. Specimens dated after 1900, and some earlier ones, are valued primarily for their bullion content.

QUARTER EAGLES — LIBERTY CAP, 1796 - 1807

1796
No Stars

1797-1807
With Stars

1796-1807

DATE	MINTAGE	ABP in F-12	F-12 Fine	EF-40 Ex. Fine	MS-60 Unc.
☐ 1796 No Stars	963	6500.00	9000.00	18750.00	42500.00
☐ 1796 With Stars	432	4500.00	6000.00	14000.00	33000.00
☐ 1797	427	2750.00	4500.00	9650.00	27000.00
☐ 1798	1,094	1750.00	2650.00	6375.00	15750.00
☐ 1802 over 1	3,033	1500.00	2300.00	5750.00	14500.00
☐ 1804 14 Star Reverse	3,327	1500.00	2300.00	5750.00	14500.00
☐ 1804 13 Star Reverse		2250.00	3325.00	7900.00	15000.00
☐ 1805	1,781	1500.00	2300.00	4200.00	14250.00
☐ 1806 over 4	1,616	1500.00	2300.00	4200.00	14250.00
☐ 1806 over 5		2500.00	4000.00	6500.00	19000.00
☐ 1807	6,812	1425.00	2200.00	4100.00	14000.00

QUARTER EAGLES — BUST TYPE, TURBAN HEAD, 1808 - 1834

1808
Draped
Bust
Round Cap

1821-1834
Undraped
Liberty
Round Cap

1808-1834
Motto
Over Eagle

DATE	MINTAGE	ABP in F-12	F-12 Fine	EF-40 Ex. Fine	MS-60 Unc.
☐ 1808	2,710	1900.00	3500.00	17500.00	42500.00
REDUCED SIZE (18.5 mm. dia.)					
☐ 1821	6,448	1300.00	2250.00	5475.00	13000.00

DATE	MINTAGE	ABP in F-12	F-12 Fine	EF-40 Ex. Fine	MS-60 Unc.
☐ 1824 over 21	2,600	1650.00	2375.00	5375.00	13750.00
☐ 1825	4,434	1650.00	2375.00	5375.00	13500.00
☐ 1826 over 25	760	2300.00	3750.00	7200.00	18000.00
☐ 1827	2,800	1650.00	2375.00	5375.00	13000.00
☐ 1829	3,403	1200.00	1850.00	4600.00	12750.00
☐ 1830	4,540	1200.00	1850.00	4600.00	11500.00
☐ 1831	4,520	1200.00	1850.00	4600.00	11500.00
☐ 1832	4,400	1200.00	1850.00	4600.00	11500.00
☐ 1833	4,160	1200.00	1850.00	4600.00	11500.00
☐ 1834 Motto	4,000	2170.00	3500.00	11750.00	23750.00

QUARTER EAGLES — LIBERTY HEAD WITH RIBBONS, 1834 - 1839
No Motto Over Eagle

Mint Mark is above Date on Obverse

DATE	MINTAGE	ABP in F-12	F-12 Fine	EF-40 Ex. Fine	MS-60 Unc.
☐ 1834 No Motto	112,234	155.00	230.00	375.00	1725.00
☐ 1835	131,402	155.00	230.00	375.00	1725.00
☐ 1836	547,986	155.00	230.00	375.00	1725.00
☐ 1837	45,080	155.00	230.00	375.00	1725.00
☐ 1838	47,030	155.00	230.00	375.00	1725.00
☐ 1838C	7,908	280.00	450.00	1500.00	5750.00
☐ 1839	27,021	150.00	220.00	370.00	1725.00
☐ 1839C	18,173	225.00	375.00	1050.00	5000.00
☐ 1839D	13,674	290.00	475.00	1400.00	5900.00
☐ 1839O	17,781	195.00	320.00	730.00	4500.00

QUARTER EAGLES — LIBERTY HEAD WITH CORONET, 1840 - 1907

Mint Mark is below Eagle on Reverse

DATE	MINTAGE	ABP in F-12	F-12 Fine	EF-40 Ex. Fine	MS-60 Unc.
☐ 1840	18,859	125.00	210.00	360.00	1375.00
☐ 1840C	12,838	170.00	320.00	900.00	3250.00
☐ 1840D	3,532	400.00	675.00	3500.00	11500.00
☐ 1840O	26,200	125.00	185.00	350.00	1325.00
☐ 1841		Stack's 1976 $40,000 in Proof			
☐ 1841C	10,297	135.00	265.00	800.00	2575.00
☐ 1841D	4,164	320.00	520.00	3100.00	8000.00
☐ 1842	2,823	165.00	330.00	975.00	2600.00
☐ 1842C	6,737	200.00	425.00	1250.00	2650.00
☐ 1842D	4,643	300.00	490.00	2500.00	7500.00
☐ 1842O	19,800	130.00	250.00	750.00	2300.00
☐ 1843	100,546	125.00	200.00	310.00	675.00
☐ 1843C Small Date	26,096	600.00	1000.00	2500.00	7500.00
☐ 1843C Large Date	26,096	160.00	305.00	800.00	2500.00
☐ 1843D	36,209	165.00	320.00	1000.00	2800.00
☐ 1843O Small Date	368,002	115.00	190.00	305.00	800.00
☐ 1843O Large Date	368,002	115.00	190.00	305.00	900.00
☐ 1844	6,784	115.00	215.00	595.00	1750.00
☐ 1844C	11,622	165.00	295.00	750.00	3250.00
☐ 1844D	17,332	160.00	310.00	1000.00	2800.00
☐ 1845	91,051	125.00	200.00	290.00	675.00
☐ 1845D	19,460	160.00	300.00	1000.00	3000.00
☐ 1845O	4,000	275.00	500.00	1750.00	5500.00
☐ 1846	21,598	125.00	200.00	475.00	1300.00
☐ 1846C	4,808	170.00	400.00	1300.00	4500.00
☐ 1846D	19,303	170.00	380.00	1100.00	4500.00
☐ 1846O	66,000	125.00	200.00	360.00	1375.00
☐ 1847	29,814	125.00	200.00	330.00	1050.00
☐ 1847C	23,226	160.00	300.00	710.00	3500.00
☐ 1847D	15,784	170.00	340.00	950.00	4000.00
☐ 1847O	124,000	125.00	200.00	385.00	1500.00
☐ 1848	8,886	150.00	280.00	780.00	2325.00
☐ 1848 Cal. above Eagle	1,389	2500.00	3500.00	8000.00	17500.00
☐ 1848C	16,788	160.00	300.00	760.00	2250.00
☐ 1848D	13,771	170.00	345.00	1000.00	2900.00
☐ 1849	23,294	125.00	200.00	370.00	950.00
☐ 1849C	10,220	160.00	310.00	875.00	3150.00
☐ 1849D	10,945	170.00	360.00	1300.00	4375.00
☐ 1850	252,923	115.00	175.00	310.00	750.00
☐ 1850C	9,148	165.00	280.00	915.00	2900.00
☐ 1850D	12,148	170.00	300.00	1030.00	3800.00
☐ 1850O	84,000	115.00	175.00	400.00	1150.00
☐ 1851	1,372,748	115.00	175.00	275.00	650.00
☐ 1851C	14,923	160.00	285.00	900.00	3400.00
☐ 1851D	11,264	170.00	330.00	1100.00	4500.00
☐ 1851O	148,000	115.00	185.00	290.00	750.00
☐ 1852	1,159,681	115.00	185.00	280.00	650.00
☐ 1852C	9,772	160.00	300.00	870.00	2650.00
☐ 1852D	4,078	180.00	360.00	1400.00	4400.00

DATE	MINTAGE	ABP in F-12	F-12 Fine	EF-40 Ex. Fine	MS-60 Unc.	PRF-65 Proof
☐1852O	140,000	115.00	180.00	310.00	1100.00	
☐1853	1,404,668	115.00	165.00	250.00	650.00	
☐1853D	3,178	190.00	360.00	1375.00	4375.00	
☐1854	596,258	115.00	170.00	265.00	650.00	
☐1854C	7,295	150.00	285.00	830.00	2500.00	
☐1854D	1,760	900.00	1600.00	4700.00	11000.00	
☐1854O	153,000	115.00	170.00	260.00	730.00	
☐1854S	246	EXTREMELY RARE—EF-40			$30,000.00	
☐1855	235,480	115.00	180.00	270.00	730.00	
☐1855C	3,677	415.00	550.00	2100.00	4600.00	
☐1855D	1,123	1100.00	2100.00	4800.00	11500.00	
☐1856	384,240	115.00	160.00	275.00	740.00	
☐1856C	7,913	225.00	380.00	930.00	2400.00	
☐1856D	874	2500.00	3900.00	9500.00	27500.00	
☐1856O	21,100	105.00	165.00	410.00	1275.00	
☐1856S	71,120	105.00	165.00	340.00	1050.00	
☐1857	214,130	105.00	160.00	290.00	675.00	
☐1857D	2,364	280.00	430.00	1450.00	5285.00	
☐1857O	34,000	105.00	160.00	310.00	1000.00	
☐1857S	68,000	105.00	160.00	310.00	1375.00	
☐1858	47,377	105.00	180.00	290.00	750.00	19500.00
☐1858C	9,056	165.00	300.00	800.00	3000.00	
☐1859	39,444	105.00	160.00	265.00	675.00	14250.00
☐1859D	2,244	320.00	500.00	2400.00	6500.00	
☐1859S	15,200	105.00	175.00	390.00	1175.00	
☐1860	22,675	105.00	160.00	290.00	975.00	9000.00
☐1860C	7,469	150.00	285.00	900.00	2675.00	
☐1860S	35,600	105.00	155.00	310.00	950.00	
☐1861	1,272,518	105.00	150.00	260.00	660.00	8500.00
☐1861S	24,000	105.00	190.00	415.00	1250.00	
☐1862	112,353	105.00	155.00	260.00	975.00	8750.00
☐1862S	8,000	105.00	270.00	850.00	2500.00	
☐1863	30	PROOFS ONLY AUCTION SALE 1978			**	36000.00
☐1863S	10,800	105.00	160.00	650.00	2300.00	
☐1864	2,874	475.00	700.00	2100.00	6000.00	14375.00
☐1865	1,545	415.00	615.00	1700.00	5000.00	14375.00
☐1865S	23,376	105.00	160.00	350.00	975.00	
☐1866	3,110	105.00	225.00	580.00	1300.00	11500.00
☐1867	3,250	105.00	175.00	490.00	1300.00	11300.00
☐1867S	28,000	105.00	155.00	450.00	975.00	
☐1868	3,625	105.00	175.00	400.00	1100.00	9500.00
☐1868S	34,000	105.00	155.00	380.00	1175.00	
☐1869	4,343	105.00	175.00	360.00	1100.00	9175.00
☐1869S	29,500	105.00	155.00	330.00	1150.00	
☐1870	4,555	105.00	175.00	380.00	1050.00	9175.00
☐1870S	16,000	105.00	155.00	290.00	1400.00	
☐1871	5,350	105.00	175.00	360.00	1150.00	9250.00
☐1871S	22,000	105.00	155.00	290.00	975.00	

DATE	MINTAGE	ABP in F-12	F-12 Fine	EF-40 Ex. Fine	MS-60 Unc.	PRF-65 Proof
☐ 1872	3,030	110.00	215.00	475.00	1200.00	9250.00
☐ 1872S	18,000	102.00	170.00	310.00	700.00	
☐ 1873	178,025	102.00	150.00	275.00	700.00	9250.00
☐ 1873S	27,000	102.00	160.00	370.00	1200.00	
☐ 1874	3,940	102.00	200.00	400.00	975.00	11500.00
☐ 1875	420	1100.00	1700.00	5500.00	9000.00	25000.00
☐ 1875S	11,600	102.00	150.00	375.00	1125.00	
☐ 1876	4,221	102.00	175.00	350.00	1700.00	9150.00
☐ 1876S	5,000	102.00	150.00	265.00	1350.00	
☐ 1877	1,652	225.00	300.00	700.00	1700.00	9150.00
☐ 1877S	35,000	102.00	150.00	250.00	685.00	
☐ 1878	286,260	102.00	150.00	250.00	685.00	8925.00
☐ 1878S	55,000	102.00	150.00	250.00	685.00	
☐ 1879	88,900	102.00	150.00	250.00	685.00	9150.00
☐ 1879S	43,500	102.00	150.00	250.00	685.00	
☐ 1880	2,996	102.00	150.00	325.00	900.00	8925.00
☐ 1881	680	400.00	625.00	2100.00	5000.00	11000.00
☐ 1882	4,040	102.00	210.00	325.00	800.00	8675.00
☐ 1883	1,960	105.00	220.00	360.00	900.00	8675.00
☐ 1884	1,993	105.00	220.00	360.00	900.00	8675.00
☐ 1885	887	350.00	475.00	1300.00	3000.00	10000.00
☐ 1886	4,088	102.00	210.00	320.00	800.00	9500.00
☐ 1887	6,282	102.00	210.00	320.00	775.00	7750.00
☐ 1888	16,098	102.00	210.00	320.00	690.00	7750.00
☐ 1889	17,648	102.00	210.00	320.00	690.00	7750.00
☐ 1890	8,813	102.00	210.00	320.00	690.00	7750.00
☐ 1891	11,040	102.00	210.00	320.00	690.00	7750.00
☐ 1892	2,545	110.00	200.00	400.00	900.00	7750.00
☐ 1893	30,106	102.00	210.00	275.00	650.00	7750.00
☐ 1894	4,122	102.00	195.00	290.00	800.00	7750.00
☐ 1895	6,119	102.00	150.00	245.00	650.00	7750.00
☐ 1896	19,202	102.00	150.00	245.00	650.00	7750.00
☐ 1898	24,165	102.00	150.00	245.00	650.00	7750.00
☐ 1899	27,350	102.00	150.00	245.00	650.00	7750.00
☐ 1900	67,205	102.00	150.00	245.00	650.00	7750.00
☐ 1901	91,323	102.00	150.00	245.00	650.00	7750.00
☐ 1902	133,733	102.00	150.00	245.00	650.00	7750.00
☐ 1903	201,257	102.00	150.00	245.00	650.00	7750.00
☐ 1904	160,960	102.00	150.00	245.00	650.00	7750.00
☐ 1905	217,944	102.00	150.00	245.00	650.00	7750.00
☐ 1906	179,490	102.00	150.00	245.00	650.00	7750.00
☐ 1907	336,448	102.00	150.00	245.00	650.00	7750.00

NOTE: Specimens dated 1905S are counterfeits, made either by die striking or applying a false Mintmark to a genuine 1905.

QUARTER EAGLES — INDIAN HEAD, 1908 - 1929

The quarter eagle was redesigned in 1908 by Bela Lyon Pratt. Liberty was removed from its obverse and replaced by a portrait of an Indian wearing a war bonnet. A standing eagle adorned the reverse. The coin has no raised edge and the designs plus inscriptions are stamped in incuse, or recessed beneath the surface, rather than being shown in high relief. The composition is .900 gold., .100 copper, with a weight of 4.18 grams. Its diameter is 18 mm. with total gold content by weight remaining at .12094 ounce. Quarter eagles were last struck in 1929, the year of this nation's financial difficulties.

Mint Mark is to Left of Value on Reverse

DATE	MINTAGE	ABP in F-12	F-12 Fine	EF-40 Ex. Fine	MS-60 Unc.	PRF-65 Proof
☐ 1908	565,057	95.00	145.00	195.00	330.00	10500.00
☐ 1908	441,899	95.00	145.00	195.00	330.00	10500.00
☐ 1910	492,682	95.00	145.00	195.00	330.00	10500.00
☐ 1911	404,191	95.00	145.00	195.00	330.00	10500.00
☐ 1911D	55,680	325.00	500.00	980.00	2500.00	
☐ 1912	616,197	95.00	145.00	195.00	330.00	10500.00
☐ 1913	722,165	95.00	145.00	195.00	330.00	10500.00
☐ 1914	240,117	95.00	150.00	210.00	425.00	10500.00
☐ 1914D	448,000	95.00	145.00	210.00	330.00	
☐ 1915	606,100	95.00	145.00	195.00	330.00	10500.00
☐ 1925D	578,000	95.00	145.00	195.00	330.00	
☐ 1926	446,000	95.00	145.00	195.00	330.00	
☐ 1927	388,000	95.00	145.00	195.00	330.00	
☐ 1928	416,000	95.00	145.00	195.00	330.00	
☐ 1929	532,000	95.00	145.00	195.00	330.00	

$3.00 GOLD PIECES
LIBERTY HEAD WITH FEATHER HEADDRESS, 1854 - 1889

Introduction and apparent public acceptance of the gold dollar in 1849 led to speculation on the possible usefulness of gold coinage in other denominations. The $3 gold piece, composed of 9/10ths gold with an alloy of 1/10th copper, was introduced in 1854. It carried an Indian Head on the obverse and a wreathed reverse. Its diameter was 20½ mm. and the weight 5.015 grams. Though the $3 gold piece continued to be struck until 1889 it had become obvious as early as pre-Civil War years that no great demand or popularity was enjoyed by this coin. The designer was James Longacre. In 1854 the word "DOLLARS" was set in smaller characters than subsequently. Total gold content by weight was .14512 ounce.

Mint Mark is Below Wreath on Reverse

DATE	MINTAGE	ABP in F-12	F-12 Fine	EF-40 Ex. Fine	MS-60 Unc.	PRF-65 Proof
☐ 1854	136,618	345.00	485.00	875.00	3275.00	
☐ 1854D	1,120	3750.00	6000.00	16750.00	27500.00	
☐ 1854O	24,000	370.00	500.00	1100.00	4150.00	
☐ 1855	50,555	370.00	500.00	900.00	3200.00	**27500.00
☐ 1855S	6,000	370.00	620.00	1450.00	3700.00	
☐ 1856	26,010	345.00	485.00	850.00	3100.00	**18000.00
☐ 1856S*	34,500	375.00	550.00	1175.00	4000.00	
☐ 1857	20,891	345.00	485.00	850.00	3000.00	**16000.00
☐ 1857S	14,000	375.00	650.00	1550.00	5275.00	
☐ 1858	2,133	500.00	800.00	1800.00	4500.00	**14000.00
☐ 1859	15,638	345.00	470.00	850.00	3000.00	21500.00
☐ 1860	7,155	345.00	480.00	1100.00	3500.00	18000.00
☐ 1860S	7,000	345.00	650.00	1350.00	5500.00	
☐ 1861	6,072	345.00	520.00	1200.00	3800.00	14750.00
☐ 1862	5,785	345.00	520.00	1200.00	4000.00	15000.00
☐ 1863	5,039	345.00	540.00	1200.00	4200.00	15000.00
☐ 1864	2,680	390.00	600.00	1250.00	4300.00	15000.00
☐ 1865	1,165	390.00	700.00	1400.00	6500.00	21000.00
☐ 1866	4,030	345.00	625.00	1100.00	4100.00	16000.00
☐ 1867	2,650	350.00	650.00	1150.00	4200.00	14750.00
☐ 1868	4,875	345.00	600.00	1075.00	3900.00	14750.00
☐ 1869	2,525	345.00	650.00	1100.00	3700.00	15750.00
☐ 1870	3,535	345.00	625.00	1000.00	3800.00	15750.00
☐ 1870S	2	One piece was in the Eliasburg Collection. The other piece is in the corner stone of the San Francisco Mint.				
☐ 1871	1,330	430.00	700.00	1250.00	3900.00	15750.00
☐ 1872	2,030	390.00	675.00	1200.00	4100.00	15750.00
☐ 1873 Open 3	25	PROOF ONLY				42500.00
☐ 1873 Closed 3 Restrike					8250.00	30000.00
☐ 1874	41,820	345.00	450.00	800.00	2875.00	21500.00
☐ 1875 Proofs Only	20					95000.00
☐ 1876 Proofs Only	†45	Bowers and Ruddy Auction Sale				27000.00
☐ 1877	1,488	520.00	770.00	1800.00	4500.00	22750.00
☐ 1878	82,324	345.00	460.00	800.00	2850.00	20000.00
☐ 1879	3,030	375.00	535.00	950.00	3475.00	15750.00

*Found in Small, Medium and Large "S" Varieties.
**Stack's Sale 1976

DATE	MINTAGE	ABP in F-12	F-12 Fine	EF-40 Ex. Fine	MS-60 Unc.	PRF-65 Proof
☐ 1880	1,036	345.00	550.00	1200.00	3750.00	15000.00
☐ 1881	550	400.00	725.00	1600.00	5000.00	17500.00
☐ 1882	1,540	345.00	600.00	1000.00	3800.00	13750.00
☐ 1883	940	345.00	630.00	1050.00	4000.00	13750.00
☐ 1884	1,106	345.00	700.00	1200.00	3700.00	14000.00
☐ 1885	910	345.00	660.00	1275.00	4500.00	14000.00
☐ 1886	1,142	345.00	680.00	1225.00	3700.00	13250.00
☐ 1887	6,160	340.00	535.00	940.00	3700.00	13250.00
☐ 1888	5,291	340.00	535.00	940.00	3700.00	13250.00
☐ 1889	2,429	340.00	535.00	940.00	3700.00	13250.00

Beware of deceiving counterfeits with the following dates: 1855, 1857, 1878, 1882, and 1888.

"STELLA" — $4.00 GOLD PIECES
LIBERTY HEAD WITH FLOWING or COILED HAIR, 1879 - 1880

In 1879 and 1880 proofs were struck, in limited quantities, of a $4 gold coin that never reached circulation. It was called "Stella" and was coined not only in gold but various other metals. The gold specimens are extremely valuable. There are two obverse types, one designed by Barber and the other by Morgan.

Flowing Hair   Coiled Hair

DATE	MINTAGE	ABP in PRF-65	PRF-65 Proof
☐ 1879 Flowing Hair (PROOFS ONLY)	415	35000.00	48500.00
☐ 1879 Coiled Hair (PROOFS ONLY)	10	74000.00	110000.00
☐ 1880 Flowing Hair (PROOFS ONLY)	15	48000.00	67500.00
☐ 1880 Coiled Hair (PROOFS ONLY)	10	70000.00	105000.00

HALF EAGLES — $5.00 GOLD PIECES, 1795 - 1908

The Half Eagle or $5 gold piece was authorized on April 2, 1792, and first struck in 1795. It has the distinction of being the first gold coin struck by the U.S. Mint. Production was limited in the early years. Its designer was Robert Scot. The composition was .9167 gold to .0833 copper alloy, yielding a weight of 8.75 grams and a diameter of (generally) 25 mm. A capped portrait of Liberty facing right adorned the obverse, with stars and date appearing below the portrait; on the reverse is a spread-winged eagle holding in its beak a wreath, surrounded by the wording "UNITED STATES OF AMERICA." Some alterations in the number of stars and size of figures in the date will be observed. These should be taken close account of as they can have a considerable bearing on value. In 1807 John Reich redesigned the Half Eagle. The bust, now "capped and draped," was turned around to face left and the eagle modified. A shortened bust was introduced in 1913. A further modification was made in 1829 but with the same basic design retained. By this time the Quarter Eagle had become an important circulating as well as banking piece, whose significance was to later increase. The year 1834 brought a revised design known as the "Classic Head," the work of William Kneass. The weight of this new coin was 8.36 grams and its composition .8992 gold to .1008 copper, with a diameter of 22½ mm. The slogan "IN GOD WE TRUST," previously used on the reverse, was dropped, probably because of a shortage of space. This was followed by Gobrecht's "Coronet" head in 1839, used until 1908. Its gold content was raised slightly to 9/10ths and the copper reduced to 1/10th. Gold content by weight was .24187 ounce. There are small and large date varieties of this coin. In 1866, following the Civil War, "IN GOD WE TRUST" was added to the rather cramped sapce between the eagle's head and the legend "UNITED STATES OF AMERICA." Composition was as before but the weight was changed to 8.359 grams and the diameter reduced to 21.6 mm. One of the longest lived of coin designs, it remained in use a full 70 years, to be replaced by Pratt's Indian head in 1908.

HALF EAGLES — LIBERTY HEAD, 1795 · 1807
Eagle on Reverse

Head Right
1795-1807

1795-1807
Large Eagle

1795-1798
Small Eagle

DATE	MINTAGE	ABP in F-12	F-12 Fine	EF-40 Ex. Fine	MS-60 Unc.
☐ 1795 Small Eagle	8,707	2800.00	4200.00	8375.00	22500.00
☐ 1795 Large Eagle	8,707	2800.00	4800.00	10500.00	31000.00
☐ 1796 over 95 Small Eagle	3,399	2800.00	4500.00	9500.00	25000.00
☐ 1797 over 95 Large Eagle	6,406	2800.00	4200.00	8100.00	19500.00
☐ 1798 Small Eagle	6 Known			EXTREMELY RARE	
☐ 1798 Large Eagle All Types	24,867	600.00	1000.00	2650.00	10000.00
☐ 1799	7,451	575.00	985.00	2100.00	9175.00
☐ 1800	37,620	575.00	985.00	2550.00	8675.00
☐ 1802 over 1	53,176	575.00	985.00	2550.00	8675.00
☐ 1803 over 2	33,506	575.00	985.00	2550.00	8675.00

DATE	MINTAGE	ABP in F-12	F-12 Fine	EF-40 Ex. Fine	MS-60 Unc.
☐ 1804 Small & Large "8"	30,475	575.00	985.00	2550.00	8675.00
☐ 1805	33,183	575.00	985.00	2550.00	8675.00
☐ 1806 (Round & PointedTop 6)	64,093	575.00	985.00	2550.00	8675.00
☐ 1807 (Head Right)	33,496	575.00	985.00	2550.00	8675.00

HALF EAGLES — DRAPED BUST, 1807 - 1812
Value 5D on Reverse

HEAD
LEFT

"Round Cap"

DATE	MINTAGE	ABP in F-12	F-12 Fine	EF-40 Ex. Fine	MS-60 Unc.
☐ 1807	50,597	675.00	1075.00	2250.00	8250.00
☐ 1808	55,578	675.00	1075.00	2250.00	8250.00
☐ 1809/8	33,875	675.00	1075.00	2250.00	8250.00
☐ 1810	100,287	675.00	1075.00	2250.00	8250.00
☐ 1811	99,581	675.00	1075.00	2250.00	8250.00
☐ 1812	58,087	675.00	1075.00	2250.00	8250.00

HALF EAGLES — LIBERTY HEAD, ROUND CAP, 1813 - 1834
Motto Over Eagle

DATE	MINTAGE	ABP in F-12	F-12 Fine	EF-40 Ex. Fine	MS-60 Unc.
☐ 1813	95,428	600.00	1175.00	2350.00	10250.00
☐ 1814 (over 13)	15,454	650.00	1250.00	2800.00	12500.00
☐ 1815	635			EXTREMELY RARE	
☐ 1818	48,588	650.00	1200.00	2400.00	10750.00
☐ 1819	51,723			RARE 45,000.00	
☐ 1820	263,806	600.00	1175.00	2300.00	10500.00
☐ 1821	34,641	1700.00	2800.00	7800.00	18500.00
☐ 1822			Only 3 Known EXTREMELY RARE		

DATE	MINTAGE	ABP in F-12	F-12 Fine	EF-40 Ex. Fine	MS-60 Unc.
☐ 1823	14,485	1300.00	1850.00	3800.00	14500.00
☐ 1824	17,340	2900.00	4750.00	15000.00	25000.00
☐ 1825 over 21	29,060	1700.00	2600.00	6900.00	16250.00
☐ 1825 over 24	29,060				EXTREMELY RARE
☐ 1826	18,069	1800.00	2750.00	8370.00	19500.00
☐ 1827	24,913	4500.00	7000.00	18200.00	40000.00
☐ 1828	28,029				RARE
☐ 1828 over 27	28,029	4175.00	6000.00	17000.00	39000.00
☐ 1829 Small Date	57,442				RARE
☐ 1829 Large Date			1976 STACK'S AUCTION		65,000
☐ 1830	126,351	1300.00	1900.00	4700.00	14250.00
☐ 1831	140,594	1300.00	1900.00	4700.00	14250.00
☐ 1832**	157,487	1900.00	3100.00	8300.00	18000.00
☐ 1833	193,630	1325.00	1950.00	4850.00	14000.00
☐ 1834***	50,141	1325.00	1950.00	4850.00	14750.00

**1832 Square Based 2, 13 Stars   ***1834 Crosslet 4: Same Price

HALF EAGLES — LIBERTY HEAD WITH RIBBON, 1834 - 1838
No Motto Over Eagle

4 Plain 4

4 Crosslet 4

Mint Mark is Above
Date on Obverse

DATE	MINTAGE	ABP in F-12	F-12 Fine	EF-40 Ex. Fine	MS-60 Unc.
☐ 1834 Plain 4*	682,028	150.00	220.00	430.00	3075.00
☐ 1835	371,534	150.00	220.00	430.00	2550.00
☐ 1836	553,147	150.00	220.00	430.00	2550.00
☐ 1837	207,121	150.00	280.00	520.00	2875.00
☐ 1838	286,588	150.00	235.00	430.00	2600.00
☐ 1838C	12,913	575.00	825.00	2800.00	6000.00
☐ 1838D	20,583	575.00	800.00	2700.00	8200.00

*1834 Crosslet 4 Worth More. MS-60 Unc. $7000.00

HALF EAGLES — LIBERTY HEAD WITH CORONET, 1839 - 1908

1839-1908 | 1839-66 No Motto | 1866-1908 With Motto

Mint Mark is Below Eagle on Reverse

DATE	MINTAGE	ABP in F-12	F-12 Fine	EF-40 Ex. Fine	MS-60 Unc.	PRF-65 Proof
☐ 1839	118,143	112.00	200.00	400.00	2250.00	
☐ 1839C	23,467	175.00	410.00	1350.00	5800.00	
☐ 1839D	18,939	150.00	370.00	1400.00	6000.00	
☐ 1840	137,382	112.00	170.00	375.00	2250.00	
☐ 1840C	19,028	170.00	400.00	1150.00	5300.00	
☐ 1840D	22,896	160.00	380.00	1100.00	6275.00	
☐ 1840O	30,400	112.00	275.00	750.00	4250.00	
☐ 1841	15,833	112.00	170.00	375.00	2300.00	
☐ 1841C	21,511	130.00	350.00	1000.00	6300.00	
☐ 1841D	30,495	130.00	350.00	1100.00	6500.00	
☐ 1841O	50		EXTREMELY RARE 2 Known			
☐ 1842	27,578	112.00	165.00	500.00	3175.00	
☐ 1842C (Large Date)	27,480	112.00	350.00	800.00	4500.00	
☐ 1842C (Small Date)	59,608	170.00	400.00	950.00	4675.00	
☐ 1842O	16,400	112.00	240.00	750.00	3900.00	
☐ 1843	611,205	112.00	150.00	225.00	1200.00	
☐ 1843C	44,353	165.00	400.00	1075.00	4900.00	
☐ 1843D	98,452	112.00	380.00	1000.00	5250.00	
☐ 1843O	101,075	112.00	190.00	525.00	3000.00	
☐ 1844	340,330	112.00	150.00	280.00	1225.00	
☐ 1844C	23,631	165.00	450.00	1200.00	6200.00	
☐ 1844D	88,982	115.00	400.00	850.00	5800.00	
☐ 1844O	364,600	112.00	225.00	460.00	2000.00	
☐ 1845	417,099	112.00	150.00	250.00	1150.00	
☐ 1845D	90,629	165.00	400.00	850.00	5500.00	
☐ 1845O	41,000	125.00	260.00	550.00	4700.00	
☐ 1846	395,942	112.00	140.00	230.00	1200.00	
☐ 1846C	12,995	155.00	425.00	1400.00	6750.00	
☐ 1846D	80,294	150.00	410.00	900.00	3500.00	
☐ 1846O	58,000	120.00	280.00	550.00	3300.00	
☐ 1847	915,981	112.00	140.00	230.00	1200.00	
☐ 1847 Impression of extra 7				VERY RARE		
☐ 1847C	84,151	155.00	410.00	1200.00	5800.00	
☐ 1847D	64,405	155.00	435.00	1050.00	5500.00	
☐ 1847O	12,000	155.00	400.00	1075.00	5375.00	

DATE	MINTAGE	ABP in F-12	F-12 Fine	EF-40 Ex. Fine	MS-60 Unc.	PRF-65 Proof
☐1848	260,775	105.00	150.00	280.00	2200.00	
☐1848C	64,472	185.00	425.00	1175.00	4375.00	
☐1848D	47,465	190.00	430.00	1000.00	3800.00	
☐1849	133,070	110.00	140.00	230.00	1600.00	
☐1849C	64,823	150.00	370.00	750.00	4500.00	
☐1849D	39,036	150.00	380.00	1500.00	6800.00	
☐1850	64,941	105.00	185.00	350.00	1850.00	
☐1850C	63,591	150.00	370.00	775.00	3200.00	
☐1850D	53,950	150.00	380.00	1400.00	5350.00	
☐1351	377,505	105.00	150.00	280.00	1675.00	
☐1851C	49,176	150.00	360.00	850.00	3700.00	
☐1851D	62,710	150.00	360.00	900.00	4100.00	
☐18510	41,000	130.00	290.00	520.00	3300.00	
☐1852	573,901	105.00	140.00	225.00	1075.00	
☐1852C	72,574	150.00	350.00	750.00	4150.00	
☐1852D	91,452	150.00	350.00	800.00	4300.00	
☐1853	305,770	105.00	150.00	280.00	1575.00	
☐1853C	65,571	150.00	350.00	775.00	5000.00	
☐1853D	89,687	150.00	350.00	815.00	4900.00	
☐1854	160,675	105.00	160.00	320.00	1675.00	
☐1854C	39,291	155.00	380.00	900.00	3500.00	
☐1854D	56,413	150.00	360.00	850.00	4850.00	
☐18540	46,000	140.00	275.00	575.00	2875.00	
☐1854S	268				EXTREMELY RARE	
☐1855	117,098	105.00	150.00	285.00	1325.00	
☐1855C	39,788	165.00	390.00	800.00	2750.00	
☐1855D	22,432	175.00	400.00	975.00	4750.00	
☐18550	11,100	160.00	375.00	800.00	4200.00	
☐1855S	61,000	130.00	160.00	550.00	2500.00	
☐1856	197,990	105.00	145.00	220.00	1150.00	
☐1856C	28,457	150.00	375.00	830.00	5175.00	
☐1856D	19,786	150.00	365.00	950.00	5350.00	
☐18560	10,000	165.00	390.00	1300.00	7000.00	
☐1856S	105,100	105.00	175.00	520.00	2750.00	
☐1857	98,188	105.00	150.00	220.00	1250.00	
☐1857C	31,360	145.00	325.00	800.00	3100.00	
☐1857D	17,046	150.00	375.00	980.00	5850.00	
☐18570	13,000	145.00	330.00	750.00	3900.00	
☐1857S	87,000	110.00	170.00	420.00	2850.00	
☐1858	15,136	130.00	195.00	360.00	1850.00	26500.00
☐1858C	38,856	160.00	350.00	800.00	2500.00	
☐1858D	15,362	170.00	380.00	1100.00	5850.00	
☐1858S	18,600	140.00	310.00	750.00	2450.00	
☐1859	16,814	130.00	195.00	550.00	2300.00	18500.00
☐1859C	31,487	150.00	330.00	830.00	3500.00	
☐1859D	10,366	175.00	400.00	950.00	3900.00	
☐1859S	13,220	175.00	420.00	1350.00	5700.00	
☐1860	19,825	130.00	195.00	490.00	2175.00	16750.00

DATE	MINTAGE	ABP in F-12	F-12 Fine	EF-40 Ex. Fine	MS-60 Unc.	PRF-65 Proof
☐1860C	14,813	185.00	380.00	1600.00	6500.00	
☐1860D	14,635	185.00	380.00	1575.00	6000.00	
☐1860S	21,200	140.00	260.00	1350.00	4500.00	
☐1861	639,950	100.00	150.00	200.00	1050.00	13500.00
☐1861C	6,879	400.00	775.00	2500.00	7200.00	
☐1861D	1,597	2000.00	3000.00	8500.00	15000.00	
☐1861S	9,500	180.00	375.00	1500.00	3600.00	
☐1862	4,465	210.00	430.00	975.00	2500.00	13500.00
☐1862S	9,500	300.00	650.00	2500.00	4800.00	
☐1863	2,472	240.00	475.00	1450.00	4100.00	13500.00
☐1863S	17,000	140.00	330.00	1500.00	3700.00	
☐1864	4,220	150.00	350.00	700.00	3450.00	13500.00
☐1864S	3,888	750.00	1150.00	3200.00	5000.00	
☐1865	1,295	210.00	450.00	1500.00	4000.00	14250.00
☐1865S	27,612	140.00	325.00	1400.00	3125.00	
☐1866S No Motto	43,020	140.00	325.00	1575.00	3650.00	
☐1866S With Motto***	43,020	120.00	260.00	1075.00	2800.00	
☐1866	6,720	180.00	340.00	840.00	2000.00	13250.00
☐1867	6,920	140.00	300.00	750.00	2000.00	13100.00
☐1867S	29,000	250.00	360.00	1475.00	3400.00	
☐1868	5,725	130.00	275.00	850.00	2000.00	13100.00
☐1868S	52,000	100.00	235.00	1100.00	2900.00	
☐1869	1,785	210.00	400.00	1000.00	2700.00	13100.00
☐1869S	31,000	120.00	300.00	1300.00	3400.00	
☐1870	4,035	180.00	320.00	850.00	2700.00	13100.00
☐1870CC	7,675		UNKNOWN IN UNC			
☐1870S	17,000	200.00	410.00	1700.00	3800.00	
☐1871	3,230	180.00	340.00	1150.00	3000.00	14000.00
☐1871CC	20,770	300.00	450.00	1400.00	3900.00	
☐1871S	25,000	110.00	235.00	750.00	1000.00	
☐1872	1,690	190.00	375.00	900.00	2100.00	13100.00
☐1872CC	16,980	230.00	480.00	1600.00	4200.00	
☐1872S	36,400	110.00	230.00	750.00	900.00	
☐1873	112,505	90.00	150.00	375.00	2000.00	13100.00
☐1873CC	7,416	300.00	585.00	1700.00	5300.00	
☐1873S	31,000	140.00	330.00	1100.00	3200.00	
☐1874	3,508	250.00	350.00	800.00	2700.00	13250.00
☐1874CC	21,198	270.00	410.00	975.00	3500.00	
☐1874S	16,000	120.00	360.00	1400.00	3100.00	
☐1875	220		VERY RARE			†60000.00
☐1875CC	11,828	280.00	540.00	1600.00	4000.00	
☐1875S	9,000	110.00	215.00	1475.00	4000.00	
☐1876	1,477	250.00	480.00	1300.00	2300.00	12850.00
☐1876CC	6,887	240.00	460.00	1175.00	2300.00	
☐1876S	4,000	260.00	550.00	2000.00	4000.00	
☐1877	1,152	220.00	450.00	1050.00	2850.00	14000.00
☐1877CC	8,680	230.00	480.00	1500.00	2725.00	
☐1877S	26,700	90.00	160.00	675.00	2000.00	
☐1878	131,740	80.00	110.00	200.00	500.00	13500.00

***From 1866 to 1908 — All have Motto "IN GOD WE TRUST" Over Eagle on Reverse.
† only 20 proofs struck in 1875

DATE	MINTAGE	ABP in F-12	F-12 Fine	EF-40 Ex. Fine	MS-60 Unc.	PRF-65 Proof
☐ 1878CC	9,054	450.00	850.00	3000.00	6000.00	
☐ 1878S	144,700	89.00	118.00	220.00	650.00	
☐ 1879	301,950	89.00	118.00	182.00	400.00	13000.00
☐ 1879CC	17,281	150.00	230.00	800.00	2000.00	
☐ 1879S	426,200	89.00	135.00	220.00	415.00	
☐ 1880	3,166,436	89.00	118.00	182.00	285.00	12850.00
☐ 1880CC	51,017	140.00	215.00	750.00	2300.00	
☐ 1880S	1,348,900	89.00	118.00	182.00	280.00	
☐ 1881	5,708,800	89.00	118.00	182.00	280.00	12500.00
☐ 1881CC	13,886	150.00	230.00	750.00	2700.00	
☐ 1881S	969,000	89.00	118.00 *	182.00	285.00	
☐ 1882	2,514,560	89.00	118.00	182.00	285.00	12250.00
☐ 1882CC	82,817	100.00	165.00	300.00	1600.00	
☐ 1882S	969,000	89.00	118.00	182.00	285.00	
☐ 1883	233,440	89.00	118.00	182.00	500.00	12125.00
☐ 1883CC	12,958	135.00	210.00	750.00	2800.00	
☐ 1883S	83,200	89.00	118.00	182.00	620.00	
☐ 1884	191,048	89.00	118.00	182.00	700.00	12125.00
☐ 1884CC	16,402	150.00	230.00	875.00	3500.00	
☐ 1884S	177,000	88.00	118.00	280.00	620.00	
☐ 1885	601,506	88.00	118.00	182.00	280.00	12125.00
☐ 1885S	1,211,500	88.00	118.00	182.00	280.00	
☐ 1886	388,432	88.00	118.00	182.00	310.00	12125.00
☐ 1886S	3,268,000	88.00	118.00	182.00	280.00	
☐ 1887	87				RARE	24750.00
☐ 1887S	1,912,000	88.00	118.00	182.00	280.00	
☐ 1888	18,296	88.00	118.00	225.00	850.00	12125.00
☐ 1888S	293,900	88.00	118.00	300.00	1100.00	
☐ 1889	7,565	100.00	150.00	450.00	920.00	12125.00
☐ 1890	4,328	140.00	215.00	630.00	1575.00	12125.00
☐ 1890CC	53,800	110.00	165.00	300.00	875.00	
☐ 1891	61,413	88.00	118.00	182.00	750.00	12125.00
☐ 1891CC	208,000	110.00	165.00	290.00	675.00	
☐ 1892	753,572	88.00	118.00	182.00	280.00	12125.00
☐ 1892CC	82,968	110.00	165.00	320.00	875.00	
☐ 1892O	10,000	200.00	375.00	750.00	2200.00	
☐ 1892S	298,400	88.00	118.00	230.00	1000.00	
☐ 1893	1,528,197	88.00	118.00	182.00	280.00	12125.00
☐ 1893CC	60,000	110.00	165.00	320.00	1300.00	
☐ 1893O	110,000	88.00	140.00	300.00	900.00	
☐ 1893S	224,000	88.00	118.00	182.00	450.00	
☐ 1894	957,955	100.00	140.00	182.00	280.00	12125.00
☐ 1894O	16,660	88.00	140.00	350.00	700.00	
☐ 1894S	55,900	120.00	230.00	600.00	1800.00	
☐ 1895	1,345,936	88.00	118.00	182.00	280.00	12125.00
☐ 1895S	112,000	88.00	135.00	280.00	900.00	
☐ 1896	59,063	88.00	118.00	200.00	375.00	12125.00
☐ 1896S	115,400	88.00	135.00	300.00	1100.00	
☐ 1897	867,883	88.00	118.00	182.00	280.00	12125.00

*** From 1866 to 1908 - all have motto "In God We Trust" over Eagle on reverse.

DATE	MINTAGE	ABP in F-12	F-12 Fine	EF-40 Ex. Fine	MS-60 Unc.	PRF-65 Proof
☐ 1897S	345,000	85.00	117.00	250.00	850.00	
☐ 1898	633,495	85.00	117.00	180.00	270.00	12125.00
☐ 1898S	1,397,400	85.00	117.00	180.00	325.00	
☐ 1899	1,710,729	85.00	117.00	180.00	270.00	11075.00
☐ 1899S	1,545,000	85.00	117.00	180.00	300.00	
☐ 1900	1,405,730	85.00	117.00	180.00	270.00	11075.00
☐ 1900S	329,000	85.00	120.00	220.00	700.00	
☐ 1901	616,040	85.00	117.00	180.00	270.00	11075.00
☐ 1901S	3,648,000	85.00	117.00	180.00	270.00	
☐ 1901S 1 over 0					2375.00	
☐ 1902	172,562	85.00	117.00	180.00	270.00	11075.00
☐ 1902S	939,000	85.00	117.00	180.00	270.00	
☐ 1903	227,024	85.00	117.00	180.00	270.00	11075.00
☐ 1903S	1,885,000	85.00	117.00	180.00	270.00	
☐ 1904	392,136	85.00	117.00	180.00	270.00	11075.00
☐ 1904S	97,000	85.00	125.00	200.00	500.00	
☐ 1905	302,308	85.00	117.00	180.00	270.00	11075.00
☐ 1905S	880,700	85.00	125.00	200.00	625.00	
☐ 1906	348,820	85.00	117.00	180.00	270.00	11075.00
☐ 1906D	320,000	85.00	117.00	180.00	270.00	
☐ 1906S	598,000	85.00	117.00	180.00	350.00	
☐ 1907	626,192	85.00	117.00	180.00	270.00	11075.00
☐ 1907D	888,000	85.00	117.00	180.00	270.00	
☐ 1908	421,874	85.00	117.00	180.00	270.00	

***1866 to 1908 — All have motto ''In God We Trust'' over Eagle on reverse.

INDIAN HEAD, 1908 - 1929

Bela Lyon Pratt's Indian Head design replaced the Liberty Head half eagle in 1908. Like the Quarter Eagle these coins are uniquely without raised edges and have designs stamped in incuse or recess rather than raised from the surface. A standing eagle adorns the reverse, with mintmark beneath the wording "E PLURIBUS UNUM." These half eagles contained 90% gold and 10% copper with a weight of 8.359 grains. The diameter is 21.6 mm. and the gold content by weight is .24187 ounce each. Striking of half eagles was suspended during World War I and not resumed until 1929, their final year of production.

Mint Mark is to Left of Value on Reverse

was dropped. For many years no motto appeared on the reverse until the installation, in 1866, of "IN GOD WE TRUST." The composition and other specifications remained unaltered. No change was made until 1907 when the Indian Head obverse, designed by Augustus Saint-Gaudens, was introduced.

EAGLES — LIBERTY HEAD, SMALL EAGLE, 1795 - 1797

DATE	MINTAGE	ABP in F-12	F-12 Fine	EF-40 Ex. Fine	MS-60 Unc.
☐ 1795	5,583	2100.00	3850.00	11750.00	29500.00
☐ 1796	4,146	2100.00	3850.00	11750.00	29500.00
☐ 1797 Part of Liberty Head, Small Eagle	3,615	2100.00	3850.00	11750.00	29500.00

EAGLES — LIBERTY HEAD, LARGE EAGLE, 1797 - 1804

4 Stars Right   6 Stars Right   Large Eagle

DATE	MINTAGE	ABP in F-12	F-12 Fine	EF-40 Ex. Fine	MS-60 Unc.
☐ 1797 Large Eagle	10,940	1250.00	2275.00	5175.00	16250.00
☐ 1798 over 97 9 Stars Left—4 Right	900	5800.00	9750.00	13250.00	25000.00
☐ 1798 over 97 7 Stars Left—6 Right	842	AUCTION SALE EF-45			46000.00
☐ 1799	37,449	1300.00	2300.00	4175.00	13850.00
☐ 1800	5,999	1300.00	2300.00	4350.00	14500.00
☐ 1801	44,344	1300.00	2300.00	4175.00	14175.00
☐ 1803	15,017	1300.00	2300.00	4350.00	14500.00
☐ 1804	3,757	1575.00	2850.00	6100.00	19250.00

DATE	MINTAGE	ABP in F-12	F-12 Fine	EF-40 Ex. Fine	MS-60 Unc.	PRF-65 Proof
☐ 1908	578,012	115.00	170.00	270.00	835.00	14500.00
☐ 1908D	148,000	115.00	170.00	270.00	850.00	14500.00
☐ 1908S	82,000	165.00	230.00	470.00	2275.00	
☐ 1909	627,138	115.00	170.00	270.00	835.00	14500.00
☐ 1909D	3,423,560	115.00	170.00	270.00	815.00	
☐ 1909O*	34,200	250.00	350.00	900.00	6800.00	
☐ 1909S	297,200	115.00	200.00	375.00	1675.00	
☐ 1910	604,250	115.00	170.00	270.00	830.00	14500.00
☐ 1910D	193,600	115.00	185.00	280.00	1100.00	
☐ 1910S	770,200	115.00	185.00	350.00	1950.00	
☐ 1911	915,139	115.00	170.00	275.00	850.00	
☐ 1911D	72,500	115.00	250.00	500.00	3500.00	14500.00
☐ 1911S	1,416,000	115.00	180.00	320.00	1250.00	
☐ 1912	790,144	115.00	170.00	235.00	830.00	
☐ 1912S	392,000	115.00	190.00	350.00	1675.00	
☐ 1913	916,099	115.00	170.00	285.00	830.00	14500.00
☐ 1913S	408,000	115.00	210.00	335.00	2400.00	
☐ 1914	247,125	115.00	170.00	275.00	860.00	14500.00
☐ 1914D	247,000	115.00	170.00	275.00	860.00	
☐ 1914S	263,000	115.00	180.00	320.00	1275.00	
☐ 1915**	588,075	115.00	170.00	275.00	830.00	16000.00
☐ 1915S	164,000	115.00	180.00	330.00	2300.00	
☐ 1916S	240,000	115.00	175.00	300.00	1250.00	
☐ 1929	662,000	900.00	1300.00	3200.00	6600.00	

*Some ''O'' Mint Marks are false. **Coins marked 1915D are not authentic.

EAGLES, $10 GOLD PIECES, 1795 - 1907

Gold pieces valued at $10 were released for general circulation in 1795. Despite the large face value and the super-large buying power ($10 in the 1790's was equivalent to about $200 in present-day money), this coin was struck in substantial numbers, chiefly as a banking piece. Though bullion shortages, speculation, and world economic conditions made the Eagle's career far from sedate, it retained great influence throughout most of its history. The first design, conceived by Robert Scot, comprised a capped bust of Liberty facing right with the so-called Small Eagle reverse, depicting an eagle holding a wreath in its beak. The shield or heraldic eagle replaced this type in 1797 and production was stepped up, output reaching more than 37,000 in 1799. The content was .9167 gold to .0833 copper, with a weight of 17½ grams and diameter generally of 33 mm. From 1805 to 1837 no eagles were struck. When production resumed in 1838 the portrait of Liberty had undergone a thorough alteration, at the hands of Christian Gobrecht. This was the Coronet type, with modified shielded eagle on the reverse. It weighed 16.718 grams with a 9-to-1 gold content (alloyed with copper) and diameter of 27 mm. The gold content by weight was .48375 ounces. The slogan "E PLURIBUS UNUM," previously used on the reverse,

EAGLES — LIBERTY HEAD WITH CORONET, 1838 - 1907

1862

1838-1866
No Motto

1866-1907
With Motto

Mint Mark is Below Eagle on Reverse

DATE	MINTAGE	ABP in F-12	F-12 Fine	EF-40 Ex. Fine	MS-60 Unc.	PRF-65 Proof
☐ 1838 Large Letters 7,200		350.00	510.00	2000.00	7175.00	
☐ 1839 Large Letters 25,800		240.00	420.00	1300.00	5700.00	
☐ 1839 Small Letters 12,447		280.00	550.00	1900.00	6300.00	
☐ 1840 47,338		180.00	335.00	650.00	3900.00	
☐ 1841 63,131		180.00	335.00	650.00	3900.00	
☐ 1841O 2,500		350.00	700.00	2300.00	6000.00	
☐ 1842 81,507		160.00	280.00	575.00	3750.00	
☐ 1842O 27,400		160.00	280.00	575.00	3750.00	
☐ 1843 75,462		175.00	315.00	625.00	3750.00	
☐ 1843O 175,162		165.00	280.00	550.00	2300.00	
☐ 1844 6,361		240.00	440.00	1600.00	4500.00	
☐ 1844O 118,700		175.00	310.00	550.00	2900.00	
☐ 1845 26,153		240.00	390.00	820.00	3275.00	
☐ 1845O 47,500		180.00	335.00	700.00	3275.00	
☐ 1846 20,095		270.00	500.00	1650.00	4800.00	
☐ 1846O 81,780		180.00	335.00	650.00	2900.00	
☐ 1847 862,258		160.00	260.00	520.00	1875.00	
☐ 1847O 417,099		170.00	280.00	540.00	2100.00	
☐ 1848 145,484		170.00	285.00	650.00	3500.00	
☐ 1848O 35,850		240.00	415.00	1300.00	3650.00	
☐ 1849 653,618		190.00	260.00	525.00	2100.00	
☐ 1849O 23,900		240.00	415.00	1275.00	3850.00	
☐ 1850 291,451		190.00	260.00	525.00	1825.00	
☐ 1850O 57,500		180.00	315.00	650.00	3400.00	
☐ 1851 176,328		190.00	295.00	635.00	2650.00	
☐ 1851O 263,000		190.00	260.00	550.00	2000.00	
☐ 1852 263,106		180.00	310.00	675.00	2625.00	
☐ 1852O 18,000		210.00	360.00	1000.00	3650.00	
☐ 1853 201,253		190.00	250.00	530.00	2100.00	
☐ 1853O 51,000		200.00	300.00	650.00	2750.00	
☐ 1854 54,250		200.00	315.00	675.00	2750.00	
☐ 1854O 52,500		200.00	285.00	620.00	2750.00	
☐ 1854S 123,826		190.00	265.00	530.00	1975.00	
☐ 1855 121,701		190.00	265.00	530.00	2100.00	40000.00
☐ 1855O 18,000		240.00	350.00	950.00	3650.00	

DATE	MINTAGE	ABP in F-12	F-12 Fine	EF-40 Ex. Fine	MS-60 Unc.	PRF-65 Proof
☐1855S	9,000	250.00	470.00	1600.00	4650.00	
☐1856	60,490	220.00	315.00	600.00	3000.00	40000.00
☐1856O	14,500	220.00	375.00	1175.00	3700.00	
☐1856S	26,000	220.00	315.00	650.00	3700.00	
☐1857	16,606	220.00	320.00	750.00	3700.00	
☐1857O	5,500	350.00	510.00	1400.00	5275.00	
☐1857S	26,000	220.00	360.00	850.00	3700.00	
☐1858*	2,521	2000.00	3000.00	7000.00		40000.00
☐1858O	20,000	220.00	310.00	625.00	3700.00	
☐1858S	11,800	250.00	460.00	1300.00	3700.00	
☐1859	16,093	220.00	325.00	650.00	3700.00	40000.00
☐1859O	2,300	675.00	975.00	3900.00	9500.00	
☐1859S	7,007	375.00	750.00	2100.00	6250.00	
☐1860	11,783	220.00	340.00	630.00	3700.00	23900.00
☐1860O	11,100	220.00	375.00	750.00	3700.00	
☐1860S	5,500	400.00	550.00	2500.00	6000.00	
☐1861	113,233	195.00	265.00	430.00	2000.00	23900.00
☐1861S	15,500	210.00	400.00	1100.00	3700.00	
☐1862	10,995	195.00	275.00	615.00	3700.00	22000.00
☐1862S	12,500	260.00	575.00	1500.00	3700.00	
☐1863	1,248	1275.00	2000.00	5000.00	9250.00	24000.00
☐1863S	10,000	330.00	650.00	1600.00	4500.00	
☐1864	3,580	420.00	700.00	1800.00	5500.00	19000.00
☐1864S	2,500	850.00	1275.00	4500.00	8900.00	
☐1865	4,005	350.00	700.00	1600.00	5500.00	19500.00
☐1865S	16,700	320.00	650.00	1550.00	4750.00	
☐1866 With Motto	3,780	250.00	550.00	1000.00	2000.00	20000.00
☐1866S No Motto	8,500	575.00	925.00	2500.00	6000.00	
☐1866S With Motto	11,500	275.00	420.00	1300.00	1900.00	
☐1867	3,140	350.00	700.00	1600.00	2000.00	17000.00
☐1867S	9,000	375.00	750.00	3000.00	6150.00	
☐1868	10,655	220.00	435.00	975.00	1600.00	17500.00
☐1868S	13,500	225.00	450.00	1475.00	3800.00	
☐1869	1,855	500.00	800.00	2000.00	4000.00	17750.00
☐1869S	6,430	350.00	700.00	1700.00	4000.00	
☐1870	2,535	300.00	575.00	1300.00	3500.00	17000.00
☐1870CC	5,908	800.00	1350.00	4500.00	8750.00	
☐1870S	8,000	250.00	450.00	1900.00	3800.00	
☐1871S	1,780	375.00	600.00	1500.00	3500.00	21000.00
☐1871CC	7,185	450.00	750.00	2400.00	4300.00	
☐1871S	16,500	315.00	500.00	1550.00	3200.00	
☐1872	1,650	725.00	1300.00	4100.00	6000.00	17500.00
☐1872CC	5,500	400.00	725.00	2500.00	3975.00	28000.00
☐1872S	17,300	200.00	400.00	1500.00	3000.00	
☐1873	825	1000.00	1600.00	5000.00	8850.00	32500.00
☐1873CC	4,543	500.00	800.00	2500.00	5000.00	
☐1873S	12,000	220.00	450.00	1350.00	2700.00	
☐1874	53,160	150.00	275.00	460.00	1000.00	21750.00
☐1874CC	16,767	300.00	485.00	2175.00	3650.00	

* Check for removed Mint Mark.

DATE	MINTAGE	ABP in F-12	F-12 Fine	EF-40 Ex. Fine	MS-60 Unc.	PRF-65 Proof
☐1874S	10,000	210.00	425.00	1475.00	1275.00	
☐1875	120	1979 GARRETT COLLECTION AUCTION				91000.00
☐1875CC	7,715	450.00	700.00	1800.00	3200.00	
☐1876	732	1350.00	2000.00	4000.00	8250.00	21500.00
☐1876CC	4,696	500.00	800.00	3500.00	5500.00	
☐1876S	5,000	300.00	475.00	1450.00	2900.00	
☐1877	817	1200.00	1900.00	3000.00	7500.00	27500.00
☐1877CC	3,332	500.00	825.00	1900.00	4000.00	
☐1877S	17,000	210.00	450.00	1475.00	3175.00	
☐1878	73,800	172.00	220.00	450.00	875.00	21000.00
☐1878CC	3,244	750.00	1050.00	2200.00	4000.00	
☐1878S	26,100	175.00	380.00	1175.00	2800.00	
☐1879	384,770	172.00	190.00	300.00	600.00	17500.00
☐1879CC	1,762	1800.00	2500.00	5250.00	12000.00	
☐1879O	1,500	1200.00	2000.00	3300.00	6000.00	
☐1879S	224,000	172.00	200.00	300.00	575.00	
☐1880	1,644,876	172.00	200.00	260.00	400.00	17000.00
☐1880CC	11,192	240.00	330.00	700.00	1375.00	
☐1880O	9,500	225.00	290.00	575.00	1075.00	
☐1880S	506,205	172.00	200.00	280.00	450.00	
☐1881	3,877,260	172.00	200.00	250.00	400.00	17000.00
☐1881CC	24,015	175.00	245.00	550.00	1600.00	
☐1881O	8,350	175.00	250.00	600.00	1750.00	
☐1881S	970,000	172.00	200.00	250.00	400.00	
☐1882	2,324,480	172.00	200.00	250.00	400.00	16750.00
☐1882CC	6,764	220.00	350.00	750.00	2500.00	
☐1882O	10,280	175.00	225.00	650.00	1900.00	
☐1882S	132,000	172.00	220.00	380.00	950.00	
☐1883	208,740	172.00	200.00	300.00	400.00	16750.00
☐1883CC	12,000	200.00	315.00	675.00	2750.00	
☐1883D	800	1100.00	2000.00	3300.00	7150.00	
☐1883S	38,000	172.00	220.00	375.00	975.00	
☐1884	76,017	172.00	220.00	375.00	975.00	31250.00
☐1884CC	9,925	215.00	350.00	650.00	1375.00	
☐1884S	124,250	172.00	200.00	340.00	975.00	
☐1885	124,527	172.00	200.00	290.00	850.00	15000.00
☐1885S	228,000	172.00	200.00	275.00	650.00	
☐1886	236,160	172.00	200.00	360.00	975.00	15000.00
☐1886S	826,000	172.00	200.00	275.00	400.00	
☐1887	53,680	172.00	200.00	290.00	850.00	15000.00
☐1887S	817,000	172.00	200.00	290.00	575.00	
☐1888	132,996	172.00	220.00	360.00	1100.00	15000.00
☐1888O	21,335	172.00	200.00	290.00	500.00	
☐1888S	648,700	172.00	200.00	290.00	400.00	
☐1889	4,485	200.00	290.00	600.00	1000.00	16750.00
☐1889S	425,400	172.00	200.00	290.00	400.00	
☐1890	58,043	172.00	220.00	370.00	700.00	15000.00
☐1890CC	17,500	175.00	215.00	450.00	900.00	

DATE	MINTAGE	ABP in F-12	F-12 Fine	EF-40 Ex. Fine	MS-60 Unc.	PRF-65 Proof
☐1891	91,868	172.00	190.00	290.00	500.00	15000.00
☐1891CC	103,732	185.00	215.00	300.00	600.00	
☐1892	797,552	172.00	190.00	280.00	410.00	14500.00
☐1892CC	40,000	200.00	280.00	450.00	1100.00	
☐18920	28,688	175.00	210.00	315.00	550.00	
☐1892S	115,500	172.00	215.00	330.00	520.00	
☐1893	1,840,895	172.00	195.00	265.00	400.00	14250.00
☐1893CC	14,000	200.00	275.00	500.00	1500.00	
☐18930	17,000	180.00	210.00	300.00	530.00	
☐1893S	141,350	165.00	215.00	330.00	520.00	
☐1894	2,470,782	165.00	190.00	285.00	375.00	13750.00
☐18940	197,500	165.00	190.00	265.00	425.00	
☐1894S	25,000	165.00	200.00	360.00	1100.00	
☐1895	567,826	165.00	190.00	235.00	400.00	13750.00
☐18950	98,000	165.00	190.00	285.00	400.00	
☐1895S	49,000	165.00	300.00	600.00	1900.00	
☐1896	76,348	165.00	190.00	285.00	400.00	13750.00
☐1896S	123,750	165.00	300.00	600.00	2000.00	
☐1897	1,000,159	165.00	190.00	285.00	400.00	13750.00
☐18970	42,500	165.00	190.00	285.00	400.00	
☐1897S	234,750	165.00	190.00	330.00	850.00	
☐1898	812,197	165.00	190.00	285.00	400.00	13750.00
☐1898S	473,600	165.00	190.00	285.00	400.00	
☐1899	1,262,305	165.00	190.00	285.00	400.00	13750.00
☐18990	37,047	165.00	190.00	285.00	400.00	
☐1899S	841,000	165.00	190.00	320.00	400.00	13750.00
☐1900	293,960	165.00	190.00	285.00	400.00	13750.00
☐1900S	81,000	165.00	190.00	285.00	400.00	
☐1901	1,718,825	165.00	190.00	285.00	400.00	13750.00
☐19010	72,041	165.00	190.00	285.00	400.00	
☐1901S	2,812,750	165.00	190.00	285.00	850.00	
☐1902	82,513	165.00	190.00	285.00	400.00	13750.00
☐1902S	469,500	165.00	190.00	285.00	400.00	
☐1903	125,926	165.00	190.00	285.00	400.00	13750.00
☐19030	112,771	165.00	190.00	285.00	400.00	
☐1903S		165.00	190.00	285.00	400.00	
☐1904	162,038	165.00	190.00	285.00	400.00	13750.00
☐19040	108,950	165.00	190.00	285.00	400.00	
☐1905	201,078	165.00	190.00	285.00	400.00	13750.00
☐1905S	369,250	165.00	190.00	285.00	700.00	
☐1906	165,496	165.00	190.00	285.00	400.00	13750.00
☐1906D	981,000	165.00	190.00	285.00	400.00	
☐19060	86,895	165.00	190.00	285.00	600.00	
☐1906S	457,000	165.00	190.00	285.00	400.00	
☐1907	1,203,973	165.00	190.00	285.00	400.00	13750.00
☐1907D	1,020,000	165.00	190.00	285.00	400.00	
☐1907S	210,000	180.00	250.00	360.00	800.00	

EAGLES — INDIAN HEAD, 1907 - 1933

A. Saint-Gaudens, a noted sculptor and really the first artist of international repute to design an American coin, strove to inject a touch of creative feeling in coin design. True to the artistic spirit of the times he sacrificed such supposedly old-fashioned qualities as balance to achieve imagination of line and composition. His eagle, on the reverse, is totally stylized, its strength and symmetry purposely over-emphasized. At first the motto "IN GOD WE TRUST" was omitted, owing to President Theodore Roosevelt's opinion that the name of God was not suitable for use on coinage in any context. He was overruled by Congress in 1908 and the motto appeared shortly thereafter. Striking of eagles, which had reached as high as nearly 4½ million pieces in a single year ($45,000,000 face value), was discontinued in 1933. The Saint-Gaudens Eagle contained 90 percent gold and 10 percent copper, with a diameter of 27 mm. and a weight of 16,718 grams. The bullion weight is .48375 of an ounce.

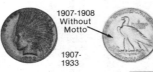

1907-1908 Without Motto

1907-1933

1908-1933 With Motto

Mint Mark is Left of Value on Reverse

DATE	MINTAGE	ABP in F-12	F-12 Fine	EF-40 Ex. Fine	MS-60 Unc.	PRF-65 Proof
☐ 1907 W/O Periods	239,406	235.00	330.00	460.00	850.00	
☐ 1907 Wire Rim with Periods Before and After U.S.A.	500				10000.00	
☐ 1907 Rolled Rim, Periods	42				36750.00	
☐ 1908 No Motto	33,500	235.00	340.00	590.00	1200.00	
☐ 1908 W/ Motto	341,486	235.00	340.00	440.00	800.00	21000.00
☐ 1908D No Motto	210,000	235.00	340.00	550.00	975.00	
☐ 1908D	386,500	235.00	340.00	580.00	1000.00	
☐ 1908S	59,850	275.00	400.00	700.00	3175.00	
☐ 1909	184,863	235.00	340.00	475.00	875.00	21000.00
☐ 1909D	121,540	235.00	340.00	475.00	900.00	
☐ 1909S	292,350	235.00	340.00	475.00	1600.00	
☐ 1910	318,704	235.00	340.00	475.00	800.00	22750.00
☐ 1910D	2,356,640	235.00	340.00	430.00	750.00	
☐ 1910S	811,000	235.00	340.00	450.00	1300.00	
☐ 1911	505,595	235.00	340.00	400.00	775.00	22000.00
☐ 1911D	30,100	385.00	590.00	925.00	5100.00	
☐ 1911S	51,000	250.00	360.00	500.00	2300.00	
☐ 1912	405,083	235.00	340.00	425.00	800.00	22500.00
☐ 1912S	300,000	235.00	340.00	480.00	2100.00	
☐ 1913	442,071	235.00	340.00	410.00	800.00	22500.00
☐ 1913S	66,000	295.00	475.00	850.00	6900.00	

DATE	MINTAGE	ABP in F-12	F-12 Fine	EF-40 Ex. Fine	MS-60 Unc.	PRF-65 Proof
☐ 1914	151,050	235.00	340.00	400.00	800.00	24750.00
☐ 1914D	343,500	235.00	340.00	400.00	800.00	
☐ 1914S	208,000	235.00	340.00	450.00	1500.00	
☐ 1915	351,075	235.00	340.00	415.00	800.00	24750.00
☐ 1915S	59,000	235.00	340.00	500.00	2800.00	
☐ 1916S	138,500	235.00	340.00	400.00	1500.00	
☐ 1920S	126,500	4000.00	5575.00	8000.00	18500.00	
☐ 1926	1,014,000	235.00	340.00	400.00	750.00	
☐ 1930S	96,000	2250.00	3200.00	5000.00	11250.00	
☐ 1932	1,463,000	235.00	340.00	400.00	750.00	
☐ 1933	312,500			15000.00	45000.00	

The rare dates of this series are heavily counterfeited. Be sure that you buy from a reputable dealer.

DOUBLE EAGLES, $20.00 GOLD PIECES

The Double Eagle or $20 gold piece was the largest denomination coin issued for regular use by the U.S. Mint. It was introduced in 1849, as a direct result of the California gold strikes. Discovery of gold at Sutter's Mill had not only made vast new supplies available to the government, but focused increased attention on gold as a medium of exchange. Necessity for a $20 face value coin was further prompted by the fact that the Treasury Department was not yet issuing paper currency.

These coins are known as "Double Eagles," as a result of being twice the size of Eagles or $10 gold pieces. Their composition was exactly the same as the lower denomination gold coins, .900 fine, or nine parts of 24K gold alloyed with one part copper. The Double Eagle contained .96750 of an ounce of pure gold, or just a slight fraction under one full ounce. With the copper content added, the coin's weight was more than an ounce — making it not only our highest denomination coin, but the heaviest physically. However it was smaller in diameter than the Silver $1, at 34 mm.

The first Double Eagles carried a portrait of Liberty facing left, by James B. Longacre, with a heraldic eagle on the reverse. Two significant changes were made during the use of this design, which was removed in 1907. In 1866 the motto "IN GOLD WE TRUST" was added above the eagle, and in 1877 the statement of value (on the reverse) was changed from "TWENTY D." to "TWENTY DOLLARS."

DOUBLE EAGLES-LIBERTY HEAD, 1849 - 1866

DATE	MINTAGE	ABP in F-12	F-12 Fine	EF-40 Ex. Fine	MS-60 Unc.	PRF-65 Proof
☐ 1849		Unique	— only 1 known in U.S. Mint Collection			
☐ 1850	1,170,261	280.00	365.00	610.00	1775.00	

Mint Mark is below Eagle on Reverse

DATE	MINTAGE	ABP in F-12	F-12 Fine	EF-40 Ex. Fine	MS-60 Unc.	PRF-65 Proof
☐ 18500	141,000	300.00	415.00	800.00	3725.00	
☐ 1851	2,087,155	290.00	375.00	600.00	1375.00	
☐ 18510	315,000	300.00	400.00	850.00	3300.00	
☐ 1852	2,053,026	290.00	375.00	630.00	1375.00	
☐ 18520	190,000	290.00	380.00	820.00	2950.00	
☐ 1853	1,261,326	290.00	360.00	600.00	1450.00	
☐ 18530	71,000	310.00	430.00	1000.00	3725.00	
☐ 1854	757,899	290.00	360.00	620.00	2250.00	
☐ 18540	3,250			35000.00	*52500.00	
☐ 1854S	141,469	290.00	370.00	630.00	2400.00	
☐ 1855	364,666	290.00	360.00	615.00	2000.00	
☐ 18550	8,000	1000.00	1900.00	7000.00	11000.00	
☐ 1855S	879,675	280.00	350.00	570.00	2475.00	
☐ 1856	329,878	280.00	350.00	570.00	2000.00	
☐ 18560	2,250					EXTREMELY RARE
☐ 1856S	1,189,750	280.00	350.00	550.00	1700.00	
☐ 1857	439,375	280.00	350.00	630.00	2150.00	
☐ 18570	30,000	300.00	400.00	1850.00	4000.00	
☐ 1857S	970,500	280.00	350.00	570.00	2650.00	
☐ 1858	211,714	280.00	350.00	600.00	2775.00	47500.00
☐ 18580	35,250	350.00	650.00	1800.00	4000.00	
☐ 1858S	846,710	280.00	350.00	570.00	2650.00	
☐ 1859	43,597	310.00	475.00	1500.00	3500.00	40000.00
☐ 1859S	636,445	280.00	350.00	600.00	3150.00	
☐ 18590	9,100	1000.00	1800.00	4200.00	7200.00	
☐ 1860	577,670	280.00	350.00	600.00	1500.00	40000.00
☐ 18600	6,600	2000.00	3100.00	7000.00	8000.00	
☐ 1860S	544,950	280.00	350.00	630.00	3250.00	
☐ 1861	2,976,453	280.00	350.00	525.00	1375.00	42500.00
☐ 18610	5,000	1000.00	1500.00	2800.00	7500.00	
☐ 1861S	768,000	280.00	350.00	615.00	3250.00	
☐ 1862	92,133	290.00	375.00	950.00	3750.00	29000.00
☐ 1862S	854,173	280.00	350.00	680.00	3500.00	
☐ 1863	142,790	300.00	380.00	650.00	3200.00	25000.00
☐ 1863S	966,570	280.00	330.00	590.00	2750.00	
☐ 1864	204,285	290.00	370.00	650.00	3200.00	27500.00
☐ 1864S	793,660	280.00	350.00	630.00	2750.00	
☐ 1865	351,200	290.00	360.00	630.00	2750.00	30000.00
☐ 1865S	1,042,500	280.00	350.00	575.00	4100.00	
☐ 1866S Part of	842,250	310.00	465.00	1175.00	5000.00	

*Stack's Auction 1979

DOUBLE EAGLES — LIBERTY HEAD, 1866 - 1876
With Motto and "TWENTY D" on Reverse

Mint Mark is below Eagle on Reverse

DATE	MINTAGE	ABP in F-12	F-12 Fine	EF-40 Ex. Fine	MS-60 Unc.	PRF-65 Proof
☐1866	698,775	265.00	315.00	630.00	2750.00	26750.00
☐1866S	842,250	265.00	315.00	630.00	1500.00	26750.00
☐1867S	920,250	260.00	315.00	630.00	1300.00	
☐1868	98,600	260.00	340.00	775.00	3000.00	26750.00
☐1868S	837,500	260.00	315.00	630.00	2750.00	
☐1869	175,155	260.00	315.00	630.00	2750.00	26750.00
☐1869S	686,750	260.00	315.00	630.00	1800.00	
☐1870	155,185	260.00	315.00	630.00	2900.00	26750.00
☐1870CC	3,789		Auction — 1973 — $28,000.00*			
☐1870S	982,000	260.00	315.00	600.00	1800.00	
☐1871	80,150	260.00	315.00	650.00	2900.00	26000.00
☐1871CC	14,687	1000.00	1400.00	3800.00	6500.00	
☐1871S	928,000	260.00	315.00	625.00	1600.00	
☐1872	251,880	260.00	315.00	625.00	1100.00	26000.00
☐1872CC	29,650	270.00	375.00	1100.00	2375.00	
☐1872S	780,000	260.00	315.00	600.00	1675.00	
☐1873	1,709,825	260.00	300.00	550.00		26750.00
☐1873CC	22,410	390.00	600.00	1275.00	3800.00	
☐1873S	1,040,600	260.00	315.00	590.00	1400.00	
☐1874	366,800	260.00	315.00	590.00	1400.00	27500.00
☐1874CC	115,085	260.00	350.00	850.00	3600.00	
☐1874S	1,241,000	260.00	300.00	520.00	975.00	
☐1875	295,740	260.00	330.00	590.00	1200.00	65000.00
☐1875CC	111,151	270.00	390.00	800.00	1500.00	
☐1875S	1,230,000	260.00	300.00	520.00	775.00	
☐1876	583,905	260.00	300.00	520.00	775.00	26000.00
☐1876CC	138,441	260.00	375.00	800.00	2100.00	
☐1876	1,597,000	260.00	300.00	520.00	750.00	

1861 and 1861-S both with A. C. Paquet Rev.
61-5 rare 61 ex. rare
*Stack's Auction in AU-50 condition

DOUBLE EAGLES — LIBERTY, 1877 - 1907
With Motto and "TWENTY DOLLARS" on Reverse

Mint Mark is below Eagle on Reverse

DATE	MINTAGE	ABP in F-12	F-12 Fine	EF-40 Ex. Fine	MS-60 Unc.	PRF-65 Proof
☐1877	397,670	255.00	310.00	560.00	900.00	23750.00
☐1877CC	42,565	260.00	370.00	825.00	2450.00	
☐1877S	1,735,000	255.00	300.00	560.00	950.00	
☐1878	534,645	255.00	310.00	560.00	850.00	23750.00
☐1878CC	13,180	260.00	420.00	1100.00	3375.00	
☐1878S	1,739,000	255.00	300.00	560.00	975.00	
☐1879	207,5630	255.00	310.00	580.00	975.00	23750.00
☐1879CC	10,708	500.00	800.00	1300.00	3700.00	
☐1879O	2,325	900.00	2000.00	4500.00	9750.00	
☐1879S	1,223,800	255.00	300.00	560.00	975.00	
☐1880	51,456	255.00	300.00	580.00	2500.00	23250.00
☐1880S	836,000	255.00	300.00	580.00	975.00	
☐1881	2,260	1000.00	2450.00	6000.00	14000.00	32000.00
☐1881S	727,000	280.00	400.00	580.00	1200.00	
☐1882	630	3500.00	6000.00	14000.00	35000.00	50000.00
☐1882CC	39,140	270.00	390.00	800.00	1825.00	
☐1882S	1,125,000	255.00	300.00	560.00	1075.00	
☐1883	40		PROOFS ONLY			85000.00
☐1883CC	59,962	270.00	375.00	775.00	1475.00	
☐1883S	1,189,000	255.00	310.00	510.00	700.00	
☐1884	71		PROOFS ONLY			70000.00
☐1884CC	81,139	270.00	375.00	775.00	1650.00	
☐1884S	916,000	255.00	320.00	520.00	700.00	
☐1885	828	2800.00	4000.00	9000.00	25000.00	40000.00
☐1885CC	9,450	625.00	900.00	1900.00	6175.00	
☐1885S	683,500	255.00	310.00	560.00	700.00	
☐1886	1,106	3000.00	6000.00	10000.00	22500.00	48500.00
☐1887	121		PROOFS ONLY			55000.00
☐1887S	283	255.00	300.00	550.00		
☐1888	226,266	255.00	300.00	550.00	850.00	23250.00
☐1888S	859,600	255.00	300.00	550.00	850.00	

DATE	MINTAGE	ABP in F-12	F-12 Fine	EF-40 Ex. Fine	MS-60 Unc.	PRF-65 Proof
☐ 1889	44,111	255.00	300.00	560.00	850.00	23250.00
☐ 1889CC	30,945	260.00	360.00	900.00	1750.00	
☐ 1889S	774,700	260.00	310.00	520.00	700.00	
☐ 1890	75,995	260.00	320.00	580.00	850.00	23250.00
☐ 1890CC	91,209	265.00	400.00	775.00	1580.00	
☐ 1890S	802,750	255.00	355.00	565.00	1000.00	
☐ 1891	1,442	1200.00	1850.00	3800.00	9800.00	24750.00
☐ 1891CC	5,000	750.00	1000.00	2300.00	7000.00	
☐ 1891S	1,288,125	255.00	310.00	490.00	650.00	
☐ 1892	4,523	500.00	800.00	1350.00	3800.00	24250.00
☐ 1892CC	27,265	300.00	450.00	850.00	1600.00	
☐ 1892S	930,150	255.00	310.00	490.00	675.00	
☐ 1893	344,399	255.00	310.00	490.00	700.00	22500.00
☐ 1893CC	18,402	280.00	430.00	850.00	2400.00	
☐ 1893S	996,175	255.00	310.00	490.00	660.00	
☐ 1894	1,368,990	255.00	310.00	490.00	660.00	21750.00
☐ 1894S	1,048,550	255.00	310.00	490.00	660.00	
☐ 1895	1,114,656	255.00	310.00	490.00	660.00	21750.00
☐ 1895S	1,143,500	255.00	310.00	490.00	660.00	
☐ 1896	792,663	255.00	310.00	490.00	660.00	21750.00
☐ 1896S	1,403,925	255.00	310.00	490.00	660.00	
☐ 1897	1,383,261	255.00	310.00	490.00	660.00	22000.00
☐ 1897S	1,470,250	255.00	310.00	560.00	775.00	
☐ 1898	170,470	255.00	310.00	490.00	660.00	21000.00
☐ 1898S	2,575,175	255.00	310.00	490.00	660.00	
☐ 1899	1,669,384	255.00	310.00	490.00	660.00	21000.00
☐ 1899S	2,010,300	255.00	310.00	490.00	660.00	
☐ 1900	1,874,584	255.00	310.00	490.00	660.00	21000.00
☐ 1900S	2,459,500	255.00	310.00	490.00	660.00	
☐ 1901	111,526	255.00	310.00	490.00	660.00	21000.00
☐ 1901S	1,596,000	255.00	310.00	490.00	660.00	
☐ 1902	31,254	255.00	330.00	530.00	800.00	21000.00
☐ 1902S	1,753,625	255.00	310.00	490.00	660.00	21000.00
☐ 1903	287,428	255.00	310.00	490.00	660.00	21000.00
☐ 1903S	954,000	255.00	310.00	490.00	660.00	
☐ 1904	6,256,797	255.00	310.00	490.00	660.00	21000.00
☐ 1904S	5,134,175	255.00	310.00	490.00	660.00	
☐ 1905	59,011	255.00	330.00	550.00	975.00	21000.00
☐ 1905S	1,813,000	255.00	310.00	490.00	700.00	
☐ 1906	69,690	255.00	310.00	490.00	740.00	21000.00
☐ 1906D	620,250	255.00	310.00	490.00	660.00	
☐ 1906S	2,065,750	255.00	310.00	490.00	660.00	
☐ 1907	1,451,864	255.00	310.00	490.00	660.00	21000.00
☐ 1907D	842,250	255.00	310.00	490.00	660.00	
☐ 1907S	2,165,800	255.00	310.00	490.00	660.00	

DOUBLE EAGLES, $20 GOLD PIECES, 1907 - 1933

The Longacre Liberty design was replaced by the Saint-Gaudens in 1907, featuring a striding figure of Liberty holding a torch on the obverse and an eagle in flight on the reverse. A fact seldom mentioned is that this, of all representations of Liberty on our coins, was the only full-face likeness, the others being profiles or semi-profiles. Composition and weight remained as previously. The motto "IN GOD WE TRUST," at first omitted on request of Theodore Roosevelt, was added by Act of Congress in 1908. Striking of Double Eagles ceased in 1933. This final version of the mighty coin had a 90% gold/10% copper composition, with a weight of 33.436 grams (of which .96750 of an ounce was pure gold — almost a full ounce). Its diameter was 34 mm.

As a speculative item for gold investors, the double eagle has enjoyed greater popularity and media publicity in recent months than ever in its history. This should not be surprising as it contains very nearly an exact ounce of gold and its worth as bullion can be figured easily based upon daily gold quotations.

DOUBLE LIBERTY STANDING " ST. GAUDENS"
Roman Numerals MCMVII

Roman Numeral High Relief, Wire Rim,
Plain Edge, 14 Rays over Capitol.
Three Folds on Liberty's skirt.

DATE	MINTAGE	ABP in F-12	F-12 Fine	EF-40 Ex. Fine	MS-60 Unc.	PRF-65 Proof
☐1907-MCMVII Ex. High Relief— Lettered Edge		UNIQUE-STACK'S 1974 $200000.00				
☐1907-MCMVII Ex. High Relief— Plain Edge		VERY RARE $500000.00				
☐1907 Flat Rim*		2000.00	2850.00	4100.00	12250.00	
☐1907 Wire Rim*	11,250	2000.00	2850.00	4100.00	12250.00	

*NOTE: Separate mintage figures were not kept on these varieties.

DOUBLE EAGLES — LIBERTY STANDING "ST. GAUDENS,"
1907 - 1908
Date in Arabic Numerals, No Motto on Reverse

Mint Mark is Below Date on Obverse

DATE	MINTAGE	ABP in F-12	F-12 Fine	EF-40 Ex. Fine	MS-60 Unc.
☐1907*	361,667	290.00	430.00	575.00	1050.00
☐1908	4,271,551	290.00	430.00	575.00	1050.00
☐1908D	66,750	290.00	430.00	575.00	1050.00

*Small Letters on Edge. Large Letter on Edge-Unique.

DOUBLE EAGLES — LIBERTY STANDING "ST. GAUDENS,"
1908 - 1933
With Motto on Reverse

Motto
"In God
We Trust"

Mint Mark is Below Date on Obverse

DATE	MINTAGE	ABP in F-12	F-12 Fine	EF-40 Ex. Fine	MS-60 Unc.	PRF-65 Proof
☐1908	156,359	290.00	410.00	575.00	850.00	34000.00
☐1908D	349,500	290.00	410.00	580.00	800.00	
☐1908S	22,000	290.00	450.00	900.00	3500.00	
☐1909	161,282	290.00	410.00	590.00	1025.00	34000.00
☐1909 over 8	161,282	290.00	410.00	550.00	1025.00	
☐1909D	52,500	290.00	460.00	750.00	2400.00	
☐1909S	2,774,925	290.00	410.00	550.00	735.00	
☐1910	482,167	290.00	410.00	550.00	735.00	
☐1910D	429,000	290.00	410.00	550.00	735.00	

DATE	MINTAGE	ABP in F-12	F-12 Fine	EF-40 Ex. Fine	MS-60 Unc.	PRF-65 Proof
☐1910S	2,128,250	295.00	400.00	550.00	710.00	
☐1911	197,350	295.00	400.00	560.00	760.00	
☐1911D	846,500	295.00	400.00	560.00	750.00	
☐1911S	775,750	295.00	400.00	560.00	750.00	
☐1912	149,824	295.00	400.00	570.00	800.00	32000.00
☐1913	168,838	295.00	400.00	560.00	725.00	32000.00
☐1913D	393,500	295.00	400.00	560.00	725.00	
☐1913S	34,000	295.00	430.00	600.00	1250.00	
☐1914	95,320	295.00	400.00	560.00	1300.00	32000.00
☐1914D	453,000	295.00	400.00	560.00	750.00	
☐1914S	1,498,000	295.00	390.00	560.00	700.00	
☐1915	152,050	295.00	400.00	580.00	1175.00	32000.00
☐1915S	567,500	295.00	400.00	560.00	750.00	
☐1916S	796,000	295.00	400.00	560.00	800.00	
☐1920	228,250	295.00	400.00	560.00	800.00	
☐1920S	558,000	2800.00	4500.00	7000.00	15000.00	
☐1921	528,500	3500.00	6000.00	8500.00	18000.00	
☐1922	1,375,500	295.00	380.00	560.00	700.00	
☐1922S	2,658,000	315.00	390.00	600.00	1050.00	
☐1923	566,000	310.00	380.00	560.00	775.00	
☐1923D	1,702,000	295.00	370.00	560.00	800.00	
☐1924	4,323,500	295.00	370.00	560.00	775.00	
☐1924D	3,049,500	315.00	430.00	925.00	1900.00	
☐1924S	2,927,500	320.00	485.00	890.00	2050.00	
☐1925	2,831,750	320.00	485.00	560.00	975.00	
☐1925D	2,938,500	325.00	580.00	1100.00	3300.00	
☐1925S	2,776,500	325.00	580.00	900.00	4175.00	
☐1926	816,750	295.00	380.00	560.00	775.00	
☐1926D	481,000	325.00	560.00	1150.00	2200.00	
☐1926S	2,041,500	320.00	530.00	1075.00	1700.00	
☐1927	2,946,750	295.00	380.00	560.00	775.00	
☐1927D	180,000				125000.00	
☐1927S	3,107,000	1325.00	2300.00	4175.00	11000.00	
☐1928	8,816,000	295.00	370.00	560.00	775.00	
☐1929	1,779,750	850.00	1600.00	3500.00	7500.00	
☐1930S	74,000	2150.00	4100.00	9000.00	17000.00	
☐1931	2,938,250	1800.00	3400.00	7100.00	13000.00	
☐1931D	106,500	1600.00	3200.00	6900.00	16500.00	
☐1932	1,101,750	3200.00	5300.00	7900.00	14750.00	
☐1933	445,525	NEVER PLACED IN CIRCULATION BECAUSE OF GOLD RECALL LEGISLATION.				

THE SILVER COMMEMORATIVE COINAGE
OF THE UNITED STATES

Commemorative coinage — that is, coins whose designs present a departure from the normal types for their denomination — was first struck in the ancient world. Roman emperors delighted in issuing coins portraying members of the family or topical events; they served an important propaganda purpose. Commemorative coins must be distinguished from medals, as the former have a stated face value and can be spent as money while the latter serve a decorative function only. During the Mint's first century it coined no commemoratives whatever. Its first was the Columbian half dollar of 1892, issued in connecton with the Columbia Exposition. To date the total has reached 158 pieces, of which one is a silver dollar; one a silver quarter; 143 are half dollars (comprising 48 major types); two are $2.50 gold pieces; two are $50 gold pieces; and nine are $1 gold pieces. There is some objection to including the $50 "Quintuple Eagles" as commemorative *coins,* as regular coins of this denomination were never issued. They do however bear a statement of face value and were spendable.

Commemorative coins are issued by a special act of Congress and overseen by a committee established for the purpose. Sale of commemoratives is made to the public (and coin dealers) at an advance in price over the face value, this advance being excused on grounds that specimens supplied as choice and uncirculated have, presumably, sufficient collector appeal to be worth more than their stated denomination. While commemoratives, have certainly not all advanced in price at a comparable pace, all have shown very healthy increases and proved excellent investments for their original or early purchasers.

A pair of medals are traditionally collected in conjunction with commemorative silver coins and careful note should be taken of them. These are the "Octagonal Norse American Centennial, 1828-1925," designed by Opus Fraser, struck on thick and thin planchets in a total issue of 40,000 (the latter are scarcer); and the "Wilson Dollar," designed by George T. Morgan of Morgan Dollar fame in connection with opening of the Phillipines Mint. The 2 Kroner commemorative of 1936 issued by Sweden is also frequently collected with our commemoratives, though small in size and quite plentiful, as it relates to the Delaware Tercentenary or 300th anniversary.

The extent to which commemorative coins have been used as money is not precisely determined but is thought to be very limited. As the original owners paid a premium for these coins it is not likely that many — except in time of dire need — would have cared to exchange them merely at face value. It should not automatically be presumed that specimens in less than uncirculated condition were indeed used as money and passed through many hands. Their substandard preservation could well be the result of injury, ill-advised cleaning or mounting procedures, or wear received from handling in traveling from collection to collection. Nevertheless, discriminating buyers expect commemoratives to be in uncirculated state and anything inferior is worth much less (the discount being sharper than for a circulating coin).

The existence of proofs among the commemorative series has aroused much debate. Commemoratives are occasionally seen as proofs, notably the Columbian and Isabella quarters, but this is no evidence that all or even a majority of commemoratives were available in proof state. It is easy to be confused on this point as well-struck uncirculated specimens frequently have a proof-like appearance.

SILVER COMEMORATIVE, 1892 - 1954
ISABELLA QUARTER DOLLAR

Comparatively little notice was at first taken of this handsome commemorative, because the Columbian Exposition (at which it was issued) had already produced a commemorative and a larger one, in 50¢ denomination. The Isabella Quarter Dollar, originally sold at the exposition for $1, soon became a popular favorite of collectors. Agitation for it was made by the fair's Board of Lady Managers, which may explain why it portrays a female on the obverse — Isabella of Spain, who helped finance Columbus' voyage round the world — and a symbol of "female industry" on its reverse. The coin was designed by C. E. Barber and struck in 1893.

DATE	MINTAGE	ABP in MS-60	MS-60 Unc.	MS-65 Unc.
☐1893	24,214	370.00	500.00	2075.00

LAFAYETTE DOLLAR

The celebrated Lafayette Dollar holds a special rank among commemoratives, being the first $1 denomination coin of its sort and the first to portray an American President. On its obverse is a profile bust of General Lafayette, the French officer so instrumental to our efforts in ending colonial domination, over which a profile of Washington is superimposed. The reverse carries a fine equestrian likeness of Lafayette, adapted from a statue put up at Paris as a gift from the American people. This coin was designed by C. E. Barber and struck in 1900. They were sold originally at twice the face value, with proceeds going to the Lafayette Memorial Commission.

DATE	MINTAGE	ABP in MS-60	MS-60 Unc.	MS-65 Unc.
☐ 1900	36,026	550.00	875.00	5750.00

SILVER COMMEMORATIVE HALF DOLLARS

COLUMBIAN
EXPOSITION
HALF DOLLAR

1892-1893

DATE	MINTAGE		ABP in MS-60	MS-60 Unc.	MS-65 Unc.
☐ 1892 Columbian Expo	950,000		19.00	31.00	280.00
☐ 1893 Columbian Expo	1,550,405		19.00	31.00	280.00
☐ 1921 Alabama Centennial	59,038		160.00	265.00	1525.00
☐ 1921 Same w/2 x 2 on Obverse	6,006		250.00	345.00	1600.00
☐ 1936 Albany, N.Y.	17,671		150.00	240.00	700.00
☐ Arkansas Centennial	Type		60.00	85.00	250.00
☐ 1935 Arkansas Centennial	13,012				
☐ 1935D Arkansas Centennial	5,505	SET	180.00	260.00	700.00
☐ 1935S Arkansas Centennial	5,506				
☐ 1936 Arkansas Centennial	9,660				
☐ 1936D Arkansas Centennial	9,660	SET	180.00	260.00	700.00
☐ 1936S Arkansas Centennial	9,662				
☐ 1937 Arkansas Centennial	5,505				
☐ 1937D Arkansas Centennial	5,505	SET	190.00	290.00	800.00
☐ 1937S Arkansas Centennial	5,506				
☐ 1938 Arkansas Centennial	3,156				
☐ 1938D Arkansas Centennial	3,155	SET	340.00	480.00	1185.00
☐ 1938S Arkansas Centennial	3,156				
☐ 1939 Arkansas Centennial	2,104				
☐ 1939D Arkansas Centennial	2,104	SET	675.00	925.00	1825.00
☐ 1939S Arkansas Centennial	2,105				
☐ 1936 Arkansas (Robinson)	25,265		85.00	125.00	300.00
☐ 1937 Battle of Antietam	18,028		225.00	350.00	625.00
☐ 1936 Battle of Gettysburg	26,030		145.00	245.00	530.00
☐ Boone Bi-Centennial	Type		72.00	120.00	280.00
☐ 1934 Boone Bi-Centennial	10,007		85.00	135.00	320.00
☐ 1935 Boone Bi-Centennial	10,010				
☐ 1935D Boone Bi-Centennial	5,005	SET	220.00	320.00	775.00
☐ 1935S Boone Bi-Centennial	5,005				

DATE	MINTAGE		ABP in MS-60	MS-60 Unc.	MS-65 Unc.
☐ 1935 Boone Bi-Cent. Sm. 1934 Rev.	10,008				
☐ 1935D Type of 1934	2,003	SET	640.00	950.00	2050.00
☐ 1935S Type of 1934	2,004				
☐ 1936 Type of 1934	12,012				
☐ 1936D Type of 1934	5,006	SET	185.00	325.00	775.00
☐ 1936S Type of 1934	5,005				
☐ 1937 Type of 1934	9,810				
☐ 1937D Type of 1934	2,506	SET	360.00	575.00	1475.00
☐ 1937S Type of 1934	2,506				
☐ 1938 Type of 1934	2,100				
☐ 1938D Same	2,100	SET	700.00	1000.00	1900.00
☐ 1938S Same	2,100				
☐ 1936 Bridgeport, Conn.	25,015		80.00	150.00	425.00
☐ 1925S California Diamond Jubilee	86,594		57.00	110.00	410.00
☐ 1936 Cinc. Music Center	Type		185.00	285.00	650.00
☐ 1936 Cinc. Music Center	5,005				
☐ 1936D Cinc. Music Center	5,005	SET	590.00	800.00	1900.00
☐ 1936S Cinc. Music Center	5,006				
☐ 1936 Cleveland Exposition	50,030		52.00	90.00	200.00
☐ 1936 Columbia, S.C.	Type		145.00	240.00	425.00
☐ 1936 Columbia, S.C.	9,007				
☐ 1936D Columbia, S.C.	8,009	SET	325.00	675.00	1325.00
☐ 1936S Columbia, S.C.	8,007				
☐ 1935 Conn. Tercentennial	25,018		115.00	230.00	625.00
☐ 1936 Delaware Tercentennial	20,993		150.00	210.00	515.00
☐ 1936 Elgin, Illinois	20,015		150.00	210.00	650.00
☐ 1925S Fort Vancouver	14,944		385.00	520.00	1225.00
☐ 1922 Grant Memorial	67,405		80.00	110.00	575.00
☐ 1922 Same w/Star on Obverse	4,256		510.00	725.00	5900.00
☐ 1928 Hawaii Sesquicentennial	9,958		620.00	850.00	2750.00
☐ 1935 Hudson Sesquicentennial	10,008		365.00	560.00	1475.00
☐ 1918 Illinois Centennial	100,058		70.00	120.00	525.00
☐ 1946 Iowa Centennial	100,057		48.00	85.00	190.00
☐ 1925 Lexington-Concord	162,013		32.00	50.00	275.00
☐ 1936 Long Island	81,826		50.00	85.00	240.00
☐ 1936 Lynchburg, Va.	20,013		140.00	200.00	650.00
☐ 1920 Maine Centennial	50,028		75.00	130.00	600.00
☐ 1934 Maryland Tercentennial	25,015		85.00	150.00	550.00
☐ 1921 Missouri Centennial	15,428		295.00	480.00	2175.00
☐ 1923 Monroe Doctrine	274,077		25.00	52.00	475.00
☐ 1938 New Rochelle	15,226		230.00	390.00	750.00
☐ 1936 Norfolk, Va.	16,936		185.00	345.00	650.00
☐ 1936 Oakland Bay Bridge	71,424		60.00	110.00	325.00
☐ 1935 Old Spanish Trail	10,008		400.00	740.00	1400.00
☐ Oregon Trail	Type		65.00	110.00	300.00
☐ 1926 Oregon Trail	47,955		65.00	115.00	320.00
☐ 1926S Oregon Trail	83,055		60.00	110.00	300.00
☐ 1928 Oregon Trail	6,028		150.00	250.00	560.00

DATE	MINTAGE		ABP in MS-60	MS-60 Unc.	MS-65 Unc.
☐ 1933D Oregon Trail	5,008		175.00	300.00	750.00
☐ 1934D Oregon Trail	7,006		135.00	210.00	600.00
☐ 1936 Oregon Trail	10,006		75.00	160.00	515.00
☐ 1936S Oregon Trail	5,006		130.00	230.00	620.00
☐ 1937D Oregon Trail	12,008		70.00	135.00	380.00
☐ 1938 Oregon Trail	6,006				
☐ 1938D Oregon Trail	6,005	SET	450.00	700.00	1000.00
☐ 1938S Oregon Trail	6,006				
☐ 1939 Oregon Trail	3,004				
☐ 1939D Oregon Trail	3,004	SET	535.00	850.00	1950.00
☐ 1939S Oregon Trail	3,005				
☐ 1915S Pan Pacific Exposition	27,134		290.00	500.00	3275.00
☐ 1920 Pilgrim Tercentennial	152,112		38.00	57.00	260.00
☐ 1921 Pilgrim Tercentennial	20,053		120.00	160.00	540.00
☐ Rhode Island	Type		80.00	117.00	350.00
☐ 1936 Rhode Island	20,013				
☐ 1936S Rhode Island	15,010	SET	200.00	350.00	1075.00
☐ 1936S Rhode Island	15,011				
☐ 1937 Roanoke Island, N.C.	29,030		95.00	190.00	500.00
☐ 1935S San Diego Exposition	70,132		55.00	95.00	300.00
☐ 1936D San Diego Exposition	30,082		75.00	125.00	330.00
☐ 1926 Sesquicentennial	141,120		30.00	50.00	425.00
☐ 1925 Stone Mountain	1,314,709		20.00	35.00	120.00
☐ Texas Centennial	Type		80.00	135.00	320.00
☐ 1934 Texas Centennial	61,413		52.00	110.00	210.00
☐ 1935 Texas Centennial	9,996				
☐ 1935D Texas Centennial	10,007	SET	185.00	380.00	975.00
☐ 1935S Texas Centennial	10,008				
☐ 1936 Texas Centennial	8,911				
☐ 1936D Texas Centennial	9,039	SET	190.00	390.00	950.00
☐ 1936S Texas Centennial	9,055				
☐ 1937 Texas Centennial	6,571				
☐ 1937D Texas Centennial	6,605	SET	205.00	400.00	1025.00
☐ 1937S Texas Centennial	6,637				
☐ 1938 Texas Centennial	3,780				
☐ 1938D Texas Centennial	3,775	SET	395.00	615.00	1275.00
☐ 1938S Texas Centennial	3,814				
☐ 1927 Vermont (Bennington)	28,162		135.00	225.00	800.00
☐ 1924 Huguenot-Walloon	142,080		60.00	110.00	500.00
☐ Washington Carver	Type		6.00	11.50	22.50
☐ 1951 Washington Carver	110,018				
☐ 1951D Washington Carver	10,004	SET	65.00	120.00	190.00
☐ 1951S Washington Carver	10,004				
☐ 1952 Washington Carver	2,006,292				
☐ 1952D Washington Carver	8,006	SET	85.00	150.00	250.00
☐ 1952S Washington Carver	8,006				

DATE	MINTAGE		ABP in MS-60	MS-60 Unc.	MS-65 Unc.
☐ 1953 Washington Carver	8,003	⎫			
☐ 1953D Washington Carver	8,003	⎬ SET	95.00	180.00	310.00
☐ 1953S Washington Carver	108,020	⎭			
☐ 1954 Washington Carver	12,006	⎫			
☐ 1954D Washington Carver	12,006	⎬ SET	70.00	130.00	200.00
☐ 1954S Washington Carver	122,024	⎭			
☐ B. T. Washington	Type		6.00	11.50	22.50
☐ 1946 B. T. Washington	1,000,546	⎫			
☐ 1946D B. T. Washington	200,113	⎬ SET	30.00	50.00	80.00
☐ 1946S B. T. Washington	500,279	⎭			
☐ 1947 B. T. Washington	100,017	⎫			
☐ 1947D B. T. Washington	100,017	⎬ SET	34.00	65.00	95.00
☐ 1947S B. T. Washington	100,017	⎭			
☐ 1948 B. T. Washington	8,005	⎫			
☐ 1948D B. T. Washington	8,005	⎬ SET	85.00	150.00	230.00
☐ 1948S B. T. Washington	8,005	⎭			
☐ 1949 B. T. Washington	6,004	⎫			
☐ 1949D B. T. Washington	6,004	⎬ SET	115.00	230.00	375.00
☐ 1949S B. T. Washington	6,004	⎭			
☐ 1950 B. T. Washington	6,004	⎫			
☐ 1950D B. T. Washington	6,004	⎬ SET	100.00	195.00	345.00
☐ 1950S B. T. Washington	512,091	⎭			
☐ 1951 B. T. Washington	510,082	⎫			
☐ 1951D B. T. Washington	7,004	⎬ SET	75.00	140.00	220.00
☐ 1951S B. T. Washington	7,004	⎭			
☐ 1936 Wisconsin	25,015		112.00	225.00	480.00
☐ 1936 York County, Me.	25,015		115.00	210.00	480.00

GEORGE WASHINGTON 250TH ANNIVERSARY

The U.S. resumed its commemorative coin program with this silver half dollar in 1982, after a lapse of 28 years. The reason for its long suspension was that the value of silver far exceeded the traditional face values of commemorative coins. However, since commemoratives are issued for collectors and not for circulation, it was finally decided that the public would not object to low face values. The year 1982 marked the 250th anniversary (technically, "sesquincentennial," though the term is seldom used) of George Washington's birth. This was considered an appropriate occasion for resumption of the commemorative series. This coin is .900 silver and has the same specifications as earlier silver commemorative half dollars, and likewise the same as circulating half dollars up to 1964. The obverse carries an equestrian portrait of Washington looking left, with a view of Mount Vernon on the reverse. The artistic style was designed to conform, at least generally, to that of the majority of earlier commemorative halves.

DATE	MINTAGE	MS-65 Unc.	PRF-65 Proof
☐ 1982P — NONE ISSUED			
☐ 1982S — PROOFS ONLY			11.00
☐ 1982D		10.00	

LOS ANGELES XXIII OLYMPIAD

The set of two commemorative silver dollars issued in 1983 and 1984 for the Los Angeles Olympic Games marked the first $1 silver commemoratives in more than 80 years. Enormous publicity and controversy surrounded these coins, concerning their designs, face values, and the method of distributing them to the public. The first coin, dated 1983, pictures a discus thrower on the obverse with a profile bust of an eagle on the reverse. The second, dated 1984, shows the entrance to the Los Angeles Coliseum (site of the 1984 games) on the obverse, and a full-length eagle on the reverse. These coins have the same specifications as the standard U.S. silver dollar, last struck in 1935, and contain approximately three fourths of an ounce of .999+ silver. Debate raged over whether or not they should show a face value and, if so, the amount. It was decided that they should have a $1 face value, in spite of the fact that they contain several times that value in silver. This virtually insured that they — unlike some commemoratives of the past — will never end up in circulation. Yet they are legal tender, and could be passed at $1 if an owner desired.

DATE	MINTAGE	MS-65 Unc.	PRF-65 Proof
☐1983P		30.00	36.00
☐1983S		30.00	36.00
☐1983D		30.00	36.00
☐1984P		30.00	36.00
☐1984S		30.00	36.00
☐1984D		30.00	36.00

SILVER COMMEMORATIVES
MEDALS COLLECTED WITH COMMEMORATIVES

NORTH AMERICAN CENTENNIAL

DATE	MINTAGE	ABP in MS-60	MS-60 Unc.	MS-65 Unc.
☐1925 (Thin)	40,000	32.00	65.00	110.00
☐1925 (Thick)	40,000	25.00	52.00	85.00

So-Called WILSON DOLLAR

DATE	MINTAGE	ABP in MS-60	MS-60 Unc.	MS-65 Unc.
☐ 1920 Silver	2,200	105.00	215.00	325.00

2 KRONER SWEDEN

DATE	MINTAGE	ABP in MS-60	MS-60 Unc.	MS-65 Unc.
☐ 1936 2 Kroner Delaware Swedish Tercentennial	500,000	15.75	27.00	38.00

GOLD COMMEMORATIVES
GOLD COMMEMORATIVES, 1903 - 1926

The gold commemorative series began not long after the silver, in 1903. Far fewer gold commemoratives were issued, as the large physical size necessary for impressive designing resulted in a coin of very high face value. Experiments were made with $1 gold commemoratives, which some critics called puny, and goliaths of $50 denomination, which were indeed eye-catching but well beyond the budgets of most citizens in those days. The final gold commemorative was coined for the 1926 Sesquicentennial or 150th anniversary of American freedom from Britain. Because of bullion market conditions it is extremely doubtful that any will ever again be attempted. The value of these pieces in extremely fine condition is about one-third the price for uncirculated — ample proof that most buying activity originates with numismatists rather than bullion speculators.

ONE AND $2.50 GOLD

1903-Jefferson   1903-McKinley   1922-Grant

DATE	MINTAGE	ABP in MS-60	MS-60 Unc.	MS-65 Unc.
☐ 1903 Jefferson Dollar	17,500	350.00	660.00	2700.00
☐ 1903 McKinley Dollar	17,500	350.00	650.00	2700.00
☐ 1904 Lewis & Clark Dollar	10,025	835.00	1175.00	4500.00
☐ 1905 Lewis & Clark Dollar	10,041	860.00	1225.00	4600.00
☐ 1915S Panama-Pacific Dollar*	15,000	360.00	675.00	2750.00
☐ 1915S Panama-Pacific $2.50 Dollar*	6,766	950.00	1650.00	5875.00
☐ 1916 McKinley Dollar	10,003	390.00	700.00	3375.00
☐ 1917 McKinley Dollar	10,004	375.00	725.00	3650.00
☐ 1922 Grant Dollar	5,016	480.00	1075.00	3400.00
☐ 1922 Grant Dollar w/star	5,000	525.00	1025.00	3575.00
☐ 1926 Philadelphia Sesquicentennial $2.50	46,019	350.00	540.00	2675.00

*Struck to Commemorate the Opening of the Panama Canal.

ONE DOLLAR GOLD

Panama-Pacific

$2.50 GOLD

Philadelphia

PANAMA-PACIFIC FIFTY DOLLARS

This huge coin, containing nearly 2½ ounces of gold, was not the world's largest goldpiece but by far the most substantial coin of that metal struck by the U.S. government. (To give some indication of changes in the market from 1915, the date of issue, until today, $50 worth of gold today is about 1/10th of an ounce.) It was issued for the Panama-Pacific Exposition and was struck in two varieties, one with round and one with octagonal edge, the former being somewhat scarcer and more valuable. Minerva is pictured on the obverse and the Athenian state symbol, the owl, representative of wisdom, on the reverse. The place of issue was San Francisco and the designer Robert Aitken. This is definitely not a piece for bullion speculators as its value is many times that of the gold content and under no circumstances would a $50 Panama-Pacific — or any U.S. gold commemorative — be melted down.

ROUND

DATE	MINTAGE	ABP in MS-60	MS-60 Unc.	MS-65 Unc.
☐1915S Round 483		22500.00	31000.00	45000.00

OCTAGONAL

DATE	MINTAGE	ABP in MS-60	MS-60 Unc.	MS-65 Unc.
☐1915S Octagonal 645		16250.00	23000.00	33000.00
☐COMPLETE SET, 50.00 Gold Round and Octagonal, 2.50 & 1.00 Gold and Half Dollar Silver		40000.00	56750.00	82500.00
☐DOUBLE SET IN ORIGINAL FRAME — Superior Sale, January 1985 - $160,000.00				

NOTE: The double sets were authorized mint issues. They consisted of two specimens of each coin, mounted so that both sides could be seen. The original price in 1915 was $400.

LOS ANGELES XXIII OLYMPIAD $10

This $10 gold commemorative, carrying the date 1984, marked U.S. reentry into commemorative gold — which many forecasters claimed would never occur. Issuance of a gold commemorative under modern circumstances called for a drastic change in approach. Traditionally (prior to the Gold Recall Act of 1933), our gold commemoratives contained slightly less than their face value in gold, just as did our gold circulating coins. With today's much higher gold prices, the Los Angeles XXIII Olympiad $10 gold commemorative contains about twenty times its face value in gold. They were distributed to the public at prices which took this factor into account, as well as including a handling fee (which many persons in the numismatic community charged to be exorbitant). A pair of torch bearers are shown on the obverse, symbolizing the ceremony of "lighting the Olympic flame" to open the games. The American eagle symbol with stars, arrows and branches is pictured on the reverse. This coin has the same specifications used in striking circulating $10 gold pieces, prior to their discontinuance.

DATE	MINTAGE	MS-65 Unc.
☐1984W*		450.00

*PROOFS — approximately same value.
NOTE: "W" mintmark indicates West Point, New York.

CONFEDERATE STATES OF AMERICA

Following its secession from the Union in 1861, the Confederate government of Louisiana took control of the federal mint at New Orleans (the only mint operating in southern territory), along with its materials and machinery. Jefferson Davis, President of the C.S.A., appointed C. G. Memminger his Secretary of the Treasury and authorized production of a "Confederate Half Dollar." This was presumably manufactured by taking ordinary half dollars and removing their reverse motif, to which was added a shield with seven stars (one for each state that had joined the C.S.A.), a Liberty cap, a wreath of sugar cane and cotton, and the wording "CONFEDERATE STATES OF AMERICAN HALF DOL." No serious effort was made to circulate this coin, only four specimens being struck. Restrikes were later made. J. W. Scott somehow got hold of the original reverse die and, having keen business aptitude, struck off 500 examples for sale to souvenir-hunters. He used his own obverse, consisting of wording without portraiture or other design.

1861
HALF DOL.

DATE	MINTAGE	ABP in MS-60	VF-20 V. Fine	MS-60 Unc.	MS-65 Unc.
☐ 1861 Half Dollar (Rare)	4				VERY RARE
☐ 1861 Half Dollar Restrike	500	375.00	625.00	1150.00	2125.00
☐ 1861 Scott Token Obverse, Confederate Reverse	500	100.00	165.00	295.00	375.00

CONFEDERATE CENT

This was the only Confedrate coin intended for general circulation — and it never got that far. Robert Lovett of Philadelphia was commissioned by agents of the C.S.A. to prepare coins in the denomination of 1¢ in 1861. He was to design the coin, engrave their dies, and do the acutal striking as well. After producing a certain quantity, of which only 12 have been discovered, Lovett ceased operations and hid both the coins and the dies from which they were struck, fearing, as a resident of the North, arrest by authorities on grounds of complicity with the enemy. Restrikes were subsequently made, in gold, silver and copper, by John Haseltine. The figures given here for mintages of the restrikes are based on best available information. Haseltine, in his memoirs of the affair, states that the die broke on the 59th coin. There are nevertheless believed to be 72 restrikes in existence. Haseltine made a point of striking no reproductions in nickel for fear they might be taken for originals.

ORIGINAL

RESTRIKE

DATE	MINTAGE		MS-60 Unc.	MS-65 Unc.
☐ 1861 Cent (original)	12		6000.00	9000.00
☐ 1861 Restrike, Silver	12	PROOF	2750.00	3825.00
☐ 1861 Restrike, Copper	55		1500.00	2375.00

U.S. PROOF SETS, 1936 TO DATE

The technical definition of a Proof is a coin made for presentation or collector purposes. Beginning in the second half of the 19th century the Mint struck proofs of many of its coins; some, but not a great number, appeared previously. A proof is not made from a specially manufactured die but rather an ordinary die set aside exclusively for use in proofs. The dies are cleaned and polished more frequently than those used for ordinary circulating coins. When any sign of wear or imperfection appears the die is scrapped. This is why proofs have a somewhat higher surface relief (bas-relief) than uncirculated specimens, leading to the conclusion — mistakenly — that more deeply engraved dies are employed. After coming from the press, proofs are not touched except with gloves or special tongs made for the purpose, and are inspected for uniformity. Any exhibiting flaws of any nature are rejected. Proofs that pass inspection are housed into holders, so that nothing may interfere with their finish.

Frosted proofs are no longer produced. These have a lustrous shining ground but the design and lettering is non-reflective or frosted. So-called "matte" proofs have a granular finish. These too are a thing of the past. Brilliant proofs, those struck from 1936 to date, are mirrorlike over the entire surface, not only the ground but design and lettering. It is well to keep in mind (for beginners) that a coin found in circulation is never a proof, regardless of the brilliance of its lustre or perfection of its condition. It is simply a "proof-like" coin.

Proof sets have been struck by the Mint since 1936, though none were issued in the years 1943-49. Beginning in 1968 they were issued in stiff plastic holders rather than pliable vinyl. Proof sets are now struck only at the San Francisco mint and all coins carry the "S" mintmark.

DATE	MINTAGE	ABP	MS-65 Proof
☐ 1936	3,837	3400.00	4900.00
☐ 1937	5,542	2500.00	3600.00
☐ 1938	8,045	950.00	1500.00
☐ 1939	8,795	850.00	1400.00
☐ 1940	11,246	750.00	1100.00
☐ 1941	15,287	700.00	1075.00
☐ 1942 One Nickel		700.00	1075.00
☐ 1942 Two Nickels	21,120	825.00	1350.00
☐ 1950	51,386	425.00	590.00
☐ 1951	57,500	235.00	350.00
☐ 1952	81,980	115.00	195.00
☐ 1953	128,800	85.00	130.00
☐ 1954	233,300	40.00	75.00
☐ 1955	378,200	37.00	70.00
☐ 1956	699,384	23.00	40.00
☐ 1957	1,247,952	13.00	25.00
☐ 1958	875,652	18.00	33.00
☐ 1959	1,149,291	15.00	24.00
☐ 1960 Small Date		17.50	31.00
☐ 1960 Large Date	1,691,602	14.00	22.00
☐ 1961	3,028,244	13.00	20.00
☐ 1962	3,218,019	13.00	20.00

DATE	MINTAGE	ABP	MS-65 Proof
☐ 1963	3,075,645	13.00	20.00
☐ 1964	3,949,634	12.00	17.00
☐ 1968S	3,041,508	3.15	5.50
☐ 1968S Without "S" 10¢		5500.00	7750.00
☐ 1969S	2,360,000	2.75	5.00
☐ 1970S	2,600,000	6.00	10.00
☐ 1970S Small Date ¢		55.00	90.00
☐ 1970S Without "S" 10¢	2,200	450.00	700.00
☐ 1971S	3,244,138	2.75	4.50
☐ 1971S Without "S" 5¢	1,655	600.00	1000.00
☐ 1972S	3,267,667	2.75	4.50
☐ 1973S	2,769,624	3.00	6.00
☐ 1974S	2,617,350	3.00	6.00
☐ 1975S	2,850,715	4.00	8.00
☐ 1976S (40%-3 pieces)	3,215,730	9.00	15.00
☐ 1976S	4,150,210	3.50	7.00
☐ 1977S	3,251,125	3.00	6.00
☐ 1978S	3,127,781	3.50	7.00
☐ 1979S	3,677,175	6.00	11.00
☐ 1979S TYPE 2		55.00	110.00
☐ 1980S	3,547,130	3.50	7.00
☐ 1981S		3.75	7.50
☐ 1982S	3,857,479	6.00	11.00
☐ 1983S	3,139,000	6.50	12.75
☐ 1984S		6.50	12.75

NOTE: Some mintage totals for Proof Sets represent estimates based upon best available information.

U.S. MINT SETS, 1947-1981

Beginning collectors habitually confuse the terms "proof set" and "mint set." It is important to recognize the distinction between them, especially as the values are quite different. The buyer who thinks he has a bargain on a proof set, when in fact he has bought a mint set, may have paid too much.

Mint sets originated well after the selling of special proof sets had become established. Manufacture of proof sets was suspended during World War II. Following conclusion of the war (1945), the mint chose not to immediately resume proof sets, but instead to sell mint sets as a substitute. They were introduced in 1947, sold well, and continued to be produced after proof sets were reinstated in 1950. The most recent mint set is that of 1981 and at present there are no immediate plans for sales of further sets.

Mint sets contain the same coins as proof sets (one of each denomination, from each mint, for that year), but the coins are not proofs. They are standard "business strikes," just like coins released into general circulation. Naturally they are uncirculated, as the mint takes specimens from its assembly lines that have not gone into circulation. In terms of specific grade, this is really a matter of luck. Some coins in mint sets are flawless and merit a full MS-70 rating. The vast majority are not quite so fine, and would grade between MS-60 and MS-65. In buying a mint set from a dealer, you can be certain that all the coins will be uncirculated, but a condition grade higher than MS-60 should not be anticipated for any of them. In offering mint sets, dealers do not mention condition grade, as it can vary from coin to coin within a set. During the final few years of the manufacture and sale of such sets by the mint (late 1970s to 1981), the level of customer complaints greatly increased concerning scratched, nicked, and otherwise disappointing coins.

To carry the values indicated, sets must be in the original sealed holders in which they were sold. In the years 1965, 1966 and 1967, when no proof sets were struck, mint sets were placed in rigid plastic holders and called "Special Mint Sets," in hopes they would appeal to the regular buyers of proof sets. The standard packaging for mint sets was originally a cardboard holder, which was abandoned in favor of plastic envelopes in 1959.

Mintage figures are not recorded for mint sets, as the coins involved are not specially produced for that purpose.

DATE	ABP	MS-60 Or Better
☐ 1947	620.00	925.00
☐ 1948	160.00	250.00
☐ 1949	620.00	925.00
☐ 1950*	—	—
☐ 1951	280.00	450.00
☐ 1952	195.00	300.00
☐ 1953	170.00	250.00
☐ 1954	80.00	130.00
☐ 1955	47.00	72.00
☐ 1956	37.00	65.00
☐ 1957	50.00	80.00
☐ 1958	42.00	70.00
☐ 1959	21.50	35.00
☐ 1960	16.00	25.00
☐ 1961	16.00	25.00
☐ 1962	16.00	25.00
☐ 1963	15.00	23.00
☐ 1964	9.00	15.00
☐ 1965 Special Mint Set	2.75	4.00
☐ 1966 Special Mint Set	2.80	4.25
☐ 1967 Special Mint Set	4.75	8.00
☐ 1968	2.00	3.25
☐ 1969	2.00	3.30
☐ 1970	14.00	24.00
☐ 1971	2.00	3.00
☐ 1972	1.85	2.85
☐ 1973	7.00	13.00
☐ 1974	3.50	5.25
☐ 1975	3.70	5.50
☐ 1976	3.50	5.25
☐ 1976S (25¢, 50¢, $1 only — no 1¢, 5¢, 10¢)	5.50	7.75
☐ 1977	3.50	5.25
☐ 1978	3.50	5.25
☐ 1979	3.30	5.00
☐ 1980	4.50	6.75
☐ 1981	7.00	13.00

*No mint sets were sold this year, only proof sets. Many mint sets were, however, assembled by dealers and placed in packaging similar to that of the mint's. In cases where the coins in these privately assembled mint sets are strictly uncirculated, they will have a slight premium value.

SPECIAL REPORT ON BU ROLLS

BU rolls are now among the most talked about and heavily traded of all numismatic items. The total quantity of coins sold in rolls far exceeds all other coin sales combined. They have become the favorite numismatic investment among thousands of investors. To a lesser extent they are also bought by collectors, though sales to collectors have not appreciably increased. For the first time in its history the Blackbook presents a market report on BU rolls.

What is a BU roll? The term BU, which has been used in coin collecting for more than two generations, stands for Brilliant Uncirculated. Some define it as Best Uncirculated, or Bright Uncirculated. Regardless of the way one interprets it, the important point about a BU coin is that it is uncirculated. Its condition grade is a minimum of MS-60 on the ANA grading scale. It may be higher than MS-60 but in buying rolls advertised only as BU, with no grade specified, do not expect any of the coins to grade higher than MS-60. It is possible to get BU rolls in MS-63 and MS-65 but of course the price is higher.

A roll comprises coins of the same denomination and, almost always, the same type. If Indian Head and Lincoln Cents were mixed in the same roll this would be advertised as a "mixed roll." Most BU roll trading occurs in *solid date rolls.* A solid date roll is one in which all the coins are of the same date and same place of manufacture: 1946-D, 1948-S, 1982-P, etc. The number of coins in a roll varies by denomination: Cents, fifty; coins; Nickels, forty; Dimes, fifty; Quarters, forty; Half Dollars, twenty. The roll may be wrapped in bank paper or contained in a lucite holder.

All rolls passing through the coin market are "assembled rolls." They were not put together at the Mint but by coin dealers, collectors, and investors. The possibility always exists that a circulated coin might have slipped in, so it is advisable to examine all the coins in a roll.

Because new rolls are constantly being made up and old ones broken, the scarcity factor is difficult to determine. While the vast majority of BU rolls are of twentieth century coins, they are also available for most of the common-date coins of the late nineteenth century as well. Generally they are not available for scarce coins of the nineteenth century, nor even for some scarce dates of the twentieth. If the coin is very common, with a mintage of 100 million or more, there will be literally thousands of BU rolls passing through the market. It may seem paradoxical, but the common coins are often preferred by investors, who feel that their low prices make them an ideal speculation. Some rolls can be had for less than $1, such as late-date Lincolns, and these too are bought by investors. At the other end of the spectrum are rolls bringing $10,000 or more, such as the 1941-S Walking Liberty Half Dollar. Rolls, like single coins, come in all price ranges.

It is important to note that the price of a BU roll does not necessarily reflect the value of the same coin when sold singly. You cannot multiply the single coin price to arrive at the roll price. BU rolls find their own value levels in trading, and the price can sometimes be quite far out of line with that of the individual coin. There are various reasons for this, chiefly tied to supply and demand. At any given time there may be a huge surplus of certain BU rolls on the market, or such an extreme shortage that dealers cannot buy them fast enough to fill orders. The availability of any coin in BU rolls may be a very different story than its availability as a single specimen. Also, investors will frequently "bandwagon" a group of coins in BU rolls, all buying the same rolls. They do not buy the single specimens, so the shortage of supply is not reflected in single specimens. This is becoming more pronounced in today's coin market, now that BU rolls have become so popular with investors. Of course the dealers also influence the prices. When a dealer is buying common to medium-scarce coins for his stock, he prefers to buy in rolls, regardless of whether he intends to sell the coins in rolls or individually. It is more convenient for him and, in many cases, more economical.

The following prices for BU rolls were current at the time of going to press.

LINCOLN CENTS — 1940 $21.50, 1940-D $46.85, 1940-S $63.75, 1941 $30, 1941-D $123, 1941-S $119, 1942 $21.60, 1942-D $24.15, 1942-S $267, 1943 $49, 1943-D $86.50, 1943-S $164.20, 1944 $21.05, 1944-D $21.05, 1944-S $18.25, 1945 $15.50, 1945-D $15.50, 1945-S $18.60, 1946 $12.30, 1946-D $10, 1946-S $15.70, 1947 $14.90, 1947-D $11.40, 1947-S $16.55, 1948 $17.20, 1948-D $32.40, 1948-S $33.65, 1949 $29, 1949-D $34.10, 1949-S $56.15, 1950 $28.25, 1950-D $13.90, 1950-S $31.35, 1951 $26.20, 1951-D $15.50, 1951-S $42.15, 1952 $16.60, 1952-D $12.45, 1952-S $22.10, 1953 $10.15, 1953-D $8.90, 1953-S $17.10, 1954 $21.70, 1954-D $6.80, 1954-S $8, 1955 $5.65, 1955-D $5.30, 1955-S $17.60, 1956 $3.20.

JEFFERSON NICKELS — 1946 $16.90, 1946-D $23.30, 1946-S $19.15, 1947 $13.85, 1947-D $23.50, 1947-S $20.95, 1948 $13.40, 1948-D $29.40, 1948-S $23.60, 1949 $24.40, 1949-D $25.15, 1949-S $57.80, 1950 $46.30, 1950-D $288, 1951 $25.15, 1951-D $33, 1951-S $58.70, 1952 $18.15, 1952-D $27.40, 1952-S $27.35, 1953 $7.20, 1953-D $6.90, 1953-S $12.90, 1954 $6.75, 1954-D $6.75, 1954-S $11.65, 1955 $15.10, 1955-D $4.35, 1956 $4.05, 1956-D $4.40, 1957 $4.80, 1957-D $4.85, 1958 $5.30, 1958-D $4.30, 1959 $4.30, 1959-D $4, 1960 $4.40, 1960-D $4.40, 1961 $4.40, 1961-D $4.40, 1962 $4.40, 1962-D $8.75, 1963 $3.60.

MERCURY DIMES — 1940 $910, 1940-D $1325, 1940-S $965, 1941 $815, 1941-D $1265, 1941-S $995, 1942 $835, 1942-D $1155, 1942-S $1480, 1943 $810, 1943-D $1020, 1943-S $1080, 1944 $835, 1944-D $890, 1944-S $905, 1945 $760, 1945-D $915, 1945-S $855.

ROOSEVELT DIMES — 1946 $96.50, 1946-D $171, 1946-S $342, 1947 $206, 1947-D $310, 1947-S $338, 1948 $440, 1948-D $490, 1948-S $480, 1949 $1195, 1949-D $620, 1949-S $2870, 1950 $209, 1950-D $209, 1950-S $1140, 1951 $119, 1951-D $137, 1951-S $835, 1952 $128, 1952-D $156, 1952-S $318, 1953 $124, 1953-D $84, 1953-S $115, 1954 $82, 1954-D $89, 1954-S $116, 1955 $161, 1955-D $101, 1955-S $86, 1956 $72, 1956-D $71, 1957 $70, 1957-D $108, 1958 $103, 1958-D $74, 1959 $73, 1959-D $107, 1960 $74, 1960-D $71, 1961 $65, 1961-D $65.

WASHINGTON QUARTERS — 1944 $284, 1944-D $763, 1944-S $731, 1945 $440, 1945-D $595, 1945-S $458, 1946 $258, 1946-D $309, 1946-S $486, 1947 $390, 1947-D $421, 1947-S $500, 1948 $270, 1948-D $388, 1948-S $391, 1949 $1572, 1949-D $610, 1950 $277, 1950-D $302, 1950-S $465, 1951 $223, 1951-D $209, 1951-S $715, 1952 $208, 1952-D $214, 1952-S $455, 1953 $199, 1953-D $176, 1953-S $270, 1954 $177, 1954-D $172, 1954-S $211, 1955 $145, 1955-D $239, 1956 $137, 1956-D $137, 1957 $137, 1957-D $137, 1958 $280, 1958-D $141, 1959 $146, 1959-D $133, 1960 $136, 1960-D $136, 1961 $124, 1961-D

$119, 1962 $108, 1962-D $108, 1963 $108, 1963-D $108, 1964 $99, 1964-D $99, 1965 $17.90, 1966 $18.65, 1967 $17.80, 1968 $17.80.

WALKING LIBERTY HALVES — 1941 $2675, 1941-D $4230, 1941-S $11,670, 1942 $2660, 1942-D $4770, 1942-S $7270, 1943 $2650, 1943-D $4950, 1944-S $6630, 1944 $2650, 1944-D $4585, 1944-S $4585, 1945 $2650, 1945-D $4390, 1945-S $3675, 1946 $2895, 1946-D $2710, 1946-S $3585, 1947 $4675.

FRANKLIN HALVES — 1950 $1460, 1950-D $995, 1951 $535, 1951-D $1270, 1951-S $1165, 1952 $450, 1952-D $430, 1952-S $1045, 1953 $830, 1953-D $400, 1953-S $735, 1954 $340, 1954-D $340, 1954-S $510.

KENNEDY HALVES — 1964 $103, 1964-D $108, 1965 $46.75, 1966 $46.75, 1967 $46.75, 1968 $46.75, 1969 $46.75.

COIN INVESTING

Coin investing from a purely speculative point of view — buying coins solely for the purpose of making money on them — is no longer confined to professional dealers. In fact it is likely that the volume of coins bought for profit by the public exceeds purchases by dealers. Investment groups have sprung up, in which investors band together and contribute sums toward the purchase of expensive rarities that they could not individually afford. They then own "shares" of the coin, shares which of course pay no dividends until the coin is sold. There are coin investment clubs and dealers who make a specialty of "investment parcels," sometimes with a guarantee to buy back the coins at full cost or a slight advance after a stated period of time.

This kind of coin investment thrives regardless of gold and silver bullion prices. It concentrates upon coins of established numismatic popularity, in VF or better condition.

It is undeniable that coin investing offers the potential for very satisfactory capital growth, based on past market performances. Frank Pick of Barron's Magazine went so far as to call rare coins "the number one hedge against inflation." The following increases in average retail values of certain coins (not all of them terribly rare by any means) from 1948 to 1986 can be matched by few commodities or other types of investments:

	MS-60 1948 value	MS-60 1986 value
1853 Half Dime w/arrows	1.50	310.00
1880 $3 Gold	50.00	3,750.00
1804 Half Cent	16.50	500.00
1901 Quarter	4.00	250.00
1864 2¢ Piece	1.00	460.00

As is clearly evident, these coins are not all extremely old, nor are they all made of precious metal. It should not be assumed that *every* U. S. coin has advanced at this rate, which is certainly not the case. Most, however, have demonstrated healthy price jumps.

There are many questions the potential investor should ask before plunging ahead.

Is coin investing "safe"?

No investment is 100% safe. In numismatics the safer investments are coins that are not valued chiefly for their metallic content. This shouldn't be taken to mean gold and silver coins are bad investments. They can be quite the reverse, provided coins are chosen in which the numismatic value is greater than the metal value. For example: common-date silver dollars are not good speculative investments. Their value is almost entirely in their metal. To gain a worthwhile profit on common date silver dollars (or any common date silver coins), silver would need to double its current price. It may do this. But this could take a very long time, during which inflation would probably be rising, and the resulting net gain would be negligible. On the other hand, key-date or key-mark silvers are an attractive investment as they tend to appreciate at a fairly steady rate regardless of the bullion market's ups and downs. Why? Because of these two important factors:

1. Many investors are buying them.
2. In addition to investors, these coins always have a demand with collectors.

Why have certain coins, whose values inched slowly upward for years, suddenly doubled and tripled in price?

Because of increased investor activity. Coin collectors alone — people buying coins strictly as a hobby with no thought of profit — could never make such sharp impacts on the market. Collectors have an influence and their influence is growing but investors account for most of the wildly spiraling prices. The more investors, the higher prices will go.

Don't prices come down just as far when investors sell as they were before they bought?

No. It isn't necessary that a coin be scarcer on the market to be more valuable. So long as buying activity is increased, the same coins can keep coming up for sale and still gain in price. Buying activity is the key.

How long must coins be held to show a satisfactory profit?

This depends on what is meant by satisfactory. The question is difficult to answer at any rate because there is no established or reliable growth rate. In a boon year, such as 1979, rare coins in general can double in price in just twelve months. Some even did better. But there have been years, even in the recent past, when the overall rate of increase was less than 20%. It is impossible to forecast what the future holds. This, however, should be taken into account. Just as with any investment, the paper profit on coins is not necessarily the actual profit. For coins to be converted into cash they must be sold and the dealer or agent to whom you sell will not pay the full retail price. When you buy you pay the full retail price but in selling you receive the retail price less the dealer's margin of profit, which is figured into the next sale. Unlike you, the dealer is not interested in holding his coins for years until they appreciate greatly in value. He wants to sell them immediately, as soon as they reach his hands, and would rather have a 20% profit on a coin today than wait a year and sell it for much more. The margin of profit depends on the type of coin and its value. For a popular U.S. key coin worth $1,000 in uncirculated condition, which the dealer knows he will have no trouble selling quickly, you are likely to be paid as much as 80% of the retail value, especially if you sell at a time of strong demand. If the coin is not so popular, or is less than VF in condition, the dealer will probably pay from 60% to 70% of his retail selling price.

You can calculate your potential success as an investor based upon this situation *plus* the rate of inflation. Obviously, future trends taken by the inflation rate are very difficult to predict. Assuming it to be 10% annually over the next five years, this would present the following prospects:

```
Coin bought for $1,000 in 1986 . . . . . . . . . . . . . . . . . . . . . . . . . . . . . . $1,000
Coin increases to $5,000 by 1991, Coin is sold for $5,000 less 20%   4,000
Inflation has reduced buying power of the dollar, by 50%,
so your $4,000 becomes . . . . . . . . . . . . . . . . . . . . . . . . . . . . . . . . . . . .   2,000
                                                            net profit   $1,000
```

This is a very simplistic example which should not be taken too serious-ly. It merely shows how to operate the arithmetic.

Assuming one has decided to invest in coins, should he trust his own abilities or rely on the services of a numismatic broker?

While brokers are of invaluable aid to persons uninformed about coins and the coin market there is no question but that a well-educated investor can do as well, or better, on his own. Often, "investment parcels" made up by so-called brokers (a title that can be used indiscriminately, without license) consist of coins that a broker, in his regular trading as a coin dealer, was unable to sell profitably. The likelihood of their being sound investments is slim. If you need advice, a reputable dealer is usually the best source, one to whom you can speak personally. If you purchase good key coins from his stock in uncirculated condition they are likely to prove as good an investment as any broker could supply.

What price range should the investor buy in? If I have $1,000 to spend, should I buy a single $1,000 coin or five for $200? Or ten for $100?

There is no established "best way" in this situation. Generally, a $1,000 coin with a proven record of growth would be a more attractive investment than several coins of lower value. Selection of the coins to buy is more important than their price range. You must confine yourself to VF or Uncir-culated only. It is true that many early coins are not available in such high grades of condition but these are not considered prime investment pieces. Be careful that the coins are not overgraded and that you aren't buying above the market. Shop around and compare prices but don't take too long doing this: the price may go up.

Do we advise coin investment? We neither advise or discourage it. The purpose of this book is to point out the realities of buying and selling coins and provide potential buyers (investors and collectors) with the information they need to make their own decisions.

PRIMARY METALS

COPPER

Copper has the distinction of use in more U.S. coins than any other metal. In fact there has only been one coin in U.S. history — the 1943 cent — which did not contain copper. Copper was used in its pure state for the early Half Cent and Large Cent; alloyed into bronze for the later Small Cent; alloyed with nickel for the 5¢ piece; and, usually in a 1-to-9 ratio, as an alloy metal for all our silver and gold coins from the eighteenth to twentieth centuries. The most notable use of copper for our coins was in the Half Cent and Large Cent. As these coins were entirely unalloyed, they show the true beauty of pure copper, many specimens having toned to remarkable shades of red, yellow, burgundy, violet, orange, and virtually every known color. A brief copper shortage during World War II, when it became a vital material in war production, resulted in the non-copper 1943 cent, as well as a reduction in the copper content of 5¢ pieces for several years. Inflation and the heavy industrial demand for copper made it necessary, in 1982, for the cent's composition to be changed to zinc with a copper coating.

SILVER

From the earliest days of the Mint, silver was regarded as the chief metal for coins in general circulation. It was used in coins having face values from 1¢ to $1, those of higher value being struck in gold. Problems arose during the administration of Thomas Jefferson, when silver bullion carried a high value abroad than in the U.S. Huge quantities of our silver coins were exported by speculators, for the purpose of melting. This brought about a long suspension of the silver $1. Then in 1965, the rising market price of silver in both the U.S. and Europe prompted its removal from the 10¢ and 25¢. It remained in the 50¢ in reduced quantity, but was later removed from that coin, too. Silver has traded for as much as $50 per ounce on the bullion market (early 1980) and currently is in the neighborhood of $6 to $8.

GOLD

The most glamorous of the metals used in U.S. coinage, gold was employed by the Mint in striking coins of $1, $2.50, $3, $4, $5, $10 and $20 denominations, as well as a commemorative coin with $50 face value. The $10 gold piece, struck for more than 100 years, was called an Eagle, and its subdivisions were similarly named: Quarter Eagle ($2.50) and Half Eagle ($5), with the $20 termed Double Eagle. The standard fineness for all these coins, during most of their years of manufacture, was .900 with an alloying of .100 copper to give stability. Though all gold denominations were available for general circulation, their actual use in circulation became limited after the Civil War, when paper currency was introduced. The Great Depression of this century caused President Roosevelt to halt all striking of gold coins and to "call in" all gold coins for redemption (Gold Recall Act of 1933). Prohibition against private ownership of gold was removed in the Presidency of Gerald Ford, resulting in its widespread purchase by investors and others. In January, 1980, gold was being traded for as much as $800 per troy ounce. At the time of compiling this edition, the price is approximately $325.

SILVER COIN VALUE CHART
Prices Reflect Melt Value of Individual Coins

Silver Price Per Ounce	Amount of Pure Silver	5.00	10.00	15.00	20.00	25.00	30.00	35.00	40.00	45.00	50.00	55.00	60.00	Change in Value per Dollar
1942-45 5¢ U.S.	.05626 oz.	.28	.56	.85	1.13	1.41	1.69	1.97	2.25	2.54	2.82	3.10	3.38	.056
1965-70 U.S. 50¢ (40%)	.14792 oz.	.74	1.48	2.22	2.96	3.70	4.44	5.18	5.92	6.66	7.40	8.14	8.88	.148
U.S. $1.00 (40%)	.31625 oz.	1.58	3.16	4.75	6.33	7.91	9.49	11.07	12.65	14.24	15.82	17.40	18.98	.316
1964 & Earlier U.S. 10¢	.07234 oz.	.36	.72	1.09	1.45	1.81	2.17	2.54	2.90	3.26	3.62	3.98	4.34	.072
1964 & Earlier U.S. 25¢	.18084 oz.	.90	1.80	2.72	3.62	4.53	5.43	6.33	7.24	8.14	9.05	9.95	10.85	.18
1964 & Earlier U.S. 50¢	.36169 oz.	1.81	3.62	5.43	7.24	9.05	10.85	12.66	14.47	16.28	18.09	19.90	21.71	.362
1935 & Earlier U.S. $1	.77344 oz.	3.87	7.73	11.61	15.47	19.34	23.21	27.07	30.94	34.81	38.68	42.54	46.41	.772

Dealers who purchase silver coins to be melted normally pay 15% to 25% under melt value in order to cover their cost of handling.

GOLD COIN VALUE CHART
Prices Reflect Melt Value of Individual Coins

Gold Price Per Ounce	Amount of Pure Gold	200.00	300.00	400.00	500.00	550.00	600.00	650.00	700.00	800.00	900.00	1000.00	Change in Value per Dollar
U.S. $1.00	.04837 oz.	9.68	14.52	19.35	24.19	26.61	29.03	31.44	33.86	38.70	43.54	48.37	.048
U.S. $2.50	.12094 oz.	24.19	36.29	48.38	60.47	66.52	72.57	78.62	84.66	96.76	108.85	120.94	.121
U.S. $3.00	.14512 oz.	29.03	43.54	58.05	72.56	79.82	87.08	94.33	101.59	116.10	130.61	145.12	.145
U.S. $5.00	.24187 oz.	48.38	72.57	96.75	120.94	133.03	145.13	157.22	169.31	193.50	217.69	241.87	.242
U.S. $10.00	.48375 oz.	96.75	145.13	193.50	241.88	266.07	290.25	314.44	338.63	387.00	435.38	483.75	.484
U.S. $20.00	.96750 oz.	193.50	290.25	387.00	483.75	532.13	580.50	628.88	677.25	774.00	870.75	967.50	.967

Dealers normally purchase U.S. Gold Coins for a premium over melt. As an example, with Gold at $635.00/ounce you could expect a dealer to pay $700.00 for a common dated twenty dollar gold coin in extremely fine or better condition.

WEIGHTS AND MEASURES
WEIGHTS OF U.S. COINS

DENOMINATION	DATE OF ISSUE	WEIGHT GRAINS	WT. TOL. + OR − GRAINS
Half Cent	1793-1795	104.0	
	1796-1857	84.0	
Large Cent	1793-1795	208.0	
	1795-1857	168.0	
Small Cent	1856-1864	72.0	2.0
	1864-	48.0	2.0
	1943	42.5	2.0
Two Cent	1864-1873	96.0	2.0
Three Cent Nic.	1865-1889	30.0	
Three Cent Sil.	1851-1854	12.345	
	1854-1873	11.574	
Half Dime	1794-1837	20.8	
	1837-1853	20.625	
	1853-1873	19.2	
Five Cents	1866-	77.16	3.0
Dime	1796-1837	41.6	
	1837-1853	41.25	1.5
	1853-1873	38.4	1.5
	1873-1964	38.58	1.5
	1965-	35.0	1.5
Twenty Cent	1875-1878	77.162	
Quarter	1796-1838	104.0	
	1838-1853	103.09	3.0
	1853-1873	95.99	3.0
	1873-1964	96.45	3.0
	1965-	87.5	3.0
Half Dollar	1794-1836	208.0	
	1836-1853	206.17	4.0
	1853-1873	192.0	4.0
	1873-1964	192.9	4.0
	1965-1970	177.5	4.0
	1971-	175.0	4.0
	1976S (Sil.)	177.5	4.0
Silver Dollar	1794-1803	416.0	
	1840-1935	412.5	6.0
Clad Dollar	1971-	350.0	8.0
40% Silver	1971-1976	379.5	8.0
Trade Dollar	1873-1885	420.0	
Gold Dollar 1	1849-1854	25.8	0.25
Gold Dollar 2	1854-1856	25.8	0.25
Gold Dollar 3	1865-1889	25.8	0.25
$2½ Gold	1796-1834	67.5	0.25
	1834-1929	64.5	0.25
$3 Gold	1854-1889	77.4	0.25
$5 Gold	1795-1834	135.0	0.25
	1834-1929	129.0	0.25
$10 Gold	1795-1834	270.0	0.50
	1834-1933	258.0	0.50
$20 Gold	1849-1933	516.0	0.50

1 Gram = 15.432 grains

FAST-FIND COIN REFERENCE INDEX

DESCRIPTION	DATE PURCHASED	COST	DATE SOLD	PRICE	CONDITION

DESCRIPTION	DATE PURCHASED	COST	DATE SOLD	PRICE	CONDITION

MEMBERSHIP IN THE ANA COULD BE YOUR BEST INVESTMENT THIS YEAR.

As a rare coin collector or hobbyist, you continually deal with a variety of questions. How can you know that the coin you're about to purchase is not counterfeit? How can you find the detailed, current information you need to build your collection? There is no authority to help you solve all these problems. Unless you belong to the American Numismatic Association.

Coin Certification. ANA specialists examine rare coins to safeguard you against counterfeiting and misrepresentation, and provide you with a certificate of authenticity.

Library Service. The largest circulating numismatic library in the world is maintained by the ANA. Its sole purpose is to provide you with free access to invaluable information that can't be found anywhere else.

The Numismatist. The Association's fully-illustrated magazine, considered *the* outstanding publication devoted exclusively to all phases of numismatics, is mailed free to all members.

And there are more benefits available through the ANA. Like coin insurance, special seminars, free booklets and photographic services. You can't find benefits like these anywhere else. Don't you owe it to yourself to join today?

JOIN US!

Application for Membership

Check one: ☐ Reg. ☐ Jr. ☐ Assoc. ☐ Life ☐ Club

Check one: ☐ Mr. ☐ Mrs. ☐ Ms. ☐ Club

_____
Name (please print and use first name)

_____
Street

_____
City

_____
State   Zip Code

_____
Birth Date   Occupation

ANA Bylaws require the publication of each application. If you DO NOT wish your STREET address published, please check this box. ☐

I herewith make application for membership in the American Numismatic Association, subject to the Bylaws of said Association. I also agree to abide by the Code of Ethics adopted by the Association.

_____
Signature of Applicant   Date

_____
Signature of Proposer (optional)   ANA No.

_____
Signature of Parent or Guardian
(Must sign for Junior applicants)

To charge to your credit card, please complete the following:

Account No. (All Digits) ☐ MasterCard ☐ Visa

☐☐☐☐☐☐☐☐☐☐☐☐☐☐☐☐☐☐☐

☐☐☐☐

Exp. Date of Card / MasterCard Interbank No.

DUES

Regular (adult)—_U.S. only_ . . . . $	21*
Regular (adult)—_all other countries_	23*
Club—_any country_	25*
Junior (11-17 years old).	11
Associate (child or spouse of R or LM member living at member's address) . .	4
Life (adult individual)	350
Installment, $60 with application,** plus $25 per month for 12 months	
Life (club) . . . . $	1000

* **Add $5 application fee, first year only**

** Includes $10 bookkeeping fee, deducted from final payment if made within 90 days of application. Life Membership is not effective until full $350 fee is paid.

Nonmember annual subscription—_U.S. only_ $28

Subscription—_all other countries_ $33

Foreign applications must be accompanied by U.S. funds drawn on a U.S. bank.

Send your application to:

American Numismatic Association
P.O. Box 2366
Colorado Springs, CO 80901

THE OFFICIAL PRICE GUIDES TO:

			Price
☐	465-6	American Silver & Silver Plate 4th Ed.	10.95
☐	482-8	Antique Clocks 3rd Ed.	10.95
☐	450-0	Antique & Modern Dolls 2nd Ed.	9.95
☐	483-6	Antique & Modern Firearms 5th Ed.	10.95
☐	271-X	Antiques & Other Collectibles 6th Ed.	9.95
☐	466-6	Antique Jewelry 4th Ed.	10.95
☐	270-1	Beer Cans & Collectibles, 3rd Ed.	7.95
☐	262-0	Bottles Old & New 9th Ed.	10.95
☐	255-8	Carnival Glass 1st Ed.	10.95
☐	454-4	Collectible Cameras 1st Ed.	10.95
☐	277-9	Collectibles of the Third Reich 2nd Ed.	10.95
☐	542-2	Collectible Toys 3rd Ed.	9.95
☐	490-9	Collector Cars 6th Ed.	11.95
☐	267-1	Collector Handguns 3rd Ed.	11.95
☐	459-3	Collector Knives 7th Ed.	11.95
☐	266-3	Collector Plates 4th Ed.	10.95
☐	476-3	Collector Prints 6th Ed.	11.95
☐	489-5	Comic Books & Collectibles 8th Ed.	9.95
☐	433-X	Depression Glass 1st Ed.	9.95
☐	472-0	Glassware 2nd Ed.	9.95
☐	492-5	Hummel Figurines & Plates 5th Ed.	9.95
☐	451-8	Kitchen Collectibles 2nd Ed.	10.95
☐	467-7	Military Collectibles 4th Ed.	10.95
☐	268-X	Music Collectibles 5th Ed.	11.95
☐	491-7	Old Books & Autographs 6th Ed.	10.95
☐	452-6	Oriental Collectibles 2nd Ed.	11.95
☐	461-5	Paper Collectibles 4th Ed.	10.95
☐	276-0	Pottery & Porcelain 5th Ed.	10.95
☐	263-9	Radio, T.V. & Movie Memorabilia 6th Ed.	11.95
☐	484-4	Records 6th Ed.	9.95
☐	485-2	Royal Doulton 4th Ed.	10.95
☐	418-6	Science Fiction & Fantasy Collectibles 1st Ed.	10.95
☐	477-1	Wicker 3rd Ed.	9.95

THE OFFICIAL:

			Price
☐	463-1	Collector's Journal 1st Ed.	4.95
☐	413-5	Identification Guide to Glassware 1st Ed.	9.95
☐	448-8	Identification Guide to Gunmarks 2nd Ed.	9.95
☐	412-7	Identification Guide to Pottery & Porcelain 1st Ed.	9.95
☐	415-1	Identification Guide to Victorian Furniture 1st Ed.	9.95

THE OFFICIAL (POCKET SIZE) PRICE GUIDES TO:

			Price
☐	479-8	Antiques & Flea Markets 3rd Ed.	3.95
☐	442-9	Antique Jewelry 1st Ed.	3.95
☐	264-7	Baseball Cards 5th Ed.	4.95
☐	487-9	Bottles 2nd Ed.	4.95
☐	468-2	Cars & Trucks 2nd Ed.	4.95
☐	260-4	Collectible Americana 1st Ed.	4.95
☐	463-1	Collectible Records 2nd Ed.	3.95
☐	469-0	Collector Guns 2nd Ed.	4.95
☐	474-7	Comic Books 3rd Ed.	3.95
☐	486-0	Dolls 3rd Ed.	4.95
☐	462-3	Football Cards 4th Ed.	4.95
☐	258-2	Glassware 2nd Ed.	3.95
☐	487-9	Hummels 3rd Ed.	4.95
☐	441-0	Military Collectibles 2nd Ed.	3.95
☐	480-1	Paperbacks & Magazines 3rd Ed.	4.95
☐	443-7	Pocket Knives 2nd Ed.	4.95
☐	479-8	Scouting Collectibles 3rd Ed.	3.95
☐	439-9	Sports Collectibles 2nd Ed.	3.95
☐	494-1	Star Trek/Star Wars Collectibles 3rd Ed.	4.95
☐	493-3	Toys 3rd Ed.	4.95

THE OFFICIAL BLACKBOOK PRICE GUIDES TO:

			Price
☐	284-1	U.S. Coins 24th Ed.	3.95
☐	286-8	U.S. Paper Money 18th Ed.	3.95
☐	285-X	U.S. Postage Stamps 8th Ed.	3.95

THE OFFICIAL INVESTORS GUIDE TO BUYING & SELLING:

			Price
☐	496-8	Gold, Silver and Diamonds 2nd Ed.	9.95
☐	497-6	Gold Coins 2nd Ed.	9.95
☐	498-4	Silver Coins 2nd Ed.	9.95

TOTAL